Painter 8 Creativity: Digital Artist's Handbook

Dear Deb,

Enjoy the book.

Happy Painting!

Jeremy

San Francisco 2004

Painter 8 Creativity: Digital Artist's Handbook

Jeremy Sutton

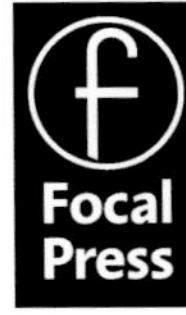

Focal Press is an imprint of Elsevier Science.

Jeremy Sutton
Painter Creativity
465 Utah Street #1
San Francisco, CA 94110
Tel: 415-626-3971
Fax: 415-626-3901
jeremy@paintercreativity.com
www.paintercreativity.com

∞ Recognizing the importance of preserving what has been written, Elsevier Science prints its books on acid-free paper whenever possible.

Library of Congress Cataloging-in-Publication Data
Sutton, Jeremy
Painter 8 Creativity : digital artist's handbook / Jeremy Sutton
p. cm.
Includes index.
ISBN 0-240-80511-9 (pbk : alk paper)
1. Computer graphics. 2. Fractal design painter. I. Title: Painter eight creativity. II. Title.

T385.S8374 2003
006.6′869—dc21

2002192745

British Library Cataloguing-in-Publication Data
A catalogue record for this book is available from the British Library.

The publisher offers special discounts on bulk orders of this book.
For information, please contact:

Manager of Special Sales
Elsevier Science
200 Wheeler Road
Burlington, MA 01803
Tel: 781-313-4700
Fax: 781-313-4882

For information on all Focal Press publications available, visit our World Wide Web home page at: http://www.focalpress.com

10 9 8 7 6 5 4 3 2

Printed in China.

In loving memory of Brad Sexton, Let Bijkersma, Renuka Seshadri, and Anne Marie Almeida, whose passion for life will always be an inspiration and whose unbounded joy and creativity embody the spirit of this book.

In casting your inspirational net as an artist, you become familiar with the humility that comes with watching your best-laid plans veer sideways. So, you set out to travel to Rome . . . and end up in Istanbul. You set off for Japan . . . and you end up on a train across Siberia. The journey, not the destination, becomes a source of wonder.

In the end, I wonder if one of the most important steps on our journey is the one in which we throw away the map. In jettisoning the grids and brambles of our own preconceptions, perhaps we are better able to find the real secrets of each place.

—Loreena McKennitt

Contents

Preface

The Goal

The goal of this book is for you to realize your full creative potential and express yourself in your art with soul and passion.

What You'll Learn

You will learn how to use the amazing paint program Corel Painter 8 to create expressive portraits, to animate paintings, to transform photographs, and to construct evocative collage.

Unlimited Creative Possibilities

Painter 8 is a wonderful creative tool, which allows you to express your heart and soul in your artwork. Painter, used with a pressure-sensitive tablet, is a magical medium that opens up unlimited creative possibilities. It is this exciting world that I want to share with you. Creating artwork on the computer offers a wonderful vehicle for accessing your creative potential and learning useful skills that you can apply in other aspects of your life. By overcoming the fears you may associate with digital art tools, you expand and empower your creativity.

Imagine yourself let loose in a magical art studio where you can do exactly what you want without any concern about cleaning brushes, using up precious paper and paint, or cleaning up the mess. That is the world you are about to enter. Enjoy your journey of creative exploration. Experiment and take risks. There is no such thing as a mistake or a bad painting. You are not trying to please or impress anyone. Be empowered. Be bold. Have fun and enjoy!

A Personal Approach

In this book I share my personal approach to using Painter. Everything I suggest is based on what works for me. It may work for you, or you may find a better way to do things. (In which case, please let me know!) Every artist develops his or her own particular way of using tools. There is no right or wrong way to create artwork. There are no absolute rules. What I share here is one perspective that I hope you will find useful, educational, fun, and inspiring. I encourage you to draw on diverse resources and stimuli, to follow the ways of different artists and different teachers, and then to develop your own unique personal style and way of doing things. Learning from others creates an opportunity to find and express your own voice.

Focus on Creativity

This book has evolved from more than 20 years of drawing portraits and the human figure, from more than 12 years of experience using the computer as my main art medium, and from more than 8 years of teaching Painter classes (online and offline), workshops, and training courses. I am sharing in this book an organized, structured approach to learning Painter that I have found works well. My analytical physics training has influenced my approach to structuring information in an organized and systematic way. I have included individual exercises and class projects that you can use either as a solo student or as an instructor teaching a group class. The focus throughout is on creativity and making art, rather than simply learning tools. Learning Painter, the premier digital art painting tool, is a means to an end, not an end in itself.

Filling a Gap

Books on graphics software tend to be either expanded user manuals or technique recipe books. In expanded user manual books, features are explained. In technique recipe books, step-by-step recipes are provided. What is generally missing in both types of books is attention to the improvised spontaneity of the actual creative process and an overall structure with exercises that allows the book to be used as a basis for a computer art curriculum. Understanding and exploring the creative process is particularly pertinent to learning Painter, because it is a program ideally suited to experimentation and improvisation. I have heard over the years of many requests from teachers and schools for a Painter curriculum and educational material—here it is! This book is also a response to the repeated requests from students for detailed, step-by-step instructions so they can concentrate on making art rather than taking notes.

This book is a tool to develop and enhance your creativity on the computer by using Painter and is a complement to other Painter books, courses, and resources. This book is not a replacement for the Painter 8 User Guide or for other Painter resources. Although you will gain a lot of knowledge about the inner workings and subtleties of Painter as you work through the exercises, this book is not intended to cover everything there is to know about Painter.

Who This Book Is For

This book is aimed at all levels of artists, ranging from first-time Painter users who wish to explore and expand their creative potential to professional fine artists, illustrators, photographers, videographers, and designers, who wish to enhance, personalize, and creatively enliven their professional product and services.

If you are unsure what the terms *cursor, file, image, canvas, folder, window, icon, menu, pop-up menu, pull-down menu, slider, palette, click, double-click,* or *drag* mean in the context of basic computer operations, then please familiarize yourself with these basic computer operations and terms before proceeding with the exercises in this book. There are many excellent books (I recommend any by author Robin Williams), videos, CD-ROMs, and courses designed to introduce you to the fundamentals of using a computer. The material in this book assumes a basic understanding of all these terms quoted. Having said that, let me welcome and reassure you if you are coming to the computer for the first time and feel intimidated, confused, or frustrated by the technology. If you have used traditional art media, you will be amazed by how natural Painter feels once you get into it and get used to the computer. In fact, you are likely to find yourself getting addicted to this wonderful new medium!

This book is designed to be suitable for college-level digital art classes, as well as for individual study and self-development. Most exercises are designed for a student working individually. Every now and then I've included a group exercise suitable for a classroom situation. In those cases the exercise is clearly labeled as a group exercise and can be ignored if you are studying on your own. I explain everything from the basics without assuming familiarity with Painter.

How This Book Is Structured

This book is divided into sessions, each one a mini-workshop in itself:

1 Painter Basics: *Getting Started*

2 Painter Empowerment: *The Four Guiding Principles*

3 Painting Portraits I: *Generating Form*

4 Painting Portraits II: *Unleashing the Power of Color*

5 Painting Portraits III: *Expressing Personality*

6 Animating Paint: *Generating Artistic Transitions*

7 Transforming Photographs I: *Achieving a Hand-Painted Look*

8 Transforming Photographs II: *Walking on the Wilder Side*

9 Creating Collage: *Evocative Storytelling*

Each session is divided into a series of lessons. Throughout the lessons are action steps, exercises, projects, and questions. The questions are designed to get you to think, serving an important balance to learning set methods, techniques, and recipes.

I am methodical in building a solid foundation. Thorough preparation is vitally important for making the most of your tools. I recommend that even an advanced power user carefully skim the first two sessions for useful tips. The time you invest upfront in technical and organizational matters, such as customizing your palette arrangements, loading extra brushes, and deciding on a consistent naming methodology, will pay big dividends down the road and help make your art creation experience all the more fun and productive.

Sessions 3 to 9, that each deal with separate application areas, are designed to be self-contained, and can be followed independently of each other. Having said that, a lot of material can be applied from one session to another. For instance, the portrait painting skills can be applied to transforming photographs into paintings, and photo transformation techniques can be applied to creating collage.

I am a great believer in the power of process. I love recording my painting sessions and playing them back—a great facility that Painter offers (known as *scripting*). Although not complicated, scripting does add some extra work and potential for errors. Therefore, I've placed the detailed instructions for scripting in session 6, Animating Paint: *Generating Artistic Transitions*. In teaching I normally introduce scripting as an integral part of a painting exercise early on. It is up to you as the student, or the instructor, whether or when to include this aspect of Painter in your study. If you are adventurous, I recommend you look over session 6 early on, before you tackle the portrait sessions, and then make a habit of recording all your paintings. If you are less daring and want to keep things as simple and easy as possible, then just ignore session 6.

At the end of the book you'll find the appendices, which contain practical information that you may wish to refer to. The first three appendices address questions I am frequently asked in class, namely, which software to use when, what size to make your files, and how to get colors to look right when you print.

Appendix IV explains how to load the extra brushes and art materials from the companion CD. Appendix V gives additional insight into my portrait painting process. Appendix VI is a troubleshooting summary, which I recommend you briefly scan so you know in advance what to watch out for and precautions to take. Appendix VII is a summary of useful keyboard shortcuts. Many of these are also on the shortcuts card that comes with Painter.

The index is designed to allow you to quickly locate where a specific topic is discussed.

Rather than include a comprehensive bibliography or resources page, I have (with great assistance from Den Laurent) created a companion web site to go with this course: www.paintercreativity.com. The companion web site includes links to useful educational Painter and art resources (including courses, DVDs, and books), plus updates, tutorials, tips, a gallery, and Painter goodies. Please visit the companion web site and extend your educational experience beyond this course.

The Painter Creativity Companion CD that accompanies this book contains custom brush libraries; extra art materials (collections of my favorite papers and patterns plus some custom color sets); project folders for saving your work, some of which contain tutorial images; and a slideshow of my work.

Instructor Notes

I have added specific notes for instructors who are using this book as a basis for teaching a computer art class or providing Painter training. For teaching purposes I recommend reviewing the whole book and then selecting those sections that fit in with the skill level and needs of your students, and with the scope of your curriculum. There is sufficient material here for several semesters of classes or many days of intensive workshop/training course instruction.

The key underlying lessons throughout this book are:

1. It's okay to experiment.
2. Trust your senses and intuition.

With these beliefs instilled in your students, they will have the confidence to develop their own style and express their own individual voices. As a teacher, always be encouraging and enthusiastic—both are infectious.

I like to arrange my classroom with computers facing outward. This creates a good space in the center of the computer laboratory for both the instructor and the students to move around in and look at each other's work. The informal exchange and interaction among students can be an important part of their learning process. Whenever possible, I avoid the schoolhouse rows of computers all facing forward.

My ideal workshop format is a five-day, Monday-to-Friday course. This is a good amount of time for learning new information and having an opportunity to integrate that new information through hands-on experience.

My typical five-day, art-oriented curriculum looks something like this:

Monday: Painter Basics

Tuesday: Painting and Cloning

Wednesday: Pop Art Techniques and Effects

Thursday: Collage

Friday: Final Project

My typical photography-oriented curriculum looks something like this:

Monday: Painter Basics

Tuesday: Oil and Watercolor Transformations

Wednesday: Wilder Hand-Painting and Effects

Thursday: Collage

Friday: Final Project

The details of these curricula will vary according to the level of the students and the emphasis of the class.

Notation and Terminology

This book is cross-platform, suitable for both Macintosh and Windows users. In this book Mac commands precede Windows commands. For instance, the keyboard shortcut for Edit > Undo is Cmd/Ctrl-Z. This abbreviation means Macintosh users hold the Command (Cmd) or Apple key down and click once on 'Z', whereas Windows users hold the Control (Ctrl) key down and click once on 'Z'. Where there is a series of steps that differ significantly between platforms, I have provided separate sets of instructions for the Macintosh and Window platforms.

For simplicity's sake I refer to *folders* (rather than *directories*) for both the Mac and for Windows. Occasionally the names of some items or folders that I refer to may be abbreviated or capitalized on Windows systems.

There are several occasions when I refer to the Painter 8 application folder; this means the folder called Corel Painter 8 that is installed on your hard drive when you install Painter.

I use the '>' symbol to indicate that you need to drag from one item in a menu to another. Spelling follows American English (e.g., *color* instead of *colour*).

Generally, I follow the Painter 8 User Guide conventions for terminology and capitalization. To keep things simple and avoid unnecessary repetition, I sometimes use the shorthand Category > Variant. For instance, I may say "choose the Blenders > Runny variant" rather than "choose the Runny variant in the Blenders category of brushes in the Brushes palette."

One exception to the use of the Painter 8 User Guide terminology is the terms *Primary* and *Secondary* colors. I refer to these as *Regular* and *Additional* colors to avoid confusion with the terms *primary color* and *secondary color* in color theory.

There are two units commonly used to specify resolution:

ppi, pixels per inch, specifically refers to digital files, which are made up of pixels. This unit is used as the default in programs such as Photoshop and Painter.

dpi, dots per inch, comes from the printing industry and refers to the density of dots of ink per inch on a printed surface. It is a characteristic of a printing device.

For clarity, in this book I use ppi when referring to pixels and dpi when referring to a printed image, even though many people use dpi for everything.

I also instruct you, in session 2, to make a Shortcuts custom palette with Save As and Clone command buttons. I refer to these throughout the book, so it is important to ensure that you have this custom palette set up.

Screen Shots and Tutorial Images

The screen shots used are captured on a Macintosh computer with system Mac OS X. The precise look and feel of the icons and the interface may differ slightly on other Macintosh operating systems and on Windows PCs.

All the tutorial images needed for following the exercises in this book are on the accompanying CD that comes with this book.

Taking Notes

I encourage you to always keep a notebook close at hand when using Painter. When you come across questions, write them down in your notebook. When you find a particular brush variant or paper texture you really love, make a note of it. When you come across a problem, note down the exact sequence of events leading up to it and the content of any error messages that appear. You will find these notes an invaluable source of reference information at a later date.

Besides using your notebook for written notes, I encourage you to also use it for sketching from nature. This will help develop your drawing skills and complement the exercises you do on the computer as part of this course. Jot down quick sketches, scribbles, and doodles of scenes or people that catch your eye. Don't worry about details or perfection.

Acknowledgments

I'd like to extend my heartfelt thanks to the many people who assisted me on the journey of creating this book.

The following contributors have kindly allowed me to use their paintings and photographs as illustrations and project samples, or allowed me to share their custom brushes and colors set: Barbara Buchner, Brandon Bastunas, Carol Mooney, Cathleen C. Savage, Celeste Dobbins, Cheri MacCallum, Chris Cimonetti, Darin, David Taylor, Denise Laurent, Dezraye Choi, Don Seegmiller, Dwight E. Goode, Eddie Tapp, Elizabeth Fenwick, Elsa Vera, Ernest Love, Gisele Bonds, Jeff Peterson, Jane Conner-ziser, Jenny Lovett, Jim and Judi Paliungas, Laura Garner, Laura Ruppersberger, Lesley Fountain, Leslie Howard Jacob, Lisa Evans, Lois Freeman-Fox, Lorne Chisholm, Marge Stewart, Paulo Roberto Purim, Peg Buckner, Rheba Mitchell, Robert Strong, Ron Kempke, Selina Topham, Sharon Moran, Sherron Sheppard, Sidne Teske, Simon Fong, Susan LeVan, Thomas Barron, Tom Deininger, Valerie Markle, and Victor de Leon.

You will find a full listing of their contact information and references to their specific contributions in the Contributors listing at the back of this book. To every one of these contributors I extend my sincere thanks: your creative contributions have enriched and enhanced this book. Your paintings, photographs, brushes, and color sets have all served as inspiration for me and will, I'm sure, do so for others.

This book is the culmination of several years of development and gestation. I thank the following people, listed alphabetically by first name, for their enthusiastic help, support, and encouragement over that time:

Claire Barry—for first introducing me to the joy of making art on the computer

Claude Szwimer—a long-time enthusiastic supporter of this project who believed in me from the very beginning

David Hunter (www.pilotmarketing.com)—for his advice on color calibration

Den Laurent (www.imagine.co.uk)—for contributing some amazing oil brushes (Den's Oil Funky Chunky is one of my all-time favorites!), for helping ensure that a Mac user like me treats Windows users to accurate cross-platform instructions and compatible files, and for generously creating the interface for the companion web site, www.paintercreativity.com

Diane Walters (www.grammarlady.com)—for diligently wading through the early stages of my manuscript and keeping it true to the rules of English grammar and spelling

Elizabeth, Debbi, and Ros Sutton—for their wonderful sisterly support, encouragement, and love—and thanks Debbi for your pull-no-punches artist/writer/teacher/big-sister insights!)

Elizabeth Fenwick (www.elizabethfenwick.com)—for generously donating her time

Jane Conner-ziser (www.janesdigitalart.com)—for being a joy to teach with and learn from, for introducing me to the wonderful community of professional photographers and helping ensure that I address their specific needs within this book, and for contributing artwork, ideas, and a wonderful essay

Jinny Brown (www.pixelalley.com)—an indefatigable Painter evangelist and fountain of Painter knowledge on all of the Painter lists and forums; I thank Jinny for helping me with cross-platform compatibility editing and suggestions

Laura Garner—for generously contributing her time, effort, design skills, and encouragement during the early stages of the book

Lisa Evans—for loving support, encouragement, inspiration, and patience

Margaret Sutton—for giving me the valuable perspective of a gifted and experienced fine artist, for helping me with indexing and, of course, for being a loving, supportive Mum!

Mona Meisami (www.monameisami.com)—for sharing her valuable perspective as an experienced designer

Olaf Malver—for sharing his fascinating insights into the Inuit troubleshooting strategies

Rheba Mitchell (www.lair-wildscape.com)—an enthusiastic former student of mine (you can try her custom color sets out from the companion CD); I thank Rheba for keeping on at me until I finally completed the book

Robin Williams (www.ratz.com)—for her great advice and inspiration on indexing

Stephanie Robey—for giving me access to PhotoSpin's complete stock photo library

Zina Kao—for kindly helping translate my portrait painting process into words

Thank you to all my students over the years for being such a source of joy and inspiration, and for leading me to the development of this book.

A key creative tool for which I am thankful is the fabulous Wacom tablet. Thank you to all my friends at Wacom: Jim McCartney, Will Reeb, KellyAnn Schroeder, Michelle Lindsey, and Weston Maggio, for their consistent and generous support and encouragement.

None of this would have been possible without the existence of the amazing creative tool, Painter. A big thank you goes out to the geniuses behind Painter, namely Mark Zimmer, Tom Hedges, and John Derry. You guys rock! (Special thanks, John, for your inspiring foreword.)

I wish to thank everyone at Corel for being supportive of this book and, of course, for doing such a great job with Painter. Special thanks to Tanya Staples, Roe McFarlane, Kathleen O'Neill, Wes Pack, and Kimberly Elko.

Thank you to everyone else who has helped me along the way.

Finally, I thank the whole team at Focal Press and Elsevier Publishing who helped bring this book to fruition. Thanks to Keith Roberts at Graphic World Publishing Services for help in production. Thanks to Christine Degon and the marketing team at Elsevier. I wish to specially thank Amy Jollymore, my editor, for being such a pleasure to work with over the last two years (yes, it's been that long!), for believing in me, and for her infinite patience.

Foreword

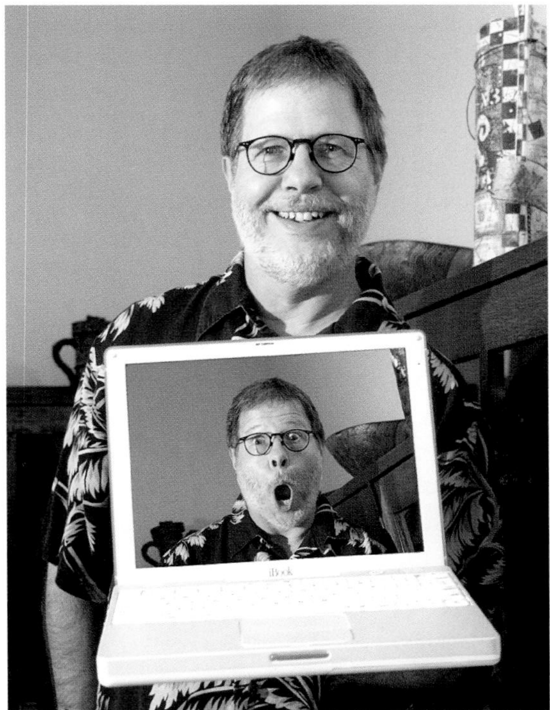

John Derry is one of the original creators of Painter.

Have you ever lost something in your youth—perhaps a treasured toy—only to discover it many years later, tucked away in a box hiding in the corner of an attic or basement? Instantly, you are immersed in a flood of memories and emotions. Everything around you takes on a new light. Through a simple childhood toy, you are reconnected with the innocent awe of youth.

Creativity can also hide from us. Many people inadvertently cast aside their natural creative self on their way to adulthood. You'll hear these individuals say "I can't draw" or "I'm not talented." Through no fault of their own, they now believe that you're either talented or you're not, and it is no use attempting to learn creativity now. In actuality, these folks were not born creative-less. They have simply tucked it away in some emotional attic or basement. There it hides, awaiting rediscovery.

The book you are now holding in your hands, *Painter 8 Creativity: Digital Artist's Handbook*, can act as a personal torch of sorts to light your way in search of your own personal creative powers. Jeremy Sutton has generously organized his tried-and-true system for coaxing creativity out of our emotional corners. He presents it here to help you rediscover the creativity you've had in you all along.

Throughout, Jeremy has utilized his years of group and classroom teaching experience by providing a set of notes for instructors and teachers. These are invaluable by the manner in which they present a clear focus to the exercises. Additionally, Jeremy offers an experienced insight into the inner mechanics of the creative process. Even the student will find these sections useful and illuminating.

This book is not a manual. It will not automatically provide easy answers. Like a real classroom, you will be called on to answer many questions. Good learning comes about through both guidance and self-questioning, and Jeremy does both very well. Instead of easily providing the solution to a problem, Jeremy coaxes you through a series of questions. This makes you *think*, and thinking leads to learning. And you'll learn quite a bit about yourself along the way!

The subject of portraiture is a fascinating one; our physical appearance is the ultimate form of self-expression, whereas creating a portrait—like all art—is an act of personal *self*-expression. A portrait, then, is a combination of these two forms of expression. Painter was designed to offer its users a wide variety of mark-making tools for the purpose of creatively expressing oneself. In this book, Jeremy has neatly wrapped all of these concepts together to provide both amateurs and professionals alike with a systematic approach to the art of the portrait. Conveniently, many of the specifics of portraiture can be applied to expressive image-making in general.

If you are ready to begin a fascinating, creative journey into your inner self, then I suggest that you now sit down at your computer, strap on your seat belt, and enjoy the marvelous ride Jeremy has in store for you. You won't regret the effort, and you'll have plenty of great pictures of your trip when you're done!

John Derry
Overland Park, Kansas

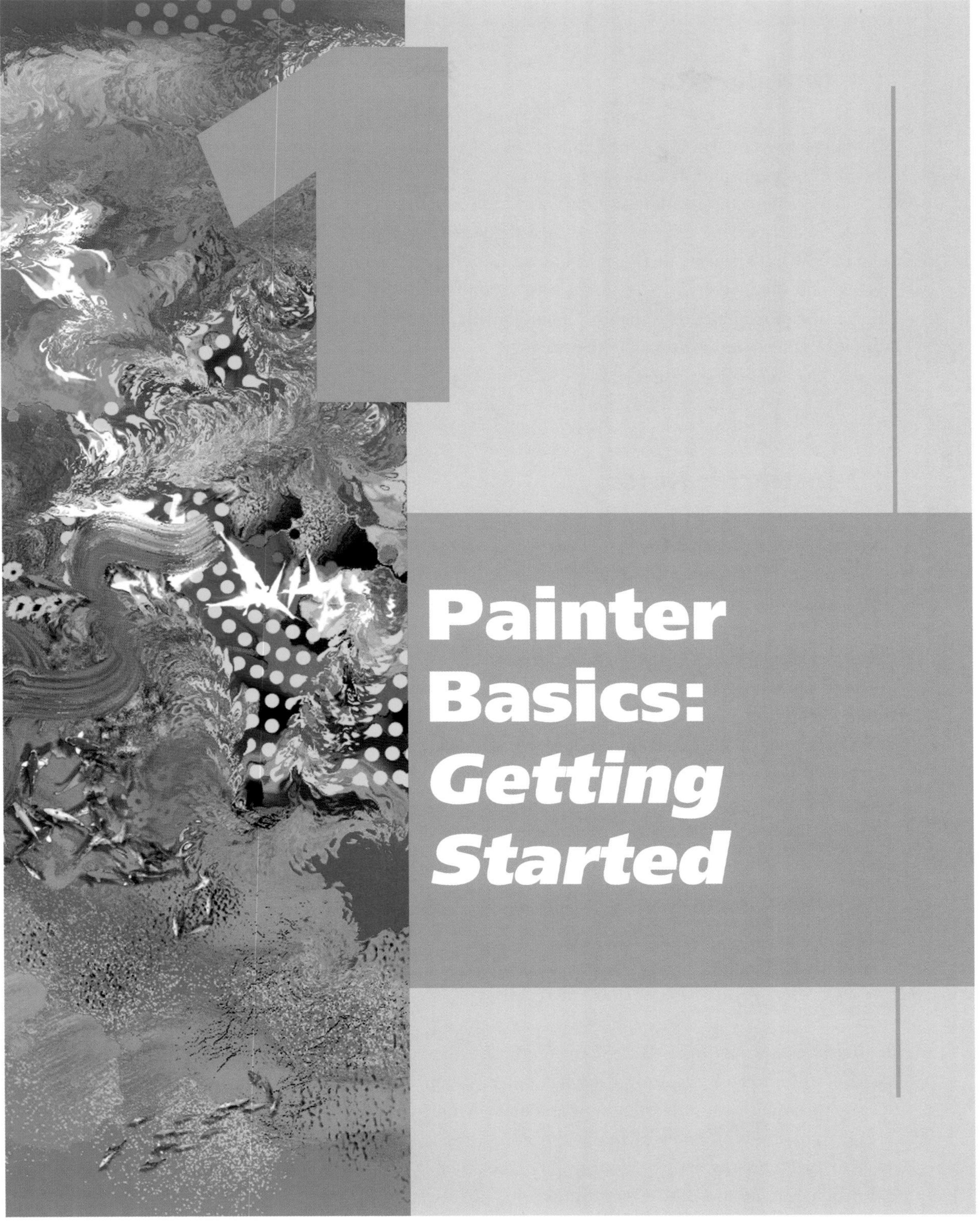

1 Painter Basics: *Getting Started*

1.1 Introduction

This session is aimed at first-time Painter users. If you are already a Painter user, I suggest you skim this session briefly and then dive into session 2.

This session starts with a summary of what you'll need. You are going to do some initial setting up of Preferences and Control Panels, and then dive into Painter and become familiar with what's what and what's where. You'll get to know the "where to" and "how to" for basic operations, such as opening a new canvas, selecting a brush, changing a color, clearing your canvas, saving your image, and much more. The session concludes with an exploration of some types of brushes that can initially confuse the first-time Painter user.

By the end of this session you'll be familiar with the Painter interface and you'll be comfortable choosing and applying Brushes and Art Materials.

1.2 Instructor Notes

This session is designed for someone who is experiencing Painter for the first time. At most schools, colleges, and companies, Painter will already be installed and the memory management issues dealt with, so the instructions pertaining to memory allocation can be overlooked in class.

The structure and content of your first lesson will depend on the duration of the course you are teaching, the objectives of the class, and the level of experience of your students.

For workshops I recommend starting off with students briefly introducing themselves, giving some insight into their background and experience, and explaining why they are there and what they hope to get out of the class. This exchange is valuable both for other class members to learn about the experience resources that exist within their fellow students and for you to gauge the students' experience level and expectations. This information allows you to shape the curriculum to suit the students' needs and objectives.

I always establish four rules from the outset:

Rule 1: There's no such thing as a mistake.

Rule 2: There's no such thing as a dumb question.

Rule 3: Be bold and take risks—you won't break the computer!

Rule 4: Have FUN!

If your class is a short one-off session, designed to give students a superficial taste of Painter, then I strongly recommend preparing each computer station by adjusting the Wacom Control Panel to disable the stylus two-function button and make double-clicking easier.

If your class is an extensive in-depth training, designed to equip your students with the skills they need to use Painter as a professional graphics tool, then I recommend you take your students through the detailed preparation and customization of Painter (explained in the first two sessions of this book). This can be hard work for the students, but the preparation provides an essential foundation for students who wish to continue and grow with Painter in the professional work environment. In such a situation I explain this to my students and run through the setup with them at a brisk pace. The advantage of having all the steps written down here is that they can always refer back to this text if they fall behind or didn't fully comprehend any part of the procedure.

In either case, whether a one-off session or an in-depth training, I recommend diving quickly into a fun, yet challenging, expressive exercise where students have a chance to play with brushes and get used to the interface. The advantages of getting the students to do this initial exercise are that:

1. It gives students an immediate hands-on experience, which most are keen to have.
2. It gives students a chance to explore and discover the program in their own time.
3. It gives students a chance to encounter and, with your help, overcome problems.
4. It gives students a reference point to look back at later and gauge their own progress.
5. It gives you, the instructor, an opportunity to assess your students' artistic and technical skill level and thus helps you know how to structure and pace the class.

An hour is typically a suitable duration for this first exercise. At the completion of the exercise, have your students save their images. Have them mount the images (Cmd/Ctrl-M) and hide their palettes, and then walk around and look at each other's work. This is also a good time for a class break. After the class break, sit down with your students and ask what they liked and disliked in the exercise, and ask them to share with the class anything they discovered, such as cool brushes.

1.3 What You'll Need

Basic Computer Skills

It is assumed that you have an understanding of basic computer system operations such as clicking, double-clicking, dragging, opening and closing folders and files, renaming folders and files, and accessing your desktop, Painter 8 folder, and Control Panels. If you don't have this knowledge, there are many excellent books and courses that can help you. One of my favorite introductory books for Mac users is *The Mac Is Not a Typewriter* by Robin Williams (Peachpit Press, 1995). Any books by Williams are well worth reading.

Minimum System Requirements

Macintosh

Mac OS 9 (version 9.2. or higher), Mac OS X (version 10.2 or higher)

Power Macintosh G3 or higher

128 MB RAM (more recommended)

24-bit color display

1024 × 768 screen resolution

CD-ROM drive

125 MB HD space for minimum installation (at least 1 GB free space recommended)

Windows

Windows 2000 or Windows XP

Pentium II, 200 MHz or higher

128 MB RAM (more recommended)

24-bit color display

1024 × 768 screen resolution

CD-ROM drive

125 MB HD space for minimum installation (at least 1 GB free space recommended)

Painter 8 Software

Painter is a phenomenal image creation tool with the richest variety and versatility of brushes available anywhere. If you think of Adobe Photoshop as your digital darkroom, then Painter is your digital art studio. Imagine a magical art supply store where you can go into the workshop at the back of the store and custom make any brush you can imagine—that is Painter. The brushes are at the heart of Painter's uniqueness and strength. Besides the phenomenal painting capabilities of Painter, it also has powerful image manipulation, design, and animation capabilities. This program is a fabulous complement to your other creation tools, both digital and traditional. Painter is an intuitive, process-oriented tool that allows you to work freely as an artist. This expressive tool encourages the use of handmade brush strokes. Painter isn't a replacement for Adobe Photoshop, or any other digital tools that you use in your workflow. Instead, Painter is an integral part of your workflow process and complements your other tools.

To precisely follow the exercises in this book, you will need Painter 8. A free 30-day trial version of Painter may be downloadable from the corel.com web site. If you have an older version of Painter or have Painter Classic (which is shipped with the Wacom tablet), I recommend upgrading to the most recent version of Painter.

Pressure-Sensitive Tablet and Stylus

A graphics tablet with a pressure-sensitive stylus (the name given to the pen you hold) is a must! Many aspects of brush behavior in Painter are controlled by pressure. I highly recommend the Wacom Intuos2 6-by-8-inch tablet (A5 in Europe) for overall comfort and convenience (although the Wacom Cintiq with it's built-in screen may be more intuitive for some). See www.wacom.com for details.

Notebook/Sketchbook

Spiral-bound or hardback book with plain white pages suitable for writing and sketching

Soft pencils, crayons, pens, and oil pastels

Mirror

You will need to be able to place a mirror for self-portraits next to your computer screen so you can conveniently look from the mirror to the screen.

1.4 Preparation

Getting Comfortable

It's important to feel good about your environment. Take a look around. Is the surface on which the computer monitor and keyboard are situated clear of clutter? Is the computer screen in a position and orientation where you won't be disturbed by reflected light from a window? Adjust your environment so you feel good about it. You want to avoid distractions once you sit down to create art on the computer.

Before sitting down at your computer, do some simple stretching and relaxation exercises. These could be as simple as some deep breaths accompanied by slowly raising and lowering your arms, gently rotating your head, and softly rolling your shoulders. You may find it pleasant to put on some relaxing music to accompany this movement. When you've completed some stretching and relaxation exercises, finish by shaking out your feet and hands. Stand upright with your arms relaxed at your side. Observe your posture. Breathe deep into your diaphragm, hold your head upright, and keep your shoulders down. Now sit at your computer.

I recommend getting up and stretching (and drinking some water) at least every hour, preferably every 20 minutes. Since time flies by when you're absorbed in a project, you may find it useful to set a small kitchen timer as your stretch time reminder.

Creating should be fun! Make it easy and comfortable for yourself. Observe your posture now that you are sitting. Maintain a relaxed upright posture with your head held high (not slouched forward) and shoulders down (not hunched up). Sit comfortably facing the screen. Make sure your eyes are in line roughly with the center of your screen. If you find you are straining your neck by being forced to look up or down, then adjust your seat and/or monitor height until you are comfortable.

Tablet Stuff

Place your tablet centrally in front of you, between you and the screen. I find it most comfortable with the tablet resting on my lap, and sometimes with the upper section of the tablet resting on the edge of the desk. Rest the side of your stylus hand on the tablet active surface. Lightly hold the stylus close to the tip and slightly more upright than you would a normal pen or pencil (Figure 1.1). Your hand and arm should feel totally relaxed. There should be no strain.

Keep the side of your hand in contact with the tablet at all times. This gives you maximum comfort and much greater control. If you hold the tablet with your hand floating in the air, it is difficult to control and you'll find yourself accidentally clicking when you don't intend to (Figure 1.2).

The tablet driver installs a Control Panel. In the next section I explain the adjustments I make to the Wacom Intuos2 Control Panel before I use the tablet for creating art. Please note that if you use a different model or make of tablet, or a different version of the driver, then the precise details of what you see, and which options are available, may differ slightly from the following instructions.

Tablet Control Panel Settings (Macintosh)

In Mac OS X select Go > Applications > Wacom > Wacom Tablet. In Mac OS 9 select the Apple Menu > Control Panels > Wacom Tablet.

You may first see a graphic representation of the control panel (with inactive tabs). If so click OK.

1. Click on the Double Click tab.
2. Check Double Click Assist.
3. Set Double Click Distance to at least 8.
4. Set Double Click Speed to Slow.

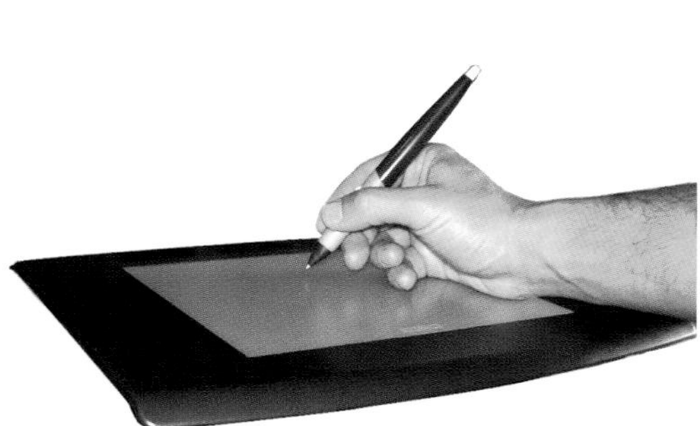

Figure 1.1 Keep the side of your hand in contact with the tablet.

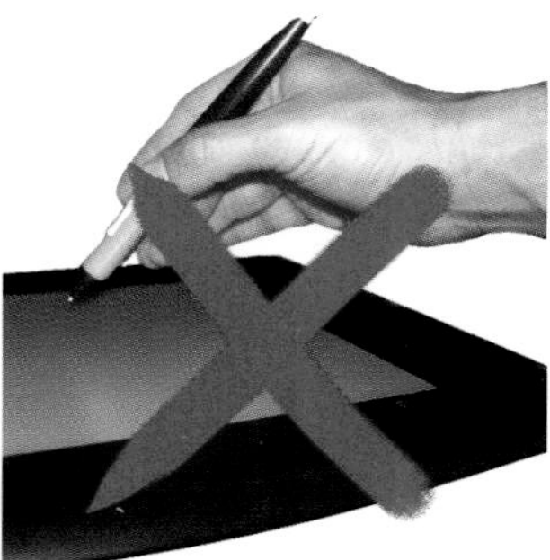

Figure 1.2 Avoid holding the stylus like a fine art pencil, with your hand floating in the air.

These Double-click settings (Figure 1.3) make double-clicking with the stylus much easier.

Now click on the Tool Buttons tab. You will see pop-up menus with lines pointing at either end of the button on the side of the stylus. I like to adjust each button menu to Ignored for simplicity and to avoid unintentionally clicking or double-clicking (Figure 1.4).

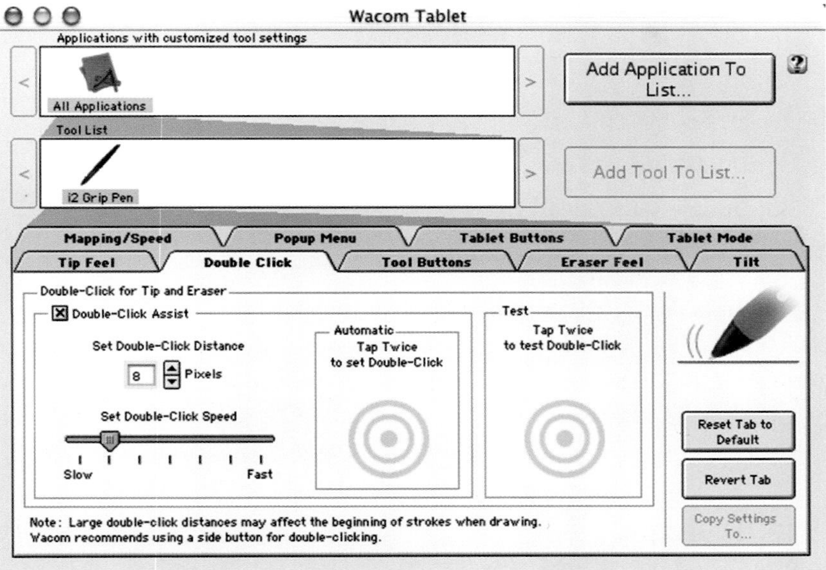

Figure 1.3 Recommended Wacom Tablet Double Click settings.

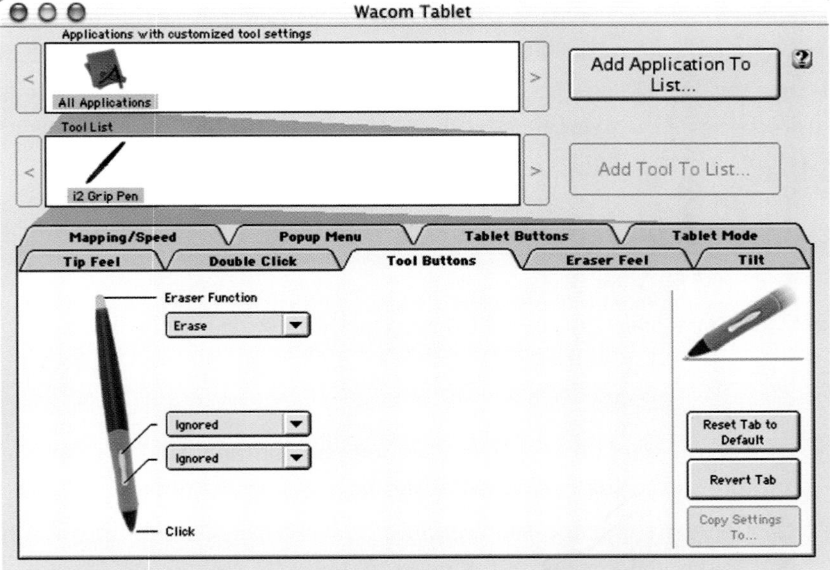

Figure 1.4 Wacom Tablet Tool Buttons suggested settings (may differ for Windows users).

Tablet Control Panel Settings (Windows)

1. Click Start > Settings > Control Panel.
2. Double-click the Wacom Tablet icon.
3. Click the Double Click tab.
4. Check Double Click Assist.
5. Set Double Click Distance to about 8.
6. Set Double Click Speed to Slow.

All these settings make double-clicking with the stylus much easier.

Now click on the Tool Buttons tab. You will see menus with lines pointing at either end of the button on the side of the stylus. Select the Right-click for one end of the button and choose from the other click options for the other end of the button. Set up your stylus in whatever way works best for you.

Using the Stylus

The stylus position determines precisely and uniquely where the cursor appears on the screen. The stylus is not relational like a mouse. There is absolute and unique correspondence between every point on the tablet surface and every point on the screen. A stylus performs all the functions of a mouse (and more). A light tap with the stylus is equivalent to a click with the mouse. Two light taps with the stylus is the same as a double-click with the mouse. The effect of a mouse click and drag is executed with a depression of the stylus at one position, maintaining the pressure while sliding the stylus to another position, and then lifting the stylus tip away from the surface of the tablet.

Basic Stylus Tasks (Macintosh)

If you are new to using a tablet, it is useful to first get used to some basic stylus tasks.

1. Click on the hard drive icon so it becomes highlighted. Then click on the desktop background so the hard drive icon is no longer highlighted.
2. Click on the top menu File and drag down to New Folder. Let go. A new untitled folder will appear on the desktop.

Continued

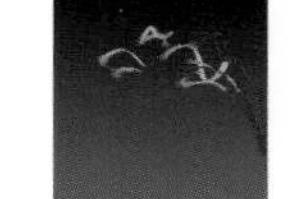

3. Double-click on the new folder icon so it opens into a window. Click on the small round red button in the top left of the window to close it (Mac OS X) or the square button in the top left (Mac OS 9 or lower).
4. Click on the untitled folder icon and drag it to the trash. Select Finder > Empty Trash (Mac OS X) or Special > Empty Trash (Mac OS 9 or lower). Click OK in the dialog box.
5. Move the cursor to each corner and along the edges of the screen, keeping the stylus tip about 1/4 inch above the tablet surface at all times. It is important to be able to move the cursor around without accidentally clicking or dragging. Get a feel for the physical relationship between the boundaries of the screen and the boundaries of the tablet.

Basic Stylus Tasks (Windows)

If you are new to using a tablet, it is useful to first get used to some basic stylus tasks.

1. Right-click in an open area of the Task Bar and choose Minimize All Windows.
2. Right-click in the open area of your desktop and choose New > Folder. A new untitled folder appears on the desktop with "New Folder" highlighted and ready to be renamed.
3. Click in the blank area of the desktop just to the right of the New Folder to disable the renaming function. The New Folder remains highlighted.
4. Click the Delete key, then click Yes to send the New Folder to the Recycle Bin.
5. Double-click the Recycle Bin icon to open it.
6. Click File > Empty Recycle Bin, then click Yes to empty it.
7. Move the cursor to each corner and along the edges of the desktop, keeping the stylus tip about 1/4 inch above the tablet surface at all times. It is important to be able to move the cursor around without accidentally clicking or dragging. Get a feel for the physical relationship between the boundaries of the screen and the boundaries of the tablet.

Copy Project Folders from the Painter Creativity Companion CD

Copy the Creativity Projects folder from the Painter Creativity Companion CD (which you will find at the back of this book) onto your hard drive. The Creativity Projects folder contains folders for each session and project images. Use this as a location to save all the work you create while following the projects in this workbook.

Memory Matters

Good Memory Habits

Always exit out of Painter when you finish a project, and reopen it afresh when you begin a new project. This clears the memory and reduces the risk of crashes.

Painter works most efficiently when it is working with files directly on a hard drive (internal or external), rather than working from files that are on removable media such as a Zip disk or CD-ROM. As you use Painter, the program creates a temporary file that takes up space on your hard drive. If you are working with very large files, it is best to make sure that Painter creates this temporary file in a volume or partition that has plenty of available memory. This may mean assigning an external hard drive, rather than the default, which is your computer hard drive, as your Temporary File Volume. You can assign the Temp File Volume in the Edit (Corel Painter 8 on Mac OS X) > Preferences > General window.

Setting Memory: Macintosh

In Mac OS X memory adjustment all happens automatically behind the scenes, and there's no need to make any changes to Painter. For Mac OS 9 and earlier, follow these instructions:

1. Select Apple Menu > Control Panels > Memory control panel.
2. Make sure that virtual memory is off.
3. Close the Memory control panel.
4. Select Apple Menu > About This Computer.
5. Note how large the largest unused block of memory is.
6. Click once on the Painter 8 application icon in the Painter folder.
7. Select Cmd-I. This opens a dialog box (Painter 8 Info).
8. Change the Show: General Information to Show: Memory. Ideally assign at least 60 MB of RAM to Painter and more if available, leaving at least 15 MB RAM free.
9. Close the Info box.

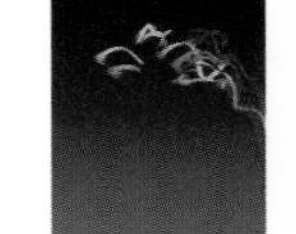

Setting Memory: Windows

1. Launch Painter.
2. Click Edit > Preferences > Windows.
3. Under Physical Memory Usage, click the appropriate radio button, depending on your needs: Maximum Memory for Painter or Half of Memory for Painter.

Regarding Virtual Memory in Windows, I suggest leaving the default settings. The issue of memory may differ depending on the particular version of Windows you are using. It is best to consult your system manual or Windows technical support if you are not sure.

Creating a Painter Alias (Mac OS X)

1. Locate the Painter 8 folder in your computer.
2. Open the Painter 8 folder and locate the Painter 8 application icon.
3. Click and drag the Painter 8 application icon into the Dock (usually located at the bottom of the screen). You will see a Painter alias appear in the Dock.
4. A single click on the Painter icon in the Dock opens Painter.
5. I like to set up the Dock with small icons on the right of my screen. You can do this through the Apple > Dock > Dock Preferences (Figure 1.5).

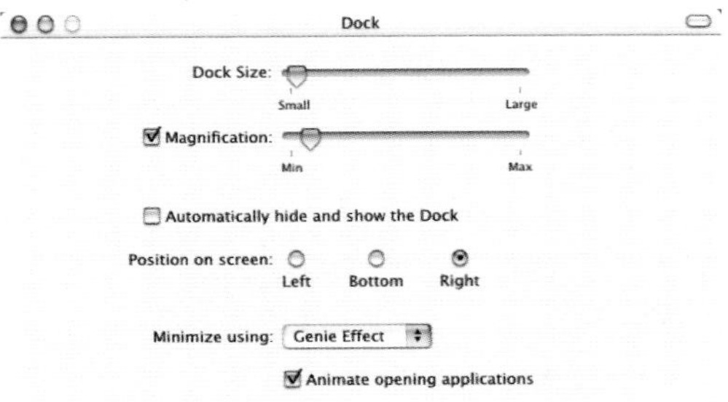

Figure 1.5 Suggested Mac OS X Dock settings.

Creating a Painter Alias (Mac OS 9)

1. Select the Painter 8 application icon in the Painter 8 application folder on your hard drive.
2. Select Cmd-M. This makes an alias, or copy, of the original icon.
3. Select the text attached to the alias icon.
4. Add a space before the P of Painter, and delete the word *alias*.
5. Drag the alias icon into the System > Apple Menu folder. This way the Painter name appears at the top of the Apple menu. To open Painter simply drag down from the Apple icon (top left corner of the Macintosh display) to the Painter alias. If you have many applications you want to be able to launch from your Apple Menu, it may be best to make a folder called Applications in the Apple Menu folder and place all of your application aliases in that Applications folder.

You can always repeat steps 1 and 2 and drag the alias onto your desktop. This way you can launch Painter either by double-clicking on the Painter alias icon on the desktop or by dragging down to the Painter alias icon in the Apple Menu.

Adding Painter to the Start Menu (Windows)

1. If a Painter shortcut icon is on your desktop, hold down the Alt key, then click and drag the Painter shortcut icon onto the Start button. Painter can now be launched from the Start menu.
2. If the Painter icon is not on your desktop, click Start > Run and type Explorer.
3. Open the Program Files folder, then open the main Painter folder.
4. Hold down the Alt key, then click and drag the Painter application icon (.exe file) over the Start button. This creates a Painter shortcut icon and places it in the Start menu. Painter can now be launched from the Start menu.

1.5 What's What and What's Where

We're going to start by opening a new canvas in Painter so you have a scratch pad to try out brushes on. You'll make some basic adjustments in the General Preferences to make things more comfortable.

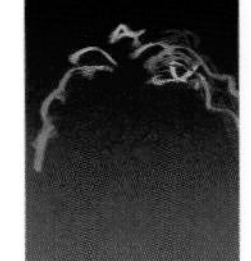

We then take a look at the Painter desktop and review what's what and what's where. We look at how you can control your desktop and explore the brushes hierarchy.

Diving Into Painter

Opening a New Canvas

1. Open Painter.
2. Select from the top menu bar File > New (Cmd/Ctrl-N).
3. In the New Picture window set the canvas size to 700 pixels wide by 750 pixels high. Leave the resolution at 72 pixels per inch, the paper color white, and the picture type as Image.
4. Click OK.

Mount and Reposition Your Canvas

1. Mount your canvas by selecting the keyboard shortcut Cmd/Ctrl-M. This is equivalent to going to the top menu Window > Screen Mode Toggle. You now see your canvas appearing against an inert gray background that you can click on and drag over without accidentally going back to the Finder (Mac users). It is also visually simpler than having the canvas border frame around the canvas. Always work in screen mode unless there's a specific reason not to.
2. Move the cursor over the canvas. The cursor arrow changes into a triangle.
3. Hold down the space bar on your keyboard. The cursor changes into a hand (the same Grabber Hand in the Tools palette). Click and drag on the canvas, still holding the space bar down, and move the canvas so it fits snugly in the top left corner.

General Preferences

1. Select Edit (or Corel Painter 8 in Mac OS X) > Preferences > General.
2. Adjust the cursor angle. I like my cursor to point toward the upper left (Figure 1.6). If you are left-handed, you may prefer it pointing to the upper right.

Continued

3 You may wish to uncheck the "Brush ghost when possible" checkbox. By default this option is checked and results in a preview of the brush shape and size, visible on the canvas when you're about to paint, which disappears when you actually paint. I find this preview distracting. Try it with and without the brush ghost and decide for yourself.

4 Click OK.

Register

If you haven't registered your copy of Painter, do so by selecting Help > Register.

The Painter 8 Desktop

The Painter 8 desktop comprises of four main interface elements: Toolbox, Property Bar, Brush Selector, and Palettes (Figure 1.7).

All of these elements can be moved around, rearranged, or hidden. Thus you have complete flexibility in controlling your Painter 8 environment.

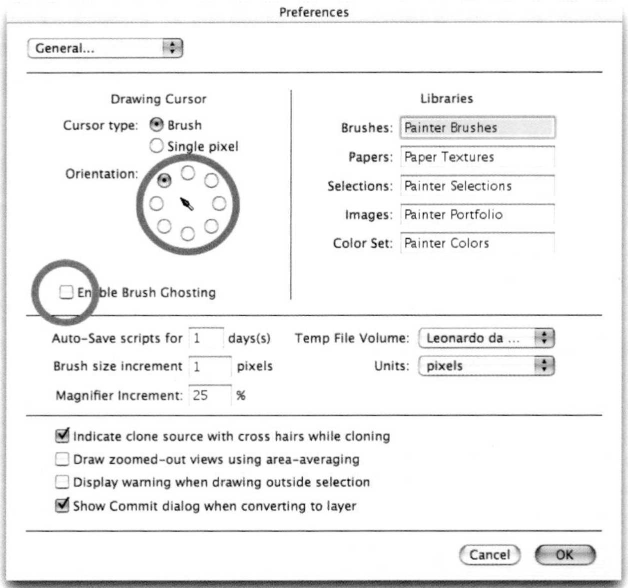

Figure 1.6 Suggested Painter General Preferences—adjust drawing cursor angle and uncheck the "Brush ghost when possible" option.

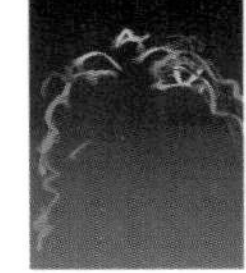

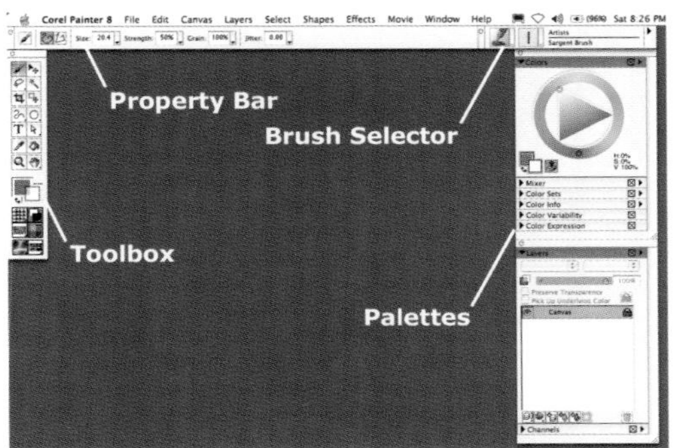

Figure 1.7 The main interface elements of the Painter 8 desktop.

Toolbox

The Toolbox lets you access the Painter 8 tools plus a variety of art materials, such as the Regular and Additional Colors, the Papers, Patterns, Gradients, Nozzles, Weaves, and Brush Looks. Note that a small triangle in the bottom right corner of a Toolbox icon indicates that more options are available if you hold your cursor down on the icon. Take a few moments to explore the Toolbox.

Property Bar

The Property Bar provides easy access to commonly needed parameters related to the currently selected tool. Notice as you change tool choice how the Property Bar changes.

Brush Selector

Brushes are at the heart of Painter's magic. The phenomenal range and ability of Painter's brushes empowers you to express yourself freely on the digital canvas. The Brush Selector is where you choose the specific brush you wish to use. It comprises a Brush Category pop-up menu (Brush Category Picker) on the left, and, immediately to the right of the Brush Category pop-up is the Brush Variant pop-up menu (Brush Variant Picker). You will always want to select Category first, followed by Variant, because each Brush Category (grouping or family of brushes with similar behaviors) is associated with a separate set of Brush Variants (individual brushes). In locating an individual brush (Figure 1.8) you first need to select the Category (left-hand menu) followed by the Variant (right-hand menu).

The consistent hierarchy of brushes in Painter is Library > Category > Variant. Understanding this hierarchy is vital to using Painter.

There is a Brushes pop-up menu accessible by holding the cursor down on the triangle in the top right of the Brush Selector window. Note that to modify and customize brushes you will need to access the Brush Creator (Cmd/Ctrl-B).

Palettes

The eighteen palettes are all summarized under the Window menu, each listed with Hide or Show, depending on whether they are already visible on your desktop. Nine of the palettes have key com-

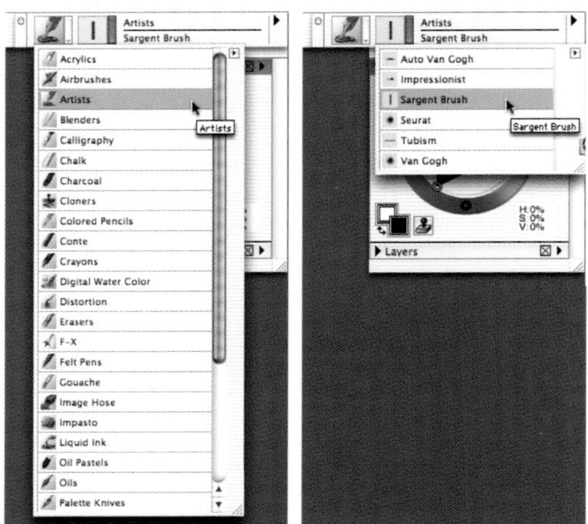

1. Select Category 2. Select Variant

Figure 1.8 Understanding the hierarchy of Categories and Variants is essential to using the Brush Selector. Always select the Category first and the Variant second.

mands that allow you to Hide or Show them without needing to go to the Window menu. Because these palettes would be overwhelming to see all at once, the default arrangement of palettes shows only eight palettes. Many palettes have pop-up menus on the far right of the palette title bar (click on the triangle). You will find that you want different combinations of palettes showing for different tasks. For instance, when painting you may just want to see Colors and Layers (in case you choose a watercolor or liquid ink brush that generates its own layer). If you are working with text you will also want to see the text palette. For working on collage, the Layers and Channels palettes will be needed. All of these palettes can be conveniently grouped or ungrouped to make the best use of your working space and avoid clutter.

For a more detailed description of the Painter desktop elements, please refer to the User Manual. My intention here is to give you a quick overview of what's there, rather than to go into detail and describe every palette and menu item.

Arranging Your Palettes

A quick way to see the standard palette arrangement is to select Window > Arrange Palettes > Default. You can move the palettes around, into and out of groups and up and down within a group, by placing your cursor in the central region of the palette title bar, to the right of the palette name and to the left of the close button (small square with an X in it), and then dragging the palette to its new position. If you close a palette, or it's not showing in the first place, you can make it visible by either using the appropriate keyboard shortcut or by going to the Windows menu and choosing Show (palette name).

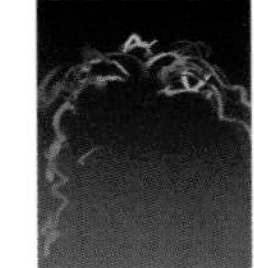

Libraries

Painter has a variety of Libraries, or collections, that can be accessed through Selectors. In the case of brushes, the Brushes Library is a collection of brush categories, each of which is a grouping of individual variants. To select a brush you use the Brush Selector to first choose the Brush Category and then decide on the brush variant.

The Papers, Gradients, Patterns, Weaves, Looks, and Nozzles Library Selectors are all accessible at the bottom of the Tools palette as well as via individual palettes listed in the Window menu. The Scripts, Selection Portfolio, and Image Portfolio Library Selectors are accessible through the Palettes listed in the Window menu.

Looking Under the Hood

You can directly observe the Brush Library > Category > Variant hierarchy by "looking under the hood," so to speak.

1. Return to your computer desktop. (Windows users, click Start > Run and type Explorer, or double click on the My Computer icon.)
2. Locate the Corel Painter 8 application folder.
3. Open the Corel Painter 8 folder and locate the Brushes folder.
4. Open the Brushes folder (Figure 1.9).
5. Within the Brushes folder is a folder called Painter Brushes. This is the default Brush Library folder.
6. Open the Painter Brushes folder.
7. Within the Painter Brushes folder are subfolders that represent the various Brush Categories, and within those Category subfolders are the individual Brush Variants themselves.

   Thus the folder hierarchy is:

   Painter 8 > Brushes > Painter Brushes **Library** > Brush **Categories** > Brush **Variants**

   At the same level as the Brush Category folders are associated .jpg files that share the same name as the Category folders (i.e., "Artists" and "Artists.jpg"). This .jpg file is used as the graphic representation of the Category in the Brushes palette drawer. If you ever replace any of these .jpg Category icon images, note that they must be 30 by 30 pixels.

Continued

8 Open one of the Brush Category subfolders and observe the mixture of .xml and other files which contain the brush data for each individual Painter 8 Brush Variant.

Make a Back-up Copy of Your Brushes Folder

At this stage make a back-up copy of your Brushes folder, the one that is within your Painter 8 application folder. On a Mac that involves just holding down your Option key while you drag the folder to another location. Rename your back-up folder "Brushes Back-up." I suggest keeping it in the Painter 8 folder. It will be useful if you ever have a brush variant file become corrupt and need replacing (which unfortunately may happen from time to time).

Trying Out Brushes

Brush Tracking

1 Choose the Artists Category > Sargent Brush Variant.

2 Make a single brush stroke that goes from applying as little pressure as you can with your stylus, to pressing as heavily as you can (Figure 1.10).

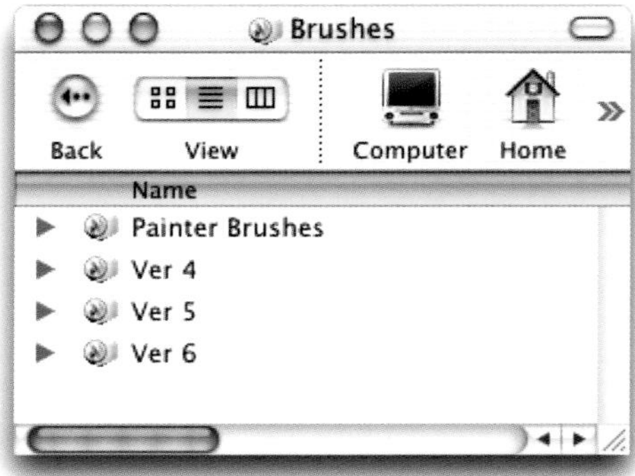

Figure 1.9 The Brushes folder, located within the Painter 8 application folder.

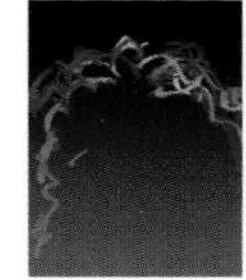

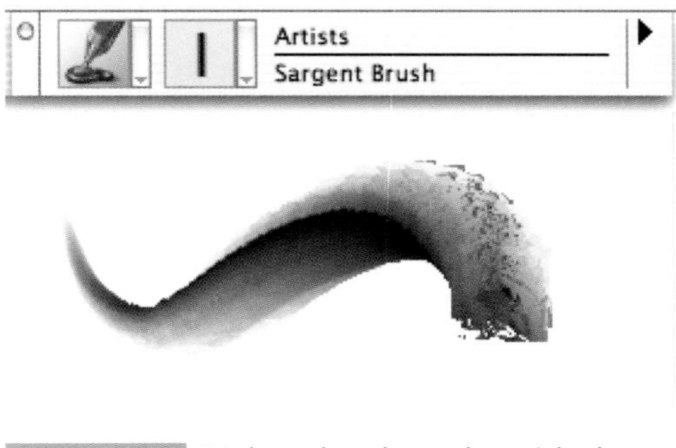

Figure 1.10 Make a brush stroke with the Sargent Brush.

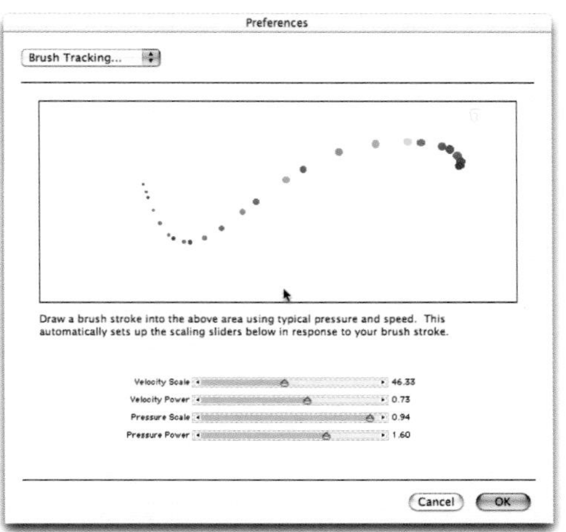

Figure 1.11 The Brush Tracking window, where you can adjust Painter's pressure sensitivity.

Don't be afraid to press hard! Note how the thickness responds to pressure. Make sure you test out the full range of thickness by going to extremes of light and heavy pressure. You should be able to comfortably control the thickness across the full range. Sometimes you may find that the brush is either too sensitive or too insensitive to the pressure you apply. This is where Brush Tracking comes into play.

We all apply a different natural range of stylus pressure when we paint. It is worthwhile to set Painter and your stylus to be sensitive to your natural pressure range. To do so, select Edit (Corel Painter 8 in Mac OS X) > Preferences > Brush Tracking.

Make a single light stroke in the Brush Tracking window (Figure 1.11).

This procedure resets the values that determine the sensitivity of your stylus. Click OK. These values are saved until you go back and reset them. You may find this helps give you much more control over your brushes. Repeat making brush strokes on your canvas. See if the sensitivity is improved. If not, repeat steps 3 and 4.

Try out the following brushes (Category > Variant):

Calligraphy > Dry Ink

Chalk > Square Chalk 35

F-X > Hair Spray

Blenders > Oily Blender 40

Image Hose > Spray-Size-P Angle-D

Do not erase or undo. You're welcome to use different colors if you wish. Paint brush strokes over each other. Push the limits of these brushes. Press very hard and very light. Note the effect of pressure. Paint with fast, gestural strokes and then with slow, smooth strokes. Paint right off the edge of the canvas. Don't be afraid of hurting the stylus! Note that some brushes add color to the canvas, whereas others only affect color that's already there.

1. Select the Chalk > Square Chalk 35.
2. Select black in the Colors palette.
3. Click on the Papers selector at the bottom of the Tools palette and select a different Paper texture from the Papers Library.
4. Choose Cmd/Ctrl-A (Select All).
5. Choose Delete/Backspace (this clears your canvas).
6. Make a brush stroke on your canvas and note the effect of the texture.
7. Adjust the Scale slider in the Papers section.
8. Make more brush strokes and note the effect of the Papers scale.
9. Check the Invert Paper checkbox in the Papers section.
10. Make more brush strokes and note the effect of inverting the paper.

Only some brushes are affected by the paper texture in Painter (all of the Chalk brushes are).

As you experiment for the first time with Painter's brushes you will inevitably run into some mysteries. Some brushes paint with a color different from that chosen in the Colors palette color picker. (For example, cloners take color from the default clone source, the currently selected pattern in the Patterns library. Cloners will be discussed later in this session.) Some brushes (Water Color and Liquid Ink) paint into special layers. When you try painting with other brushes after using either of those, you get a warning telling you that only watercolor brushes can be used on watercolor layers, and a similar message for liquid ink. Instructions are included toward the end of this session explaining how to delete, flatten or paint below those layers. First we will review some basic operations.

1.6 Basic Operations

Removing Paint

I encourage you to avoid erasing, deleting, and undoing brush strokes. Although the computer offers convenient ways to remove paint, your paintings will take on greater depth and interest if you build up your brush strokes, even when you're not happy with them, rather than delete them. Having said that, here's a brief synopsis of the options at your fingertips when you do wish to remove paint.

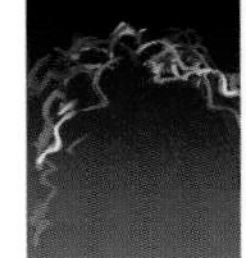

Erasing

The Eraser variants in the Erasers category of brushes erase to the paper color (which is white by default but can be set to the current regular color by selecting Canvas > Set Paper Color). The Bleach variant simply bleaches out the color on the canvas until it is white, independent of the Paper Color. The bleach gives a similar effect to the Dodge variant in the Photo category of brushes. Try the Eraser variants on your painted image. You can also simply turn your stylus over on its end and use the large eraser at the opposite end of the stylus tip (although I find this a bit cumbersome).

Deleting Selected Regions of Your Canvas

You can always use a selection tool (e.g., lasso or rectangular/oval selection tool) to select a region of canvas. If you want a soft edge to your deletion, choose Select > Feather and feather the selection by 10 pixels or so. Then select Delete/Backspace to delete to the paper color. Try this on a region of your painted image.

Clearing Your Whole Canvas

1. Select Cmd/Ctrl-A (equivalent of choosing Select > All). You'll see *dancing ants* around the perimeter of your canvas (unless the perimeter is beyond the limits of the screen).
2. Click the Delete/Backspace key on the keyboard. Your canvas clears to plain white again unless you have created any watercolor or liquid ink layers.

Deleting Water Color or Liquid Ink Layers

1. Open the Objects palette > Layers section.
2. Hold down the shift key while you click once on each layer.
3. Let go of the shift key.
4. Click on the trash can icon in the lower right of the Layers section.

Dropping Water Color or Liquid Ink Layers

1. Open the Layers palette.
2. Hold down the Shift key while you click once on each layer.
3. Let go of the Shift key.
4. Click on the left-hand icon in the lower left of the Layers palette and drag down to Drop.

This process flattens your image, placing what was in the watercolor or liquid ink Layers onto the background canvas, and allows you to paint over those marks with other brushes.

Painting Beneath Water Color or Liquid Ink Layers

1. Open the Objects palette > Layers section.
2. Click on Canvas so it is highlighted.

This deselects the layer and allows you to continue painting beneath the layer on the background canvas. You can always reselect the layer at a later time and either add to it with an appropriate variant (watercolor on watercolor layers), delete it, or drop it.

Undoing Individual Brush Strokes

My advice when painting is: Don't undo! Get used to being committed to your marks. Let every mark contribute to the fabric of your painting. To undo individual strokes, use the Cmd/Ctrl-Z.

Setting Undo Preferences

Painter is set to have a default of five levels of undo (Cmd/Ctrl-Z). You can set up to 32 levels, although this will take up more memory. For some projects, multiple undo can be useful. Plus it can be a valuable safety back-up feature. Therefore I suggest setting the Undo levels to the maximum. If Painter seems to be reacting slowly or crashing, then go back and reduce the number of levels of Undo.

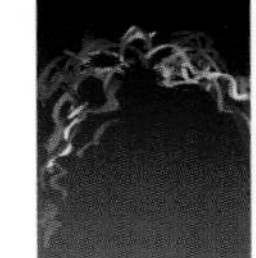

1. Select Edit > Preferences > Undo.
2. Set Allow Undo up to 32 levels.
3. Click OK.

Fading a Brush Stroke or Effect

It is also possible to partially undo a brush stroke or effect by selecting Edit > Fade. This is a particularly useful feature for effects, because the small preview windows in the effects dialog boxes often lead you to underestimate the influence of the effect when applied to the whole canvas.

Saving Your Images

1. Select File > Save As.
2. Give the file an appropriate name.
3. Select the location where you wish to save your file.
4. Click Save.

I recommend that you save your work in progress as a RIFF file, and your final image for printing as an RGB TIFF. You will find a detailed discussion regarding strategies for naming and saving your artwork in the next session. A brief discussion of strategies for selecting file formats and color modes is included in Appendix I.

Adjusting Brush Size

Some brush strokes vary in width according to the pressure you apply with your stylus. If you want more variation of brush thickness than that provided by pressure control, then you need to adjust the Brush Size. You can do this by a number of different means.

Size Preview in the Brush Creator's Stroke Designer Window

1 Choose Window > Show Brush Creator (Cmd/Ctrl-B) > Stroke Designer tab > Size section. The preview window on the upper left indicates brush diameter. The outside of the solid black circle is the brush diameter. Some brushes, such as the Artists category > Impressionist brush variant (Figure 1.12), have a variation of diameter built in (Min Size slider less than 100%). This variation is shown as an inner solid black circle, indicating the minimum diameter, and an outer gray ring, indicating the maximum diameter.

If you click on the Brush Dab Preview Window in the Size section, you see a depiction of how the pigment is distributed. Click again and it returns to the original solid circles. Have the preview set to show the solid black (or black and gray) circle.

The six small brush dab profile icons, located on the upper right of the Size preview, show the way pigment will be distributed across the stroke.

Size Selector in the Property Bar

Either type in the size in the Brush Property Bar or click on the Size box and adjust the slider that appears.

You can adjust size with the Size slider, either in this Brush Creator > Stroke Designer window or in the Brush Property Bar. I recommend using the Size slider in the Brush Creator rather than the Size slider in the Brush Property Bar, since the latter has no preview and it is easy to inadvertently try to create a brush so huge that the program crashes.

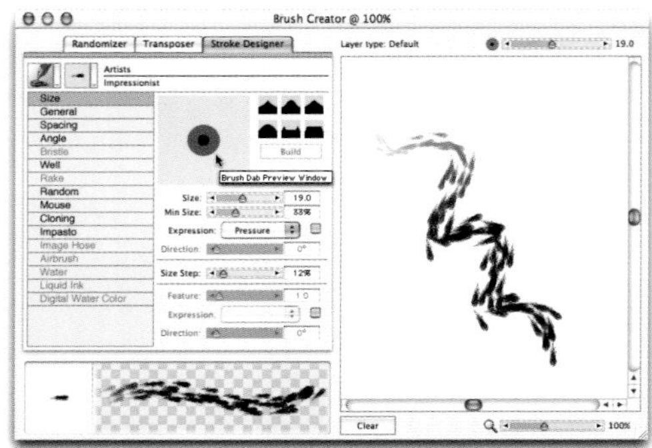

Figure 1.12 Brush Dab Preview Window for the Artists > Impressionist brush.

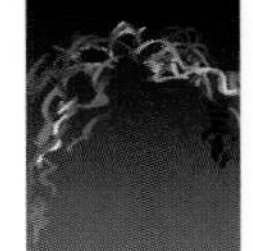

Key Commands

You can also incrementally increase or decrease the brush size using:

the [key for decrease

the] key for increase

or use the key command combination Cmd-Option-Shift / Ctrl-Alt-Shift and click and drag on the canvas.

Color

Picking Color

You can select color either by clicking on color squares in the Color Sets palette or by using the Color Picker in the Colors palette.

The Standard Colors Color Picker (Figure 1.13) has an outer Hue Ring (based on a representation of the color spectrum known traditionally as the *color wheel*) and a Saturation/Value Triangle in the center. There is another Color Picker, called Small Colors, accessible from the Colors palette pop-up menu (arrow in top right of Colors palette). The Small Colors Color Picker combines a single horizontal hue bar with a Saturation/Value Triangle. I recommend sticking with the Standard Colors Color Picker.

Hue, Saturation, and Value

Hue is the named color (e.g., red, orange, yellow, green, blue, indigo, violet).

Saturation, also known as intensity or chroma, is the brightness or dullness of the color. High saturation is a very pure color (bright). Low saturation is a more impure color (mixed with darker or lighter color).

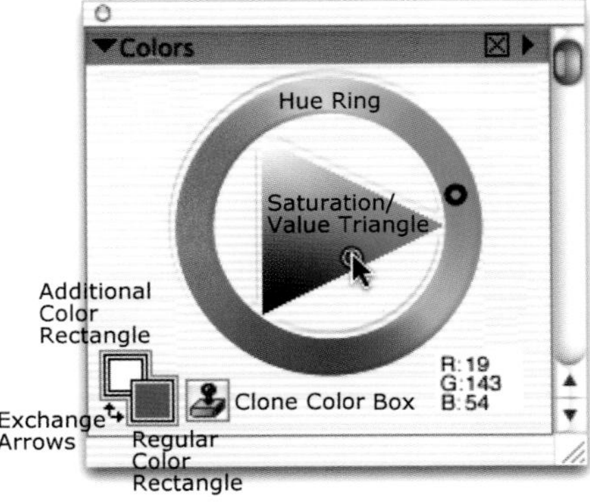

Figure 1.13 The Colors palette.

Value, also known as luminosity, is the lightness or darkness of the color. If a color were represented in a gray-scale spectrum, the value of that color would determine the lightness or darkness of the equivalent gray. The extremes in value are pure black or pure white.

A color is only uniquely defined when all three qualities—hue, saturation, and value (HSV)—are defined. There are a number of other ways of uniquely defining color, such as Red Green Blue (the colors of the luminescent phosphors in a computer screen or color TV) or Cyan Magenta Yellow Black (the colors of the standard inks used in the printing industry).

In Painter, defining a color involves adjusting both the small circular cursor in the outer Hue Ring and the one in the Saturation/Value Triangle. To select either white or black in the Color Picker, take the Saturation/Value Triangle cursor to the upper left corner for white or to the lower left corner for black. The hue is not relevant when selecting white or black. It is easy to leave the Saturation/Value Triangle cursor in one of the corners (black lower left or white upper left) and wonder why you are not getting the color indicated by the cursor position in the hue ring.

To fully understand how you can utilize the arrangement of hues, or colors, in the Hue Ring as you paint, it is useful to understand how Painter's Hue Ring relates to the traditional artist's Color Wheel. The next few sections of this session explain the basics. Color theory is a huge subject, and there are many excellent resources available. My intention here is just to give you information that can help you make the most of the Hue Ring. If you wish to understand color at a deeper level I recommend further research and much experimentation.

Primary Colors

When you create an image on the computer you can either view it on a computer display or as an actual print. When viewed on a computer screen, or using projected light, the colors you see are generated directly from a light source, such as a phosphor, and transmitted through space to your eye. Color viewed in this way is known as additive color. When you combine red, green and blue transmitted light you get pure white. These three colors are known in the world of physics as the primary colors of light.

When you view the same artwork as a print, you are seeing light that is reflected off the print. Any color seen in a print, as in traditional painting, is simply color that is not absorbed when light strikes the surface of the print. Such color is known as subtractive color. When you mix red, yellow, and blue pigments you get black (or close to black). In traditional painting these three colors—red, yellow, and blue—cannot be created by mixing others colors together. Red, yellow, and blue are known in traditional painting as the primary colors (different from the primary colors in projected light).

Color Wheel

A traditional artist's color wheel is created by initially placing dabs of the three primary colors—red, yellow, and blue—in equidistant positions on a flat circle. Adjacent primary colors are then mixed to create secondary colors (for instance, yellow and blue are mixed to create green). Dabs of the secondary colors are placed halfway between the primary colors from which they are made. This process is continued with tertiary colors, which are made by mixing primary colors with

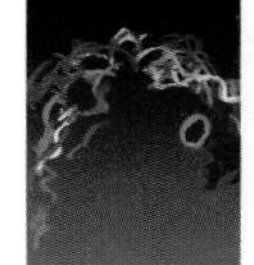

secondary colors around the wheel, and so on until there is a continuous range of colors around the wheel.

Painter's Hue Ring is a color wheel based on the physics primary colors of light: red, green, and blue. These three colors are equidistant around the wheel. The secondary colors on this Hue Ring are cyan, magenta, and yellow.

Complementary Colors

Two colors are complementary when they are exactly opposite each other on the color wheel. When juxtaposed adjacent to each other on a painting, complementary colors can have a powerful effect by bringing out a vividness in each. As painters we can take advantage of the fact that our eyes naturally seek to balance any given color with its complementary color. When the complementary color is not present, the eye spontaneously generates the complement. We can use combinations of complementary colors in a work to provide harmonious balance, as well as bring attention to specific areas of the image. An excellent book that deals with these issues, plus a lot more concerning color contrast of all kinds, is *Elements of Color* by Johannes Itten (John Wiley & Sons, 1970).

Regular and Additional Color

Notice the two overlapping rectangles of color in the lower left corner of the Colors section and also in the Tools palette. The Painter 8 User Guide refers to these as Primary and Secondary colors. I prefer to refer to these as Regular and Additional colors to avoid unnecessary confusion with the terms primary and secondary colors used in color theory.

The Regular color is indicated by the foremost of the two overlapping rectangles. Behind the Regular color rectangle is the Additional color rectangle. You can make either rectangle active by clicking on it. A bold black border highlights the active rectangle in the Tools palette. When you first open Painter the Regular color rectangle is always active.

Although these rectangles closely resemble the foreground and background color rectangles of Photoshop, they have quite different functions in Painter. Most brushes apply only the Regular color. The Additional color can be used for several purposes, such as specifying a two-color gradient (the Two Point gradient in the Gradients palette) or providing a tint color for Image Hose nozzles (when the Grain slider in the Property Bar is moved to the left). I recommend that you always have the Regular color active and use the exchange arrows to toggle between the Regular and Additional colors when you need to.

Paper Color

Do not confuse the Additional color with background or paper color. The Additional and Regular color rectangles in Painter look deceptively similar to the Background and Foreground color rectangles in Adobe Photoshop. The paper color in Painter is determined in the New File dialog box, or by choosing Canvas > Set Paper Color at which point the paper color becomes the current Regular color. The Eraser family of brushes—and the Select All > Delete commands—erase to the current paper color. When you enlarge a canvas by choosing Canvas > Canvas Size, the extra canvas added on is the color of the current paper color. You can use this technique to add colored borders to your work. The default paper color is white.

Color Management

If you are specifically interested in learning more about how to ensure consistency of color between your screen image and your printed image, and in moving an image between Painter and Photoshop, then see the Help > Tutorials and refer to Appendix III.

1.7 Brushes Close-up

Brushes That Require Deeper Understanding

Most brushes are straightforward to use and behave in logical, predictable ways. You just pick the brush and then play with it directly on the canvas. You'll typically see color painted onto the canvas, interaction with color already on the canvas, or both. You'll notice a myriad of subtle differences in behavior, such as some brushes covering up other colors, some mixing with other colors, some showing paper textures, some changing size with pressure, and so on. You don't need to know anything special, just try them and see what they do!

Every now and then you'll come across a brush that doesn't act like the others and needs a little explanation. You may need to take a few extra steps to make these brushes work or to realize their full mark-making potential. In the remainder of this session you will explore the following:

Image Hose

Cloners

Water Color

Liquid Ink

Impasto

Image Hose

Painting with Sequences of Image Elements

The Image Hose brush category is represented by the icon showing a garden hose nozzle with green clover leaves spewing out of the end. When you paint with it you will see a succession of images being painted onto the canvas (Figure 1.14).

The set of images that are being painted are known as a Nozzle. The variants for this brush category are unlike all others; they do not indicate different brush variants but simply different ways that the nozzle elements are distributed as they leave the Image Hose.

For instance, in the Spray-Size-P Angle-D variant, "Spray-Size-P" means the size of the elements, and their proximity to each other as they are sprayed out is determined by stylus pressure. "Angle-D"

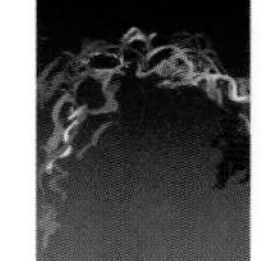

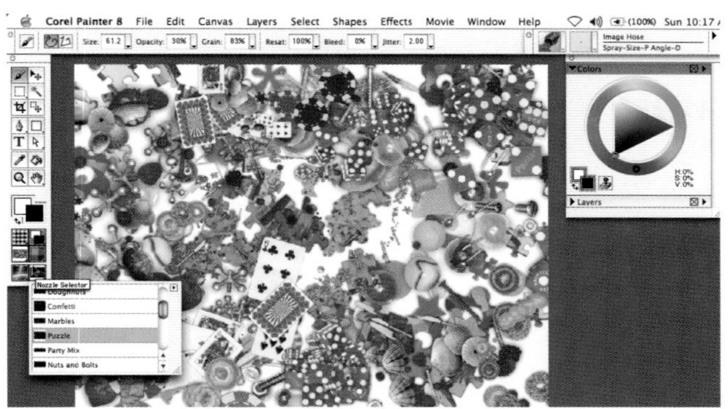

Figure 1.14 Experimenting with the Image Hose > Spray-Size-P Angle-D variant and a variety of nozzles.

means that the direction of the Nozzle image elements follows the direction of your brush stroke. You can load up different nozzles from the Nozzle selector in the Tools palette.

Select different nozzles and try them out. Choose different variant options and see their effect. Try light pressure as well as heavy pressure. Try short dabs as well as long strokes.

Advanced Image Hose Operations (Optional)

Picking up the Additional Color in the Image Hose

1. Choose a bright color in the Color Picker.
2. Click on the exchange arrows to make that bright color go to the Additional Color rectangle.
3. Move the Grain slider to the left in the Property Bar.
4. Make a brush stroke and note how the nozzle color changes when you paint.

Creating Your Own Nozzles

1. Paste your nozzle contents as layers in a file.
2. Select all the layers in the Layers palette by clicking on each one with the Shift key held down or choosing Select All in the Layers pop-up menu.

Continued

3. Select Cmd/Ctrl-G to group the layers.
4. Select Make Nozzle from Group from the Nozzles pop-up menu located in the top right of the Nozzle selector in the Tools palette.
5. Save the resulting file as a RIFF file with the name you wish to call your nozzle.
6. Choose Cmd/Ctrl-L.
7. Locate your nozzle file and click Open.
8. Apply the nozzle on your canvas.
9. Select Add Nozzle to Library. Your custom nozzle will now be part of the current Nozzle Library.

Cloners

The Default Clone Source

The Cloners Brush Variants look at a clone source for their source of color, rather than the Color Picker (which is usually grayed out when a cloner is selected). The default clone source in Painter is the currently selected pattern (Patterns palette). Thus when you first use cloners you'll often see a mysterious pattern appear on your canvas.

There are numerous different cloner variants, many of which act as artistic filters that you selectively apply by hand, rather than applying instantaneously and globally over the whole image, as you do when applying an effect.

Making Any Brush a Cloner

You are not restricted to the Brush Variants of the Cloners Brush Category to clone from one image (source image) into another (destination image). You can turn almost any brush in Painter into a cloner simply by clicking on the Clone Color icon in the Colors palette. This makes Painter a phenomenally powerful image transformation tool since you can hand-paint a clone transformation using an almost unlimited variety of brushes.

Working From a Photograph

For detailed instructions and techniques, refer to the later sessions on photography (sessions 7 and 8). Here is a brief synopsis of the basics. When you make a copy of a file by selecting File > Clone, the original file automatically becomes the clone source. This is useful when you're working from photographs. An added benefit of making a clone copy of an image is that you can apply Tracing Paper (Cmd/Ctrl-T) and see the source image showing through under the destination image (50% opacity of each).

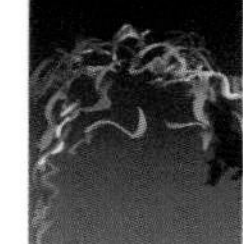

1. Go to the Creativity Projects > 1- Basics > 1–7 Brushes Close-up folder that you copied earlier from the Painter Creativity Companion CD. You will find a tutorial image called "specialmoment.jpg", a photograph by Jim Paliungas.
2. Open the specialmoment.jpg file in Painter, or any photograph of your own.
3. Choose File > Clone.
4. Choose Cmd/Ctrl-M to mount the clone copy.
5. Choose Cmd/Ctrl-A (Select > All).
6. Choose Delete/Backspace. This clears your canvas.
7. Choose Cmd/Ctrl-D (Select > None).
8. Choose Cmd/Ctrl-T (Canvas > Tracing Paper). You'll see a 50 percent opacity representation of the original image.
9. Select the Cloners Brush Category in the Brushes palette.
10. Experiment on this image (Figure 1.15) with different cloner variants, except those whose names begin with "Water Color . . ." or an "×". Have fun! Regularly turn off Tracing Paper (Cmd/Ctrl-T toggles Tracing Paper on and off) so you can see what you really have on your canvas. You can also try out brushes from other categories by clicking on the Clone Color Box in the Colors palette. The Impressionist and Sargent variants from the Artists category both work very well as cloners.

Note that the Soft Cloner variant is an excellent brush for gently bringing back the original image into your clone image.

Water Color

Water Color Layers

Water Color brushes are represented by an icon showing a glass of water in the background and a brush painting a green splodge in the foreground. They are not to be confused with the Digital Water Color brushes, represented by a similar icon. Both categories and brushes, Water Color and Digital Water Color, give beautiful, soft washes and effects. The crucial and unique aspect of working with the Water Color brushes is that they paint into special Water Color layers that are separate from, and sit above, the regular background canvas. Open the Layers palette so you can observe the Water Color layers. The Runny Water Color variants take a few moments for the paint to run, during which time you can see water droplets falling in the Layers palette. Water Color brush strokes are usually translucent, so you can see the underlying background canvas paint showing through from beneath the Wet

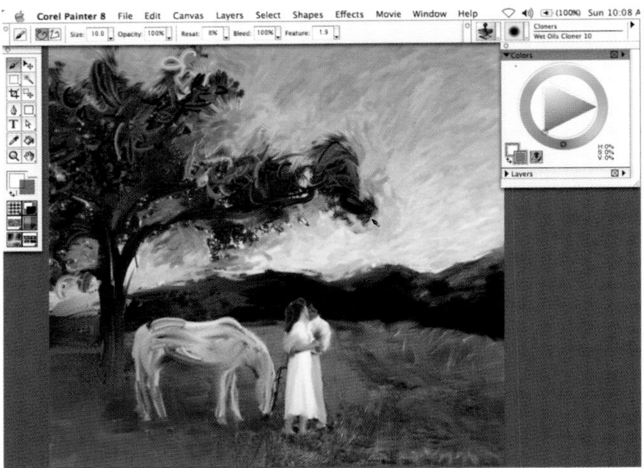

Figure 1.15 Experimenting with the Cloners brushes.

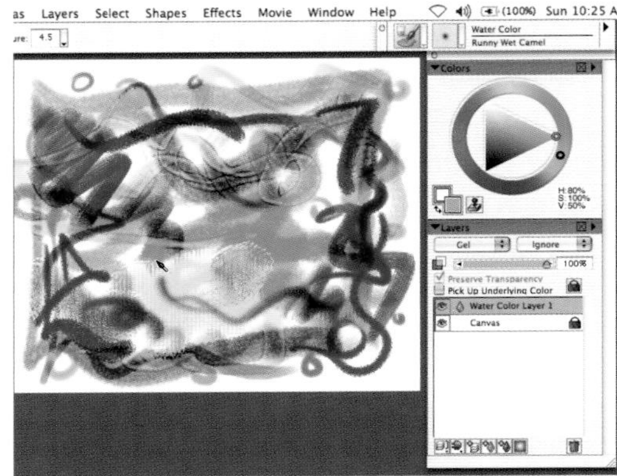

Figure 1.16 Experimenting with the Water Color brushes

layer. Open a new canvas 700 pixels wide by 600 pixels high and try out all the different Water Color variants (Figure 1.16).

After you've applied Water Color, if you then apply a non-Water Color brush stroke you'll get a warning "Only Water Color brushes can be used on Water Color layers." You must first click on the Canvas in the Layers section. When you paint on the background canvas with other brushes it appears that you're painting beneath the Water Color. Water Color layers can always be added to and changed by Water Color brushes as long as they are selected in the Layers section of the Objects palette when you apply the Water Color brushes. When you try clearing your background canvas (Select All > Delete), any Water Color layers will be left untouched.

Dropping or Deleting a Water Color Layer

To drop a watercolor layer onto the background canvas, select the layer in the Layers section and then click on the left hand of the four small icons beneath the Layers list and drag down to Drop. To

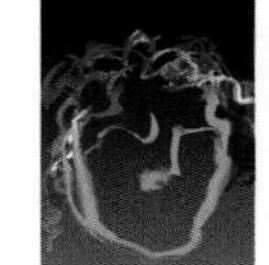

delete a Water Color layer, select the layer in the Layers section and then click on the trash can icon on the right of the four icons at the bottom of the Layers section.

Painting Beneath a Water Color Layer

If you wish, you can preserve the Water Color layer and paint underneath it with other, non-Water Color brushes. To do so just click on the Canvas layer in the Layers section. The Canvas layer will now be highlighted and you can continue painting with non-Water Color brushes on the background canvas beneath the watercolor layer. Any time you wish to add Water Color brush strokes to the Water Color layer, just reselect that layer. Water Color layers can only be edited with Water Color brushes if the canvas is preserved in the RIFF file format.

Reference Material

John Derry, one of the creators of Painter and the writer of the Foreword for this book, has written some excellent visual guides, which are available as PDF files that can be downloaded from the Web. *A Visual Guide to Corel Painter 7 Water Color* is a must-read if you really want to understand these brushes. You can download it from Jinny Brown's web site at www.pixelalley.com/tutorials/jderry-guide-pdf-downloads.html. You can also find links to this site from my resources web page.

Liquid Ink

Liquid Ink Layers

Liquid ink brushes are represented by an icon showing a silver pen nib with a silvery mercury-like liquid forming a pool at the end of the nib. Liquid Ink brushes produce some astounding graphic and resist effects (Figure 1.17). Like the Water Color brushes, the Liquid Ink brushes paint into their own Liquid Ink layers.

After you've applied Liquid Ink, if you then apply a non–Liquid Ink brush stroke you'll get a warning saying "Non-Liquid-Ink brushes cannot be used on Liquid-Ink layers." As with Water Color layers, you have the choice of dropping, deleting, or painting beneath the Liquid Ink layer. Note that the resist liquid ink variants only have a visible effect on brush strokes from nonresist liquid ink variants in the same Liquid Ink layer. Try out all the Liquid Ink variants.

Reference Material

I highly recommend you take a look at John Derry's *A Visual Guide to Corel Painter 7 Liquid Ink* to deepen your understanding of these brushes. You can download it from the same URL on Jinny's web site as mentioned previously, www.pixelalley.com/tutorials/jderry-guide-pdf-downloads.html.

Impasto

The Impasto category of brushes are a group of brushes that add three-dimensional depth to their brush strokes, almost as if you are embossing the canvas as you paint (Figure 1.18).

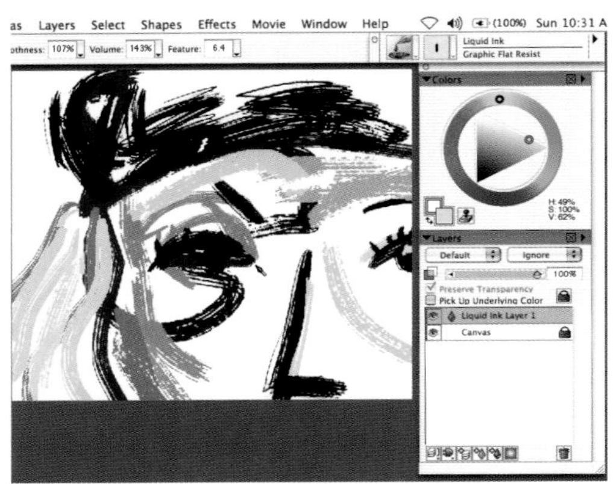

Figure 1.17 Experimenting with Liquid Ink brushes.

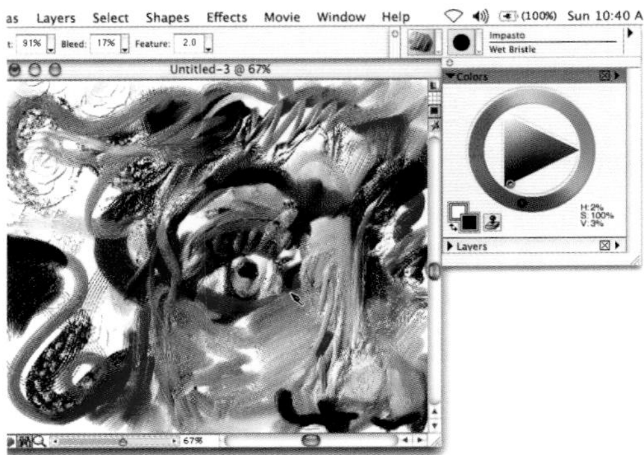

Figure 1.18 Experimenting with the Impasto brushes.

They can give you some fabulous effects but also cause much confusion and frustration. Once you have painted with an Impasto brush, the three-dimensional embossing appears to remain in your image, even when you try to paint over it with other non-Impasto brushes. It is as if the Impasto depth is recorded in a separate layer (one that does not appear in the Layers palette). You can control whether an Impasto brush actually generates the depth by going to the Impasto section of the Brush Creator > Stroke Designer window (Cmd/Ctrl-B). By changing the Draw To pop-up menu from Color and Depth to Color, you change the Impasto brush into one that doesn't add depth. Whether or not you like the depth is a matter of taste.

You can turn the Impasto effect off and on by clicking the small blue "bubble-gum" icon that appears in the upper right of the image window frame. You may have to go out of screen mode to see this icon by choosing Cmd/Ctrl-M if your canvas is mounted.

If you wish to flatten the impasto depth layer, either so you can paint over it in Painter or so you can preserve the Impasto depth effect when you open the image up in Photoshop, then choose Save As and save the file as a TIFF file. Close the TIFF file and then reopen it. This will automatically flatten the impasto depth layer.

Try-Out Abstract

1. Choose Cmd/Ctrl-N.
2. Open a new canvas 700 pixels wide by 700 pixels high.
3. Choose Cmd/Ctrl-M to mount the canvas in screen mode.

Continued

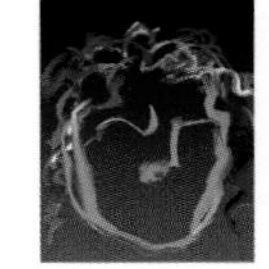

4 Play with the brushes on the canvas. Create an abstract. Don't undo or erase; just keep building up brush strokes on top of one another. Use this abstract as a way to explore the multitude of wonderful brush Variants contained in all the different brush Categories.

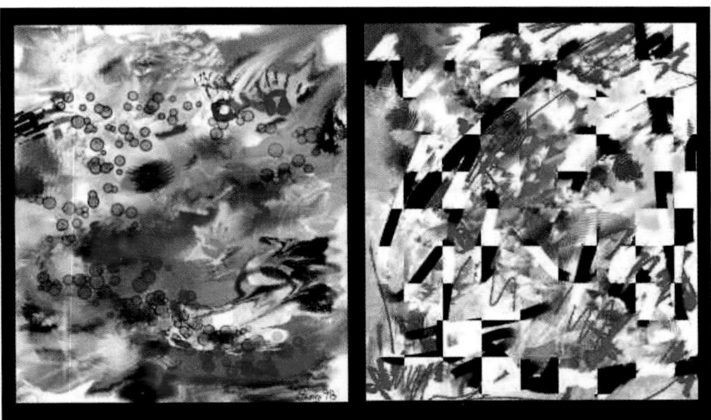

Figure 1.19 Abstracts by Sharon and Lois.

Here are a couple of abstracts two of my students, Sharon Bing and Lois Freeman-Fox, made (Figure 1.19) while exploring the brushes as part of my "Beyond the Brush" online art class.

1.8 Wrap

In this session you got your toes wet with Painter basics. You are now familiar with the palettes and know how to select and apply brushes and art materials. If you run into any problems, remember to refer to Appendix VI, Troubleshooting.

You're now ready to move on to the next step, which is not just how to use Painter, but how to use Painter smartly. In the next session you'll learn how to apply the four Guiding Principles in Painter. These principles will help you be more creative, more productive, and more efficient when using Painter.

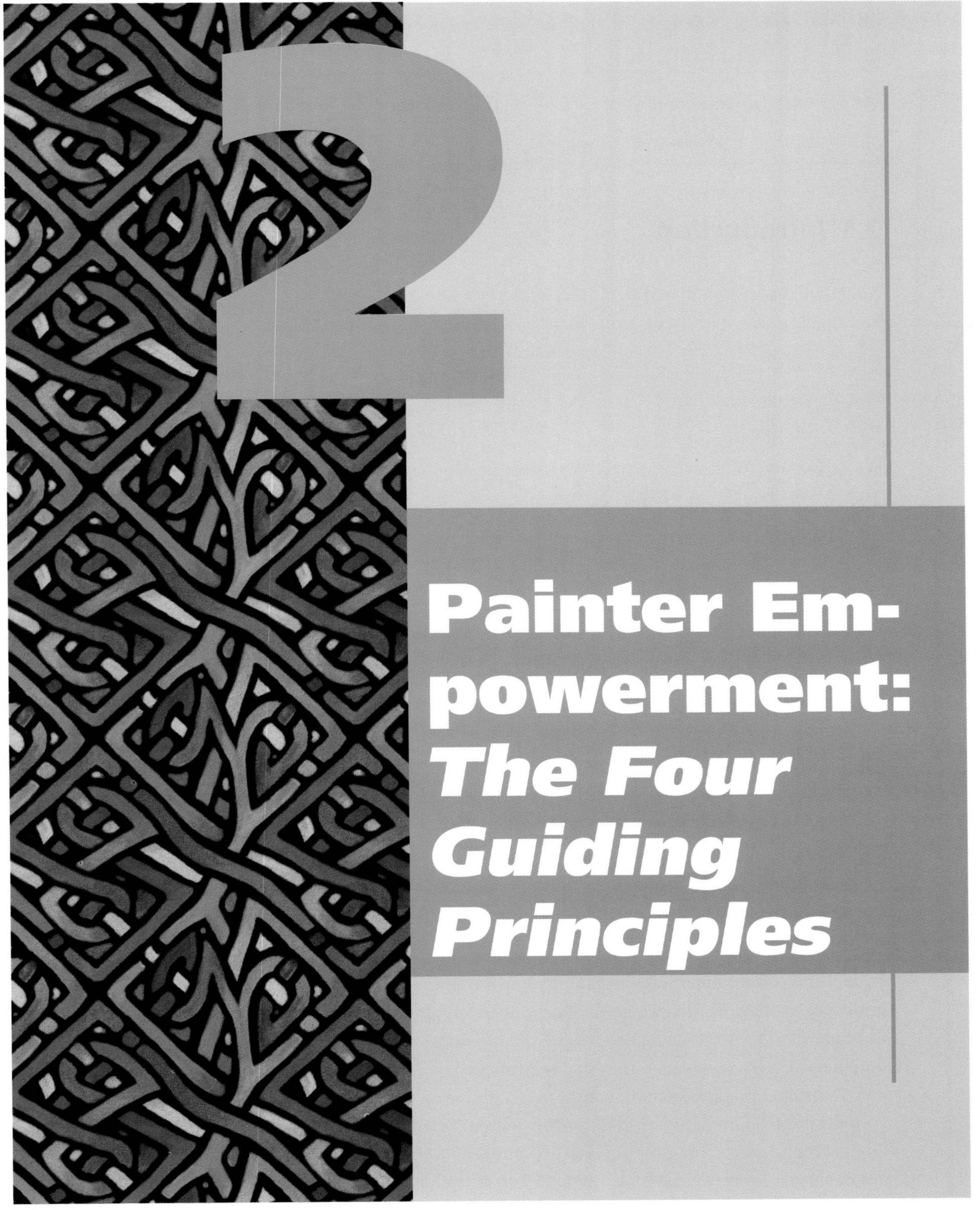

2

Painter Em-powerment: *The Four Guiding Principles*

We are what we repeatedly do. Excellence, then, is not an act, but a habit.

—*Aristotle*

2.1 Introduction

Now that you are familiar with Painter's interface and basic operations, you are ready to enact the four guiding principles for making the most of Painter. These principles are:

I Simplify

II Organize

III Optimize

IV Document

Applying these principles will help you be more creative, more productive, and more efficient when using Painter.

2.2 Instructor Notes

As an instructor, you can treat this session in one of three ways:

1. Ignore it completely, as in the case of a one-off class for beginners where you just want them to experience Painter and not get bogged down in strategic or technical detail.
2. Devote a specific class time to thoroughly covering these four guiding principles and going through all the detailed set-up involved, an approach I recommend for serious-minded, highly motivated students who want to use Painter professionally.
3. Take a halfway approach where you point out the principles as they come up, for instance in simplifying the desktop, encouraging documentation, and naming files, but don't go into specific detail or devote class time to them explicitly. This approach will fit into almost any class structure.

I adopt the second approach for almost all of my classes, because I find that by highlighting the principles to students, the principles stick in their minds. This allows reinforcement of the concepts throughout the class as examples crop up of situations where the principles can be applied or could have helped avert a problem if they had been applied.

The single practical action, contained in this session, that will make the biggest difference to your students' experience is loading the custom brushes, contained on the Painter Creativity Companion CD. If you do nothing else, I recommend that you at least load the Jeremy Faves custom brush category into your student computers so they have a greater diversity of brushes to choose from. See Appendix IV for instructions to load the extra brushes.

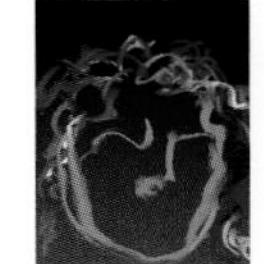

Besides my Jeremy Faves custom brush category, I have included on the Painter Creativity Companion CD a custom Brush Library called Creativity Brushes, which is full of my favorite brushes from Painter CD2, from earlier versions of Painter and also some custom Categories of brushes from artists around the world who have kindly given me permission to share them. There is also a Basic Brushes (No Layers) library that has all the brushes that automatically generate layers (Water Colors and Liquid Ink) taken out. This may be useful for a demo session where people unfamiliar with Painter are given the opportunity to try it out. The No Layers library avoids the complication and frustration of students inadvertently creating Water Color or Liquid Ink layers and then wondering why they keep getting an error message when they try to paint with other brushes. For any regular class, understanding these error messages is an important part of coming to grips with Painter.

For a basic introduction to painting, the enso exercise described in this session could be a good warm-up.

2.3 Overview

Here is an overview of the four guiding principles:

Principle I: Simplify

Keep things simple. Simplify your palette groups and save your palette layouts.

Make things easy and comfortable.

Avoid distractions. Be selective about what is visible on your desktop.

Avoid visual clutter. Work with images in screen mode whenever possible.

Principle II: Organize

Be organized (inside and outside Painter).

Always start Painter afresh when beginning a new project and close Painter at the completion of a project.

Adopt consistent, meaningful naming conventions for everything. That includes files, custom Variants, layers, scripts, custom palettes, custom libraries, and so on.

Organize and maintain a consistent file and folder hierarchy so you always know where everything is saved.

Begin with the end in mind. Work backward in determining the file size and resolution you need to begin a project with.

Principle III: Optimize

Maximize the power of Painter. Maximize your choices of Brushes and Art Materials. Take advantage of the full dynamic range and versatility of each brush you use.

Customize and save brush variants to suit your individual needs and preferences.

Customize and personalize your arrangement of variants, categories, and libraries.

Save meaningfully named, efficient Palette Arrangements to suit different tasks, operations, and, where relevant, screen resolutions.

Principle IV: Document

Meticulously document the progress of every project. Save stages and versions, each with a different file name, especially immediately prior to dropping layers or applying effects.

Where possible, record and save scripts of your painting sessions.

Back up and archive all of your data, in duplicate (stored in two separate locations), onto CD-ROM or DVD, on a regular basis. Catalog the contents of your archive disks for convenient and easy access to old files.

2.4 Principle I: Simplify

Painter can be overwhelming at first sight. The sheer preponderance and complexity of palettes, pop-ups, menus, and sliders can initially be a little intimidating. In Painter we have the capability to customize almost every aspect of brush behavior. We also have the ability to personalize and customize the interface and palette layout. Being spoiled by choice is a double-edged sword: It gives us great power but also can distract and overwhelm us.

The key to harnessing the full power of Painter and making it invisible is to simplify. Constantly simplify. Make life easy for yourself. Simplicity makes an enormous difference in the ease of use of Painter and in sorting out problems when you come across them.

Simplify Your Palettes and Minimize Your Desktop Clutter

Only have visible the palettes you need to access. You can show or hide palettes simply by choosing Windows > Hide or Show (palette name), or by using the palette keyboard shortcuts (see the Quick Reference Card). Show just the palettes you need for any given task and hide the others.

Group your Palettes to suit your task. You can group and ungroup palettes simply by placing your cursor over the central part of the palette title bar and then dragging them into or out of groups of palettes. You can hide palettes by clicking the close button (square with X in it) located on the right side of each palette title bar. Once you have selected which palettes you need for a task then I suggest you group them together so that as you open one palette it doesn't obscure any others (which happens easily if you just place ungrouped palettes on top of each other). For some tasks where you need to see more palettes, such as working with text and collage, where you may wish to see layers, text and channels all at the same time, then it may be better to make two groups of palettes and place them on either side of your screen (or on a second monitor if you have one). For straight-

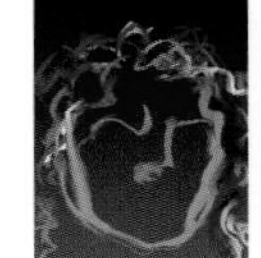

forward painting I suggest, at least initially, a simple palette group such as that illustrated here (Figure 2.1). Naturally your palette grouping may depend on your monitor size, with a larger monitor affording more flexibility.

Save Your Palette Layout

Now that you've set up your palettes in a convenient and efficient arrangement for basic painting, you are going to save your palette layout so you won't have to repeat this step again.

1. Select Window > Arrange Palettes > Save Layout.
2. Name your layout. For example I named my initial palette layout as Basic1-1024 ×768. (Figure 2.2). I included the screen resolution in my layout name for convenience.

   If I am doing a presentation my screen resolution may be smaller (800 by 600 for instance) than when I am working on a project in my studio. Including the resolution in the layout name makes it easy to get the appropriate layout to suit the screen resolution. Otherwise you may find that palettes mysteriously seem to disappear off the edge of the screen.
3. Click OK.

You can always save more layouts and delete old layouts. As you use Painter more and more, you'll find that certain layouts work well for certain tasks. It is useful to be able to just go to Window > Arrange Palettes and select your custom layout instantaneously (Figure 2.3).

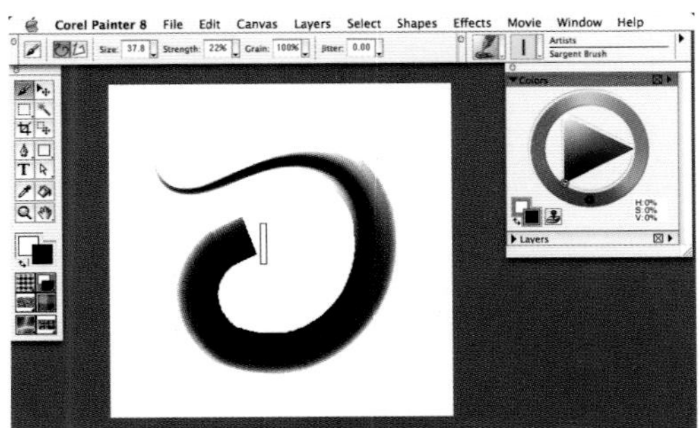

Figure 2.1 Simplified palette arrangement for 1024 pixel by 768 pixel screen resolution.

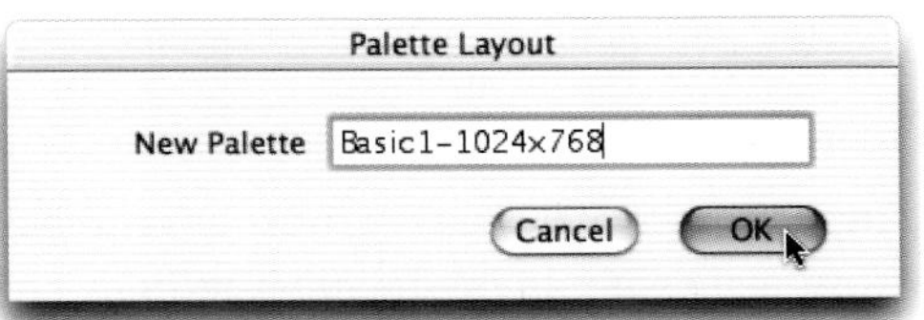

Figure 2.2 Naming the palette arrangement.

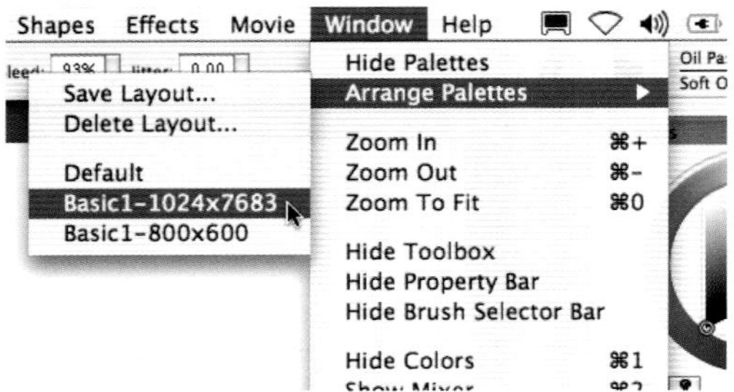

Figure 2.3 Choosing a palette arrangement.

Hiding All Palettes

Window > Hide/Show Palettes toggles between hiding and showing palettes. This can be useful during painting when you want to concentrate on the image using just a single brush. I often hide the palettes when I'm zooming in and working in great detail.

Setting up Function Keys on Your Keyboard

1. Edit (or Corel Painter 8 in Mac OS X) > Preferences > Customize Keys. Many keyboards include a set of 12 function (or F) keys. The Customize Keys preferences window allows you to set the 12 F-keys (F1 to F12), plus the same keys with the Shift command, making a total of 24 possible custom function key settings. You can select any menu item in Painter for these keys. Thus if you're more comfortable with keyboard shortcuts than clicking buttons on screen, you could set F1 to be Save As (Figure 2.4).
2. Select menu item (e.g., File > Save As).
3. Select Set.
4. Select Done.
5. Continue assigning other function key actions.

The Wacom Tablet Control Panel has a Tablet Buttons tab that allows you to assign commands and menu actions to all the function buttons placed along the top of the Wacom Tablet (Figure 2.5). I prefer to have all these tablet buttons assigned to Ignore so that I don't accidentally activate them when my cursor is selecting an item from the top menu on the screen.

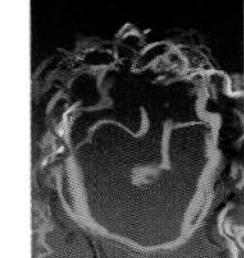

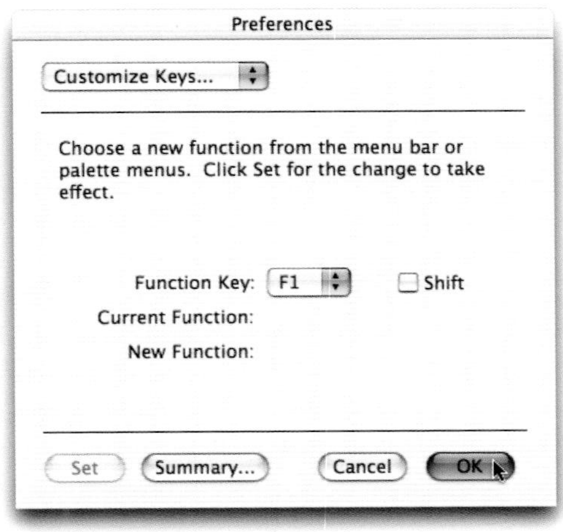

Figure 2.4 The Customize Keys Preferences Window.

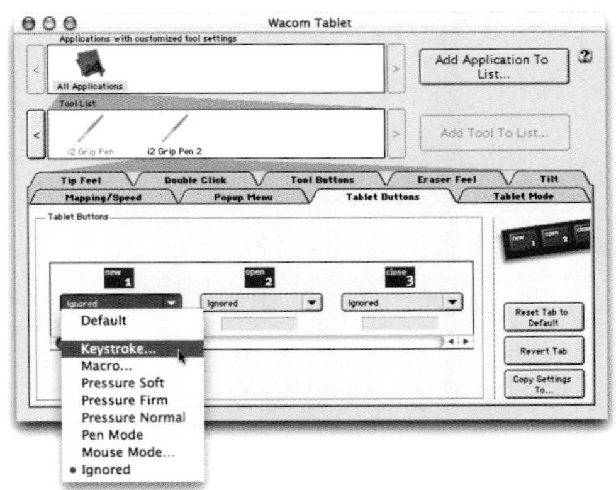

Figure 2.5 Setting the Wacom Tablet buttons in the Wacom Control Panel.

2.5 Principle II: Organize

The Feng Shui Organizing Metaphor

Adopting well-organized strategies and principles when using Painter makes all the difference between being able to flow with your creativity versus continually getting frustrated and caught up in technicalities. You can apply the organizing principles of Feng Shui (pronounced fung shway) to Painter with great success. Feng Shui is the ancient Chinese art of creating a harmonious, beautiful, and balanced environment that nurtures and supports your health, happiness, and success. Such an environment allows your creative energy, or *chi*, to flow freely. Harmony, beauty, balance, and free-flow of energy are exactly what you need within your digital environment (the virtual workspace on your computer screen) to realize your full creative potential and express yourself in your art with soul and passion.

The Painter workspace has a tendency to get cluttered and busy. It is like the law of nature that tends to increase entropy, or disorder, in the universe. After a short time of working in Painter, you may well find that confusion reigns, with palettes overlapping and obscuring each other. At this point the tools become barriers to creativity, distracting rather than empowering. That is why being organized and systematic makes such a big difference.

Adopting consistent principles, methodical strategies, and good habits makes everything flow easier and, ultimately, frees you up to be totally immersed in your creative process. Your tools should empower you, not distract you.

Files and Folders

Organize your files and folders on your hard drive. Think ahead of how you are going to name your files and folders, and where you are going to save work for different projects. Be consistent and methodical. Think about how you may want to search for and access specific files in the future. I suggest a simple system such as folders titled by project title and containing files titled by subject, version number, and file type. On the Painter Creativity Companion CD that accompanies this handbook, you'll find a folder called Creativity Projects. This folder contains folders with the session (chapter) names. The session folders in turn contain folders with project names. Copy the Creativity Projects folder onto your computer hard drive. Save your project artwork into the appropriate folders as you work. This will ensure that you can easily identify the location of any files you may wish to refer back to in the future.

Where a project file is called for in the instructions, you will find it placed in the appropriate project folder contained within the session folder contained within the Creativity Projects folder. For instance, one oil paint project in session 7 calls for a file called specialmoment.jpg. This file is found in the location: Creativity Projects > 7-Photography I > 7–14 Oil Paint.

Adopt a consistent and logical naming convention for all of your files right from the start. One naming methodology you may wish to consider is reverse date: project name: version number: file format tag. By having the reverse date (YY-MM-DD year/month/day notation, e.g., 03-10-25 for October 25, 2003) at the beginning of your file names, you ensure that your files line up chronologically when displayed as a list (providing you separate your pre–January 1, 2000 files from your post–January 1, 2000 files). An example of applying this naming methodology is: 03-10-25slfprtrt03.rif. Like Photoshop, Painter automatically adds the three-letter file format tag (e.g., .rif, .tif, .jpg) to your file names, so you do not have to do so manually. On the Macintosh I prefer to use a period rather than a dash for the reverse date and a dash before the version number, so my file names look like 03.10.25 slfprtrt-03.rif. However, on a Windows machine, it's safest to keep the file names as short as possible and avoid any non-numeric characters besides the dot in the file format tag. Whatever system you decide on, keep to it and be consistent with file naming. You'll be pleased with this approach later on when you're searching for specific files from a specific project.

Differentiating between Save As and Save and knowing which to use when. One safe approach to saving is to start with a Save As, naming that first file as version-01. As you work, regularly select the keyboard shortcut Cmd/Ctrl-S, or File > Save, which updates the file. When you are about to apply an effect, or drop a layer, or make any other significant change, do a final Cmd/Ctrl-S, make the change, and then click the Save As button and rename the file as version-02. Continue as before with regular saves until the next major transition in the image. This methodology is the safest way to avoid losing work in the event of a computer crash or program freeze. It also minimizes the versions saved to just those necessary to preserve the main transitions of the image.

This organizing principle extends to immediately and consistently renaming all custom palettes, clone copies, and layers within Painter. Painter automatically generates default names such as

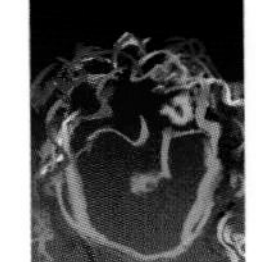

Custom 1, Clone of (name), Layer 1, etc. When working with complex projects, these default names start to get confusing, and you'll find yourself wasting a lot of time trying to work out which file is which and which layer is which. Rename meticulously and immediately whenever a default name is generated. You'll avoid any confusion and save yourself a lot of time in the long run.

File Format

In the Save As dialog box, you have a choice of file formats. I recommend that you save your works in progress in the RIFF (Raster Image File Format) format, the native format of Painter, when working in Painter. RIFF files can only be opened in Painter. RIFF files preserve the most data, including image layers, text layers, Water Color layers, Liquid Ink layers, Impasto, Mosaics, and so on. All of the functionality of these layers is preserved with the RIFF format, so that you can reopen the file later and continue adding to or editing the layers.

If you intend to go back and forth between Painter and Photoshop, then save your files in Photoshop or TIFF format; however, be aware that TIFF format will flatten your file and Photoshop format will automatically convert Water Color and Liquid Ink layers into regular bitmap image layers (you cannot use Water Color or Liquid Ink brushes on image layers). Also you will need to flatten any image containing impasto data for that data to appear in Photoshop (which doesn't support Painter's impasto layer technology). For printing purposes I suggest saving your files, when complete, in TIFF format. These can then be opened in Photoshop and converted from RGB color mode to CMYK color mode, if needed.

2.6 Principle III: Optimize

Thus far you've familiarized yourself with Painter's interface and taken care of your workspace organization. The next step is to maximize your creative power within Painter. The creative power offered by a tool is related to the variety of choices the tool offers you—for instance, the type of marks that can be made and the control you exert over those choices and how they are applied. This can be summarized as: Power = Choice × Control.

The goal here is to maximize both your choices and your control. You increase your brush choices by loading extra brushes not normally installed with Painter. You maximize your control over the brushes by creating, saving, and organizing customized brush variants.

Maximize Your Choices

Loading Extra Brushes and Art Materials

Your Painter 8 CD2 contains a wealth of fabulous extra brushes, papers, patterns, gradients, and so on that do not get automatically installed when you install Painter 8 on your computer hard drive. I have put together a special custom brush category, Jeremy Faves, and a special custom library of brushes, titled Creativity Brushes, that include my favorite brushes from CD2, from earlier versions of Painter, as well as brushes made by friends who have generously allowed me to share them with you (thanks Chris, Den, Don, Marge, Paulo, Ron, and Sherron). I have also created some custom art materials libraries with my favorite papers and patterns, plus a variety of custom color sets. The possible drawbacks of installing all these extra goodies are as follows:

1. Choice overload on you, the artist
2. Computer overload (the extra brushes and art materials will take up memory as you open and use them)

Computer overload is a less important consideration with today's powerful machines. Choice overload is always a risk with Painter, even with the default libraries; however, the extra brushes and art materials add so much richness and expand your range of creative possibilities that I recommend loading them. For detailed instructions as to how to load the extra brushes and art materials from the Painter Creativity Companion CD, see Appendix IV, Loading Extra Brushes and Art Materials. You will also find many custom brushes freely available for download on the web (see the www.paintercreativity.com companion site resource page for links).

Maximize Your Control

Controlling Your Brush Stroke: Enso Paintings

In this exercise you will follow in a Zen-painting tradition of painting circles known as *enso* (look up "zen painting enso" in the internet search engine www.google.com to find links where you can see examples of ensos and learn about their historical background). The purpose of asking you to paint circles is to focus you on controlling your stylus and, consequently, your brush stroke. Without learning to fully control a single brush stroke, all other attempts to maximize your power within Painter are meaningless.

Background

Ensos were popular expressions of spiritual vision and discipline in the sumi-e tradition (Japanese ink painting) among the Zen monks during Japan's Edo period (18th century).

The Sumi-e Society Midwest has an elegant description of the Sumi-e philosophy on their web site (http://www.silverdragonstudio.com/sumi-e). Here is an excerpt.

> **The philosophy** of Sumi-e is contrast and harmony, expressing simple beauty and elegance. The balance and integration of the two dynamically opposed forces of the Universe are the ultimate goal of Sumi-e.
>
> The art of brush painting aims to depict the spirit, rather than the semblance of the object. In creating a picture the artist must grasp the spirit of the subject. Sumi-e attempts to capture the **Chi** or "life spirit" of the subject, painting in the language of the spirit.

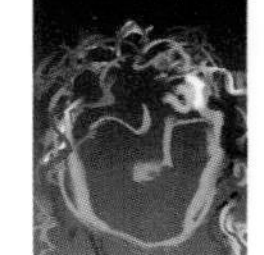

> Patience is essential in brush painting. Balance, rhythm and harmony are the qualities the artist strives for by developing patience, self-discipline and concentration.
>
> The goal of the brush painter is to use the brush with both vitality and restraint. Constantly striving to be a better person because his character and personality come through in his work.

The enso has many interpretations and levels of meaning. The expressiveness of the circle is created by a synergy of control and accident. Every enso is unique, influenced by the way the brush hairs spread out on the paper, the texture of the paper, the way the artists load their brushes with ink, and the speed and pressure variation of their brushes as they make the circle. Similarly, in Painter every enso is different, depending on the way you change pressure, the speed of your stroke, and so on. Traditionally, painting an enso was part of meditation and was a way to attain an enlightened state of mind. In more modern times the enso has been adopted as the basis for corporate logos, such as Bell Labs' Lucent Technologies division (see www.lucent.com).

The following two paragraphs are excerpts from an enso gallery web site that is no longer on the web.

How is the enso created?

> The enso is created when the Zen calligrapher (traditionally a monk) takes a large sumi brush full of ink while meditating on the emptiness of the blank paper. At the decisive "perfect moment" the monk quickly lays out the circle on the page. The circle contains both the perfection of the expressive moment and the imperfections of the ink, page and brush. Outcomes vary from thin, smooth, nearly perfect circles to fat, rough squares, triangles and spirals.

What does an enso symbolize?

> The dynamic circle of the enso symbolizes many Zen ideas. On the surface, it may represent the full moon, the empty tea cup, the turning wheel, the eye or face of the Buddha or the monk Bodhi Daruma, the dragon chasing its tail, and other poetic visual symbols. On a deeper level, the circle may symbolize the emptiness of the void, the endless circle of life, and the fullness of the spirit. Deeper still is the representation of the circle as the moment of enlightenment, the moment when the mind is free enough to simply let the body or spirit create, the moment when the perfection of the circle is committed to the emptiness of the page, and the moment of the chaos that is creation. Each enso shows the expressive movement of the spirit in time.

It is interesting, in the context of this Enso exercise, to read the comments made by the Russian painter Vasily Kandinsky in 1930 on what a circle means to him:

> Why does the circle fascinate me? It is:
>
> 1. the most modest form, but asserts itself unconditionally,
> 2. a precise, but inexhaustible, variable,
> 3. simultaneously stable and unstable,

4. simultaneously loud and soft,
5. a single tension that carries countless tensions within it.

The circle is the synthesis of the greatest oppositions. It combines the concentric and the eccentric in a single form, and in equilibrium. Of the three primary forms, triangle, circle and square, it points most clearly to the fourth dimension.

Instructions

1. Open Painter.
2. Open a new canvas 600 pixels wide by 600 pixels high (Cmd/Ctrl-N).
3. Mount your canvas (Cmd/Ctrl-M).
4. Make sure black is the selected color in the Colors palette.
5. Select the Calligraphy brush category > Dry Ink variant from the Brush Selector.
6. Start with very light pressure and slowly paint a circle, steadily increasing pressure as you go.
7. Take your time.
8. Complete the brush stroke as you just start to overlap the beginning of the stroke (Figure 2.6).
9. Choose Save As and save the enso as enso-01.rif in the Creativity Projects > 2-Empowerment folder on the Painter Creativity Companion CD.
10. You may initially find it difficult to get a smooth, gradually increasing brush diameter as you initiate the stroke. If you find that the brush goes straight into a full thickness stroke, then select Edit (or Corel Painter 8 in Mac OSX) > Preferences > Brush Tracking.
11. Make a firm single brush stroke in the Brush Tracking window scratch pad.
12. Choose OK.
13. Repeat the enso stroke and see if you can achieve a smoother, more satisfying circle.
14. Choose Save As and save the enso as enso-02.rif.
15. Repeat the enso at least eight more times, saving each enso with a sequential version number (-03, -04, etc.), varying the way you increase pressure (for instance, waiting longer before increasing pressure) and varying the speed with which you make the stroke. You may find that adjusting the brush size will give a more satisfying result.

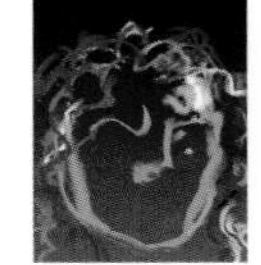

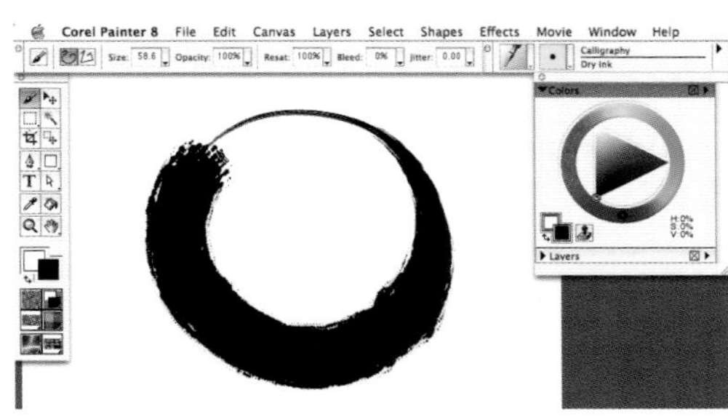

Figure 2.6 An enso.

Compare all your ensos. Which do you prefer? Why?

Customizing and Organizing Brushes

Understanding Brush Variants

Every Brush Variant has its own unique properties and characteristics. Each Variant is a unique combination of settings, accessible in the Brush Creator (show and hide using the Cmd/Ctrl-B shortcut) or in the Brush Property Bar. Variants with similar behaviors are grouped together in Categories.

Why Create Custom Variants?

With the huge number of variants provided in Painter as standard, why create more? There are two main reasons:

1. To make simple changes, (such as brush size, opacity, or both,) which you keep coming back to. In that case you may want to save the changes as variants with appropriate descriptive names (e.g., Sargent-Fine and Sargent-Huge). Minor changes, such as to brush size or opacity, can be done using the Brush Property Bar. More profound modifications to brush behavior can be made in the Brush Creator.
2. To save and be able to repeatedly use and share with others the novel brush looks and effects that you generate in the Brush Creator. The Brush Creator is accessed either through the Window menu (Window > Show Brush Creator) or with the keyboard shortcut Cmd/Ctrl-B. The Brush Creator is a separate mode of Painter that is designed exclusively for creating and experimenting with Brush Variants. As soon as you paint on an image the Brush Creator disappears.

From time to time you will make changes to sliders and settings and stumble across great brush looks that you love. If you don't save them as custom Variants at the time you come across them, then later when you want the same effect you'll wish you had. It is unlikely you'll be able to recall the exact setting from memory. There will also be projects where you want to create a specific brush look that isn't exactly captured by any of the default variants. In this case you may set out to experiment in the Brush Creator with a goal in mind and want to save the result when you find it.

Saving a Simple Custom Variant When in Painting Mode (Without Use of the Brush Creator)

Here is an example of a simple modification done using the brush Property Bar and not involving the Brush Creator.

1. Select the Distortion > Distorto brush variant in the Brush Selector bar.
2. In the brush Property Bar, adjust the Opacity from 0 percent to about 24 percent (the exact value is not critical).
3. Try this modified distorto out with different colors. Note the beautiful oily and smeary nature of the brush stroke and the way that the brush strokes drag any underlying color along with them. I like to use this brush for eyes in particular.
4. Select Save Variant from the Brush Selector pop-up menu.
5. Name the new variant Distorto-Color-Fine, or something appropriately descriptive (Figure 2.7).
6. Click OK.
7. The new variant appears as one of the variants listed in the current brush category (Distortion).

Saving a Custom Variant Using the Brush Creator

The main Brush Creator window has three tab options: Randomizer, Transposer, and Stroke Designer. The three tabs provide you with three different ways to experiment with generating new brush looks. The Randomizer randomizes properties of a Variant, the Transposer transposes the properties of one Variant with those of another, and the Stroke Designer allows you to adjust advanced control settings.

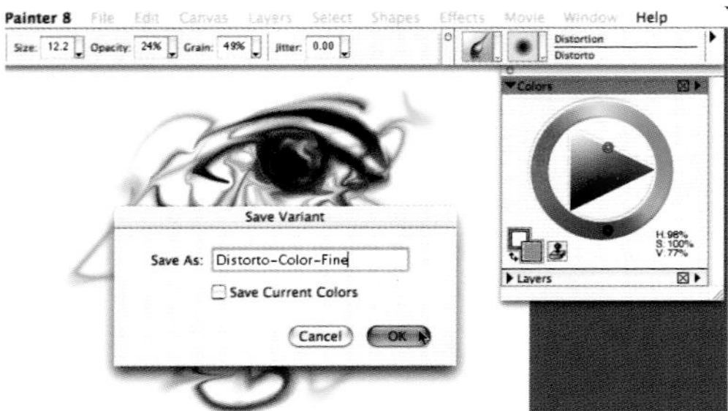

Figure 2.7 Saving a custom brush variant when in painting mode.

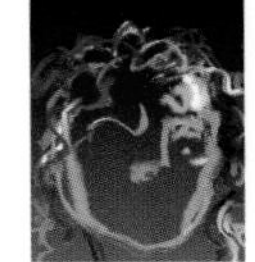

In all three tabs you can try out the current settings in the scratch pad. There is a Tracker palette that allows you to go back to any earlier versions you created along the way. The Brush Creator tools, art materials, and color palettes are accessible through the Windows menu (different from the standard painting mode Windows menu). When you are ready to save a custom Variant created in the Brush Creator you choose Variant > Save Variant from the top menu.

Restoring Default Variants

As you make changes in the Variant settings, Painter remembers those changes. The next time you open Painter and return to that Variant, you'll find it in the state you left it. Sometimes you may wish to return to the original default settings for the Variant. You can do this for an individual Variant by selecting the Variant in the brushes palette and then selecting Restore Default Variant from the Brush Selecting pop-up menu. If you'd like to restore every Variant to its original default settings, you can do so in one fell swoop by selecting Restore All Default Variants from the same Brush Selector pop-up menu (or from the Brush Creator Variant menu). This will reset all of your brush variants to Painter's default settings. It will not get rid of your custom brushes.

Creating a New Brush Category

As you use Painter you'll find there are certain brushes you love to use. You may find it useful to group these brushes together in a special "My Favorites" Brush Category. Alternatively, you may just wish to group together a collection of default or customized brushes that have common behaviors (e.g., My Favorite Smeary Brushes). Whatever way you wish to group your brushes together can be easily achieved by creating new Brush Categories and then copying Variants into those new Brush Categories.

1. Open a preexisting image, or paint an image, that you can use for the little icon, which will represent the new Brush Category in the Brush Library drawer.
2. Select the Rectangular Selection tool (middle lower row of the Tools palette, shortcut r).
3. Drag the Rectangular Selection tool over the patch of image you want to capture as the new Category icon.
4. Choose Window > Show Brush Creator (Cmd/Ctrl-B).
5. Select Brush > Capture Brush Category from the top menu.
6. Name the new Brush Category.
7. Click OK.

Note that the new Brush Category is now selected in the brushes palette and has a single Variant in it, which carries the same name as the Category.

Copying a Variant from One Category into Another

1. Select the first brush variant from another Brush Category that you'd like to copy into the new Brush Category.
2. Select Copy Variant from the Brush Selector pop-up menu (or Copy from the Brush Creator Variant menu).
3. In the Copy Variant window, select the new Brush Category from the Copy Variant to . . . pop-up menu.
4. Click OK.

Deleting an Unwanted Custom Variant

If you copied across a custom Variant, you may wish to delete the earlier version so you don't have duplicates of the same Variant.

1. Select the variant you wish to delete. Be careful not to accidentally select a default Painter Variant.
2. Select Delete Variant from the Brush Selector pop-up menu (or Delete from the Brush Creator Variant menu).
3. You'll be asked to confirm that you want to delete this Variant in this particular category. If it is the correct variant, then click Yes.

Note that you can't undo the deletion of a Variant, so always take great care. Also note that you can't delete the last Variant in a Category; there always has to be at least one Variant in the Category.

Sharing Variants between Computers

To share a Variant between computers, just copy the appropriate .xml file, together with any associated .jpg file, from one computer into the appropriate Brush Category folder of the Painter Brushes library in the other computer. It will then appear in the list of Variants for that Category

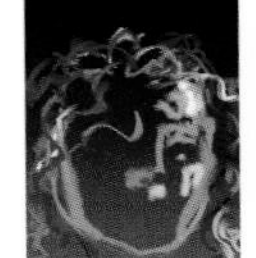

when Painter is opened. This works across platforms. When copying a Variant generated on a Macintosh computer into a Windows computer, you may need to select the Properties for the variant (right click on Variant and drag to Properties) and uncheck the Read Only box.

It is easy to get confused if you are downloading a custom brush from, say, the web, and you are not sure where to place the file you have downloaded. It's always crucial to know exactly what you are introducing to Painter:

1. Is it a Brush Variant file (.xml)? ⇒ Place in a Brush Category folder.
2. Is it a Brush Category folder (with 30 by 30 pixel .jpg icon)? ⇒ Place in a Brush Library folder.
3. Is it a Brush Library folder (containing brush category folders, which in turn contain the Brush Variants)? ⇒ Place in the Brushes folder in the Painter 8 application folder.

Creating a New Brush Library

To really make Painter work for your individual needs, it can be useful to create your own Brush Library, making sure you maintain a copy of the default library Painter Brushes in the Painter 8 > Brushes folder. If you are new to Painter I suggest you skip this. Here are the steps to make your own library:

1. Create a new folder within the Painter 8 > Brushes folder (at the same level of hierarchy as Painter Brushes, Ver 4, Ver 5, and Ver 6). This will be your new brush library folder.
2. Copy brush category folders and their associated .jpg files from the Painter Brushes library into your new library folder (holding down the Alt/Option key to make sure you leave a copy behind).
3. I recommend altering the brush category .jpg files in any new library so you can immediately see which library you have in your brushes palette.
4. Finally, if you'd like your custom brush library to be the one that appears every time you open Painter, select from the top menu bar Edit (Corel Painter 8 on Mac OS X) > Preferences > General and replace Libraries Brushes:Painter Brushes with the name of your own brush library.

Understanding the Brush Creator

It is useful to develop a deep understanding of the Brush Creator and how brush behavior is controlled, adjusted, and customized. This knowledge will allow you to create and modify any look or feel you want. Whatever you imagine is possible. Here are some experiments you can try out to explore the possibilities. These experiments can be quite time consuming. If you have limited time and are only interested in the basic use of Painter, I suggest you skip these experiments and jump ahead to the final section of this session, 2.7 Principle IV: Document.

The Plug-in Subcategory Experiment

1. Open Painter.
2. Open a new canvas 600 pixels wide by 600 pixels high (Cmd/Ctrl-N).
3. Mount your canvas (Cmd/Ctrl-M).
4. Choose any Brush Variant from any Brush Category.
5. Choose Window > Show Brush Creator (Cmd/Ctrl-B).
6. Select the Stroke Designer tab in the Brush Creator main window.
7. View the Stroke Designer > General section of the Brush Creator window.
8. See if the Dab Type is Circular, Single-Pixel, Static Bristle, or Captured. If it is, then continue to step 9. If not, change the Dab Type pop-up menu to Circular, Single-Pixel, or Static Bristle.
9. Change the Method to Plug-in.
10. Select the first choice in the Plug-in subcategory, which is the Confusion Brush (Figure 2.8).
11. Try out this brush setting on the canvas.
12. Work your way down all of the Plug-in subcategories. You are guaranteed to produce really bizarre results!
13. Try this with different Brush Variants, saving any good Variants as you go.

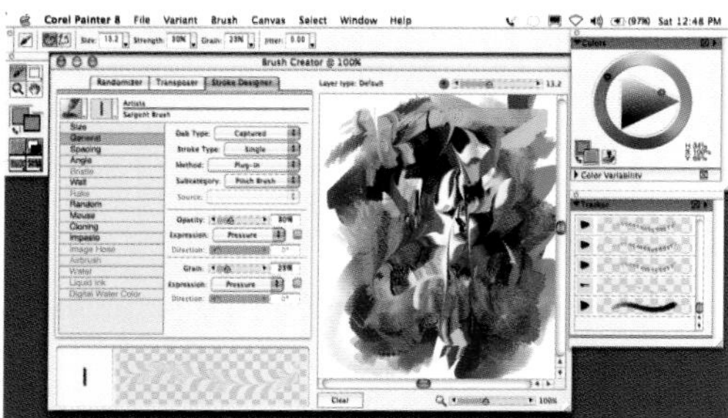

Figure 2.8 Creating a custom Variant in the Brush Creator Stroke Designer.

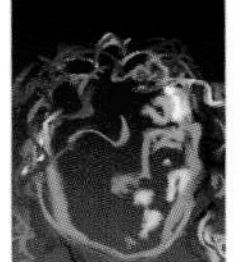

The Extreme Brush Controls Experiment

1. Open Painter.
2. Open a new canvas 600 pixels wide by 600 pixels high (Cmd/Ctrl-N).
3. Mount your canvas (Cmd/Ctrl-M).
4. Take any brush variant from any brush category.
5. Choose Window > Show Brush Creator (Cmd/Ctrl-B).
6. Select the Stroke Designer tab in the Brush Creator main window.
7. Go through all the accessible Brush Controls and adjust all the sliders to their extremes, continually testing out the effect on the brush stroke.

2.7 Principle IV: Document

What is Meant by Document?

Document in this context is used as a verb and means to:

1. Document the brush looks at your disposal.
2. Document your process and methodology meticulously as you work.
3. Back up, archive, and safeguard your data on a regular basis.

Document Your Brushes: Create an Encyclopedia of Looks

This project will briefly expose you to every brush variant. In the process, you will create your own visual encyclopedia of brush looks that will be useful to refer back to later.

1. Open Painter.
2. Open a new canvas 700 pixels wide by 600 pixels high.
3. Cmd/Ctrl-M (screen mode toggle).

Continued

4. Select the Brush Category Acrylics, which is at the top of the alphabetically ordered list of Categories in the Brush Selector Category pop-up menu (left-hand menu).
5. Methodically make at least one brush stroke on the canvas with every variant in the Category, working your way from the top of the variants pop-up menu (right-hand menu) all the way to the bottom of the menu. You may use any colors and any shape or composition of brush strokes you wish. Vary pressure as you paint to see what, if any, effect it has.
6. Save the file as looks-acrylics.rif.
7. Open a new canvas and repeat this process for every Brush Category, working your way methodically down the alphabetical list of Categories, and saving each file with the appropriate category name (e.g., looks-artists.rif, looks-brushes.rif). Note that some Categories, such as the Blenders and Photo Categories, will need to be applied to a canvas that already has marks, because many of those brushes do not add color, they just alter color that is already on the canvas. In those cases just recycle a canvas from another Category.

Document Your Work Meticulously

Keep versions as you work on a project (Do not just overwrite files). That means frequent use of Save As rather than Save. Back up regularly. Memory and storage is relatively inexpensive. The digital medium presents us with a wonderful opportunity to save a progression of stages as we create a painting. Save separate versions regularly.

Document Your Process

It is important to save separate versions regularly. I emphasize saving separate versions, each with a distinct file name, rather than simply overwriting an existing file, because of the versatility you gain in being able to go back to earlier versions of a project. As a habit click on your Save As button (equivalent to select File > Save As and save a new version number rather than File > Save (Cmd/Ctrl-S) and simply update the file. I also recommend that you get in the habit of recording scripts of your painting sessions. This is easy to do and very powerful, as well as fun. Please refer to session 6 in this book for detailed instructions regarding recording and playing back scripts.

Back up Regularly

One big difference between creating a traditional painting and a digital one is the fragility of the digital file. Almost everyone creating art on the computer has experienced the accidental loss of a

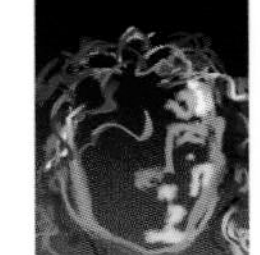

piece of artwork at some time or another. It is easy to accidentally lose your artwork at the flick of a keystroke or when your computer crashes.

Meticulous documentation and regularly backing up pays big dividends down the road, sometimes when you least expect it. For instance, you may find a new use many years later for an intermediate version of an artwork. The need to edit or repurpose artwork is not always predictable. It is better to prepare for future versatility than to regret not doing so. The bottom line is: Back up regularly!

2.8 Wrap

Congratulations! You're now ready for action. You've got all the basics behind you. You've got Painter running at optimum efficiency, like a finely tuned engine. You've started on the road of good habits, such as organized file naming and regular saving of versions, which will make life much easier for you years hence. Now it's time to put your newfound skills and knowledge to good use.

The next seven sessions deal with specific artistic and graphic applications of Painter. These sessions have been ordered specifically in a way that will lead you on a progressive path. You will start with painting from observation and pure brush work (sessions 3, 4, and 5, Painting Portraits). Then you will focus on transforming imagery and capturing your process (session 6, Animating Paint). You will apply these experiences to working with photographic imagery (sessions 7 and 8, Transforming Photographs). Finally, you will build on your photo-manipulation skills to explore photo-collage (session 9, Creating Collage).

The ideal is to work your way through all of the sessions in order. They are designed to each stand alone if you choose to just select one or two sessions to follow; however, I recommend, regardless of your interests, that you follow the next three sessions, Painting Portraits. The painting and observational skills you will develop in the next session will be valuable for everything else you do in Painter.

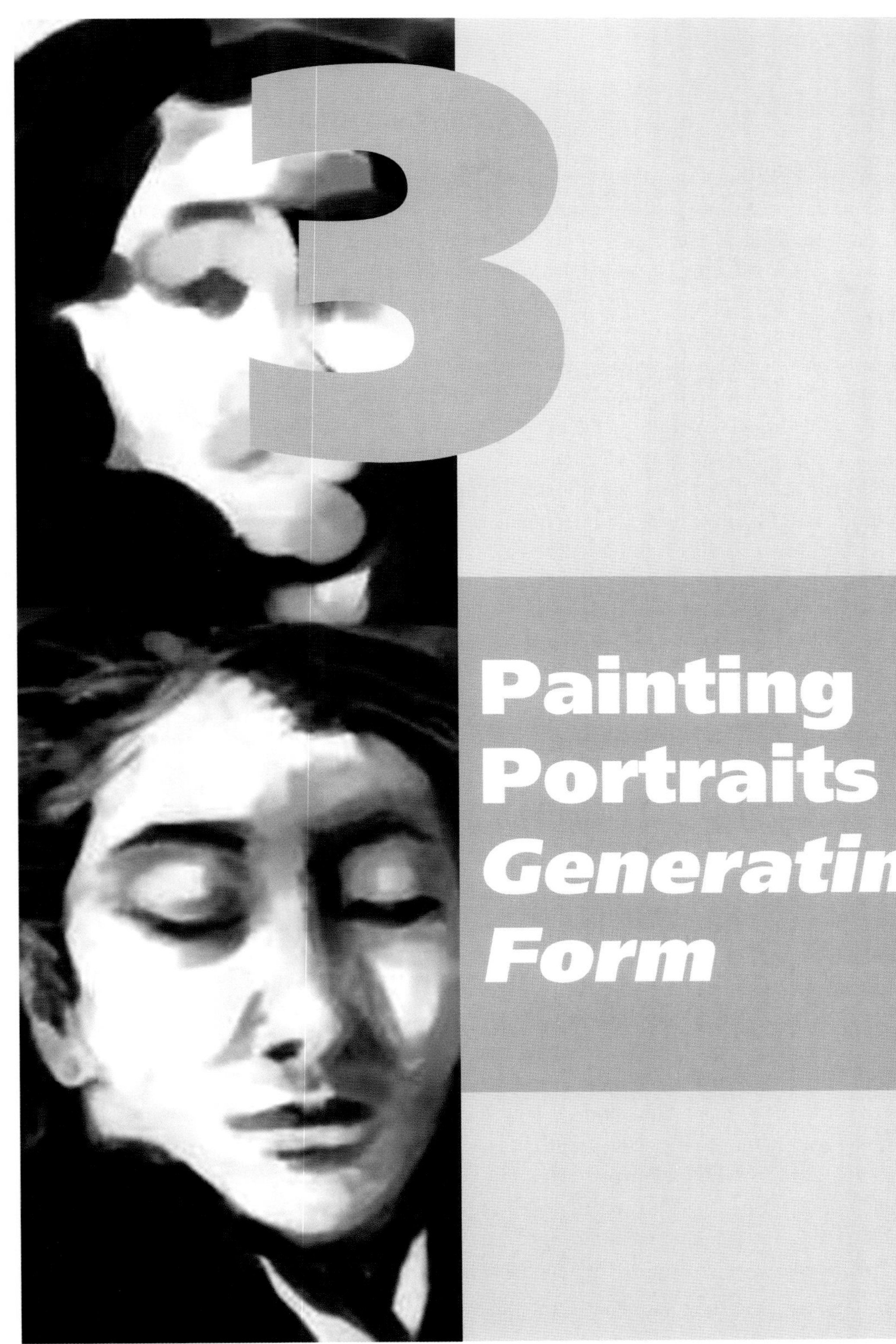

3

Painting Portraits I: *Generating Form*

3.1 Introduction

Hop on board for an exciting ride! Whether you have absolutely no drawing experience or you're a seasoned painter, in this and the following two sessions, you'll experience the joy of evoking character and personality on your digital canvas. I will share with you my own approach to painting colorful portraits from life. You will develop your observational and painting skills. The goal is to create expressive portraits that capture the personality of your subject and express your feelings about that subject.

In this session you will learn the basics of painting a portrait based on observation of a live model (as opposed to simply making up a face from your imagination or starting with a photograph and using the cloner brushes and/or tracing paper). The exercises in this session are designed to get you warmed up, help you observe carefully, and develop your use of line and tone.

If you feel you are not a natural artist, or you feel uncomfortable painting from observation, or you are uninterested in portraiture, I still recommend you persevere with this and the following sessions. The lessons you will learn can be applied to all aspects of your work with Painter, whether you are working from photographs, constructing collage, making animations, using text, or any other media. Everything that you learn about portraiture can be applied to landscapes, too. You will enjoy the exercises and gain a great deal no matter what artistic background you have. If you are an experienced painter with formal art school training, this session may cover familiar territory; although, if you are new to Painter, it will still be worthwhile.

This session begins with a discussion of what a portrait is and why the fascination with portraits. One of the barriers to painting a portrait is simply the expectation of what a portrait is and what it should look like. If the expectation is that a portrait should look like an accurate physical likeness of the subject and anything less is a failure, then it will be difficult to proceed. I want to open your mind to alternative interpretations of portraiture and thus make the process of creating a portrait less intimidating.

You will then find a summary of the basic principles that go into portrait painting. I have included these principles up front so you can gain an overview of where we are heading. Do not expect to immediately remember or apply all of these principles. It will take time. In Appendix V: Painting Portraits: Principles and Actions, you will find a more detailed analysis of the principles and actions that go into my own personal process of painting a portrait.

If you find the portrait discussion and summary of principles a bit overwhelming, just skip straight to the practical exercises that start off with the Warm-up Self-Portraits (section 3.5). You can always refer back to the discussion and principles after you have completed some of the practical exercises. This will have the advantage of giving you more context in which to base your understanding of the principles. Plus it will ensure your first self-portraits are better reflections of your natural style (before being influenced by my instruction) and will therefore be more useful to look back to as initial reference points in your development.

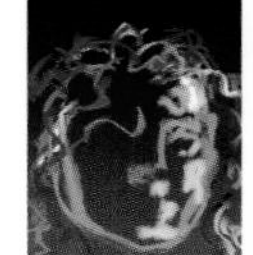

3.2 Instructor Notes

Look over this session and the following two sessions and pick and choose those parts that are relevant to your class curriculum. You could follow the three sessions in their entirety for a thorough grounding in portrait painting. If your students have already studied traditional drawing and painting skills, and have done traditional life drawing (from the nude model) and portrait painting, then it may be best to start with session 4, Painting Portraits II: *Unleashing the Power of Color*.

I like to start my portrait painting classes with a self-portrait exercise (see section 3.5) so students have a yardstick with which to compare their work from later on in the course. Their initial self-portrait can serve as a useful reference point for appreciating their progress and development. Having said that, I know that some students, if they have little painting experience, can be intimidated by the challenge of painting a self-portrait, especially if they are also struggling with mastering the digital medium at the same time. Therefore, I've started this session with the discussion on portraiture and an overview of the basic principles.

I believe that it can be beneficial to give your students a challenge and that it's part of the learning process to experience that place of uneasiness where your students feel a little out of their comfort zone.

One of the most popular group exercises I've done with my classes is the "Musical Computers" Collaborative Self-Portraits (see section 3.5). One class actually requested a repeat session of this exercise at the end of the course. I highly recommend this exercise for any group class. It is a great lesson for the students in letting go of the preciousness of their brush strokes and in experiencing the freedom to continually transform their canvas. It is also a great social mixer and generates excitement and fun!

3.3 Portraiture

What Is a Portrait?

What does the word *portrait* conjure in your mind? Grab a sheet of paper and a pen and describe in words what you think of as a portrait.

Web link Open a new Web browser window and locate the internet search engine www.google.com. Type in "portrait" and click "go" (or hit the return key). Open another new Web browser window and follow the same procedure, but this time type in "portraits." Look at the first 10 links in each category. How many of the sites conformed to what you wrote down as your understanding of the word *portrait*?

A portrait may be a likeness, representation, description, expression, symbol, portrayal, impression, or interpretation of a subject. It can also describe the orientation of a sheet of paper, computer screen, or canvas (tall, narrow "portrait" as opposed to wide, short "landscape"). A portrait of a person does not necessarily depict or describe the person's face, head, or even the figure. A portrait may show something that symbolizes or signifies a person's presence or character. In this session the word *portrait* describes a pictorial representation, or impression, of a person's face.

A portrait may be expressed in a drawing, a painting, a photograph, words, theater, music, film, sculpture, and so on. The medium we are using here is digital paint, or more precisely, Painter. Painter offers unrivaled richness, versatility, diversity, and freedom of expression. It is a phenomenal tool for exploring the art of portrait painting.

Representation versus Expression

One of the fundamental decisions we make, either consciously or subconsciously, in creating a portrait is the degree to which we focus on representing appearance versus expressing emotions. On the one hand, we can represent the appearance of our subject as we observe him or her in a literal illustrative way. Paint can be used to create an impression or illusion of three-dimensional form and can be used to accurately represent a physical likeness. On the other hand, we can express our feelings and impressions of the subject through gestural abstract forms that do not necessarily accurately depict the literal appearance of the subject. Such gestures often capture the heart and soul of the subject better then photographic realism.

When asked to explain the difference between illustration and nonillustration, painter Francis Bacon answered: "[A]n illustrational form tells you through the intelligence immediately what the form is about, whereas non-illustrational form works first upon sensation and then slowly leaks back into the fact."

Visit your local library, art museums, galleries, and the Web, and start looking at the way different artists approach portraiture: their use of media, composition, colors, scale, and so on. Is their approach more representational or expressionistic? Make a note of portraits that you particularly like or dislike. Think about why you react to them the way you do.

Web link Take a look at some of Degas' beautiful portraits in the Degas gallery of Orazio Centaro's Art Images on the Web www.ocaiw.com/degalepo.htm. Does Degas succeed in going below the surface in his portraits? Notice the feeling he captures in his portrait of Mademoiselle Dibogny (www.ocaiw.com/degalg12.htm).

The Relationship between Artist and Subject

While painting portraits, artists not only carefully visually observe their subjects, but they also sense their subjects with their other senses: touch, smell, and sound. The artists are aware of their

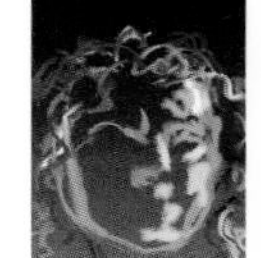

response to the subjects. They experience the subjects. A portrait reflects the whole relationship between artist and subject. A portrait of a subject is as much a portrait of the artist as of the subject. Every portrait tells its own story.

When I paint a portrait from life, there is a resonance between me and the subject. Before I make any marks on my canvas, I tune in to my subject. My subject and I enter a focused intimate space where all other distractions fade away. It is a peaceful, powerful space. This tune-in process is similar to the meditation on their subjects that Sumi-e artists do before commencing their brush stroke (see session 2 for a description of this type of art).

Web link Open a new Web browser window and locate the Van Gogh Portraits Gallery, www.vangoghgallery.com/painting/main_po.htm. Look at some of the portraits. What do Van Gogh's portraits say about Van Gogh? How much do you feel you are experiencing a reflection of the artist as much as of the subject? Now look at his self-portraits at www.vangoghgallery.com/painting/main_se.htm. Compare the feelings expressed in those self-portraits with those of his other portrait subjects. What are the similarities and differences? Which of Van Gogh's portraits or self-portraits do you find most moving, and why?

Why the Fascination with Portraiture?

Portraiture has held a special place in art and society for centuries. The visual images we are most used to looking at are the facial appearance and expressions of other people. The expressiveness of the face is programmed in biologically: the face has more muscles per square inch of skin surface area than other parts of the body, and is therefore capable of a greater variety of movement than other parts of the body. We are conditioned to see and read faces—especially eyes, the "windows to the soul." When faced with ambiguous visual data, or looking at an abstract or organic form, we naturally see faces in the abstract forms. That is how many optical illusions work, such as the famous Young Girl/Old Woman illusion (www.aspecialplace.net/illusions/young_girl.htm).

There is a fascination with reading and interpreting the face of another person. What are they feeling, thinking, experiencing? Every face is, in some ways, a reflection of our own. In others we can also experience ourselves. We can identify with them. We can be deeply affected by them.

Portraits as Cultural and Political Icons

Consider the power of the portrait in politics. Consider the huge (6 meters high by 4.5 meters wide) portrait of Chairman Mao in Tian'anmen Square, Beijing, which was first designed back in 1949. The power and symbolism of that one portrait on a whole nation was immense. Great thought and debate went into every detail, including the expression in the eyes and how much of each ear was showing. See what one of the current artists who is responsible for upkeep of the portrait has to say at www.cbw.com/btm/issue71/64–65.html.

Web link Besides the Mao portrait, many more examples of portraits have become cultural or political icons: Leonardo da Vinci's Mona Lisa, www.louvre.fr/anglais/collec/peint/peint_f.htm (click on Selected Works, Italy 16th century, to see a close-up of the Mona Lisa); Andy Warhol's Marilyn Monroe, www.1001prints-posters.com/andy_warhol_marilyn_monroe_picture.htm; and the famous Che Guevara poster. These examples all illustrate the pivotal role of portraits in society.

The Challenge of Painting a Portrait

The "I'm Not an Artist" Challenge

Portraits are notoriously hard to paint. We are so familiar with looking at and recognizing faces that we often see what we expect, not what is actually there. Many of us are conditioned from a very young age to draw stick figure faces, circles with dots for eyes, and to accept that we are not, and never can be, artists. In fact, we are all artists. Every child is born an artist. Every child is born with a natural ability to fearlessly make marks in the world (whether on canvas or on the floor or walls, that's another matter!).

The "There's Too Many Tools" Challenge

All of those tools, palettes, and menus in Painter can be intimidating. How do I know where to go or what to adjust? Part of the function of this course is to help you master the choices and feel comfortable with Painter's tools and interface.

The "The Blank Canvas Scares Me!" Challenge

In addition to the so-called difficulty of painting a portrait, there is also the fear of the blank canvas. There are so many decisions to be made. How do I start? What do I include in my picture? How much background do I include? Where do I crop the portrait? At what scale do I depict the subject? In what way do I apply brush strokes to describe the subject? It seems like an endless stream of questions. The blank canvas is both an opportunity and a challenge. These challenges can all be overcome with training, practice, and patience. Whatever our experience and conditioning, we are all capable of mastering the beautiful brushes in Painter, overcoming our fear of the blank canvas, and painting expressive portraits.

Overcoming These Challenges

The principles described as follows, some of which have been applied in painting and drawing over the centuries, can help you overcome these challenges, save you time, and empower you to achieve satisfying results. They are not firm rules. They are designed as a framework to help you make

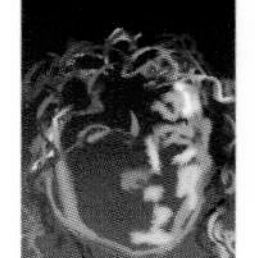

decisions in the portrait-painting process. Experiment with these principles. Apply them in your work and see the results.

3.4 Principles

The principles of portrait painting fall into three important categories: preparation, observation, and creation.

Preparation

Prepare Your Model

Put your models at ease and develop a rapport with them. Explain their participatory role in the creative process, their rights, what you expect of them (e.g., how still do they need to sit and for how long, when will there be breaks). Create a short, simple, and clear release form that you ask your models (or their guardians, if they are under 18) to sign (with date, place, and model's contact details). Sample wording may be as follows:

I, (name of model), give (name of artist) permission to paint my portrait and grant permission for the artist to use, display, transfer, or reproduce the completed image, or any stage or derivative version of it, in any way he/she wishes. The artist retains full copyright over his/her artwork. No payment is owed for use of my likeness.

Keep the signed release in your records. The release ensures that you have the freedom to do what you want with your own artwork.

Your model may ask about what clothing to wear, make-up or no make-up, hair up or down, and similar questions. Put your model at ease. Clothes and make-up are unimportant for the purposes of this course.

Once you are both seated and ready for drawing, your model may ask "How should I pose? Do you want me to smile? Should I keep completely still?" Reassure the model that there is no need to pose or smile. Ask the model to get comfortable and to feel free to move slightly—keeping completely still is not necessary. The objective is to capture the fundamental nature of the model, not a superficial smile or forced expression.

Sit the model comfortably, at the required angle and with appropriate lighting. Lighting slightly from one side and slightly from above can work well. Avoid casting shadows that are too harsh. You may find playing music in the background makes the experience more relaxing and enjoyable for both you and your model.

Prepare Your Canvas

Select Appropriate Canvas Size and Resolution

Plan ahead for your final usage. If you want to end up with a reasonably large high-quality canvas print or have the image published on a magazine cover, start off with a relatively large canvas, say 8 inches wide by 10 inches high at 300 pixels per inch (2400 by 3000 pixels). On the other hand, if you're creating a portrait that will be printed on letter-size paper, then you could work on a smaller, lower resolution canvas that is, say, 7 inches wide by 8 inches high at 125 pixels per inch (875 by 1000 pixels).

Choose Appropriate Paper Color

The default Painter paper color is white. Painting on a canvas that is non-white gives you the opportunity to paint from light values (highlights) rather than just from darker values. A white canvas will tend to wash out highlights. For me, a colored (non-white) background gives me something to "bite" against. Thus I recommend initially filling your canvas (Cmd/Ctrl-F) with a color other than white (or with a simple two color gradient). Traditional canvas background colors have been light grays (i.e., light to mid-tonal values, with the Painter Color Picker Value-Saturation triangle cursor about two-thirds of the way up), often with a cool hue such as cyan (blue-green). Hues in Painter are selected by placing the cursor in the outer hue circle. Cyan is located around "4 o'clock" on the hue circle.

Prepare Yourself

Trust Your Eyes

For the purposes of learning to paint expressive portraits and developing your observational drawing skills, avoid mechanical intervention or shortcuts such as scanning a photograph or tracing from a picture. Trust that your eyes, and other senses, can give you as much information as you need.

Trust Your Hand

Use hand-painted brush strokes wherever and whenever possible. Avoid special effects and filters. Trust your hand to convey and express what you wish to say. Your hand is much better at communicating what is in your soul than a keyboard command or special effect.

Make Yourself Comfortable

Just as you prepare your models and make them as comfortable as possible, do the same for yourself. Set up your computer so you can comfortably look back and forth between the subject and your screen.

Observation

Take Time

Take time to observe your model. Look at your subject afresh, as if you have never seen him or her before. Be aware of your feelings about the subject and what emotions you want to convey and express in your portrait. Observe the way light falls on your subject and is reflected. Notice the colors

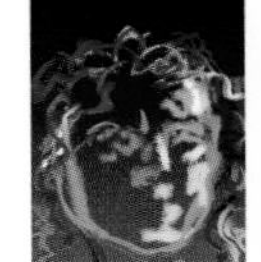

in the shadows, as well as in the highlights. Notice the different types of shadows, those caused by facing away from the light source and those cast on a surface by another object.

Identify a Focal Point

Half close your eyes and observe what stands out, what strikes you, where your eyes are drawn to. This helps you determine the main focal point of your composition, the point where the viewer's eyes will be naturally drawn. The mind likes to prioritize and categorize and be able to say "this is important and this isn't." A clear focal point in an image makes it comfortable and easy to look at. It is important to identify what you want to emphasize and where you want to lead your viewer's eyes. Just as painting a portrait is a journey, looking at a portrait is also a journey. When we paint, we lay down clues that guide viewers' eyes around our canvas, leading them naturally and subconsciously toward the focal point of the painting.

Tune In

One method for fully observing and being aware of, or tuning in to, your subject is following a process, or ritual, of "meditation-visualization." This process is personal and will differ for everyone. In my case, I momentarily close my eyes, take a deep breath, hold the breath for a few moments, and then let out a big sigh, relax, and open my eyes. I continue breathing steadily and deeply. I look into my subject. I feel my way into the portrait. I ask myself what is the mood, where is the emphasis, what moves me, where is the power? I picture the finished portrait in my mind and ask myself what does it look and feel like? What impression does it leave me with? I also feel my way into the canvas, moving both hands, palms down, on my tablet, as if feeling a sculpture. I then move the stylus tip over the tablet surface without touching the tablet, moving the cursor like a frenetic dancer, mapping out the portrait without making any marks.

This meditation-visualization process lays the foundation for the direction my painting takes. It doesn't involve picturing exactly what it's going to end up looking like, more just being aware of my reaction to this subject and of what I'd like to express in the portrait. This process also separates my painting state from my everyday state. It is a way that I let go of the many distractions that normally fill my mind, and focus exclusively on my subject and the creation of the painting.

Observe the Skull

The shape of the skull, although sometimes obscured by hair, is an important element in defining character. Is it long and narrow? Is it wide and short? How does it sit on the shoulders? Is it tilted forward or back or to one side? Are the eye sockets deep-set or shallow? Are the cheekbones high and pronounced or flat and smooth? Does the chin protrude or recede?

Observe the Skin

The pigmentation and texture of the skin can communicate a lot about a person. Also, how the skin is draped over the skull: is it loose or taut? Are there wrinkles? If so, in what direction and how deep? Are there scars, freckles, and so on?

Observe the Features

Our attention tends to naturally focus on features such as the eyes, eyebrows, hair, nose, ears, and lips. We read a lot from their orientation and relative position and scale. Getting the relative proportions and locations of these particular features is important. The relative placement and shapes of the nose and ears are important but usually less so than for the eyes and mouth.

Pay Special Attention to the Eyes

Eyes are often termed as the "windows to the soul." Besides the role they play as an important feature in creating a likeness, they also allow you to delve deeper into the personality of your subject. Looking into the amazing myriad of colors and reflections in someone's irises is a journey in itself. Depicting this richness and detail in a painting helps form the character of the portrait.

Establish Relative Proportions and Placements

Visualize the composition in your mind. Are you going to paint on a tall, narrow canvas (portrait orientation) or short, wide canvas (landscape orientation)? How are you going to use the border of the composition to add dynamism and strength to the picture? Dramatic cropping, and the use of some elements within the picture that frame the portrait, can help bring the viewer's eyes back into the central focal point of the picture. How are you going to position the face in the canvas? Centrally or off to one side? Is your subject looking straight out of the canvas or at an angle? The eye naturally likes a little asymmetry in a composition. Try placing the head off-center or cropping the composition so there are interesting shapes cut between the head and the edge of the canvas (creative use of positive and negative space).

You may choose to leave large portions of your canvas as free space, breathing space for the brush strokes you paint. This is a compositional choice. Treat the subject, background, and border with awareness to the effect of one on the other. Don't be afraid to exaggerate, go to the extremes. Be bold.

Quickly map out where you are going to place the head in the canvas and how big it will be relative to the canvas size. Start sketching in rough placement of main features and contours. In particular placement of the eyes, nose and mouth, and the main shapes cut out by the edge of the hair, jawline, cheekline, and so on.

Creation

Start Rough

Don't get distracted by detail. Start working all over the canvas, not spending too much time in any one place. Don't be timid! Cover your whole canvas with paint.

Depict Lights and Darks Continuously

As you paint, no matter what color you choose and brush you apply, use every mark to depict the relative tonal values (lights and darks) you observe. Use the Painter Color Picker Value-Saturation

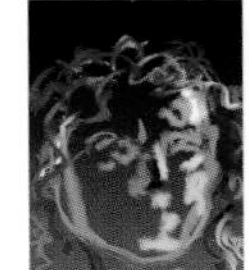

triangle to control value. Bear in mind that some colors, such as blues, are naturally darker in tonal value than others, such as yellows. The tones are the foundations of your painting. To check on relative tonal values, half-close your eyes and look back and forth between your subject and your painting. Compare the lights and darks. A portrait can be forgiving of wild color choices but less forgiving of incorrect tonal values.

Make the Most with the Least

Always try to make the most with the least ("less is more"). Walter Murch explains this principle eloquently in his book on film editing called *In the Blink of an Eye*:

> You may not always succeed, but attempt to produce the greatest effect in the viewer's mind by the least number of things on screen. Why? Because you want to do only what is necessary to engage the imagination of the audience. Suggestion is always more effective than exposition. Past a certain point, the more effort you put into wealth of detail, the more you encourage the audience to become spectators rather than participants.

The same principle applies to portrait painting with Painter.

Emphasize and Use Contrasts

Selectively depict contrasts to create focal points in your painting while striving for balance and harmony. Use contrasts to draw the attention of the viewer to specific parts of your painting and to add life and form to your work. Work with opposites, determining a balance in your picture between opposing or contrasting effects. Sharper boundaries between contrasting regions can increase their dramatic effect. I sometimes finish off a portrait with a little Burn and Dodge (variants from the Photo brush category) to bring out light-dark and intense-dull contrasts in the areas of the picture I wish to draw attention to. There are many examples of contrasts that you can use in your paintings. Here are some:

Light-Dark (Chiaroscuro)

Light-Heavy

Thick-Thin

Broad-Narrow

Transparent-Opaque

Soft-Hard

Positive-Negative

Chaos-Order

Loud-Quiet

Busy-Uncluttered

Detailed-Rough

Smooth-Rough

Large-Small

Much-Little

High-Low

Rest-Motion

Cold-Warm

Intense-Dull

Pure-Diluted

Directions (diagonals, horizontals, verticals, etc.)

Textures (texture, no texture, different texture)

Complementary Colors (pairs of colors from opposite sides of the color wheel)

Simultaneous Contrast (a sensation in the eye of the viewer that spontaneously generates the complementary color if not already present)

Note that each of these contrasts can form the basis for an exercise in which you focus on demonstrating the use of that one contrast.

Seek Balance

The eye naturally likes balance in a composition. Balance is not the same as symmetry. Balance relates to the distribution of contrasts such as lights and darks, small and big forms, and so on. Stand back and look at your composition through half-closed eyes. Ask yourself if anything jumps out. If it does, did you intent it to? If not, how can you correct the picture?

Work toward Selective Detail

An example of selective contrast is use of selective detail. Identify the areas of the image you want to bring attention to and then work in greater detail in those areas. The viewer does not need to be overwhelmed with precise detail. Leave something to the imagination. Don't make the same amount of detail everywhere. Be selective about where you zoom in, and spend more time with smaller brushes, and more variety of brush marks, working in greater detail and making features sharper and more precise. I recommend doing so in the eyes. Zoom out periodically to see the effect you are having. Think of your painting as being a snapshot taken with a very short focal length so most of the picture is out of focus and just selected parts are in focus. You can exaggerate this effect to bring more attention to your focal point.

Use All Dimensions

Use your full repertoire of dimensional representation, including depiction of dabs, lines, planes, and volumes. Use the "Five Lights of Nature," described later, to depict three-dimensional forms.

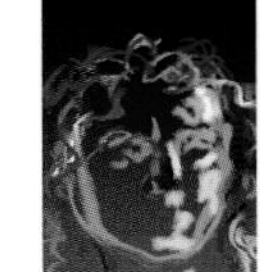

Create Movement

The viewer's eye is naturally led along the boundary between two strongly contrasting regions and along a strong linear form such as a bold line or the edge of a shape. Use this effect to create movement in your composition. Lead the viewer's eye back to your focal points. Imagine a race track with curves that lead you back to where you started. Create lines and curves in your compositions that do the same. Bear in mind that people react differently to lines in different directions. Diagonals leading upward toward the right tend to feel more positive than diagonals leading downward to the right.

Use Rhythm and Repetition

The eye naturally likes some rhythm and repetition, although not overdone. A good guide is when applying color to an image, add it in about five places around the canvas, even if it is only a small amount here or there. The more evenly spaced the dabs, the more rhythmic the effect (like beats in music). An odd number of dabs, or similar image elements, seems to work better than an even number. You can experiment with this concept. By placing similar colors around the canvas, you build up a subconscious visual resonance. When I work in the eyes I often pick up colors from all over the painting and add traces of those colors in the irises.

Intermittently Critique

Regularly stop painting, step back, and look at your picture as if seeing it for the first time. One of the advantages of working on the computer is that you can easily zoom out and see a small version of your image on the screen. Do this from time to time. Looking at a small version of your image is equivalent to an artist stepping back from their canvas to get an objective overview of the image. When looking at your image ask yourself the following questions:

What do I like and dislike about it?

What works and doesn't work?

Where is my eye led?

Is there a natural focal point?

What feelings or emotions does it evoke?

Is there any quality about it I'd like to remember when I paint a portrait?

If you see something that sticks out and looks wrong, ask yourself what's not working, what could make the portrait better. Run through this checklist of questions:

Is the shape working?

Are the lines working?

Is the composition balanced?

Is the coloring working?

Is the lighting working?

Are the details and contrast working?

Make a point of looking at portraits in galleries, books, on the Web, on billboards, anywhere, and asking these same questions.

Go for Extremes

Don't be shy! Go for the extremes. As in the theater, if you are going to make a gesture, make it big! Test the limits of your tools. You can always edit and scale back later. If you edit yourself as you paint, you contain and limit your creativity, rather than express it.

Go for Emotion

Emotion trumps all! If there's a choice between making cruder marks that express and evoke emotion versus carefully controlled marks that may accurately depict the physical likeness of a subject but flatten the emotions, go for the cruder marks. Emotion is key.

3.5 Warm-up Self-Portraits

Solo Self-Portrait

Forget the Rules!

Having reviewed some basic principles of portrait painting, I now want you to forget them and just enjoy yourself! This exercise is designed simply for you to dive in and have fun with Painter. Take your time and please don't worry about how you create the self-portrait or what it looks like.

1. Place a small mirror next to your computer angled so that you can clearly see your face.
2. Choose Cmd/Ctrl-N (File > New) in Painter and open a new canvas 875 pixels wide by 1000 pixels high with resolution 125 pixels per inch (making the physical size 7 inches wide by 8 inches high).
3. Choose Cmd/Ctrl-M (Window > Screen Mode Toggle).
4. Set up a palette arrangement (Window > Arrange Palettes > Save Layout) that includes the Colors and Layers palettes showing.

Continued

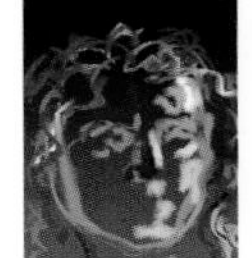

5. Paint a self-portrait. Stick to hand-painted brush strokes (as opposed to scanning in a photograph, or applying effects). Use any colors and any brushes you like. Stay loose and relaxed. Do not use the Undo command. Be committed to your brush strokes. Be adventurous! Cover the whole canvas with paint. Use this exercise as an opportunity to explore the brushes in Painter you've never used before. Don't worry about making a masterpiece!
6. When you have completely covered the canvas with paint, choose File Save As.
7. Save the resulting image with the reverse date (year.month.day) a version number in the title (e.g., 02.09.21 self-01.rif) into the Creativity Projects > 3-Portraits I > 3–5 Self-portraits folder.
8. Now transform your self-portrait into a wild image of some kind. It doesn't matter what you do to it! Try some of the fun Liquid brushes and see how they move the paint around on the canvas.
9. When you have completely transformed your self-portrait, click your Save As button.
10. Save the resulting wild image with a subsequent version number (e.g., 02.09.21-self-02.rif).

Questions

1. What was it like painting the first stage of your self-portrait?
2. What was it like transforming the "completed" self-portrait?
3. What do you like/dislike about your self-portrait (either stage)?
4. Which are your favorite brushes so far?
5. What do you like about them?

Musical Computers Collaborative Self-Portraits (Group Exercise)

This is a great warm-up exercise for a computer painting class. It's always proved to be a favorite of my students. The objectives of this exercise include:

Learn to improvise with what's already on the canvas.

Learn to overcome the preciousness of your own and other's brush strokes and images.

1. Place a number on each computer, using the double-digit system if there are more than nine computers (01, 02, 03, etc., instead of 1, 2, 3, etc.).
2. Place a small mirror next to each computer angled so that each student can clearly see his or her own face. Play music in the background.
3. Ask each student to open a new canvas 600 pixels wide by 650 pixels high.
4. Ask each student to choose Cmd/Ctrl-M.
5. Ask each student to start painting a self-portrait.
6. After 10 minutes or so, turn the music down. This is a signal for the students to click their Save As button and save the image with the name "YY.MM.DD-CC-01-studentname.rif" where YY.MM.DD is the reverse date and CC is the computer number corresponding to the computer they are sitting at.
7. Every student now gets up and chooses another computer to sit at.
8. Each student now continues transforming whatever image is on the screen into a new self-portrait. They should not erase, clear, or delete the previous image. Instead they must use, transform, distort, smear, or paint over existing marks. They must build on what is already there.
9. After another 10 minutes the music is turned down again and every student must choose File > Save As and save the image with the name "YY.MM.DD-CC-02-studentname.rif".
10. Every student now gets up and chooses another computer to sit at that they haven't sat at before.
11. Each student now continues transforming whatever image is on the screen into a new self-portrait, building up on what is already there.
12. Continue this process until each student has sat at each computer, or until there is no more time available.
13. At completion of this exercise, have the students open up every image that was created on the computers they are sitting at.
14. Put every image centrally positioned in screen mode (Cmd/Ctrl-M). Click once on an image with the space bar held down to automatically center it in the screen.
15. Select dark charcoal gray in the Color Picker.
16. Choose Edit > Preferences > Interface.
17. Click on Window Background Color: Use Current Color.
18. Choose Window > Hide Palettes.

Continued

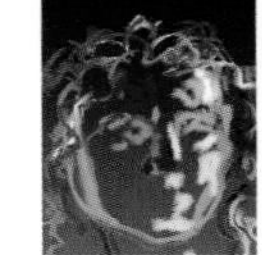

19 Use the Window drop-down menu to select the first image (YY.MM.DD-CC-01-studentname.rif).

20 Have all students gather around each computer in turn while one student shows all the self-portrait images in the order they were created. As each self-portrait is shown, invite any comments such as what the subject feels about the image, or the process of creating the image, or other people's reaction to it. Ask the following:

How did they feel about "intruding" on another person's artwork?

Did painting over a busy background affect their own marks? If so, how?

Did they discover any great new brushes in the process?

Here is a series of portrait transformations created on one computer in a classroom (in the EX'PRESSION Center For New Media, Emeryville, California, www.xnewmedia.com) during a session of Musical Computers Collaborative Self-Portraits. The students are Darin (Figures 3.1 and 3.2), Dezraye (Figure 3.3), and Simon (Figure 3.4).

Note how Darin built up one portrait and then completely transformed it. Both Dezraye and Simon ended up covering up most of what was on the canvas when they started their self-portraits.

Here is another series from another computer with the same class. This series shows the work of Thomas (Figure 3.5), Brandon (Figure 3.6), Jenny (Figure 3.7), and Laura (Figure 3.8).

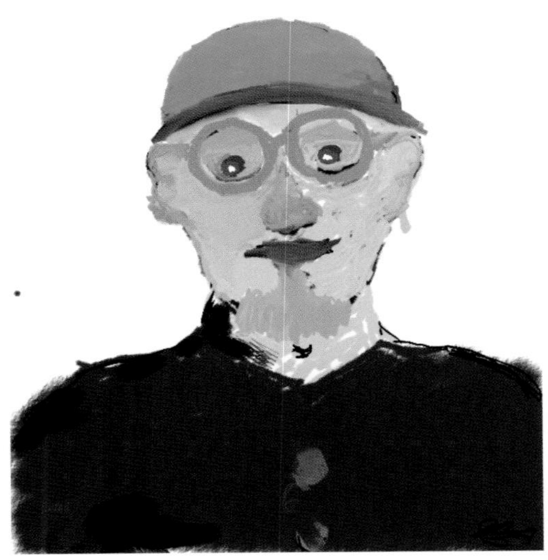

Figure 3.1 Darin's collaborative self-portrait version 1.

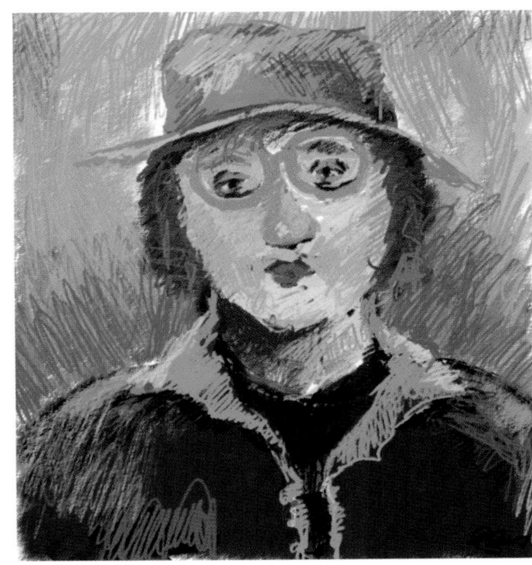

Figure 3.2 Darin's collaborative self-portrait version 2.

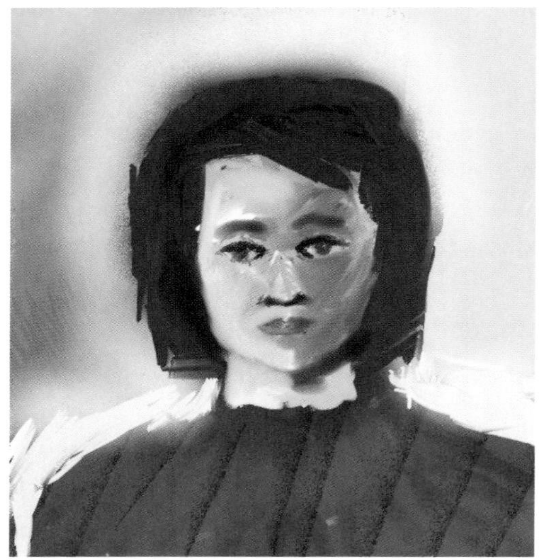

Figure 3.3 Dezraye's collaborative self-portrait.

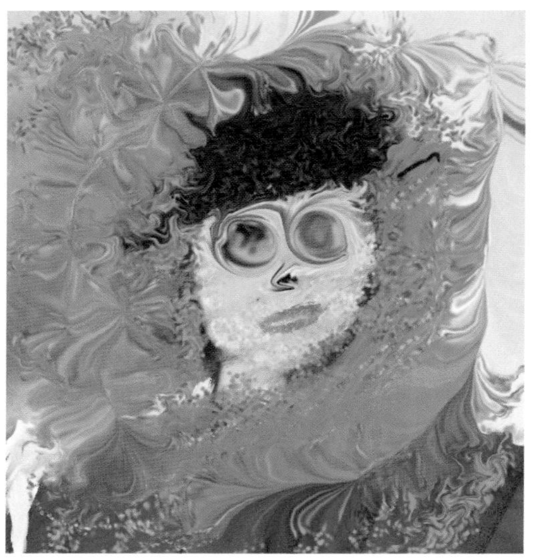

Figure 3.4 Simon's collaborative self-portrait.

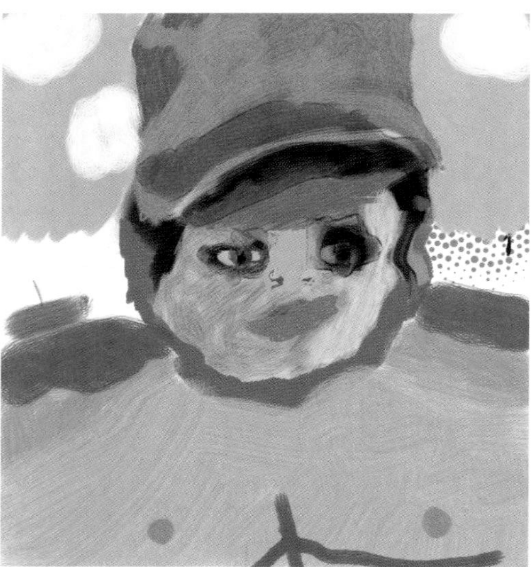

Figure 3.5 Thomas's collaborative self-portrait.

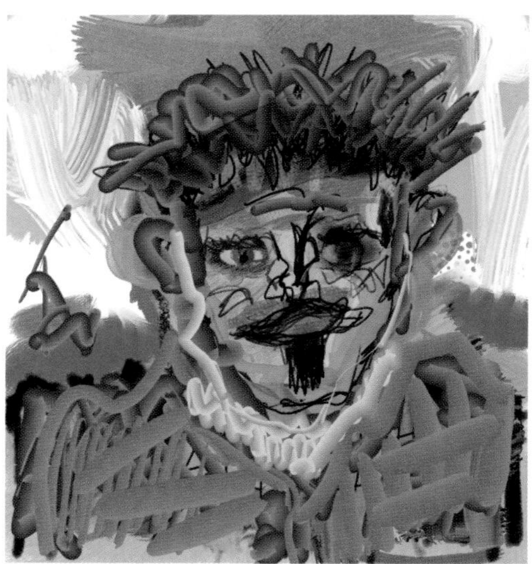

Figure 3.6 Brandon's collaborative self-portrait.

Note how Brandon built on, rather than covered up, Thomas's brushwork, while Jenny and Laura covered up the backgrounds they started with.

What struck me about the student portraits that emerged from this exercise was, irrespective of whether the students built up or covered up underlying brush work, the portraits were free and

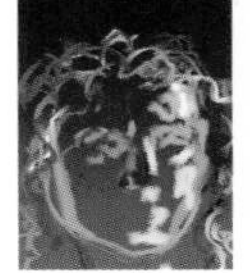

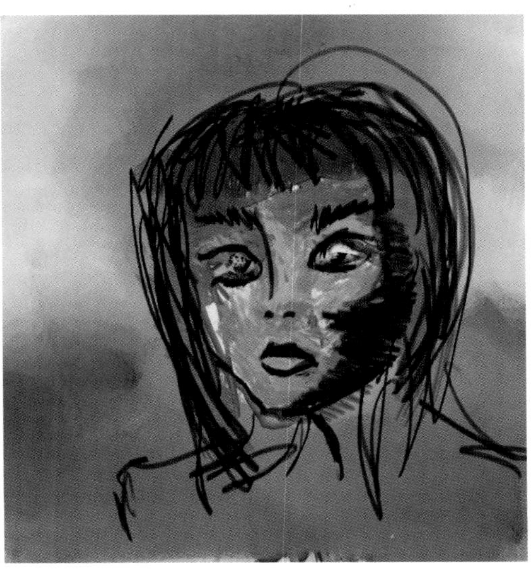

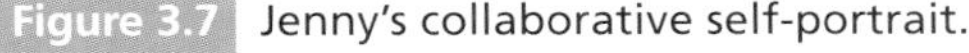

Figure 3.7 Jenny's collaborative self-portrait.

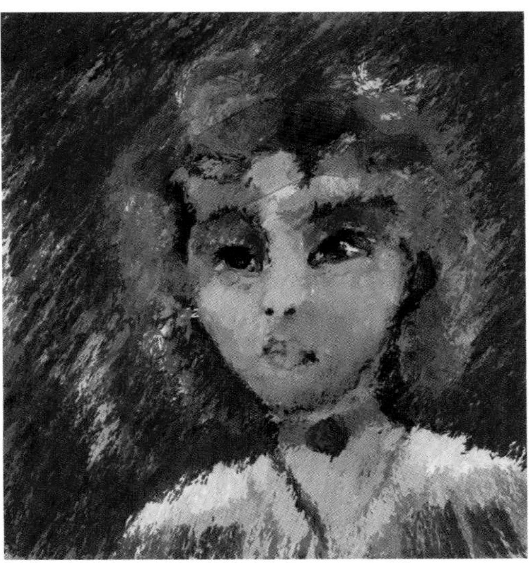

Figure 3.8 Laura's collaborative self-portrait.

expressive. The exercise succeeded in forcing each participant to take greater risks than if they were just starting from a blank canvas.

Variations on the Musical Computers Collaborative Self-Portraits

Lengthen or shorten the amount of time spent at each computer.

Have the students record the entire process as a recorded session so the transformations can be played back in continuous replay. This can be great fun and very dramatic to see; however, I have found that, especially with beginner students, the recording and replaying process may confuse, distract, or overwhelm the students. Many inadvertently stop the recording too early or fail to save the recording successfully.

3.6 The Beauty of Line

In this lesson you will follow a series of simple contour exercises designed to (1) help you loosen up and relax with your brush strokes, (2) make as wide a variety of type and quality of marks as is possible with a single brush, and (3) develop your powers of observation. Although no "Save As" instructions are included here, I recommend that you save each stage. Use a consistent file name convention, such as "YY.MM.DD-lines-01.rif," "YY.MM.DD-lines-02.rif," and so on, where YY.MM.DD is the inverse date (year.month.day).

Simple Brush Stroke

1. Open a new canvas 600 pixels wide by 650 pixels high.
2. Make sure black is the selected color.
3. Select the Sargent Brush Variant in the Artists Brush Category.
4. Select Variant > Restore Default Variant in the Brush Selector pop-up menu.
5. Make a fast, hard, single continuous brush stroke (Figure 3.9).
6. Choose Cmd/Ctrl-Z and undo the stroke you just made.
7. Make a single continuous brush stroke with varying pressure (Figure 3.10). Experience the full dynamic range of the brush. Make the most variety of marks possible with this one brush.

Single-Line Contour Drawings

1. Choose Cmd/Ctrl-Z and undo the stroke you just made.
2. Position a model by your computer, or look into a small mirror placed next to your computer.
3. Observe the contours in your subject's face. Some contours are outlines in which you see where the edge of an object meets the background. Within a subject are further boundaries, or internal contours, between lights and darks that indicate the presence of features (bumps or hollows). Note how all of these contours relate to each other—their different lengths, angles, shapes, paths, and intersections.
4. Use your favored hand (i.e., the hand you most naturally use for drawing) and make a single continuous stroke following the contours you observe, keeping your stylus on the tablet at all times. Take your line for a walk. Allow your eyes to guide your brush stroke. Think of the metaphor of throwing a ball. The ball will tend to go toward wherever you are looking. Similarly, when you draw a subject using a continuous single brush stroke, let your eye follow the natural path it takes as you look at your subject and your brush stroke will follow. You can look back and forth between the screen and the subject as you make the single contour, but spend more time looking at your subject. Take your time with this; there's no rush. Focus on varying and controlling the quality of your line, not on what the picture looks like (Figure 3.11).

Continued

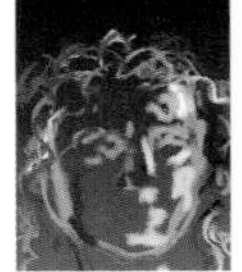

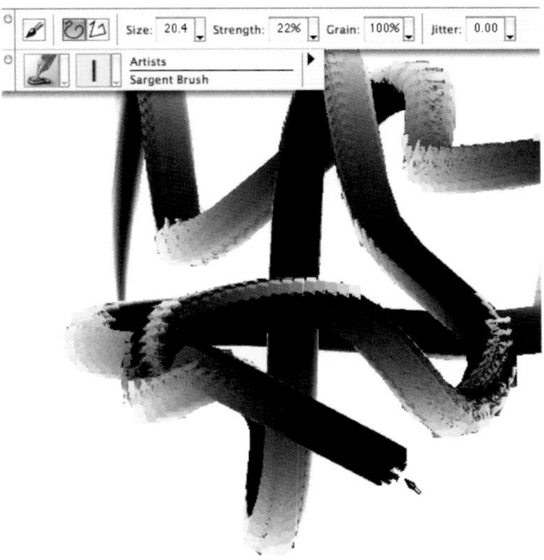

Figure 3.9 Sargent brush stroke with hard pressure.

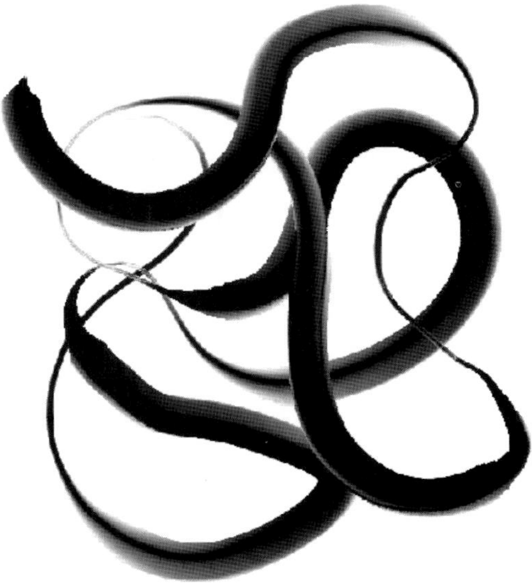

Figure 3.10 Sargent brush stroke with varied pressure.

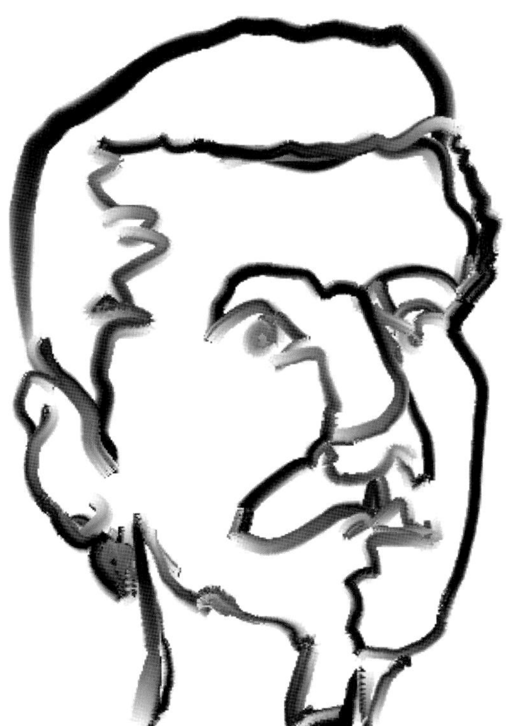

Figure 3.11 Single-line contour drawing with favored hand.

Here are some examples (Figure 3.12) of single-line contour drawings by Carol, one of my students.

5 Choose Cmd/Ctrl-Z and undo the stroke you just made.

6 Repeat this single-line contour drawing using your nonfavored hand (Figure 3.13). Don't worry about how awkward it may feel.

Blind Single-Line Contour Drawings

1 Choose Cmd/Ctrl-Z and undo the stroke you just made.

2 Select the Scratchboard Tool variant from the Pens brush category.

3 Hold the stylus in your favored hand.

4 Use the tips of your thumb and index finger of your nonfavored hand to mark two corners of your canvas on the tablet. These will act as valuable markers that will allow you to stay within your canvas while doing a blind drawing.

5 Tape a sheet of paper over your screen.

6 Look at your subject. Use the Scratchboard brush to follow the path of your eyes as they follow the contours in your subject. Keep your stylus on the tablet (Figure 3.14).

Continued

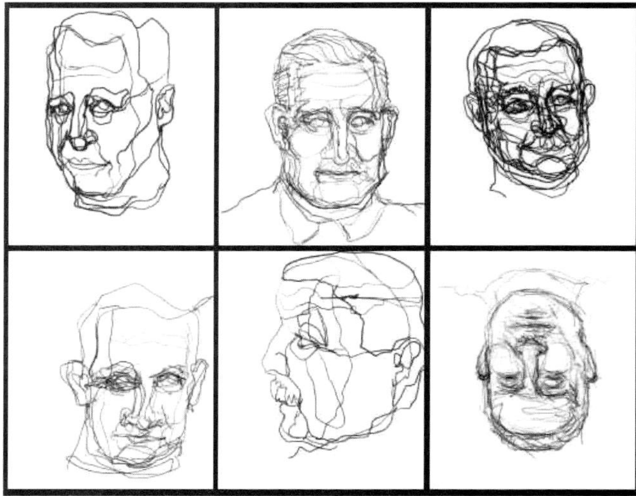

Figure 3.12 Single-line contour drawings by Carol.

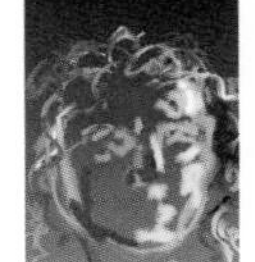

7 Choose Cmd/Ctrl-Z.

8 Make a blind single-line contour drawing with your nonfavored hand (Figure 3.15).

Nervous Pen Drawing

1 Remove the sheet of paper that was covering the screen.

2 Choose Cmd/Ctrl-Z.

3 Select the Nervous Pen variant from the Pens brush category.

4 Hold the stylus in your favored hand.

5 Sketch your subject using the Nervous Pen. There are no restrictions. Try to keep loose and don't get attached to detail (Figure 3.16).

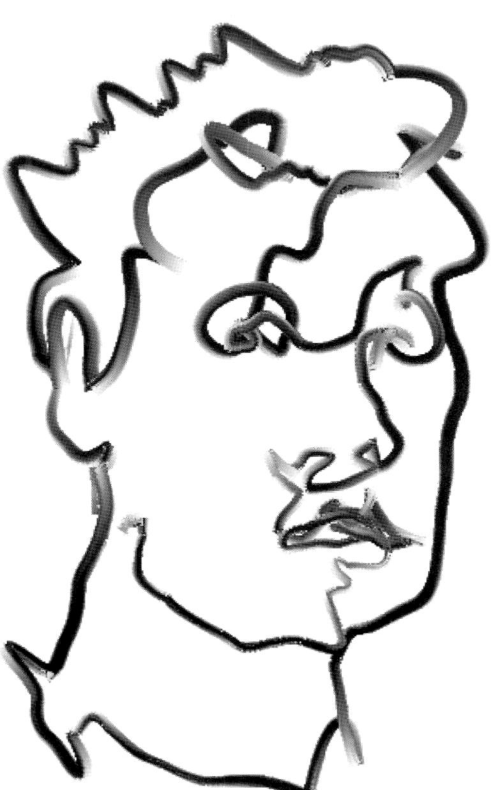

Figure 3.13 Single-line contour drawing with nonfavored hand.

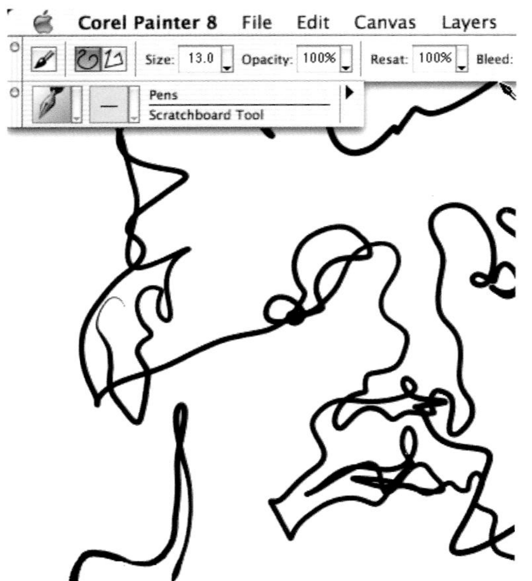

Figure 3.14 Blind single-line contour drawing with favored hand.

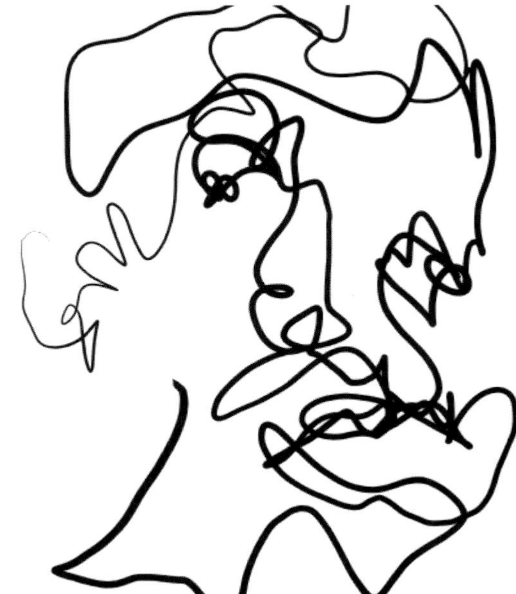

Figure 3.15 Blind single-line contour drawing with nonfavored hand.

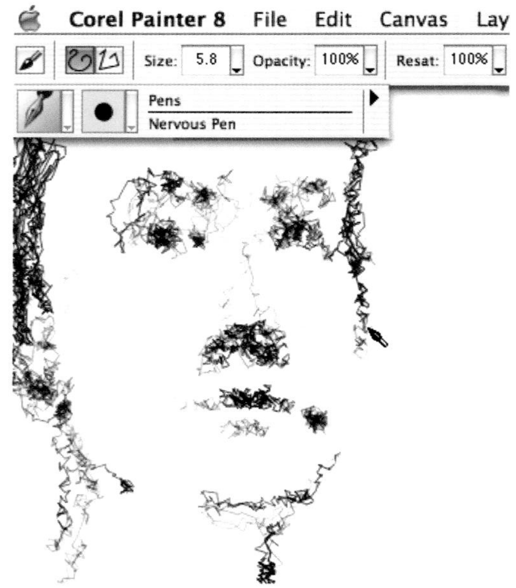

Figure 3.16 Nervous Pen drawing with favored hand.

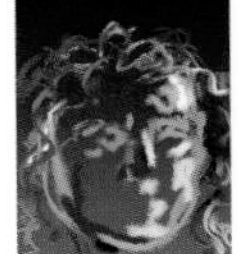

Seven Line Expressions

1. Choose Cmd/Ctrl-A.
2. Choose Delete/Backspace to clear your canvas.
3. Select the Scratchboard Tool variant in the Pens brush category.
4. Using only seven lines in each drawing, make a series of drawings of facial features that evoke the following emotions: happiness (Figure 3.17), surprise, sadness (Figure 3.18), anger, shock, and satisfaction. Make appropriate expressions in the mirror to use as a guide.

Questions

1. Which of the drawing exercises in this lesson did you enjoy the most and the least, and why?
2. What difference in the quality of the brush strokes drawn by your nonfavored hand compared to your favored hand do you notice?

Feel free to try these exercises with other brushes.

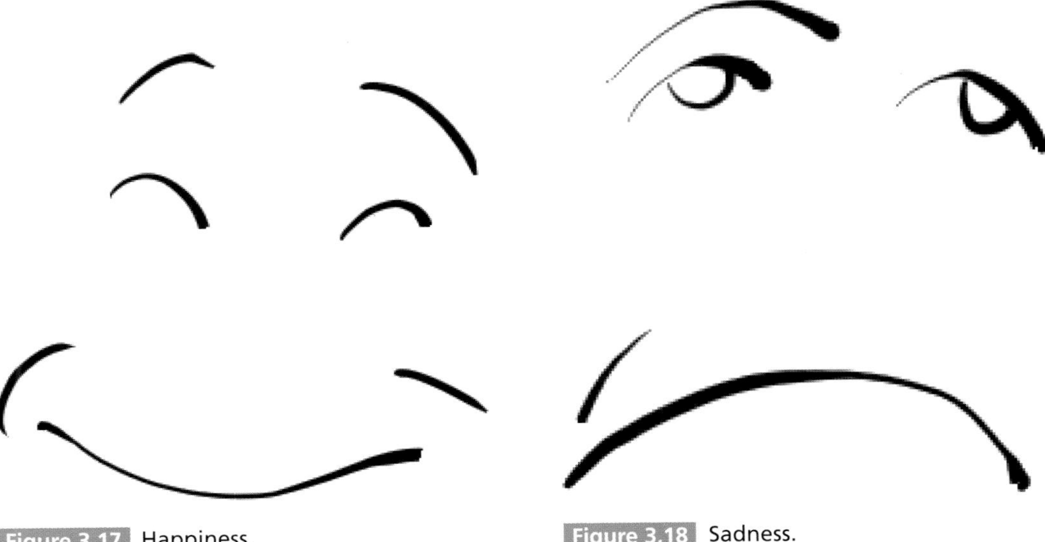

Figure 3.17 Happiness.

Figure 3.18 Sadness.

3.7 Form through Tone

What This Lesson Is About

This lesson deals with the role of the lightness and darkness, also known as the tone or value, of your brush marks in conveying the impression of three-dimensional form in your two-dimensional painting. In this lesson your focus will be on solid blocks of light and dark, rather than on contours.

Blocks of Light and Dark

Half-close your eyes and look at a face (could be your own in a mirror). Close your eyes more until you can just make out the broad forms, the main regions of light and dark. Observe the shapes of the regions of light and dark and the way they fit together. These shapes and the way they relate to each other are visual clues that help our minds perceive what we are observing. These visual clues give a sense of three-dimensional form.

Look at the shapes in the background that are intersected by the head. The head in effect cuts out a negative space surrounded by background. Look within the face and observe a series of light and dark shapes, each one helping define the neighboring one. It is the relationship between these shapes that we translate onto the canvas with our brush strokes. Our eye has to gauge the relative size, or proportions, of the shapes to each other and to the size of the canvas as we paint them.

Differentiating Shadows from Dark Colors

We have talked about shapes of light and dark tones and how they can be used to convey form; however, what happens if the surface of the subject we are looking at has dark colors in a well-lit region or light colors in a shadowy region? How do you differentiate shadows from dark colors in a painting? To differentiate these components, it is helpful to understand the way light interacts with a solid form. The following Five Lights lesson is based on one by Jane Connor-ziser and uses her illustrations.

Depicting Form: The Five Lights of Nature

Form, as a noun, is the three-dimensional shape and structure of an object as distinguished from its material and surface characteristics. *Form*, as a verb, is the action of shaping or molding something. In portraiture our marks on the canvas can convey the illusion of three-dimensional form, and in the process form a likeness of our model.

To depict a solid three-dimensional form by making marks on a flat surface, we need to carefully observe, and then accurately describe on our canvas, the way light interacts with the solid form.

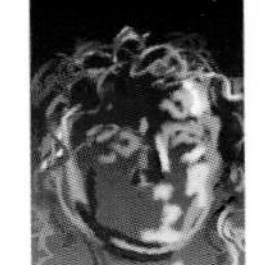

There are five specific types of light and shade that we observe on and around a solid form: base tone, specular highlights, shaded side, refracted light, and cast shadow. These are the Five Lights of Nature, also known as the Five Values. Understanding these helps us both observe and paint better.

Base Tone

Let's start with a simple form, that of an egg (Figure 3.19). Let's assume the egg surface has a particular hue associated with it, say, pink. This hue is known in traditional art as the base tone or mid-tone, or, in photography, as the diffuse highlight. Our initial blocking out of base tone establishes the main shape of our subject, in this case an oval. In reality a surface base tone has texture and variations throughout the object.

Specular Highlight

Imagine a single point light source (e.g., sun or lightbulb) located to the upper left of the egg. Imagine light as being made up of ping-pong balls (photons in physics-speak). The ping-pong balls hit the closest protrusion of the egg with the greatest density and intensity. These ping-pong balls bounce off (are reflected) in many directions, some of them striking our eyes. Hence we observe a patch of intense, bright, warm light (Figure 3.20). This patch of directly reflected light is known as the specular highlight, or sometimes just as the highlight.

Figure 3.19 Base tone.

Figure 3.20 Specular highlight.

Shaded Side

The far side of the egg to the light source is protected from the ping-pong balls and thus does not send any reflected balls in our direction. This is the shaded side, or form shadow (Figure 3.21). When depicting the shaded side, it is effective to make the shaded color a medium-dark gray made with a cool hue that is the complement of the hue in the specular highlight. Complementary colors are easy to identify in the Painter Color Picker since they are simply on opposite sides of the hue circle.

Refracted Light

Some ping-pong balls miss the egg but are reflected back onto the shaded side of the egg from the surroundings (Figure 3.22). This refracted light, or indirectly reflected light, often contains hues from the environment. For instance, you will often notice the color of a person's shirt or jacket reflected back into the shaded area under the chin or on the jawline.

Cast Shadow

The egg acts as a shield and prevents the ping-pong balls from striking the surface immediately beneath it and on the opposite side of it to the light source. This casts a shadow (Figure 3.23). The shape of a cast shadow indicates both the shape of the object or feature blocking out the light and the shape and form of the surface on which it is cast. Shadows are a useful tool for putting your portrait in an environmental context, rather than just having it float in a vacuum. Cast shadows are

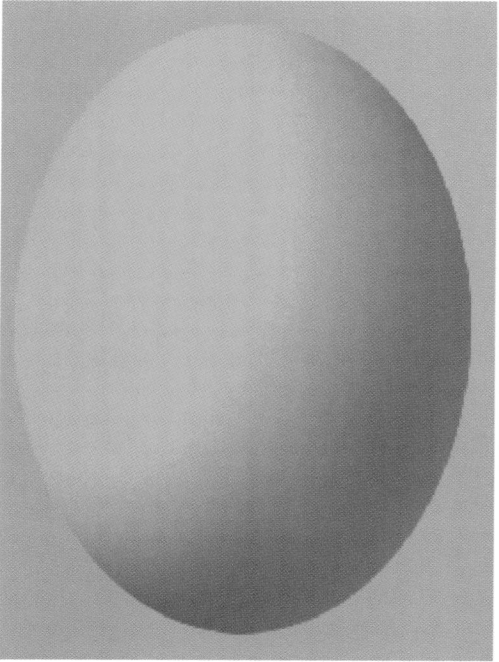

Figure 3.21 Shaded side.

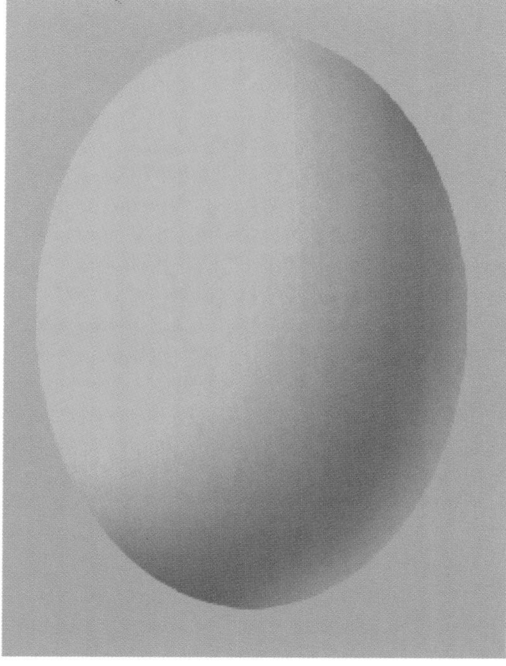

Figure 3.22 Refracted light.

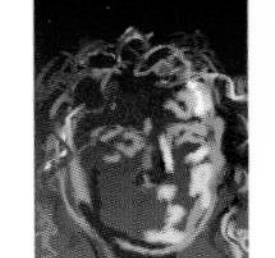

also useful for putting individual features in context with each other. The shadow is usually the darkest tone in the picture.

When all five lights of nature are present in a painting, the illusion of a three-dimensional form is created (Figure 3.24).

All Five Lights of Nature can be seen as applied to not only the whole head, but also individual protruding features on a person's face, such as the nose, lips, and chin. Indentations, such as deeply set eyes, have the same five lights but on opposite sides to the protrusions.

Five Lights of Nature Exercise

1. Choose Cmd/Ctrl-N.
2. Create a new file 600 pixels wide by 650 pixels high.
3. Choose Cmd/Ctrl-M.
4. Select New Layer from the pop-up menu in the Layers section of the Objects palette (Figure 3.25).
5. Repeat this step until you have five new layers.
6. Double-click on each layer name in turn in the layers section and rename the layers with the five lights of nature.
7. Click on the Canvas in the Layers section.
8. Choose Cmd/Ctrl-F.

Continued

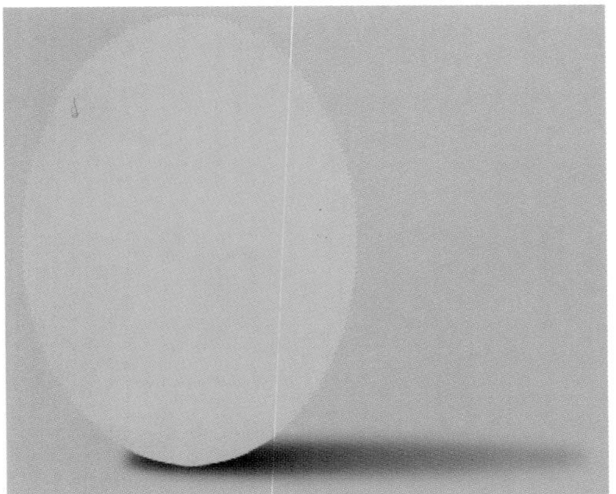

Figure 3.23 Cast shadow.

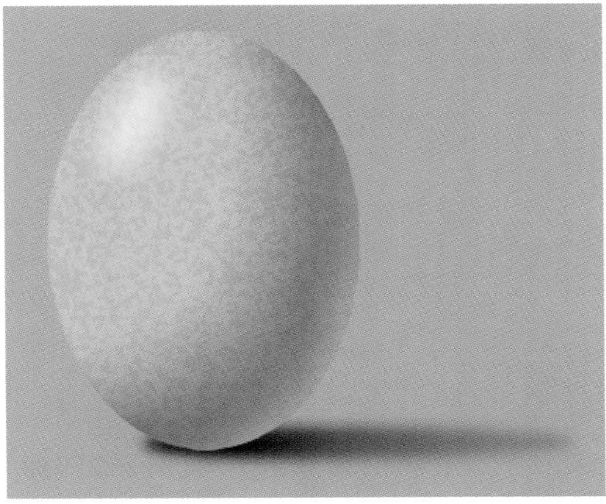

Figure 3.24 All Five Lights of Nature.

9 Pick a background color.

10 Click OK.

11 Select the Artist Pastel Chalk from the Dry Media brush category.

12 Choose a subject to paint. This could be a still life, a model, or yourself.

13 Starting with the Base Tone layer (by clicking on it in the Layers section) and working your way upward, paint each layer the appropriate color (Figure 3.26).

14 Save the final image as a Riff so you can preserve the layers.

Progressive Statements Project

In the ancient board game of Go, the arrangement of black and white counters can be simultaneously looked at as either black surrounding white, or conversely, as white surrounding black. Similarly, we can look at regions of light and dark tone as positive and negative spaces that surround one another. In this project you observe the shapes of those tonal regions and the spatial and tonal relationships between them, and then build up the blocks of light and dark tone on your canvas, starting rough and working toward detail.

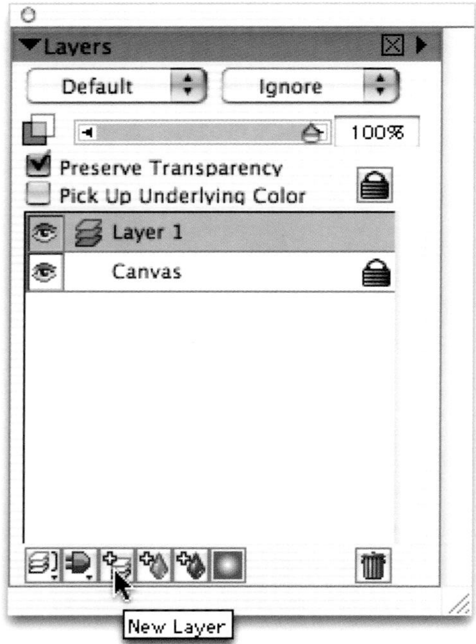

Figure 3.25 Creating a new layer.

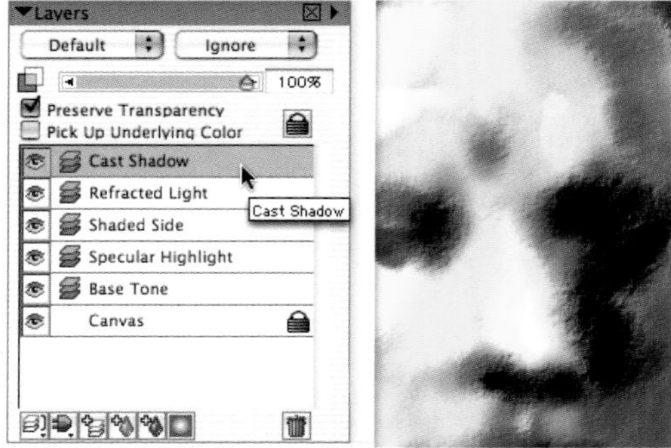

Figure 3.26 Paint on the layers.

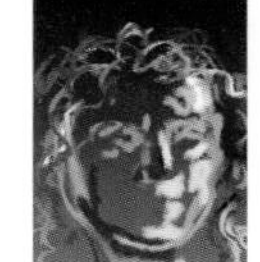

The objectives of this exercise are to:

1. Accurately observe variations in tonal values in a subject.
2. Accurately observe shapes of tonal regions and their relationship to form.
3. Learn to paint from rough forms to the details.

1. Choose Cmd/Ctrl-N to open a new canvas 600 pixels wide by 650 pixels high.
2. Choose Cmd/Ctrl-M to mount the canvas in screen mode.
3. Select a mid-gray as the current color (with the Value-Saturation Triangle cursor midway up on the left). To keep to pure tone during this exercise, keep the Value-Saturation Triangle cursor along the left (zero saturation) side of the triangle and restrict yourself to moving it up and down to alter value.
4. Select Cmd/Ctrl-F.
5. Select Fill With: Current Color in the Fill dialog box.
6. Click OK.
7. Select the Captured Bristle brush variant in the Acrylics Brush Category.
8. Sit your model down near your computer screen (or look at yourself in a mirror).
9. Look carefully at your model with half-closed eyes and visualize their face and the surroundings in terms of a few large flat blocks of tone. Identify which blocks are the lightest and which are the darkest.
10. Make broad white brush strokes that describe the lightest regions. Avoid the temptation to sketch in a line drawing of where the blocks of tone go.
11. Paint black brush strokes where you see the darkest blocks of tone. Work rapidly and loosely. Don't get attached to details. Don't worry about making a likeness of your subject. In this first stage, or first *statement* (see Figure 3.18), you are reducing the subject to the minimum number of tone areas that will convey the essence of the subject. This first statement reduces the complex array of colors, tones, and textures into a few simple shades of black, white, and gray. Intermittently zoom out (Cmd/Ctrl-'–') and see what your painting looks like when it is postage stamp size on the screen. Stop painting when you are satisfied that you have captured the essence of the subject (Figure 3.27). This initial rough painting is your first statement.
12. Choose File > Save As and save it with a file name indicating that it is the first statement.

Continued

13 Reduce the brush diameter.

14 Now look even more carefully at your subject and observe the subtler changes in tone. You can probably see several smaller blocks of tone within the regions that you painted as large, rough blocks in the first statement. Paint over the large blocks of tone with these smaller blocks. This is your second statement (Figure 3.28), which is more detailed than the first and conveys more subtle differences in tone. Notice the Five Lights of Nature as you paint.

15 Choose File > Save As and save the image with a file name indicating that it is the second statement.

16 You can continue this process, developing a series of statements, each one more detailed.

Questions

1. How have you found this exercise?
2. What were the challenges?
3. What do you feel about the results?

Here's an example (Figure 3.29) of first and second statements from Sharon, a student of mine.

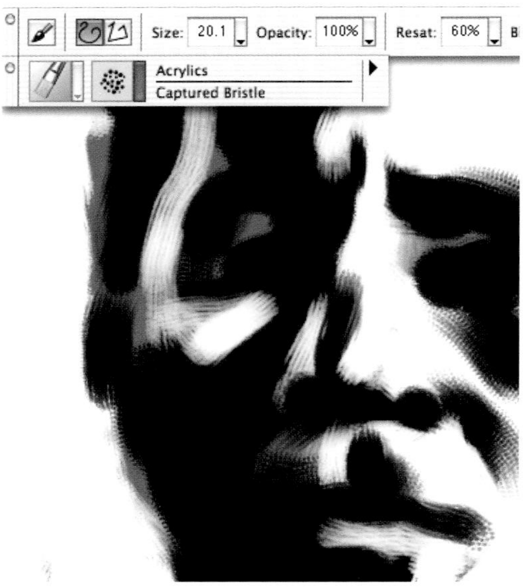

Figure 3.27 First statement.

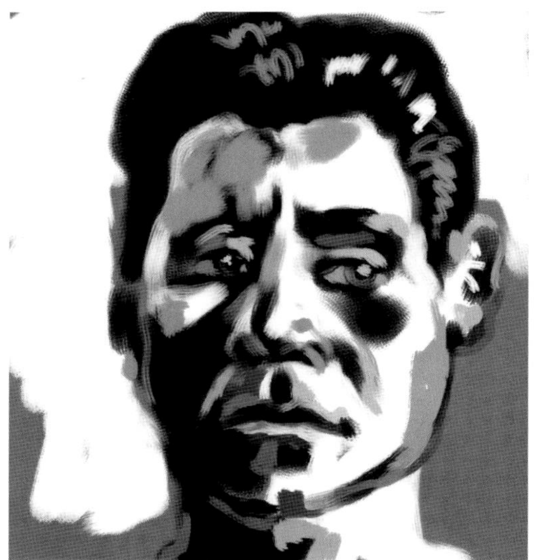

Figure 3.28 Second statement.

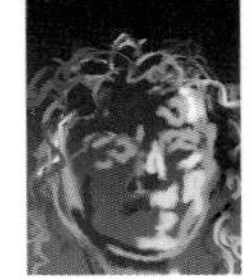

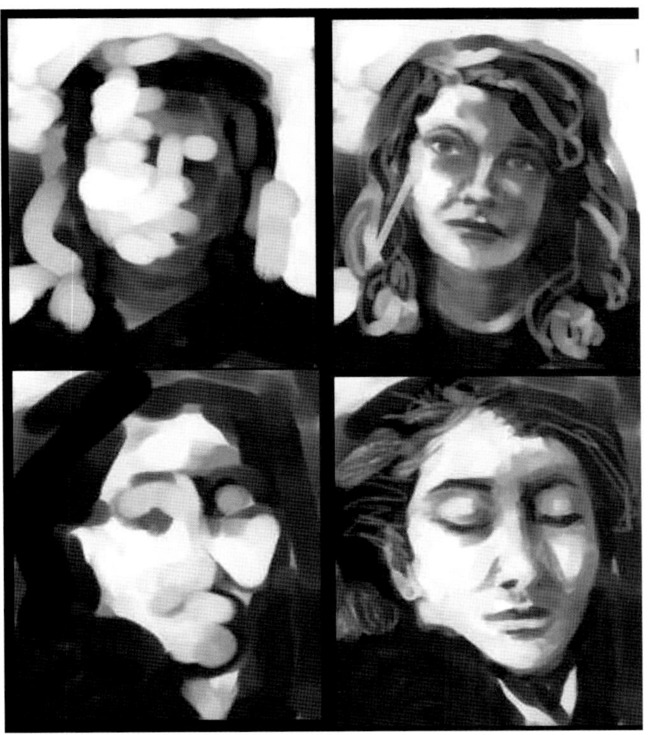

Figure 3.29 Sharon's first and second statements.

3.8 Wrap

In this session you have explored some of the basic visual vocabulary that you will subsequently be putting to use in your paintings. For instance, gaining greater control over the quality of a brush stroke allows you to get much more expression into your paintings. Learning to accurately observe and perceive tone and build up progressive tonal statements is essential to creating the illusion of three-dimensional form. An excellent source of exercises that can help you overcome our mind's tendency to get in the way of seeing is Betty Edward's book *Drawing on the Right Side of the Brain*. The same skills of seeing and perceiving that you've built up in this session will be applied with color in the following session.

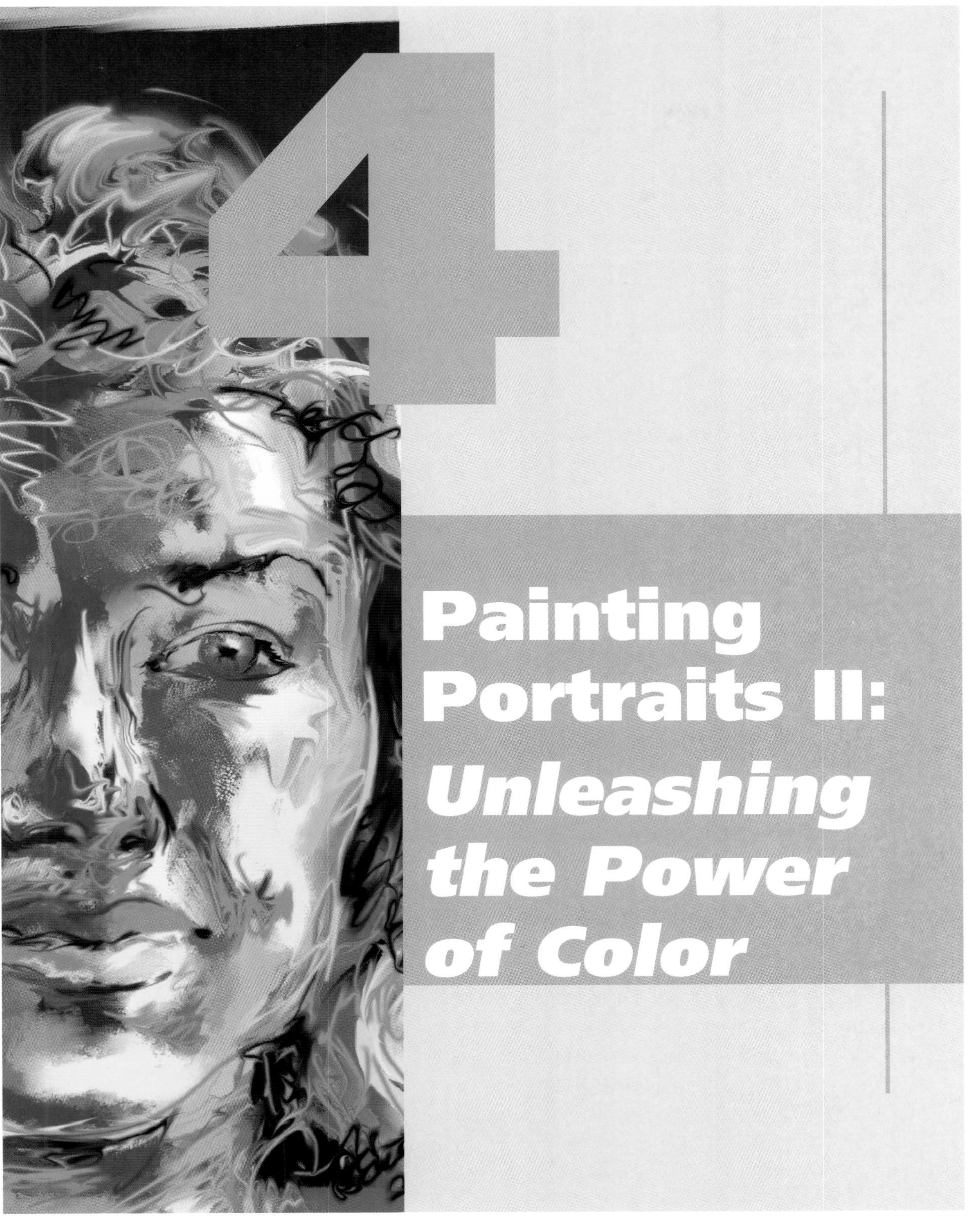

4

Painting Portraits II: *Unleashing the Power of Color*

4.1 Introduction

In the last session you encountered the challenge of seeing contours, shapes, and tonal variations and using the relationship between them to depict three-dimensional form on a two-dimensional canvas. As you will have discovered, your mind filters what you see, tells you what to expect to see, and gets in the way of accurate observation. To overcome your knowledge of what you expect to see, you either had to play tricks on your mind (drawing with your nondrawing hand, etc.) or you had to make a real effort to accurately observe. The same challenge of overcoming your mind's expectations applies to seeing and describing color.

This session focuses on the power of color. You will experiment with different approaches to adding the dimension of color to your paintings. Color offers great opportunities for expression, while being challenging and intimidating due to the vast range of possibilities at your fingertips. A typical computer system offers around 24 million possible colors for each pixel in your image. That's a lot of choice! When you make color choices you need to be clear about your goal. Are you trying to render as accurately as possible the colors you see in real life or are you are using color to express emotion in your paintings (for instance by use of bright happy colors, dull sad colors, angry colors, or calm colors)? Both goals are equally valid but can lead to quite different results.

In this session the goal is to use color to express yourself in your paintings. The exercises are designed to help you choose and apply color, to become confident in making color decisions, and to realize the full power of color in expressing yourself and your impression of your subject.

4.2 Instructor Notes

The following exercises are fun, exciting ways to explore the use of color in portraiture. The same exercises can equally be applied to any other subject besides a portrait, so you can adapt the lessons to suit your particular class focus and interest.

I recommend reviewing the discussion of color in session 1 and how it relates to Painter's color picker. The use of complementary and primary colors can be explored as part of this session. I suggest referring to examples of where artists have specifically and successfully juxtaposed complementary colors, such as artists of the Fauvist movement.

The one exercise in this session that, in my experience, has made the most difference to students is the "Wild Color!" project. I have found this exercise is helpful in getting students to be more free and confident in their use of color. The key underlying lesson throughout this session, and worthwhile reminding your students of, is that it's okay to take risks and to experiment with color.

The last lesson of this session deals with color sets. This session is optional, although color sets can offer a powerful tool in shaping and limiting the student's color palette.

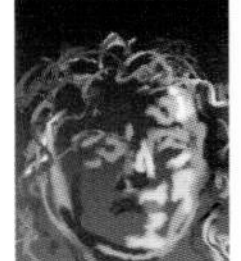

4.3 About Color

There Is Color Everywhere

Everything you see has a hue (color) associated with it, in addition to its purity or saturation (brightness/dullness) and tonal value (lightness/darkness). In general there is no such thing as pure black or pure white or pure gray in nature.

When we see shadows on a face, there are many reflected colors within those shadows, even within the darkest shadows. Look carefully at the world around you and observe the myriad of colors contained in every highlight, every shadow, and, in fact, in everything we see.

Color Perception

Our perception of color, when looking at a region of color in a subject, is influenced by the colors in the environment immediately around that region. Every color is influenced by every other color. This is an effect you can use to your benefit when applying color in a painting. A touch of color here and there can affect the whole mood and feel of the painting. The underlying issue in perceiving color is color relationships. How do we relate the colors and tones we see to the colors we put down on the canvas? How do the colors on our canvas relate to, and contrast with, each other and affect our perception of the image? These are questions we are constantly addressing in our paintings.

Color Spots

One way to deal with the complexities of color relationships is to think of the world as a vast pattern of interlocking colored areas, a dazzling patchwork of "colored spots," as they were called by artist Charles Hawthorne. If you put the right color and shape of color spot in the right place on the canvas, the color spots will link up in the viewer's eye to give a convincing image of the subject.

Computer Color

Luminescent phosphors or liquid crystals emit the colors we see on our computer screen. This type of color is known as *luminescent* or *additive color*. The colors we see in our environment (whether from objects or printed materials) are observed via reflected and refracted light after some wavelengths are absorbed or dispersed. They are known as *reflective* or *subtractive colors*. The color ranges, or gamuts, of the two types of color—additive versus subtractive—are quite different. Thus we will never see on our computer screens the exact same colors we see around us in the environment or in print. For details and suggestions on the issues of color consistency between your screen image and your printed image, please see Appendix III: Getting Colors to Look Right When You Print, and the Color Management PDF documents contained in the Painter Creativity Companion CD.

Color Tone

All colors, even pure 100 percent saturated colors, have inherent tone (lightness and darkness). For instance, yellow has an inherently lighter tonal value than blue. The inherent value of a color is independent of the value adjustments you can make in Painter's Saturation Value (SV) triangle to lighten or darken, or saturate or desaturate, a color. Whether we do so intentionally or not, every color we paint on our canvas depicts a tonal value.

If you are unsure of what the tonal value of your colors are at any time, you can always employ the gray-scale "cheater" technique of temporarily turning your color painting into a gray-scale (black and white) image. To check color tonality, choose Effects > Tonal Control > Adjust Colors and set the Saturation slider all the way to the left (−139%). After you've examined the image and noted any areas that need darkening or lightening, select Cmd/Ctrl-Z to undo the effect.

4.4 Progressive Color Statements

The Progressive Color Statements project is about identifying and then painting the color and shape and relative position of color spots to build up an image. You do this by using the same progressive statement approach used in the previous session. Start off painting big, rough forms with few colors and then refine the painting in stages toward greater detail and a larger range of colors. Throughout this exercise, be conscious of selecting the tone of the colors you apply to suit the appropriate tonal value of the section of the portrait you are painting.

1. Choose Cmd/Ctrl-N.
2. Open a new canvas 700 pixels wide by 900 pixels high (7 inches by 9 inches at 100 dpi).
3. Choose Cmd/Ctrl-M to mount the canvas.
4. Choose Window > Zoom to Fit. Zoom out further, using the Cmd/Ctrl-"−" command, to suit your screen size and palette arrangement.
5. Hold down the space bar and drag your canvas into a convenient position on the screen.

Continued

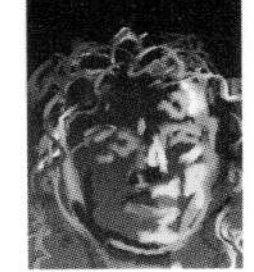

6 Select a mid-gray-yellow as the current color, with a yellow selected in the Hue Wheel and the Value-Saturation Triangle cursor mid-way up on the left and slightly to the right (Figure 4.1).

7 Select Cmd/Ctrl-F.

8 Select Fill With: Current Color in the Fill dialog box.

9 Click OK.

10 Select the Captured Bristle brush variant in the Brushes brush category.

11 Set the brush size to be about 30.

12 Sit your model down near your computer screen (or look at yourself in a mirror).

13 Look carefully at your model with half-closed eyes and visualize their face and the surroundings in terms of blocks of tone. Identify which blocks are the lightest and which are the darkest.

14 Using light and dark colors, adjusting the SV-triangle cursor as you do so, paint in the main areas of light and dark. Work rapidly and loosely. Don't get attached to details (keep your brush size relatively large), to trying to get perfectly accurate colors, or to trying to make a likeness of your subject. In this first stage, or first *color statement*, you are reducing the subject to the minimum number of colored tonal areas that will convey the essence of the subject. You are reducing the complex array of colors, tones, and textures into a few simple light and dark color spots or regions. The most important aspect of this exercise is getting used to seeing color in terms of tonal values.

15 Intermittently zoom out (Cmd/Ctrl-"–") and see what your painting looks like when it is postage stamp size on the screen.

16 Also intermittently apply the gray-scale "cheater" technique where you choose Effects > Tonal Control > Adjust Colors (Figure 4.2) and set the Saturation slider all the way to the left (–139%). After you've examined the gray-scale version of the image (Figure 4.3) and noted any areas that need darkening or lightening, select Cmd/Ctrl-Z to undo the effect.

17 Continue painting until you have completely covered the canvas with paint and have captured the essence of the subject. This initial rough painting is your first color statement (Figure 4.4).

18 Choose File > Save As and save it with a file name indicating that it is the first color statement.

19 Reduce the brush diameter to about 5.

Continued

20 Now look more carefully at your subject and observe the subtler changes in tone and colors. Observe the smaller blocks of tone and color within the regions that you painted as large rough blocks in the first statement. Paint over the large blocks with these smaller blocks. This is your second statement (Figure 4.5), which is more detailed than the first and conveys more subtle differences in tone and color.

21 Choose File > Save As and save the image with a file name indicating that it is the second color statement.

22 Continue this process, developing a series of statements, each one more detailed.

Questions

1 How did you like this exercise?

2 What were the challenges?

3 How do you feel about the results?

Here's an example (Figure 4.6) of a first and second color statement from a student of mine, Lois.

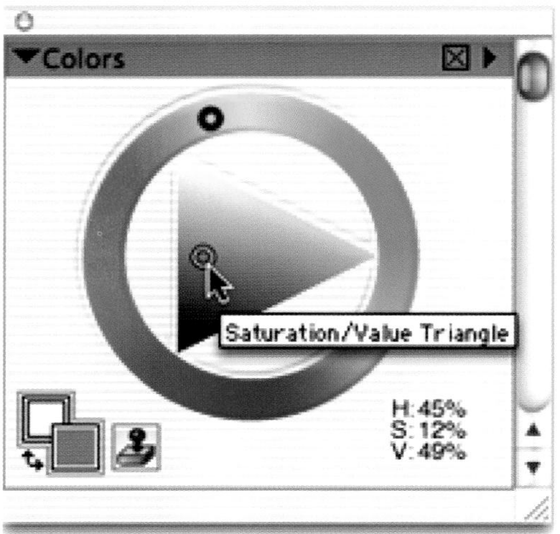

Figure 4.1 Select a mid-gray-yellow.

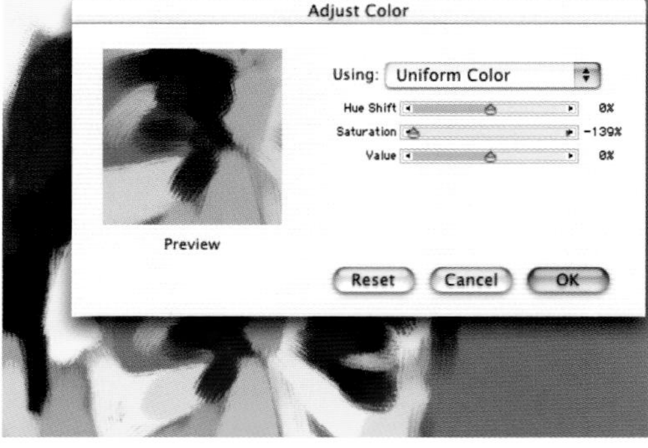

Figure 4.2 Desaturating with Adjust Color.

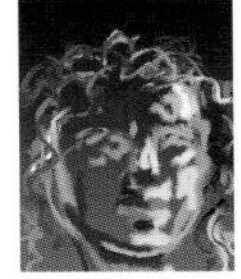

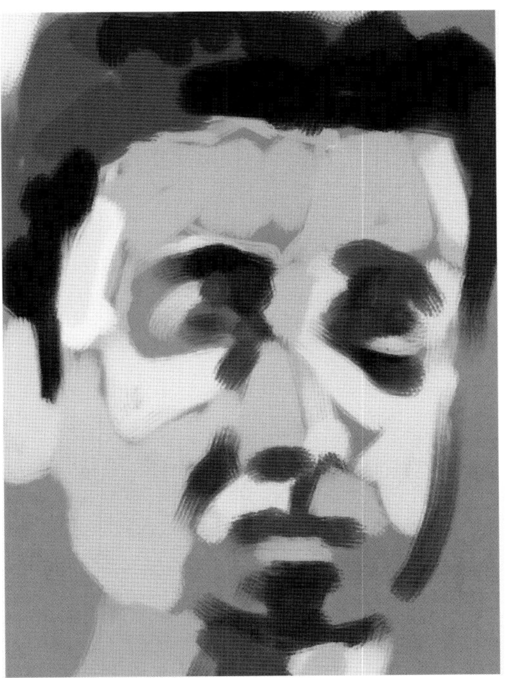

Figure 4.3 Image after temporary adjustment.

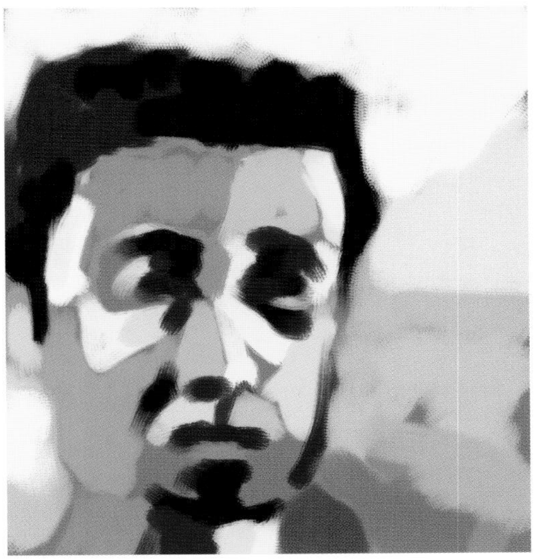

Figure 4.4 First color statement.

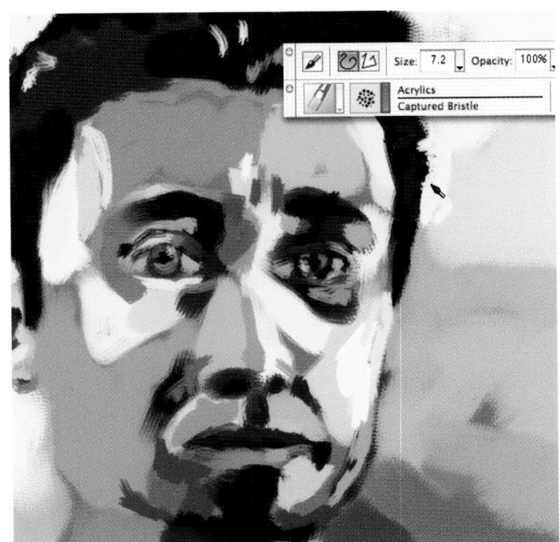

Figure 4.5 Second color statement.

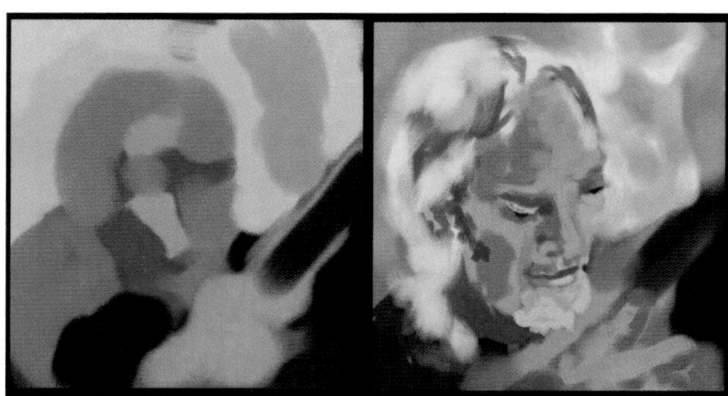

Figure 4.6 Lois's first and second color statements.

4.5 Wild Color!

This assignment is totally the opposite of the previous one. Instead of striving to accurately observe and depict color, this exercise is about letting go of rules and shoulds, and instead giving yourself license to be free and expressive with color. Play with different combinations of colors next to each other. Test out the effect of juxtaposing complementary colors from opposite sides of the color wheel/hue circle. Paint in a way that you may not have dared to before. This is an exercise where you are being given permission to step out from being safe. Your canvas is a laboratory for experimentation. Make the most of it and enjoy it!

In summary, the objectives of this exercise are to:

Throw all rules and restrictions out the window!

Be free from worry about what color should be where.

Have fun!

1. Choose Cmd/Ctrl-N.
2. Open a new canvas 700 pixels wide by 900 pixels high (7 inches by 9 inches at 100 dpi).
3. Choose Cmd/Ctrl-M to mount the canvas.
4. Choose Window > Zoom to Fit. Zoom out further, using the Cmd/Ctrl-"–" command, to suit your screen size and palette arrangement.
5. Hold down the space bar and drag your canvas into a convenient position on the screen.
6. Use whatever brushes you like. Paint a portrait using as many different colors as possible. The colors you choose need not bear any relationship or resemblance to the actual colors you see. Be bold, be daring, be crazy, be WILD!

Continued

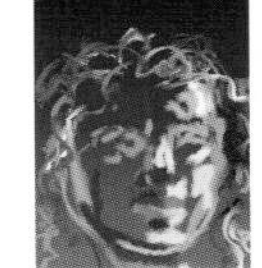

7 When you've finished, Choose File > Save As. Save the resulting image as a RIFF file.

Questions

1. Did you have fun?
2. Was choosing color easy or difficult?
3. What's your impression of the end result?

Here are several examples of "Wild Color!" self-portraits by three of my students, Lesley, Sidne, and Den (Figures 4.7, 4.8, 4.9).

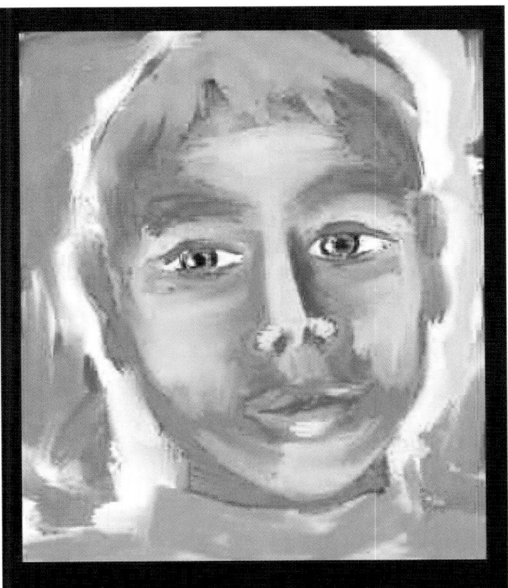

Figure 4.7 Lesley's wild color self-portrait.

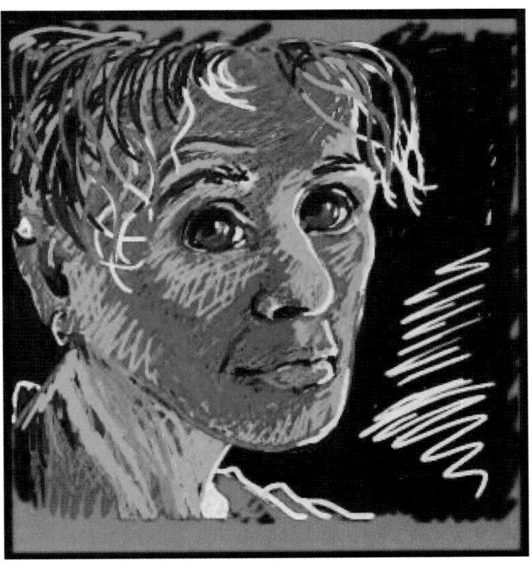

Figure 4.8 Sidne's wild color self-portrait.

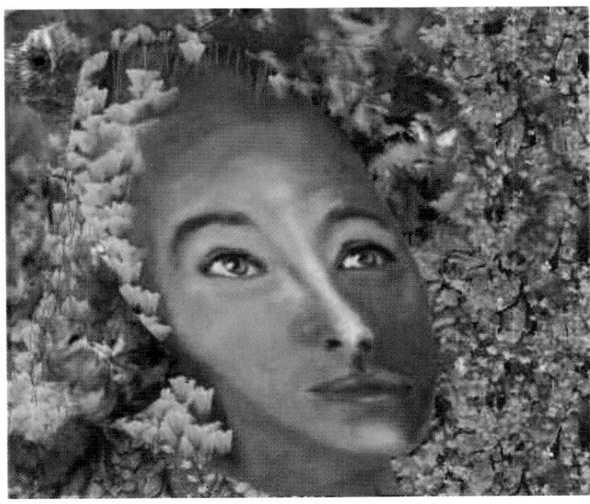

Figure 4.9 Den's wild color self-portrait.

4.6 Using Color Sets

Advantages of Using Color Sets

The use of color sets in Painter can offer you power, elegance, and consistency in your choice and application of color. Up until now you've picked your color using the Standard Colors hue-wheel/SV-triangle Color Picker in the Colors palette. This color picker is a handy, intuitive way to pick color; however, there can be advantages in using color sets. Color sets allow you to restrict your palette to a particular range of colors and easily pick those colors just by clicking on the color squares. These colors may be your favorite colors or colors you need to apply with consistency for a particular project. They may be colors you know from experience will print well or will be good for certain jobs, such as skin colors, and so on. To see the default color set (Painter Colors), if it's not already visible on your screen, select Window > Show Color Sets (Cmd/Ctrl-3).

Exploring the Standard Color Sets

Before making your own customized color sets, it's a good idea to explore the standard color sets that come with Painter. To access, modify, and create color sets, open the Color Sets section of the Art Materials palette (Figure 4.10).

1. Choose Open Color Set from the Color Sets palette pop-up menu.
2. Select the Color Sets folder within the Painter 8 folder.
3. Choose the "72 Pencils" color set.
4. Click Open. You'll see the "72 Pencils" color set appear.
5. Try out the colors from the "72 Pencils" color set using any brushes you choose.
6. Repeat steps 1 through 5 with all the other color sets.

Loading Color Sets from Another Computer or Removable Media

To add color sets that you've downloaded from the Web or have on removable media such as CD-ROM, just copy the color set data into the Color Sets folder within your Painter 8 application folder. Then just open the color sets following the previous steps (using the Library button in the Color Sets section).

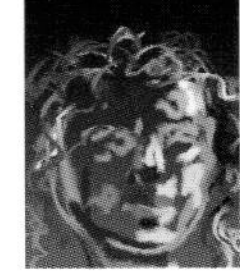

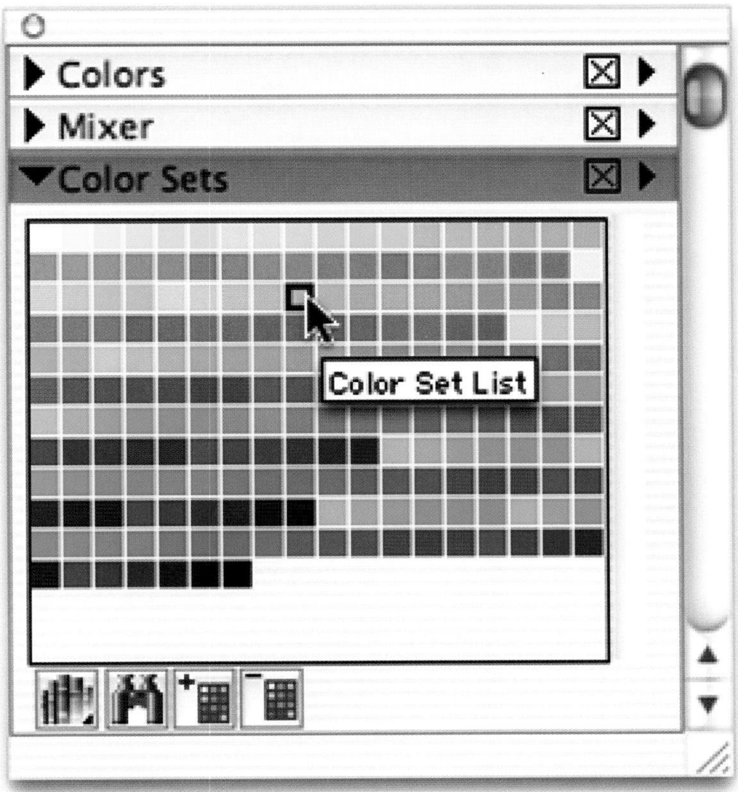

Figure 4.10 The default "Painter Colors" color set and Color Set section of the Art Materials palette.

1. Place the Painter Creativity Companion CD in your computer.
2. Drag the Extra Color Sets folder into the Painter 8 application folder on your computer hard drive.
3. Choose Open Color Set in the Color Sets palette pop-up menu.
4. Select the Extra Color Sets folder within the Painter 8 folder.
5. Choose the "50s RnB" color set.
6. Click Open. You'll see the "50s RnB" color set appear.
7. Try out the colors from the "50s RnB" color set using any brushes you choose.
8. Repeat steps 1 through 5 with all the other extra color sets.

Creating a Custom Color Set Manually by Mixing and Picking Your Own Colors

1. Choose Cmd/Ctrl-N.
2. Set the new canvas to be 600 pixels wide by 600 pixels high at 72 dpi.
3. Click OK.
4. Choose Cmd/Ctrl-M to mount the canvas.
5. Choose Window > Zoom to Fit. Zoom out farther, using the Cmd/Ctrl-"–" command, to suit your screen size and palette arrangement.
6. Hold down the space bar and drag your canvas into a convenient position on the screen.
7. Select the Captured Bristle brush variant in the Acrylics category.
8. Open the Color Sets palette.
9. Choose the Open Color Set Library button in the Color Sets pop-up menu and select the Fine Art Oils color set from the Extra Color Sets folder.
10. Select colors from this color set and make dabs on the canvas, placing different colors adjacent to each other. There are many different ways you can approach mixing and blending colors in Painter, including using the Mixer palette. The sample shown here was created by Rheba. In the Color Sets Galore folder on the companion CD, you'll find a color set called "Ron's Old Masters Mix," which was generated with a different approach to mixing color based on Old Master techniques.
11. Choose Pointed Stump 30 from the Blenders Brush Category.
12. Blend the colors together (Figure 4.11).
13. Click on the left-hand square button (has icon with array of vertical and horizontal lines) in the Color Sets palette section and choose the first pop-up menu option Create New Empty Color Set (Figure 4.12).

    This generates an empty color set (Figure 4.13).
14. Select the Dropper tool ('d' on the keyboard).
15. Click with the Dropper tool on the first color in your blended image that you wish to select. This chooses that color.
16. Click on the "+" button in the Color Sets palette. This adds the chosen color to the current color set.

Continued

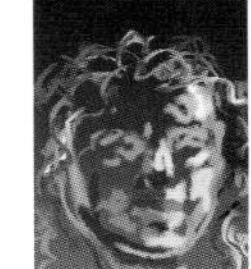

17 Continue this process until you have saved all the colors you wish in your color set.

18 When finished, choose Save Color Set from the Color Sets palette pop-up menu (Figure 4.14).

19 You will see a Save Color Set window.

20 Name the Color Set.

21 Choose Save, saving it in the Color Sets folder in your Painter 8 folder.

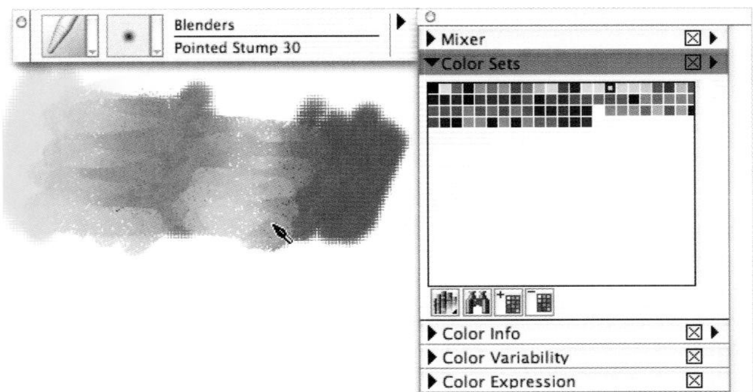

Figure 4.11 Blended colors (courtesy of Rheba).

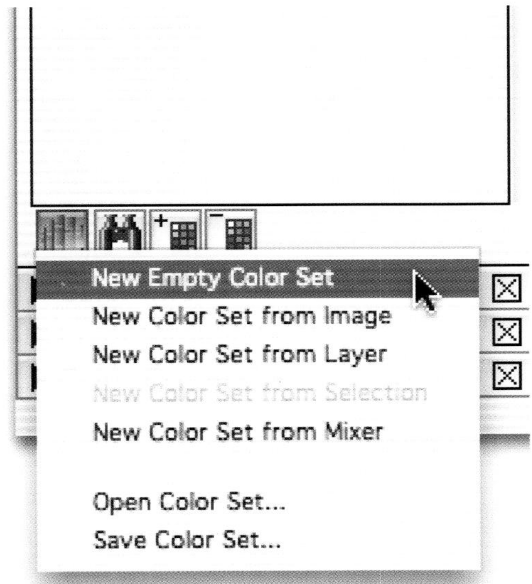

Figure 4.12 Creating a new empty color set.

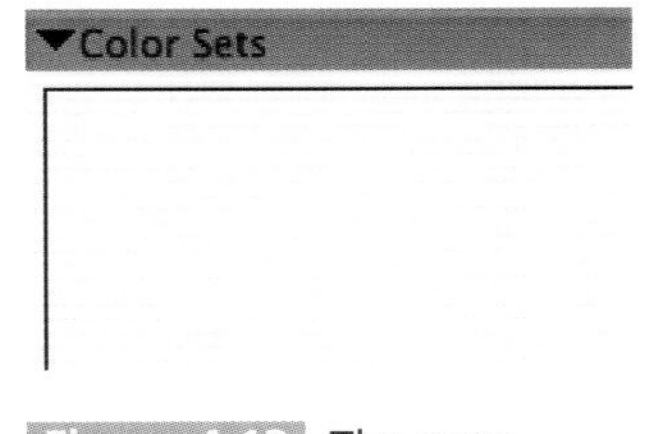

Figure 4.13 The new empty color set.

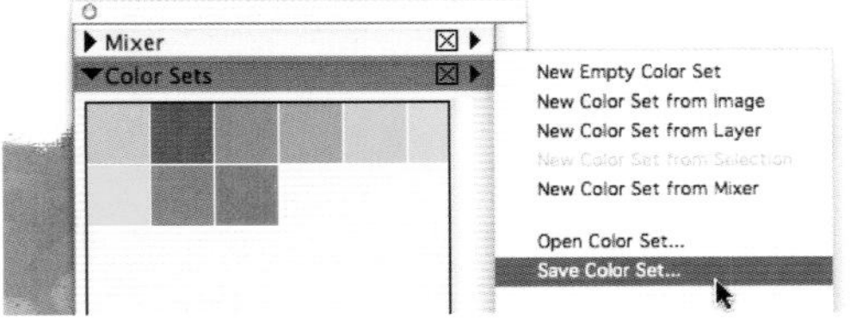

Figure 4.14 Saving a new color set.

You can apply the previous methodology of picking colors from an image and saving them in a custom color set, to any image, including digitized photos. You can also add to an existing color set at any time. This can be useful in building up a color set of your favorite colors over time. One artist, Susan LeVan (see her portfolio on www.bruckandmoss.com), has built up a color set of bright saturated colors that she knows reproduce well in print, having tested them out. This allows her to paint on the computer with the knowledge that her colors will come out consistently and predictably when she outputs her images. I have included two color sets, "LeVan's Lively Favorites" and "LeVan's Lively Mix," based on her colors in the Extra Color Sets folder on the companion CD.

Generating a Color Set Automatically Using the Colors Contained in an Image

1. Open an image in Painter that you wish to use as a basis for automatically generating a new color set.
2. Click on the left-hand square button (has icon with array of vertical and horizontal lines) in the Color Sets palette and choose the second pop-up menu option "New Color Set from Image." This instantly generates a color set based on the colors in the active image.
3. Choose Save Color Set from the Color Sets pop-up menu.
4. You will see a Save Color Set window.
5. Name the Color Set.
6. Choose Save, saving it in the Color Sets folder in your Painter 8 folder.

I have used this process to generate the color sets "50s RnB," "Art Deco," "Malevich Mix," and "Rich Paint," all to be found in the Extra Color Sets folder on the Painter Creativity Companion CD.

Color Set Assignment

Create a painting using only color from a single color set (any color set of your choice) and *not* using the Standard Colors color picker (hue-wheel, SV-triangle). This would be a good exercise to try out Den's Oil Brushes and Ron's Oils Brushes (Figure 4.15).

Questions

1. Which color set did you choose?
2. How did using the color set, instead of the color picker, influence your colors and your picture?

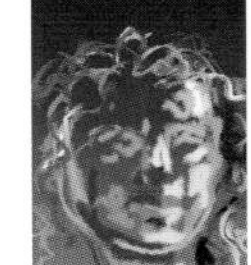

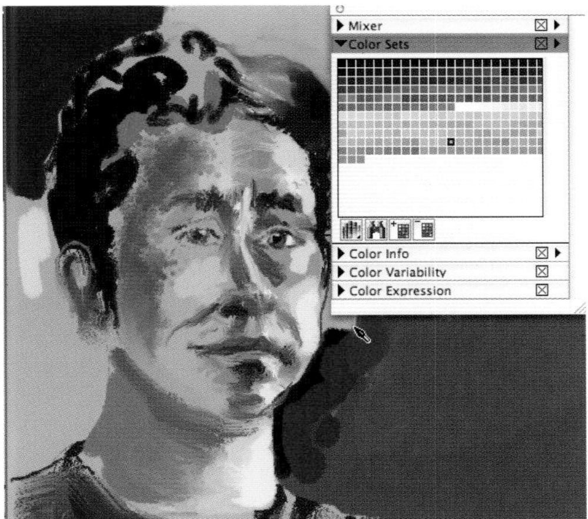

Figure 4.15 Painting with ArtDeco Grande color set.

4.7 Wrap

Having dived first into line, then tone, and now color, you are ready for the next step: namely, developing your own style and expressing your personality in your work.

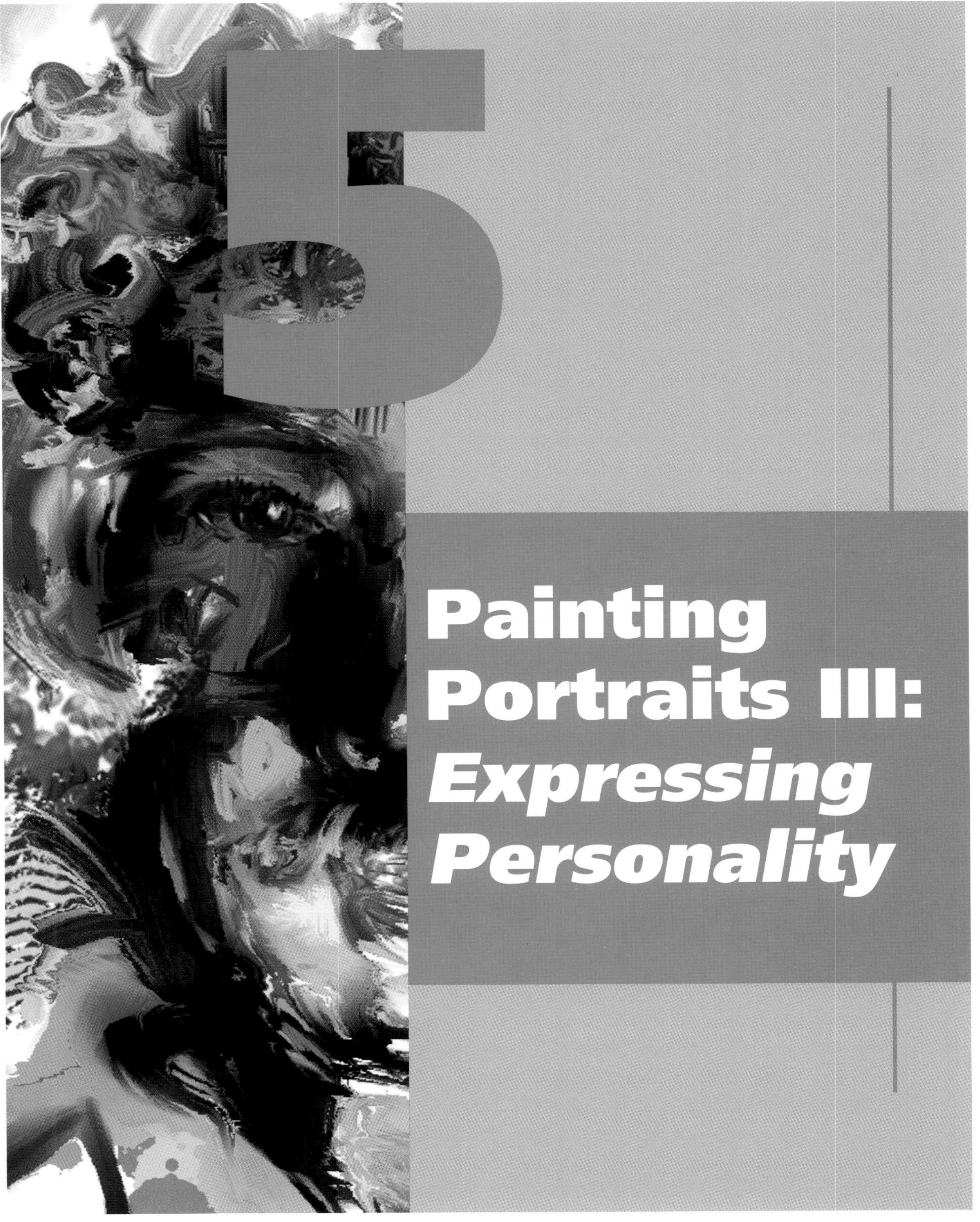

5

Painting Portraits III: *Expressing Personality*

We use a mirror to see our faces, we use art to see our soul.

—George Bernard Shaw

5.1 Introduction

The goal of this session is to help you go beyond depicting just the physical surface characteristics of color, texture, light, and shade. The goal here is to capture the essence of your subject—their soul, character, and personality—at the same time as expressing your own personality in your portraits. These inner qualities make a portrait jump from the canvas. As the opening quote from George Bernard Shaw states, art provides us with a window through which we see beyond the surface. Aim to create portraits that move the viewer, that embody emotion and feeling.

As in Sumi-e, the ancient art of brush painting, I encourage you to depict the spirit, rather than—or as well as—the semblance of the subject. Here is an apt quote from the Sumi-e Society Midwest web site philosophy page (www.silverdragonstudio.com/sumi-e/philos.html):

> The philosophy of Sumi-e is contrast and harmony, expressing simple beauty and elegance. The art of brush painting aims to depict the spirit, rather than the semblance, of the object. In creating a picture the artist must grasp the spirit of the subject.
>
> Balance, rhythm and harmony are the qualities the artist strives for by developing patience, self-discipline and concentration. The goal of the brush painter is to use the brush with both vitality and restraint.

Those paradoxical qualities of contrast and harmony, vitality and restraint, are what brings a painting to life.

5.2 Instructor Notes

The following exercises are fun, exciting ways to explore improvisation in portraiture. The same exercises can equally be applied to any other subject besides a portrait, so you could adapt the lessons to suit your particular class focus and interest. Two exercises in this session that, in my experience, have made the most difference to students are the Single-Brush Painting and the Order from Chaos Self-Portrait.

The Single-Brush Exercise has proven instructive in demonstrating to students the power and versatility that can come out of using a single brush. It also focuses their attention on the key points made earlier—the importance of being continually aware of the tonal values of your brush strokes

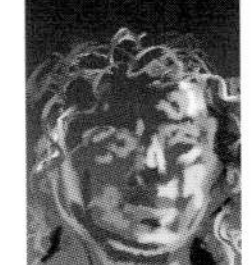

and the use of finer detail and greater contrast to attract attention and create a focal point. In the instructions for the Single-Brush exercise, I give the students a choice of selecting a visual reference, either from life (i.e., live model, still life, or looking at themselves in a mirror) or from a photo (either looking at a hard-copy print or using a digitized photo in Painter with tracing paper). In a classroom situation, I suggest the instructor makes this choice. The student examples shown were self-portraits done from life using a mirror propped up against the computer.

The Order from Chaos Self-Portrait embraces chaos as a starting point. This has the effect of liberating the students from attachment to tight, precise drawing and their need for immediate perfection and realism. This was particularly useful for students who either lacked confidence as artists or who had difficulty loosening up.

5.3 Creating a Focal Point

What This Lesson Is About

This lesson is about the use of fine detail, and tonal and color contrasts, in selected regions of the canvas to create focal points of emphasis and interest that attract the viewer's eye.

Selective Detail

By selective detail I mean choosing limited regions of your image, such as eyes, to paint in more detail compared with the rest of the image. The detailed areas draw the viewer's eyes; it generates emphasis and focus. Don't just try to fill in every detail. Think of a camera lens where you can adjust the focal length and depth of field, determining what is sharply in focus.

Think about your focus before you make any marks on the canvas. Then still work from the rough beginning statements through to the detail at the end. By thinking about it at the beginning, you will paint with direction and with a feel for how you want to express yourself on the canvas.

Resizing Up

One way to work from rough, general shapes to selective detail is to start at low resolution (e.g., 72 ppi) and gradually resize your canvas as you work to higher and higher resolution (e.g., ending up at 300 ppi), using progressively finer brushes. As you resize up to greater resolution, the existing brushwork becomes more diffuse and pixelated. (That is why it is normally not recommended to resize up since you lower the quality of your original image). This effect can be used to purposely get a sense of exaggerated focus where the finest detail is painted at the highest resolution.

1. Choose Cmd/Ctrl-N.
2. Open a new canvas 504 pixels wide by 648 pixels high (7 inches by 9 inches at 72 dpi).
3. Click OK.
4. Choose Cmd/Ctrl-M to mount the canvas.
5. Start your painting. Create the "first statement."
6. Choose Canvas > Resize.
7. Make sure the Constrain File Size box is unchecked.
8. Change the pixel width to 1050 pixels (7 inches by 9 inches at 150 dpi).
9. Click OK.
10. Continue painting on selected areas with smaller brushes and finer detail to create a second statement.
11. Choose Canvas > Resize.
12. Change the pixel width to 2100 pixels (7 inches by 9 inches at 300 dpi).
13. Click OK.
14. With very fine brush work, add the final touches to regions where you want the finest detail.

Selective Detail Project

Objectives:

Exercise control and discretion in attention to detail.

Focus on eyes.

1. Choose Cmd/Ctrl-N.
2. Open a new canvas 700 pixels wide by 900 pixels high (7 inches by 9 inches at 100 dpi).
3. Choose Cmd/Ctrl-M to mount the canvas.

Continued

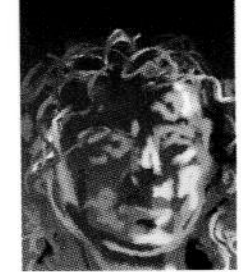

4 Choose Window > Zoom to Fit. Zoom out farther, using the Cmd/Ctrl-"–" command, to suit your screen size and palette arrangement.

5 Hold down the space bar and drag your canvas into a convenient position on the screen.

6 Sit your model down next to your computer screen. Ask your model to look at you (or use your own image looking into a mirror).

7 Spend a minute to look carefully at your model's eyes. What do you see? What structures, textures, colors, subtleties, and reflections can you see? What feelings do your model's eyes convey? Are they happy, sad, thoughtful, reflective?

8 In your mind visualize a close-cropped composition in which your subject's face fills, or almost fills, your canvas.

9 Now paint a first statement. Use whatever brushes and colors you like. Paint loosely. Cover the whole canvas quickly with paint. Don't go into detail anywhere (not even the eyes . . . yet). You are welcome to use the first and second statement technique explored earlier. In any case, work over the painting until you are satisfied that the shapes and proportions are reasonably accurate (Figure 5.1).

10 Save this stage of the portrait.

11 Now focus in on the eyes and the region immediately around the eyes. Make your brush sizes much smaller and zoom into the eye region on your computer screen using the keyboard shortcut Cmd/Ctrl-+. Paint as much detail as you can. Really look closely at the iris, the pupil, capture the subtle reflection of the room, and so on. A very small airbrush can be useful for this stage of your painting. Spend at least as much time on the eyes as you have on the rest of the portrait (Figure 5.2). For more specific techniques regarding painting catchlights and colorizing the iris, refer to session 7, lesson 7.11, Enhancing Eyes (page 195).

12 Every now and then, zoom out and see what your painting looks like as a whole. If you want to continue working on it, zoom back in.

13 When you are satisfied, save your image.

Questions

1 What did you see when you looked into your subject's eyes?

2 How has selectively focusing on the subject's eyes affected the final portrait?

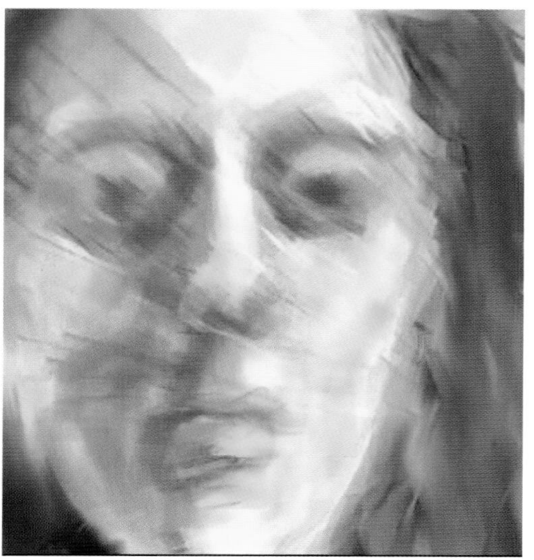

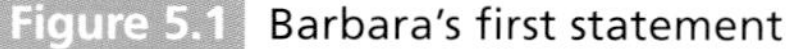

Figure 5.1 Barbara's first statement.

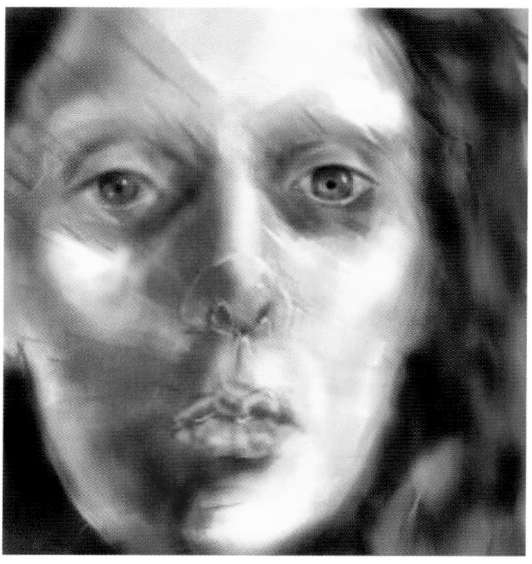

Figure 5.2 Barbara's portrait with details added.

5.4 One-Brush Painting

In this exercise you will make an entire painting using just a single brush. The objective is to apply the maximum range of marks you can obtain from this single brush to create a focal point to your painting, conveying three-dimensional form and express emotion. The only adjustments to this brush you can make, besides your choice in color and the pressure you apply with your stylus, are adjusting the brush size and the opacity. You may be surprised at the versatility of a single brush using just these adjustments.

1. Select a visual reference, either from life (i.e., live model, still life, or looking at yourself in a mirror) or from a photo (either looking at a hard-copy print or using a digitized photo in Painter with tracing paper).
2. Open a blank canvas in Painter. For a reasonable-quality print on letter size or A4 paper, set the canvas dimensions to 7 inches wide by 8 inches high at 150 ppi (1050 pixels wide by 1200 pixels high).
3. Choose Cmd/Ctrl-M. This mounts your canvas in screen mode.

Continued

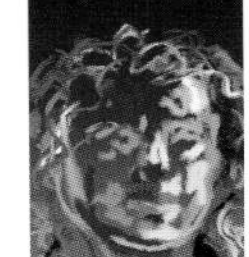

4 Set up a tidy, simple arrangement of palettes so you can see the following:

Tools

Property Bar

Brush Selector

Colors palette

5 Choose Window > Arrange Palettes > Save Layout. Save this arrangement as "Simple Brush" or something similar.

6 Choose Window > Zoom to Fit (you can also use Cmd/Ctrl-"–"/"+," the zoom out and zoom in keyboard shortcuts for fine-tuning the canvas size on your screen. Make sure you can see the entire canvas at this stage.

7 Hold down the space bar on your keyboard, which turns your cursor into a grabber hand, and click on and drag the canvas to reposition it on your screen. You should end up with a screen display that looks something like Figure 5.3.

8 Choose a Brush Variant with an interesting structure. Here are some examples of interesting brushes you could choose from the Jeremy Faves Brush Category:

Watery

Uncle Wiggly

Wood

Den's Oil Funky Chunky

Note that the brushes described here are also found in the Creativity Brushes Brush Library. Avoid any Liquid Ink or Water Color brushes because these generate special layers. Also avoid Cloners, Impasto, and Pencil brushes. Choose

Continued

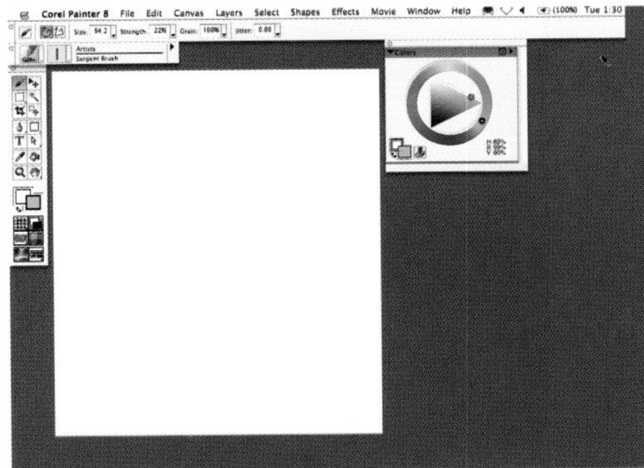

Figure 5.3 Simple palette layout for one-brush painting.

a brush that puts down paint, rather than just moves paint around. Take a moment to experiment with some brushes if you're not sure which to choose. Most important, choose a brush that will be challenging, not one that will be easy or comfortable! The more challenging the brush (i.e., the less like a normal brush or pencil), the more you will learn from this exercise.

9 Select a suitable color, such as a light blue-cyan or light orange-sandy, to fill your canvas background with.

Alternately, you may find it more interesting to fill your paper with a two-color gradient rather than just a single, flat color. The purpose of the fill is to give yourself something to paint against, which makes it easier and more natural for you to express highlights (compared with painting against a bright white default background). You will end up painting over the entire background, so in the end the initial background won't make much difference, but in the beginning it can make a lot of difference.

To make a two-tone gradient you will need to select two different regular and additional colors in the Colors palette (first selecting one regular color, using the arrows to interchange the regular and additional colors, and then picking another regular color). Then open the Gradients palette. Select the Two-Point gradient (which is usually selected by default). Move the tiny red sphere around the gradient preview to adjust the direction of the gradient (you may find a vertical gradient that goes from dark at the top to light at the bottom works well).

10 Choose Cmd/Ctrl-F. In the Fill window make sure you have Fill With: Current Color if you are doing a plain single color fill, or Fill With: Gradient if you are going to fill with a gradient.

11 Click OK. Your canvas will now be filled with your selected background color or gradient. As an optional extra you may, if you wish, record a script of your session. See session 6, Animating Paint: *Generating Artistic Transitions*, for detailed instructions.

12 Look at your subject with half-closed eyes and observe where you see the main regions of light and dark.

13 Start with a large brush size and low to medium opacity. This exercise is designed to make you use your brush to its full extent, getting the maximum variety of lines, looks, and effects out of the single brush. Your main adjustments will be to size, color, and opacity. Vary these as you paint. Start by filling in the canvas with bold, gestural brush strokes that define the main blocks of tone (first statement). Work into the painting, layering brush strokes

Continued

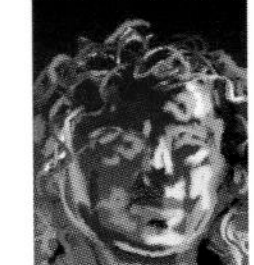

over brush strokes, covering the entire canvas with paint. Don't worry about 116detail. Take your brush to extremes: Make the brush very large (although watch out, you can crash Painter if you make it too large!) and the opacity very low (try the lowest setting of 1%). Don't be afraid of testing the extremes. Click Save As regularly as you paint, saving separate RIFF files with sequential version numbers into an appropriately named project folder.

14 Selectively start defining more detail and contrast in your painting. Reduce the brush size and increase the brush opacity as you do so.

15 Regularly zoom out and look at your image when it is the size of a postage stamp on your screen. This is equivalent to an artist stepping back from the canvas to get an overview of how it is looking. Look at the zoomed-out canvas and ask yourself if the painting is working from a tonal and compositional perspective. Then choose Window > Zoom to Fit to return your canvas to filling the screen.

16 Regularly select Effects > Tonal Control > Adjust Colors. Take the Saturation slider in the Adjust Color window all the way to the left (–139%). Click OK. You will see your image as if it were just in gray-scale (although in reality it is still an RGB image). This can tell you whether your relative tonal differences are working. When you've looked carefully at the result of this operation, choose Cmd/Ctrl-Z to undo the Adjust Colors and return your image to full color.

Think about incorporating the following as you build up and enhance your image:

Lighting and Shading: *Creating Volume by Applying the Five Lights of Nature.*

Work with the specular highlights (light source is reflected from surface), base tone/diffuse highlight (light skims across the object here), shaded side (darkened side of object), refracted light (light reflected from surroundings), and cast shadow (surroundings shielded from light source) to create the effect of solid three-dimensional form.

Contrast, Color, and Detail: *Creating Selective Focus.*

Apply your sharpest contrasts (lights against darks, sharp edges, etc.), your brightest, warmest colors (yellows, oranges, reds), and your finest level of detail in the regions of your image you want to draw the viewers eye toward (e.g., eyes in a portrait). For the finest details, usually in the eyes, your brush size will be at, or close to, the minimum (1.0) and your opacity at, or close to, 100 percent. A lower opacity and slightly larger brush size will give a more diffuse look, which can be useful in painting colorations and radial striations in the iris and depicting a diffuse catch light in the eye.

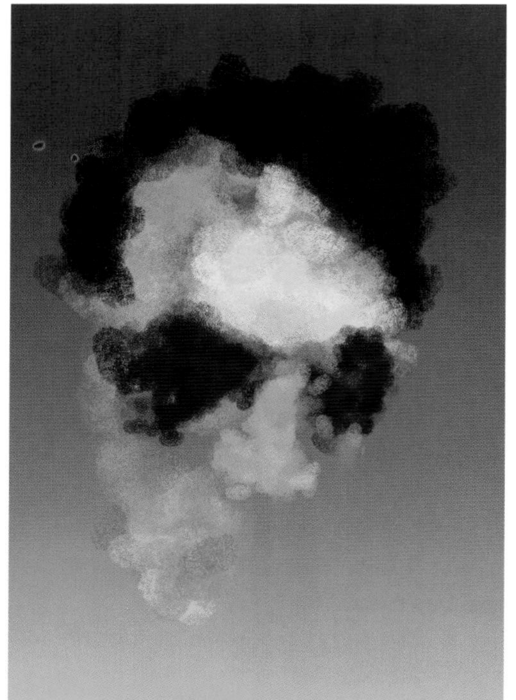

Figure 5.4

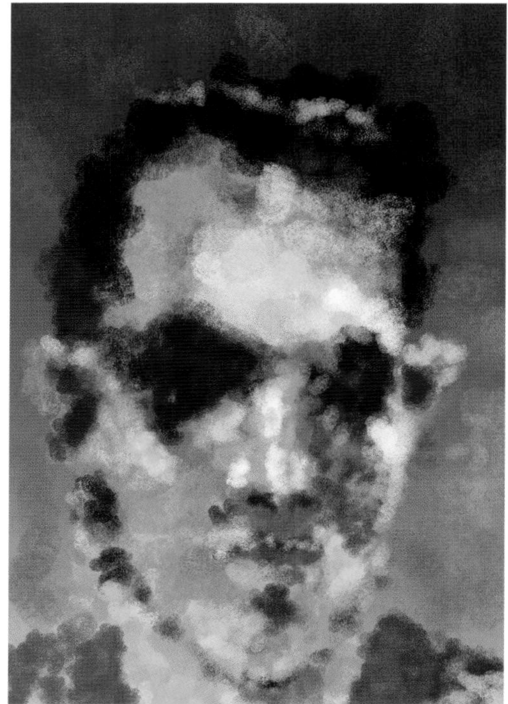

Figure 5.5

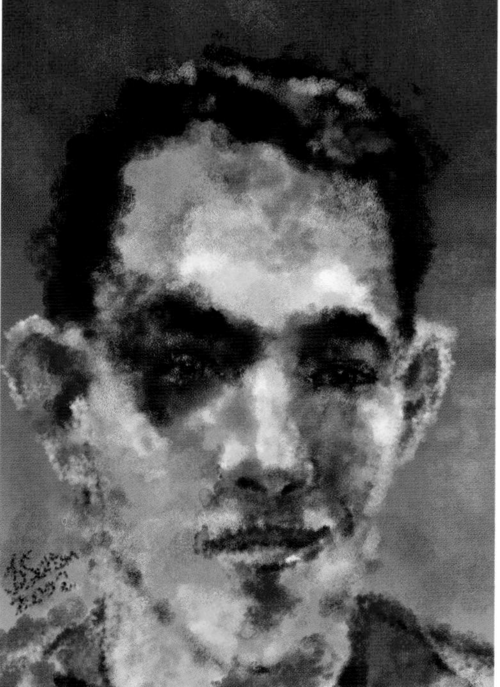

Figure 5.6

Three stages of a portrait of Bradford created by Jeremy using only the Fingerpaint variant (Graphic Design category in the Creativity Brushes library).

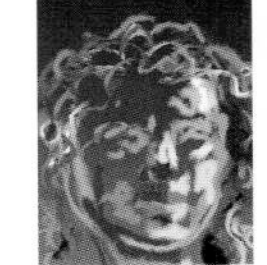

Line, Shape, Balance, Perspective, Composition, and Lighting: *Generating Feeling and Mood.*

Utilize the direction and form of your lines (straight, curved, diagonals, horizontals, verticals), the structure of your shapes, the balance or unbalance of your image, the perspective you view your subject from, the way you compose your subject within your canvas, and the way you light your subject to generate feeling and mood.

Spend about two hours on this exercise.

Here is an example of several stages (Figures 5.4 to 5.6) of a portrait I painted while demonstrating Painter at the Macworld Expo in San Francisco in January 2002. It is painted using only the Fingerpaint variant in the Graphic Design category.

Here are examples of One-Brush Paintings by students (Figures 5.7 to 5.10).

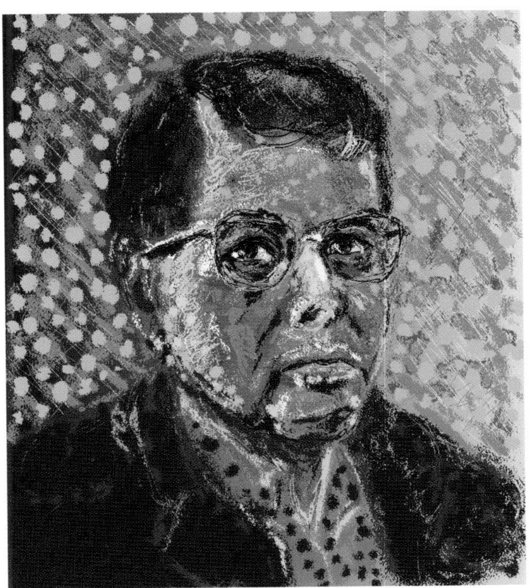

Figure 5.7 One-brush self portrait by Jeff, created using only the Graphic Paintbrush Soft variant (Brushes category in the Creativity Brushes library).

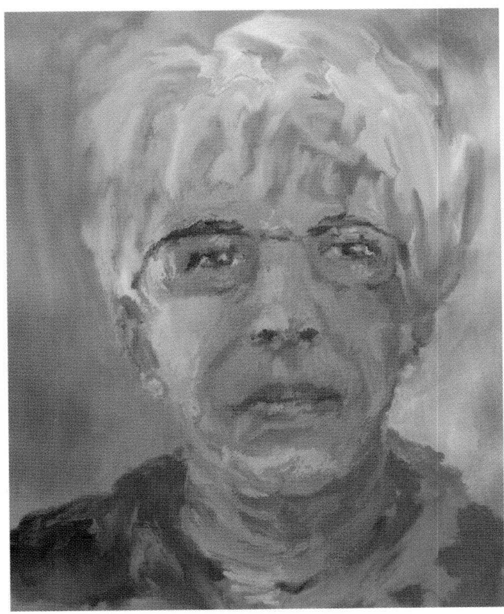

Figure 5.8 One-brush self portrait by Sherron, created using only her own custom variant, Blender Wood (Sherron's Brushes category in the Creativity Brushes library).

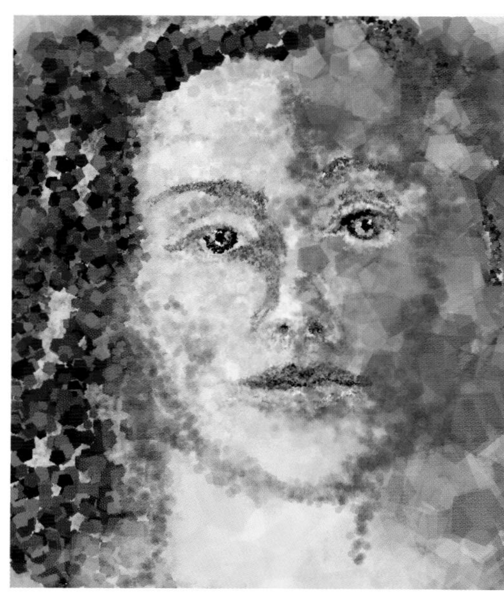

Figure 5.9 One-brush self portrait by Lois, created using only the Pentagonia variant (Fun Brushes category in the Creativity Brushes library).

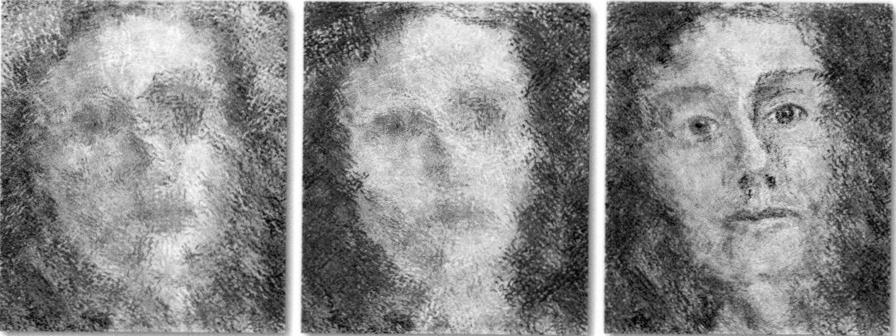

Figure 5.10 One-brush self portrait (showing three stages) by Lois, created using only the Uncle Wiggly variant (Nature Brushes category in the Creativity Brushes library).

5.5 In the Style of Other Artists

Finding Your Own Voice

In this lesson you learn from copying the style of other artists. In the Introduction to this workbook I listed the goals of the course. The fourth goal was to "express your own voice in your artwork." That means being true to yourself and expressing who you are in your artwork.

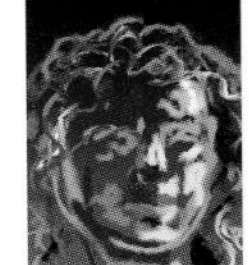

Expand Your Vocabulary

Paradoxically, exploring other people's voices can help you find your own voice. In this section the focus is on how other people have expressed their voices through their art. It is the unique, individual, and recognizable style of an artist that expresses their voice. By emulating the style of other artists in this exercise, you can feel what works for you and what doesn't. Doing this expands your expressive vocabulary.

In the Style of Other Artists Project

Objectives:

Expose you to different approaches to portraiture.

Put yourself in the mindset of the other artist.

Imagine the process the other artist went through.

Expose you to a wide range of exciting stylistic possibilities.

Explore stylistic choices you may not make otherwise.

1. Research different approaches to portraiture. Visit the library, surf the Internet, look at art postcards, art books, and art magazines, and visit art museums and galleries. Select two artists with contrasting and distinctive styles.
2. Choose Cmd/Ctrl-N.
3. Open a new canvas 700 pixels wide by 900 pixels high (7 inches by 9 inches at 100 dpi).
4. Choose Cmd/Ctrl-M to mount the canvas.
5. Choose Window > Zoom to Fit. Zoom out farther, using the Cmd/Ctrl-"–" command, to suit your screen size and palette arrangement.
6. Hold down the space bar and drag your canvas into a convenient position on the screen.
7. Use whatever brushes you like. Paint two portraits of a live model emulating the style of the two artists you have selected.
8. When you complete each portrait, click your Save As button. Save the resulting images as RIFF files.

Questions

1. Which artists did you select?
2. Why did you select these artists?
3. How did you find the task of trying to emulate other artists' styles?
4. Which did you find easier and why?
5. Has this experience influenced how you want to approach portraiture?

Here are results of this exercise from some of my online students (Figures 5.11 through 5.14).

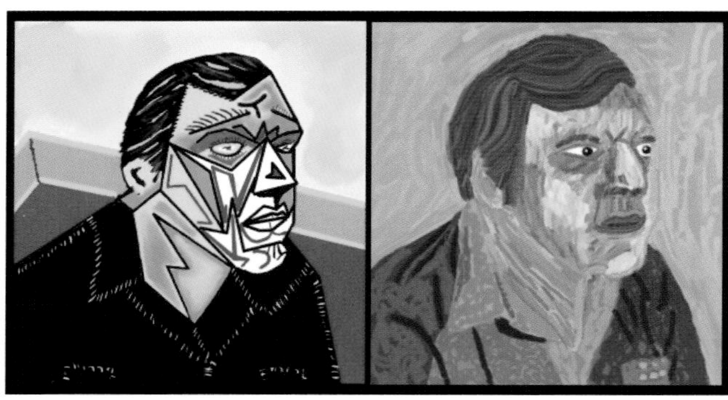

Figure 5.11 Sel's paintings in the style of Pablo Picasso and Vincent Van Gogh.

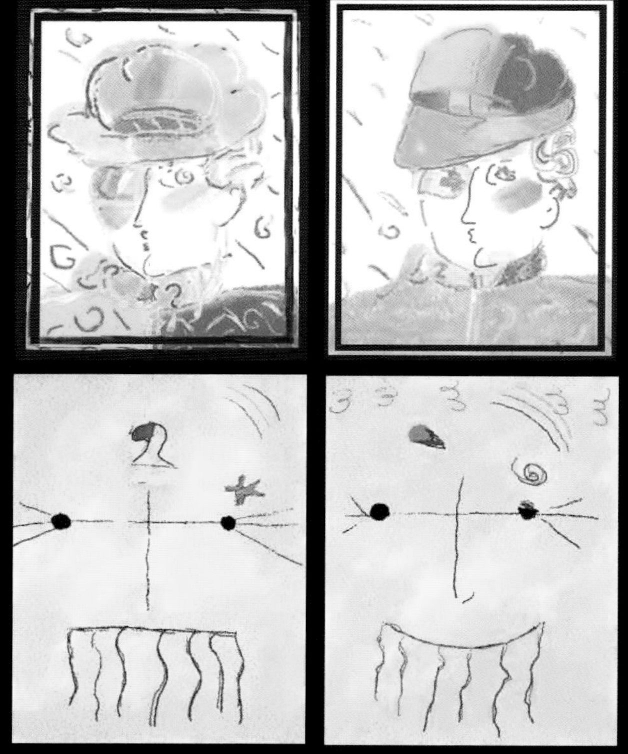

Figure 5.12 Sharon's paintings in the style of Peter Max and Paul Klee.

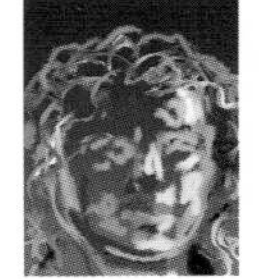

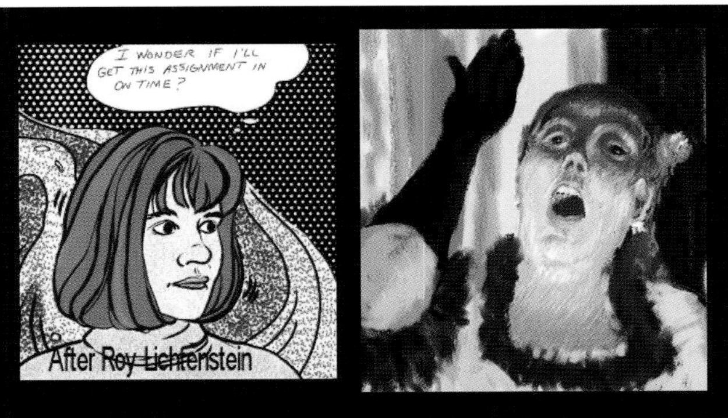

Figure 5.13 Cathleen's and Lois's paintings in the style of Roy Lichtenstein and Edgar Degas.

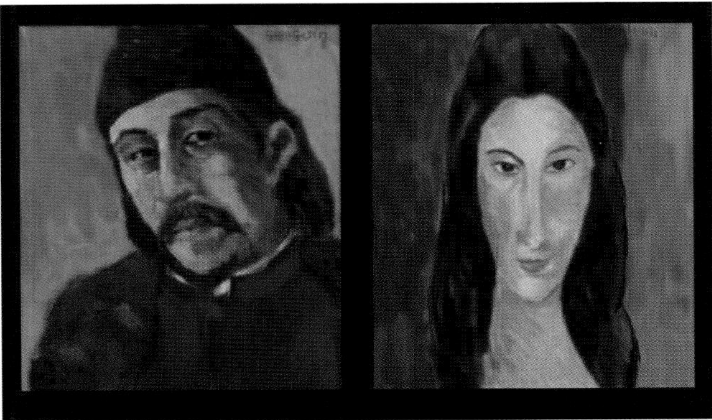

Figure 5.14 Carol's paintings in the styles of Paul Gauguin and Amedeo Modigliani.

5.6 Creative Improvisation

Flowing and Forgetting

This lesson deals with transformation and trust in your creative process. Now is the time to allow yourself the luxury of forgetting everything you've done prior to this. You are going to focus on enjoying flowing with the organic nature of the painting process. Don't try to get things right. Trust yourself to integrate all of your experiences over time and to allow newly learned skills to become second nature. This is the point where you fully immerse yourself in the creative process.

Understanding the Creative Process

What is written here could equally well apply to any creative, expressive activity such as dance, making music, writing, and so on. Understanding the nature of the creative process will help you make the most out of Painter's incredible potential. Using Painter is unlike using Photoshop and other digital imaging tools in that it is not a formula- or technique-driven activity. The beauty and power of Painter is as much what emerges that is unexpected as it is achieving a predetermined result or effect.

Process of Continual Transition

The Merriam-Webster's Dictionary describes *creativity* as a quality of making, or an ability to make, something original rather than copied. For me creativity is a journey or a way or a path or a process, not a destination or quality or ability. Creativity is a process of continual transition and discovery where the end result evolves in an organic way, taking on a life and voice of its own. A good analogy is to imagine yourself surfing on a wave of creativity, where you have to continually respond to and improvise around ever-changing and unpredictable forces of nature. Awareness, balance, vision, trust, and intuition all come into play. You know the end result will be (hopefully) traveling from one location to closer to the shore, but the exact place you end up and the experience along the way are different every time.

When you diligently follow a formula or recipe or set of instructions, you take a single fixed path to achieving a predetermined result. This may involve fighting the unexpected, suppressing and ignoring surprises, and getting frustrated when the end result differs from your original expectation. By contrast, creativity welcomes and celebrates the unexpected.

Discovery of a Path

Walter Murch, in his fascinating book *In the Blink of an Eye* (Silman James Press, 2001), beautifully describes the process of surfing the wave of creativity. Murch makes the point in discussing the enormous task of editing the film *Apocalypse Now* that the actual rate of cuts per editor per day turned out to be 1.47, a process which takes under 10 seconds. It took Murch a year to edit his sections of the film. If he'd known exactly where he was going at the beginning, he could have just come in for 10 seconds of work each day and taken the same time! His point is that creativity, in this case film editing, "is not so much a putting together as it is a discovery of a path."

Murch describes the creator/editor as evaluating different pathways. The more possibilities that compound on each other, the more pathways there are and the more time is needed for evaluation. This made me think of the way I paint in Painter. Whatever my visual goal, I find myself entering a path of creativity that's always full of surprises and discoveries. I find myself exploring many different pathways and possibilities, trying this brush, trying that effect, tweaking this slider, and so on.

Surfing the wave of creativity is discovering a path. This is true even when you have a specific visual destination, or end result, in mind. Treat the digital canvas as an ever-changing, continually malleable clay or liquid surface. Let intuition, spontaneity, improvisation, and serendipity guide your

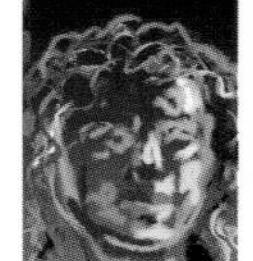

creative process. Value the creative process as highly as the end result or final product. Part of the magic of Painter is that it allows you to continuously utilize and recycle your creative process to generate new possibilities for evaluation.

Surfing the wave of creativity is an ongoing process and attitude, not just an end result. There are countless potential end results along the way. This applies whether you are painting a portrait or transforming a photograph.

Surfing the wave of creativity frees you from the tightness and fears associated with needing to get things right. It allows you to let go of the preciousness of the end product. Your artwork will show more life and integrity by taking a process-oriented approach to creativity.

Improvising in the Moment

Surfing the wave of creativity involves improvising in the moment. The unexpected will always happen. The only question is how we react to the unexpected. Surfing the wave of creativity involves flowing with what *is* rather than giving up. It involves seeing the unexpected as an opportunity rather than a barrier. Treat your journey in creating a painting as a path of continual improvisation. When something happens that you don't like, see it as an opportunity to make your picture more interesting. The unexpected can often be a launching point or catalyst for creative growth.

Overcoming Fear

The biggest barrier to surfing the wave of creativity is fear: fear of letting go, fear of missing out, fear of starting, fear of completion, fear of imperfection, fear of failure, fear of inadequacy, fear of computers, fear of the unknown, and fear of other people's judgment. Do any of these ring a bell? They certainly do for me! As Earl Wilson once said: "Courage is the art of being the only one who knows you're scared to death."

The blank canvas can elicit both fear and excitement. To start creating, we need to overcome our fears and open ourselves to being vulnerable and exposed. We also need to forget old patterns, attitudes, and habits. This is always easier said than done.

Every time I am about to begin a live digital portrait in front of an audience, I face fear. A voice in me asks: "What if it ends up looking nothing like the subject?" "What if I make a fool of myself?" and so on. Yet it is that very risk, of plowing into the unknown, of being vulnerable, of creating something spontaneous and unrehearsed, that excites and interests the audience, and that keeps me learning and developing. The presence of the audience may amplify my fear, but those fears are present to some extent even when I'm on my own and no one is watching. Thus my creative process is a continual dance with letting go and overcoming fears. The keys to overcoming these fears are commitment, trust, and acceptance.

An excellent book that explores the fears that get in the way of artmaking is *Art & Fear: Observations on the Perils (and Rewards) of Artmaking* by David Bayles and Ted Orland (Image Continuum, 1993).

Helen Keller expressed a simple truth regarding the futility of fear: "Avoiding danger is no safer in the long run than outright exposure. Life is a daring adventure or nothing at all."

Commitment

Commitment has power. Be committed to the process of learning and experimenting. Be committed to taking risks. Be committed to persevering even when the going gets tough! The easiest way to be committed is to be highly motivated. The easiest way to be highly motivated is to focus on something you care about. Passion is the great motivator. When you care and are passionate about what you are doing, the creative process becomes an exciting and energizing journey. In this situation there is no effort in appreciating the process: work becomes pleasure.

Commitment applies on the micro as well as the macro level. Be committed not only to the creative process in general, but in the case of painting also be committed to your individual brush strokes. I recommend avoiding undoes and erasing. Commit yourself to your marks on the canvas. When you hit a block, when you feel like giving up, when it's no longer fun, be committed to pushing a little further, to entering the region of discomfort, to not giving up immediately.

Every brush stroke and mark on your canvas added richness and depth to your painting, even those marks that you may feel were wrong. There's no such thing as a mistake, only transitions in the creative process.

Trust

Trust in yourself and in the creative process. We are all born artists. Babies are not separated into artists and nonartists. All children will naturally draw when they get their hands on mark-making tools (after chewing and eating them, of course!). If you have any doubts about being an artist, just think back to being a child when the label *artist* didn't matter. Allow yourself the freedom to be creative. Listen to your inner voice. In trusting the creative process you become one with the creative process—totally absorbed. It is safe to be vulnerable. It is safe to honestly express your emotions in the creative process.

Acceptance

Acceptance means acceptance of how we are, who we are, and what we create. Do not be overcritical of yourself. You may initially struggle with finding your way around the Painter palettes, you may not be satisfied with your artwork, you may get frustrated, and you may get stuck—that's okay. Sometimes it's necessary to go through discomfort to be able to progress.

Accept imperfection. Accept that the creative process sometimes involves frustration. Acceptance allows us to open ourselves to the intuitive, to flow with the organic unfolding of the painting, to enjoy improvisation, to relish the role of serendipity, the accidental, and the unintentional. There is no such thing as a mistake in your creative process, simply marks that add to the richness and character of your creation.

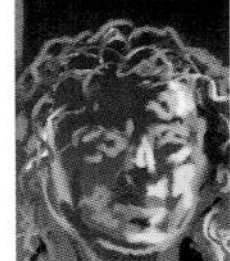

Studies, Not Masterpieces

All of the exercises in this book are intended to help you learn and develop. The artworks you create along the way are incomplete studies, byproducts of the learning process. They are not intended to be finished masterpieces. Let go of the "masterpiece mentality," which is the inner critic that says everything you do has to be a masterpiece. Accept whatever emerges on your canvas for what it is—a study, nothing more, nothing less.

Take Time to Smell the Roses

Surfing the wave of creativity can result in unintended positive consequences that go far beyond realizing your creative potential in using Painter. You may find yourself being less attached to perfect end results in other aspects of your life. Take time to "smell the roses" on and off the digital canvas!

Order From Chaos Self-Portrait

Objectives:

Expose you to living on the edge, to trusting your intuitive creative flow.

Free you from the fear of making a mess or a mistake.

Embrace chaos and generate order out of chaos.

Exercise the freedom of transformation and regeneration on the digital canvas.

Experience the perpetual destruction-creation cycle in the creative process.

Express your voice, your personality, your feelings, and your individuality.

1. Choose Cmd/Ctrl-N.
2. Open a new canvas 700 pixels wide by 900 pixels high (7 inches by 9 inches at 100 dpi).
3. Choose Cmd/Ctrl-M to mount the canvas.
4. Choose Window > Zoom to Fit. Zoom out further, using the Cmd/Ctrl-"–" command, to suit your screen size and palette arrangement.
5. Hold down the space bar and drag your canvas into a convenient position on the screen.

Continued

6. Place a mirror next to your computer screen.
7. Spend a minute just observing yourself in the mirror. What do you see? What do you feel? What do you want to express about yourself in your self-portrait?
8. Create a chaotic mess. Have some fun. Be bold. Be wild here. Play! Don't be timid and don't try to make the picture look like a portrait at this stage.
9. When you have filled the canvas with paint and had sufficient fun, choose File > Save As and save the file at this stage.
10. Now start bringing in the influence of what you see in the mirror. Start indicating the major areas of light and dark. Be loose and free in your brush strokes. Avoid getting bogged down in detail. Try using brushes that move paint around, such as the Gooey:Pinch or the Brushes:Palette Knife, to build up the shapes you observe and to communicate form.
11. Keep working on this picture. Work through the "ugly stages." Treat the canvas as ever-transforming malleable clay. Layer paint on top of earlier strokes. Don't erase or undo, just continue painting.
12. When you have worked the entire canvas thoroughly and are satisfied that you've reached a point of closure, choose File > Save As. Save the resulting image.

Here is an example of student work (Figures 5.15), showing the earlier abstract stage followed by the final "orderly" stage.

An alternative to this exercise is to recycle other artwork and start a portrait with your canvas being another image.

Questions

1. How did you like this assignment?
2. What was challenging?

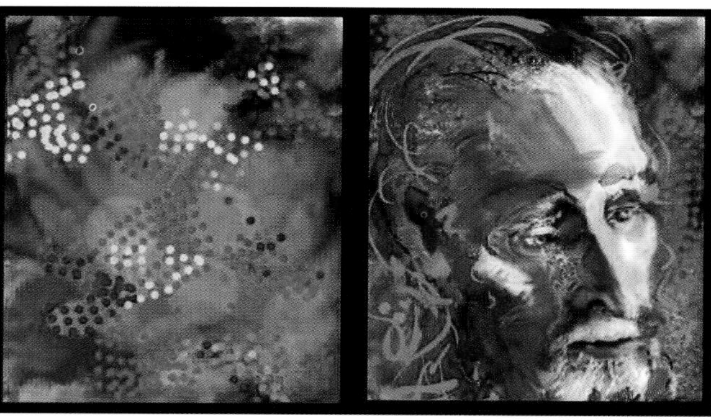

Figure 5.15 Lois's abstract and orderly stages.

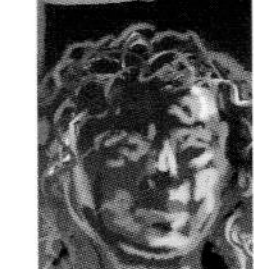

3 What did you learn?

4 What do you think of the final result?

5 How did the experience compare to the first self-portrait assignment in lesson 1 where you started orderly and ended wild?

5.7 Wrap

Congratulations on completing the three portrait sessions. As you will have discovered along the way, every painting process is full of surprises and unexpected results. This is part of the beauty of the creative process.

For a detailed analysis of my own approach to painting portraits, please refer to Appendix V, Painting Portraits: Principles and Actions.

One of the wonderful capabilities in Painter is the ability to record, play back, and even modify your entire painting process. This powerful facility, known as *scripting*, is covered in the next session. I encourage you to make recording scripts part of your process whenever you are painting.

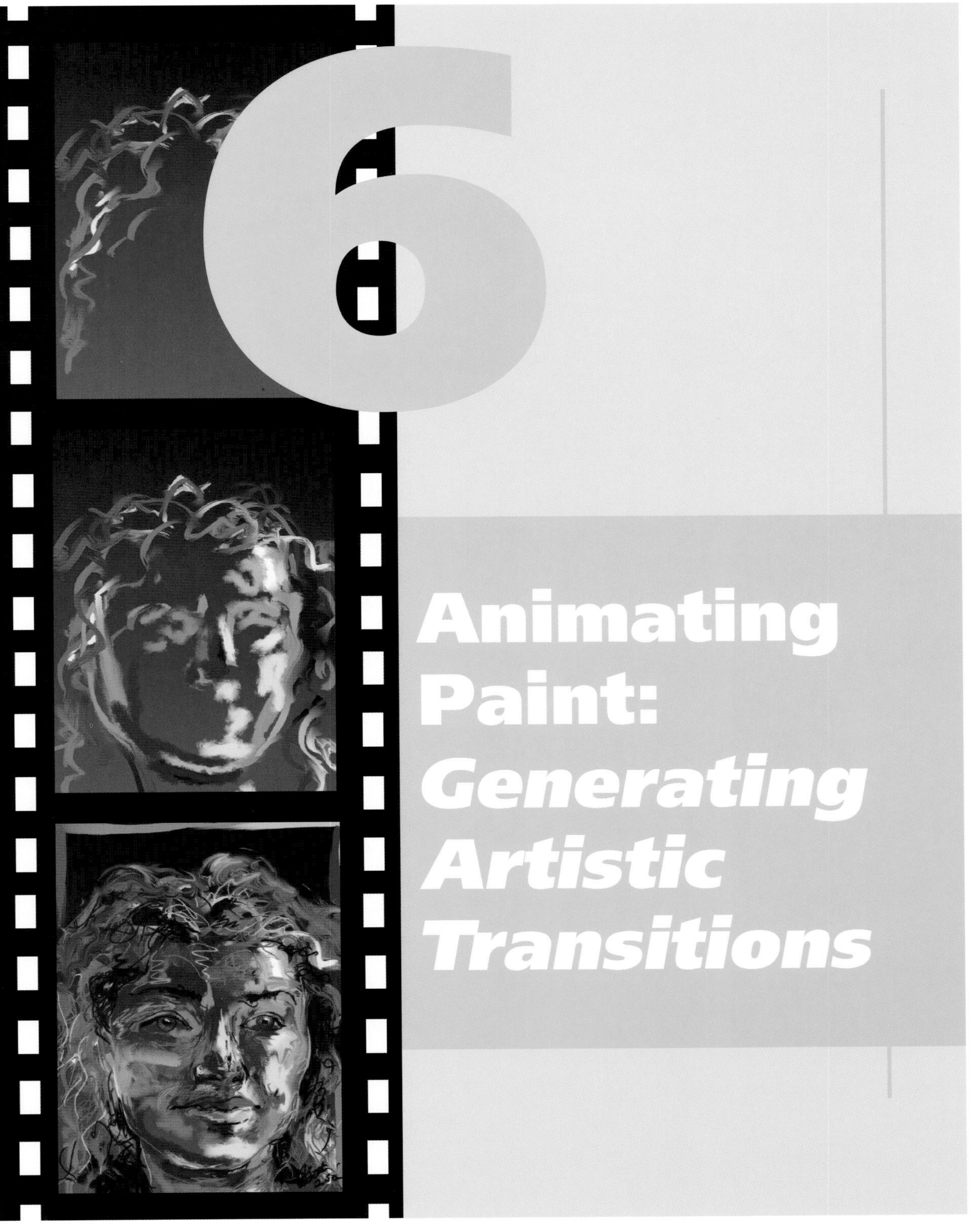

6

Animating Paint: *Generating Artistic Transitions*

6.1 Introduction

One of the hidden gems that Painter offers is the ability to record, play back, play with, and save your creative process. Painter achieves this by recording *scripts* as you create. In this session you will be introduced to the beauty and magic of working with scripts. I encourage you to experiment with scripting and to make the most of your creative process and the many beautiful transitions that your artwork goes through.

A Painter script is a small text file that documents every detail of the brushes you choose, your brush strokes, and any effects or menu commands you apply. When you play back a script, you see every action you performed being replayed continuously (not frame by frame). The speed of the playback is related to the power of your computer and the types of actions being played back. Some brushes and effects take much longer to play back than others. The script doesn't record lack of activity. Thus you can take a break while recording a script without any effect on the script.

I encourage you to get into the habit of recording scripts every time you are making a straightforward painting in a single session. The scripts can act, in effect, as an "infinite Undo" because you can pause your playback at any point and save the image at that stage. The scripts also allow you to generate unlimited variations of your paintings. For instance, you can replay a script against different backgrounds, at different resolutions, into different aspect ratios (stretched or squashed), or using different brushes (you can change the brush selections while pausing the script). Scripts also allow you to preserve, share, and recycle your creative process as movies, animations, or videos.

In this session you will learn about the three distinct stages of using scripts in Painter. These three stages are:

1. Recording a script
2. Playing back a script
3. Converting a script to a movie

A Painter script can be converted into a QuickTime Movie, AVI Movie, Animated GIF, or numbered files. Painter uses the word *movie* rather loosely, sometimes referring to Painter Frame Stacks (which can only be opened in Painter) as movies, and other times referring to regular animation formats, such as QuickTime and AVI, as movies. The animation formats (QuickTime Movie, AVI Movie, Animated GIF, or numbered files) allow you to edit and use your recorded sessions in animation and special effects programs such as Apple Final Cut Pro, Adobe Premiere, or Adobe After Effects. You can also use these movies in other media such as TV, video, or on the Web.

The basics of recording and playing back a script are simple. I have meticulously detailed step-by-step instructions here for making the most of scripting and taking it beyond just a basic replay mechanism. Please don't be intimidated by the amount of instructions! I spell out a methodical approach that gives you the most flexibility. If you just want a simple replay and nothing else, just read the sections on starting, stopping, and replaying a script and ignore everything else. There are also clear basic instructions in the Painter User Guide.

Please note that if you want to pursue the animation aspects of Painter in greater depth and generate movies from your scripts, you will need a very large amount of RAM and storage space (the maximum possible in both cases).

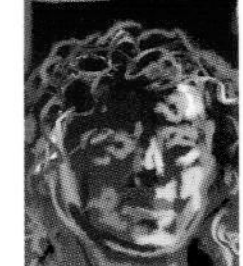

6.2 Instructor Notes

I always encourage my students to try out scripts and usually introduce scripting as an integral part of an early painting exercise; however, be aware that scripting can confuse some students. Students may have a hard time getting it to work, either because they forget to start the recorder and therefore they think they're recording a script when they're not, or they forget to stop the recorder, or they close their file before they save the script. If you do include recording and replaying scripts as part of an exercise, allow extra time to go over the steps involved at the beginning and to troubleshoot at the end. Learning how to transform the scripts into movies is a project in itself. You should allow at least an hour or two for exercises to practice the whole process.

Using scripts is a great way to get your students to think about treating their canvas as an ever-evolving experiment, a continually malleable liquid medium that undergoes continuous transitions. It is also a great way to get your students to work with transforming one image into another (and another and another), rather than just aiming to create one perfect image.

6.3 Recording a Script

Starting a Script

It is easy to record a script. For the best, most reliable results, keep everything as simple as possible. For maximum reliability always restart Painter afresh when you are about to begin a new script. Close your file and quit out of Painter when you've completed everything and after you've saved your script. For trouble-free scripts I recommend you complete your painting in a single session and paint directly on the background canvas (rather than working with layers). The steps that follow are generic steps that you can apply any time you create any painting in Painter. In this first scripting project you will record a self-portrait developing.

1. Place a small mirror next to your computer. Adjust the orientation of the mirror so that you can clearly see your face.
2. Choose Cmd/Ctrl-N (File > New) in Painter and open a new canvas 875 pixels wide by 1000 pixels high with resolution 125 pixels per inch (making the physical size 7 inches wide by 8 inches high). It is important to decide on your canvas size before starting the recorder and then stick with it for the whole session.
3. Choose Cmd/Ctrl-M (Window > Screen Mode Toggle). This sets your canvas in screen mode and simplifies the desktop.

Continued

4 Zoom out (Cmd/Ctrl-"–") until you can see the edge of the canvas on your screen.

5 Set up a palette arrangement (Figure 6.1) that includes the Tools, Property Bar, Brush Selector, and Colors and Scripts palettes.

6 Choose Window > Arrange Palettes > Save Layout.

7 Name the palette layout something like "Recording Basics." I often add the screen resolution (e.g., "Recording Basics 1024 × 768"). This is helpful if you are doing presentations and need to adjust your screen resolution for a projector. You can then select the right layout to suit your current screen resolution (otherwise some palettes may seem to disappear beyond the edge of the screen).

8 Select a canvas background color (in the Regular color rectangle of the Colors palette).

Instead of using a single plain color as a background, you could use a Two-Point gradient (which you'll find in the Gradients palette). The Two-Point gradient uses the Regular and Additional colors (front and back color rectangles, respectively) in the Colors palette and makes a gradient that blends from one color to the other. For a background I usually select two shades of a cool blue or a neutral sandy color and have the gradient blend vertically from the darker shade at the top to the lighter shade at the bottom (Figure 6.2).

9 Choose Cmd/Ctrl-F (Effect > Fill).

10 Select what you are filling with (either Current Color or Gradient) and click OK.

11 Choose File > Save As.

12 Create a new folder for this project. Save all your versions of this image in that specially named folder, noting where it is located on your computer hard drive.

13 Name the file with a name indicating this is the starting point and including a version number (e.g., subjectname-01.rif). I also add a reverse date, YY.MM.DD (year-month-day), at the beginning of all my file names so my file names always line up chronologically (e.g., February 27, 2003, would be 03.02.27). If you are using Windows you may wish to avoid using periods in the reverse date notation. You will be returning to this first version (-01) when you replay your script, so make sure you remember the file name. It may be helpful to add "B" after the version number to indicate Base, Beginning, or Background (i.e., the

Continued

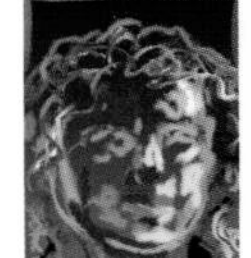

file name would then be subjectname-01B.rif). This will help you immediately recognize the original background canvas when you want to open it for replaying the script.

14 Choose Cmd/Ctrl-A (Select > All). You'll see dancing ants surrounding your canvas. This is not necessary for recording a script but adds a whole level of extra flexibility in what you can do with the script (such as replay into a higher-resolution canvas or replay into any rectangular selection).

15 Click on the central dark red, solid circular record button in the center of the five script control buttons (Figure 6.3) in the Scripts palette. The circle goes bright red (Figure 6.4), indicating that recording has begun.

16 Close, or minimize, the Scripts palette by clicking once on the little triangle on the top left of the palette. This is for safety to prevent you accidentally turning off the recorder before your image is complete. Alternatively you could close the Scripts palette (close button is small button in the top right corner of the palette) or drag the palette title bar down to the bottom of your screen so most of the palette is hidden.

17 Choose Cmd/Ctrl-D (Select > None). This gets rid of the selection and the dancing ants.

You have now started your script and you are ready to paint!

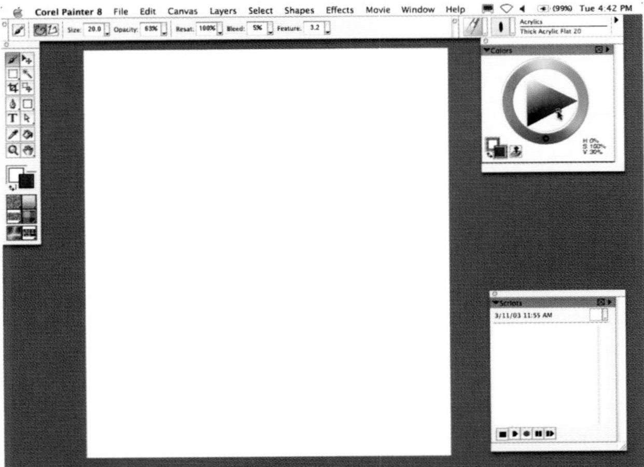

Figure 6.1 Basic palette layout for recording a script.

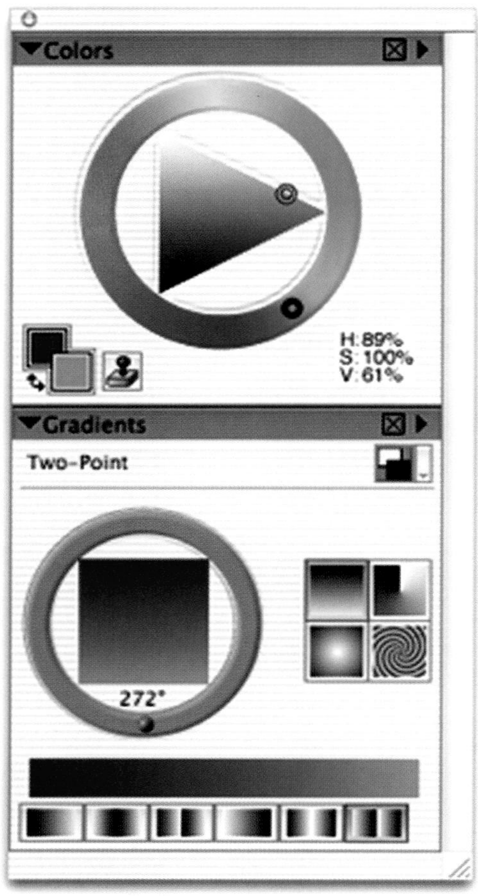

Figure 6.2 Cool blue Two-Point gradation.

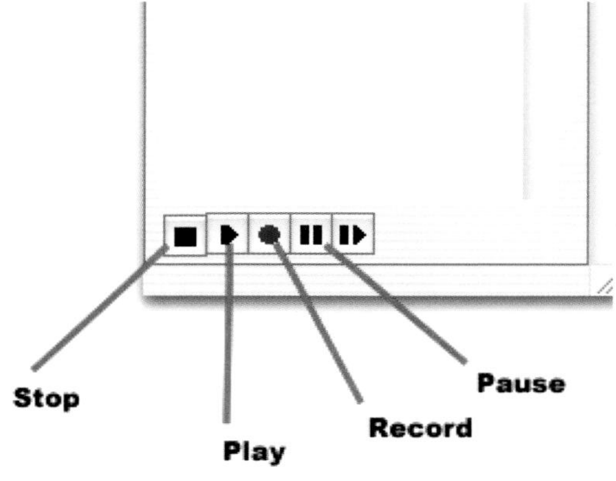

Figure 6.3 The script control buttons.

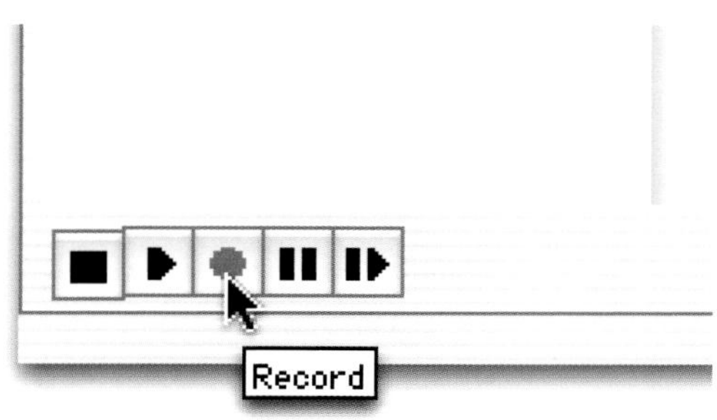

Figure 6.4 The record button goes bright red while you are recording.

While a Script Is Being Recorded

1 Start with broad, rough brush strokes. Fill in the main areas of light and dark. Don't worry about details or about creating a lifelike image. Experiment with different brushes. Use this project as a laboratory for experimentation and exploration.

Continued

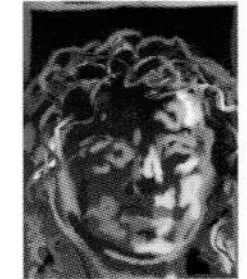

2. After filling the canvas with paint, start working toward more details using smaller brushes. Selectively increase the vibrancy of colors, the contrasts, and the level of detail in those regions of the image you wish to focus on (such as the eyes).
3. Work for at least one hour on your self-portrait. When it is "complete," after saving the image, transform your self-portrait into a wild image of some kind. It doesn't matter what you do to it! Try some of the fun Liquid brushes and see how they move paint around on the canvas.

Only have one canvas open in Painter while recording the script. Do not close your current image, or resize your canvas, or open a new canvas, or start working on another canvas, while recording a script.

Regularly choose File > Save As and save sequentially numbered versions as RIFF files into the folder you created for this project. I recommend doing this as a safety back-up, even though your script may allow you to go back to any intermediate stages. Sometimes scripts don't work properly, and you should avoid relying on a script as your only record of your work in progress.

I always end my painting sessions with a signature, copyright symbol, and year. This is not only a good habit for protecting your artwork, but it also makes it easy to see when your script replay is completed.

Stopping, Naming, and Saving a Script

1. When you have completed your image and are ready to stop the recorder, reopen the Scripts palette.
2. Click on the black square button on the left of the five Scripts buttons.
3. In the Script Name window you will see "Save As: Untitled." Untitled is highlighted.
4. Type in the name of your script, which will replace the default script name "Untitled."

Continued

I name my scripts using the same reverse date notation as my image files. For instance, for a self-portrait created on October 15, 2003, I may name the script: "03.10.15 self portrait." If I was planning to create more than one self-portrait script that day, I would add version 1, 2, 3, etc. to the end of the script name. Because this naming convention for scripts is very similar to the convention for naming the image files, I usually save myself time by copying the file name (excluding the file format tag) when I do a Save As (by highlighting the name and choosing Cmd/Ctrl-C) and then just pasting (Cmd/Ctrl-V) the name into the Script Name window.

5 Select OK. It is important not to accidentally select Cancel. You *cannot* undo Cancel. You will have lost your script forever if you do select Cancel.

Protecting Your Saved Versions

After you have saved the script, choose File > Save As again. Save one last version of your image, even if it will be exactly the same as your previously saved version, which was saved within the recording. Name this final version with a different, higher version number, and add the letter "F" for final. The "F" helps when you are looking to print the image to know immediately which was your final version. Also this will be your safety back-up in case you accidentally ruin (i.e., unintentionally modify) all the earlier versions saved within the script.

Scripts record every time you save a file. Thus if you play back a script and make any changes to the process as you do so (e.g., different background, brushes, dimensions), you run the risk of accidentally overwriting all your original saved versions. The replay will not show you any window asking if you wish to save changes, it'll just replace your original files! Thus I recommend, *before* replaying a script, that you locate the folder on your computer hard drive where you saved all the versions of the image and copy those files into a back-up folder in a different location. On a Mac you would drag your cursor over the files to select them and then, holding down the Option key, drag the files into the back-up folder.

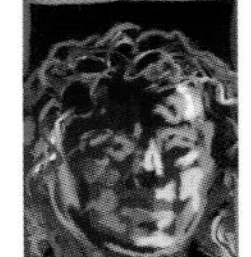

6.4 Playing Back a Script

Basic Replay

1. Select your script from the Scripts library drop-down menu in the Scripts palette.
2. Open the original background canvas (version -01B) that you started with prior to recording the script.
3. Choose Cmd/Ctrl-M (Window > Screen Mode Toggle).
4. Select the black triangular play button, second from the left of the five script control buttons. When you click on the triangle, it goes bright green (Figure 6.5), indicating that you are now replaying the currently selected script.

   You should now see your painting process replay seamlessly and continuously. Note that to get an authentic replay of exactly what you originally created you will need all the same libraries in Painter. If any of the Brush Variants or Art Materials are missing, or have different names, you'll be prompted to locate them.
5. The replay will continue until the end, at which time the green triangle button will become black again. If you did a concluding signature at the end of your session, you can also look out for that signature to appear as an indication of when the replay is complete.

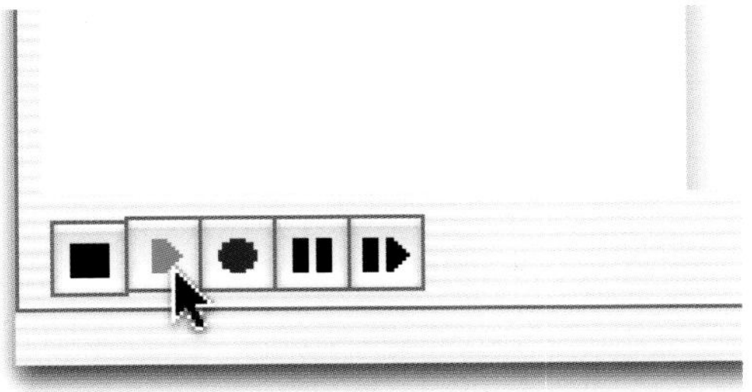

Figure 6.5 The play button goes bright green while you replay a script.

Pausing During Replay

During replay you may see a stage of your painting that you'd like to take time to look at. You may wish to save the stage or to recall which exact brush settings you were using at that moment in the creative process.

1. To pause the replay at any time, just click the pause button (two vertical black lines, the second button from the right). You'll see the pause button go bright orange (Figure 6.6), and all action will halt. During this pause you can choose Save As to save that stage, or look at all the palettes to find out exactly what Brush Variant settings and Art Materials you were using at that moment. This can be useful when you want to remind yourself of a great brush you used at a certain stage of the painting process.
2. When you wish to continue your replay, you just click the pause button once again (or click the play button) and the replay continues where it left off.

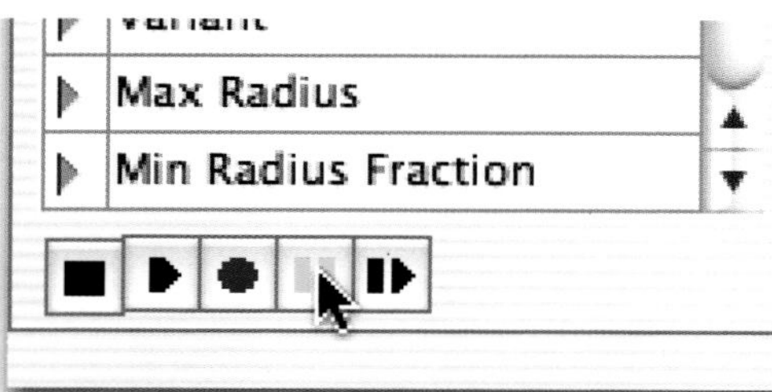

Figure 6.6 The pause button goes bright orange while you pause during the replay of a script.

Changing Background on Replay

1. Open the original background canvas (version -01B).
2. Fill the canvas with a different background.
3. Choose Save As.
4. Rename this new beginning canvas.
5. Replay the script (following instructions above).

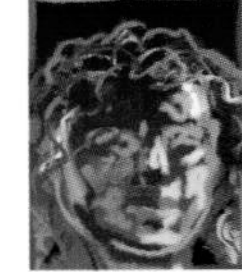

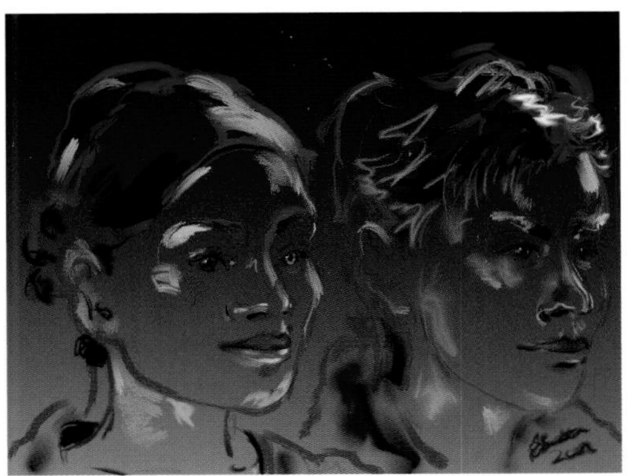

Figure 6.7 Rob and Diane, the original version.

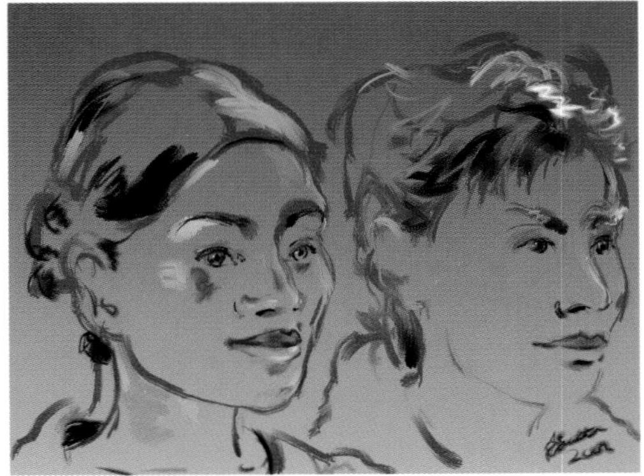

Figure 6.8 Rob and Diane, replayed over a sandy-brown gradient background.

You can see an example here (Figure 6.7) of an original painting, a portrait I did of Rob and Diane, two talented swing dance teachers (www.yeahman.com), at an event in San Francisco. My original background was a blue gradation.

After completing this portrait I replayed with a sandy-brown gradation in the background instead of the original blue gradation. I found the result (Figure 6.8) worked better than my original.

Changing Brushes during Replay

1. Click the pause button to pause the replay.
2. Change the selected brush variant. You can also alter the current color at this time.
3. Click the pause or play buttons and the replay will continue with the new brush variant.

You can see here (Figure 6.9) another original painting, this time a portrait I did of Wendell at the 2002 Macworld Expo Digital Art Class demo station in San Francisco. The original brush variant used in making Wendell's portrait was the Sargent variant in the Artists brush category.

Here is a variation of Wendell's portrait created by replaying the script, pausing at the beginning, and changing the brush variant from Sargent to the Spiral variant in the Nature Brushes category (Figure 6.10).

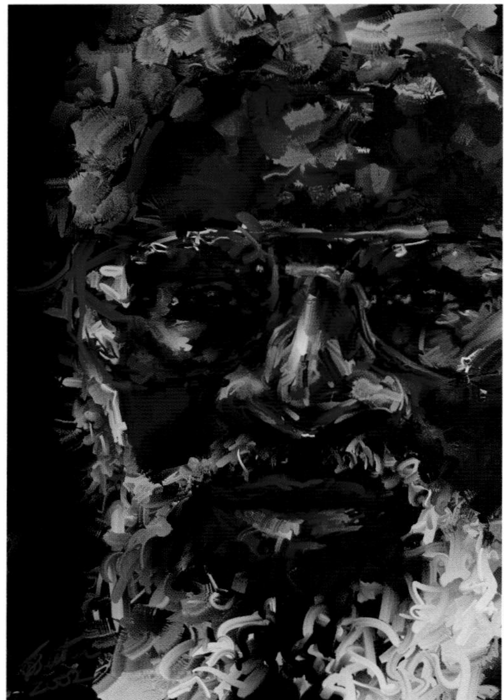

Figure 6.9 Wendell, the original portrait, created with the Sargent variant in the Artists category.

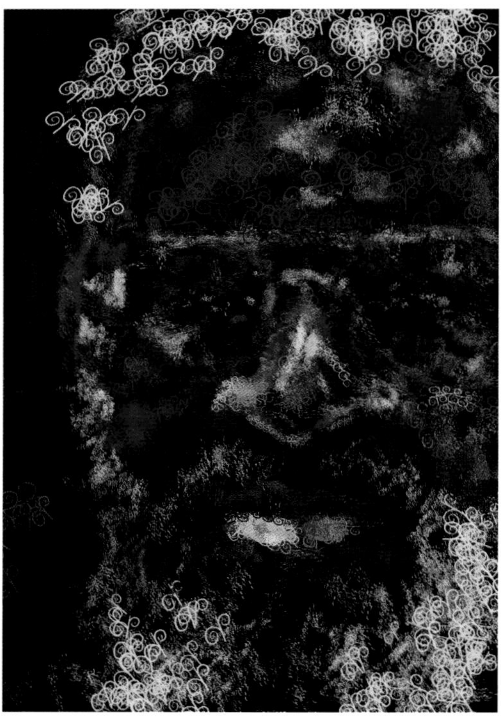

Figure 6.10 Wendell, replayed with the Spiral variant in the Nature Brushes category (found in Creativity Brushes library).

Once you have generated a series of variations based on the same recorded painting session, you can then mix and match them by treating them all as alternative cloning sources (using File > Clone Source to go between them all). Use the Soft Cloner variant in the Cloners category to clone them together. I recommend making a master working file the same size as the clone sources (the easiest way to do this is to just pick one image and choose File > Clone).

Distorting Your Image on Replay

You can stretch or squash your replayed image either vertically or horizontally, provided you remembered to "select all" immediately prior to starting the recorder. Distorted replays can lead to interesting results.

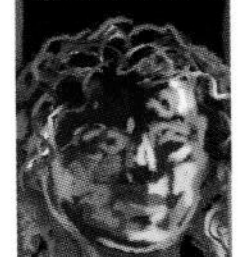

1. Open your original background canvas (version -01 or -01B).
2. Make a rectangular selection in your canvas using the Rectangular Selection tool (keyboard shortcut "r"). Make the selection wide and short or thin and tall for the most noticeable results.
3. Replay your script as normal. You will see it replay into the selection, no matter how different the shape of the selection to the original canvas.

You can see here (Figure 6.11) a portrait I did of Ralph, also at the 2002 Macworld Expo Digital Art Class demo station in San Francisco.

Here is the same portrait played back into a tall, thin rectangular selection (Figure 6.12).

Besides the convenience (and fun) of being able to make Giaccometti or Mogdilliani versions of your painting (i.e., stretched out and thin), there is another benefit to this technique of replaying into rectangular selections. If the selection contour is smaller than the size of your canvas, then the

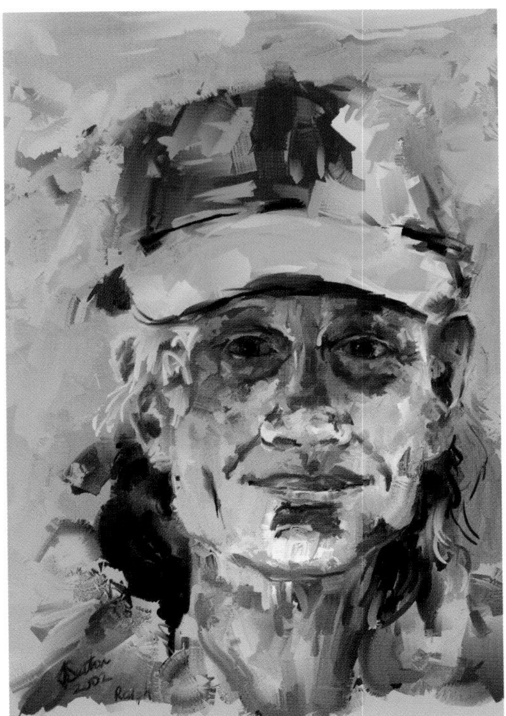

Figure 6.11 Ralph, the original portrait.

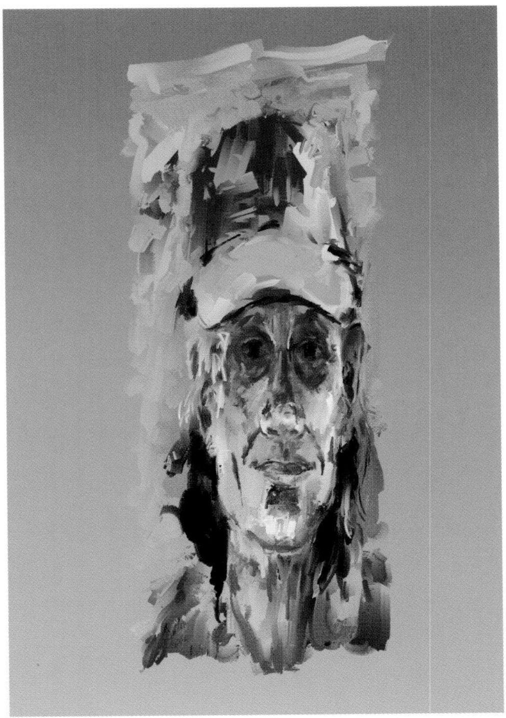

Figure 6.12 Ralph, replayed into tall, thin rectangular selection.

edge of your replayed painting can have wonderful, organic forms because the replayed brush strokes can extend beyond the selection area. You can clearly see this result if you compare the two versions of Ralph shown here.

Playing Back at Higher or Lower Resolution

One of the practical benefits of the Select All prior to the recording is that you can paint a quick gestural sketch on a small canvas and then replay the same painting onto a high-resolution canvas for printing. You can also replay a large painting into a very small canvas (as I did in preparing the frames for the flipbook images you see in this book).

1. Open your original background canvas (version -01B).
2. Choose Canvas > Resize.
3. Uncheck the Constrain File Size check box in the Resize window.
4. Set your Width and Height units to inches (the default unit is pixels).
5. Change the resolution from 72 ppi to 300 ppi.
6. Click OK.
7. Make any changes you wish to the background.
8. Choose Cmd/Ctrl-A (Select > All).
9. Replay the script. It will replay into the larger file.

If you forget to do the Select All just before you replay the script, the script will replay at the original pixel size, aligned in the top left corner of the canvas.

6.5 Converting a Script to a Movie

Converting Your Script into a Frame Stack

To do something with your recorded painting process outside Painter, you will first need to convert the script, which is a continuous record of all your actions, into a series of individual frames. That is achieved by creating, in Painter, a special file known as a *frame stack*, which, as the name suggests, is a file containing a stack of frames or images. The frame stack can only be opened within Painter and should be treated as a temporary transition state before saving the frames in a more versatile and stable format that can be opened in programs other than Painter.

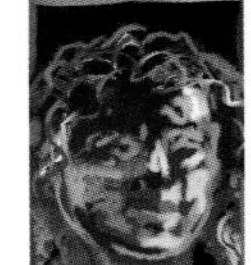

The frames that make up the frame stack can either be saved as separate sequentially numbered images or as movie files (QuickTime is the most common format, although AVI movies and GIF animations are also options). Note that within Painter the word *movie* is used to denote both frame stack and conventional movie formats such as QuickTime and AVI. This can sometimes be a little confusing, so I recommend you always be careful with your file names so it is clear whether you're dealing with a Frame stack or QuickTime movie.

1. Select Script Options from the Scripts pop-up menu (Figure 6.13) that appears when you click on the small triangle in the top right of the Scripts palette.
2. Click on the Save Frames on Playback checkbox in the Script Options window (Figure 6.14). You should now see a check appear in that checkbox.
3. Leave the Record Initial State checkbox checked (the default state). The Record Initial State means that whenever the script is replayed, the program will look for the same Libraries as were present in Painter when the script was originally started.
4. In the Script Options window you will type in a number of tenths of a second to determine how frequently Painter will save a snapshot of the image as the script is replayed.

   Each of these snapshots becomes a frame in the frame stack. It is a common misconception that the figure that you type into the "Every . . . 1/10ths of a second" represents the frame rate (frames per second) of your final movie. This is *not* the case! The figure you type in has nothing to do with the frame rate of your movie. It is only going to determine how many, or how few, frames you end up with. The default figure, which is 10 ("Every 10 1/10ths of a second"), means that at intervals of 10 tenths of a second (i.e., every second), during the replay of a script Painter will take a snapshot of the current image (assuming you have Save Frames on Playback checked). These snapshots become frames in the frame stack. If you doubled the figure from 10 to 20 ("Every 20 1/10ths of a second," i.e., every two seconds), then the interval between snapshots will be doubled, so the total number of snapshots will be halved.

   Conversely, if you halved the figure from 10 to 5 ("Every 5 1/10ths of a second," i.e., every half a second), then the interval between snapshots will be halved and the total number of snapshots will be doubled. To get the most frames you'd make the figure 1 ("Every 1 1/10ths of a second," i.e., every one tenths of a second), whereas to get a very few frames you'd make the figure

Continued

very large, e.g., 100 ("Every 100 1/10ths of a second," i.e., every 10 seconds). This is not exact science! The rate of replay of a script is determined by a number of factors, including what brushes or effects you used and how fast your computer is. Thus a slow computer, ironically, allows you to generate more frames than a super-fast one.

You may find yourself doing several trial runs in order to end up with a frame stack with the right number of frames. Painter's scripting and animation capability, which has not been developed significantly since it was first introduced in Painter back in the mid-1990s, doesn't give you precise control over things like the speed of script replay, the total number of frames in a frame stack, and the frame rate when you replay a frame stack.

5 Click OK in the Script Options window.

6 Select your script from the Scripts library drop-down menu in the Scripts palette.

7 Open the original background canvas (version -01B) that you started with prior to recording the script.

8 Choose Cmd/Ctrl-M (Window > Screen Mode Toggle).

9 Select the black triangular play button, second from the left of the five Script buttons. When you click on it the triangle goes bright green, indicating that it is replaying the selected script.

10 You will now see a window titled "Enter Movie Name" where you can name your frame stack and determine the location on your computer where the frame stack will be saved. Note that the use of the word *movie* here refers to frame stack, *not* QuickTime or AVI movie.

Remember that you may make a few trial frame stacks; therefore, it is best to name them with an indication of the Script Option setting you chose for saving frames. Also, if you are on a Macintosh, add a file format tag at the end of the file name that indicates it is a frame stack (Windows systems do this automatically). Thus if you selected "Every 10 1/10ths of a second" in Script Options, then the frame stack name may be something like "portrait-10tenths-01.frm." Put this name where you see Save As: Untitled.

Frame stacks can be very large files. Their size is simply the addition of all the images that make up the frames. So if you have a frame stack with 450 frames, each frame being about 1.5 Megabytes, then the frame stack will be about 675 Megabytes. Make sure you have plenty of free hard drive space (I recommend at least 1 Gigabyte of free space) at the location where you are saving the frame stack. I often save the frame stacks onto the desktop and then trash them as soon as I've saved my final movie in QuickTime format.

Continued

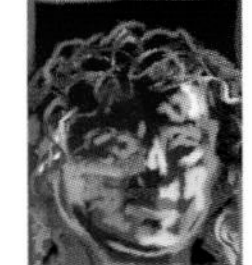

Note that when you close a frame stack you are never asked whether you wish to save changes; any changes are automatically saved. This makes the frame stacks an unreliable, as well as unwieldy, format in which to save your animation. It is better to rely on your original script and your QuickTime movie as your means of saving your movie. The QuickTime movie has the advantage of enduring with time independent of Painter. The script will only work with the exact same brushes and art materials loaded in Painter as when you originally recorded the script.

11 After you've named the frame stack and determined where it will be located, click Save.

12 You now see the New Frame Stack window (Figure 6.15). Leave the defaults Layers of Onion Skin: 2 and Storage Type: 24-bit color with 8-bit alpha. Click OK.

13 The script will now replay. You will see a Frame Stack palette (Figure 6.16) with small previews of the frames as they are saved.

When the script has replayed completely, the Script play button, located in the Scripts section of the Objects palette, will return to being black (from being bright green). At this point the frame stack is completed.

You may find that your script plays back too fast and therefore doesn't allow you to capture a sufficient number of frames (e.g., you're recording your signature and it replays into a single frame,

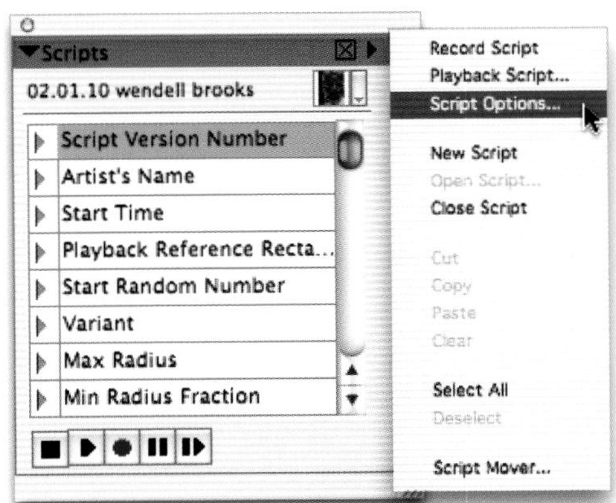

Figure 6.13 The Scripts pop-up menu.

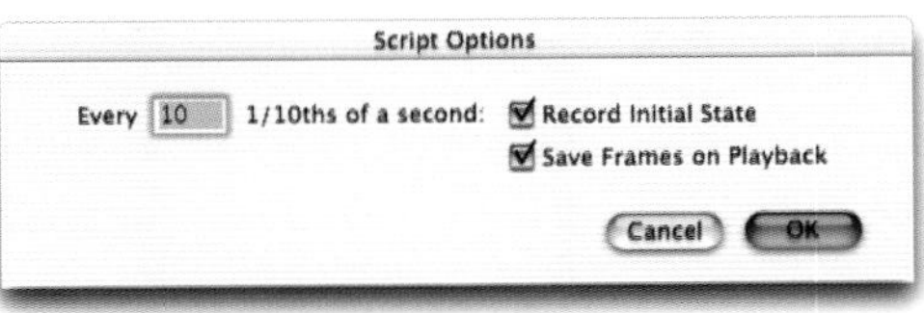

Figure 6.14 The Script Options window.

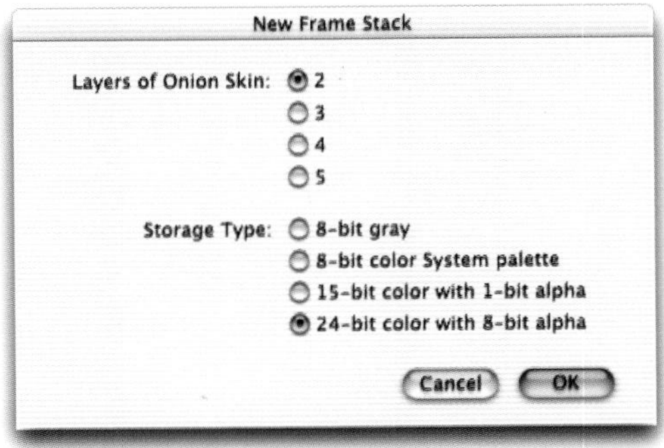

Figure 6.15 The New Frame Stack window.

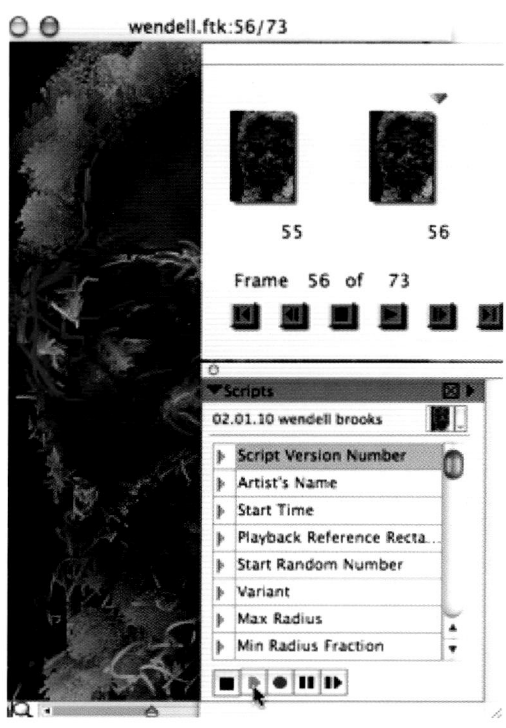

Figure 6.16 The Frame Stack palette with the Scripts palette.

even on the 1/10ths of a second setting). Unfortunately in Painter there is no replay speed control; the replay speed is a function of the speed of your computer and the memory intensiveness of your actions in Painter. In the situation where you can't capture enough frames, re-record your script on a much larger canvas (but with the same aspect ratio: width/height). This will automatically slow the replay. You will then need to alter the movie frame size in a program outside of Painter.

Converting a Frame Stack into a QuickTime Movie

1. Choose File > Save As.
2. Select your option from the Save Movie window (Figure 6.17). If you are unsure of which option to use and you want to be able to replay your movie in slide shows and presentations, I recommend selecting Save Options: Save movie as QuickTime. The rest of these instructions will be based on that choice.
3. Click OK.

Continued

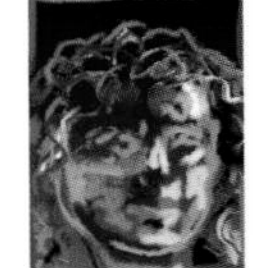

4. You now see the Enter Movie Name window. This is now referring to saving the QuickTime movie, not the frame stack. If you are on a Macintosh, name the QuickTime movie with a name ending in .qtm (Windows systems do this automatically) to identify it as a QuickTime movie.
5. Choose where you wish to save the QuickTime movie.
6. Click OK.
7. In the Compression Settings window (Figure 6.18) select Compression: Animation with Millions of Colors + and move the Quality slider to the right (Best). I suggest leaving the Frames per second at 12 and unchecking "Key frame every . . . frames," unless you have specific needs, such as a faster frame rate for video (typically 29.97 fps).
8. Click OK.

Figure 6.17 The Save Movie window.

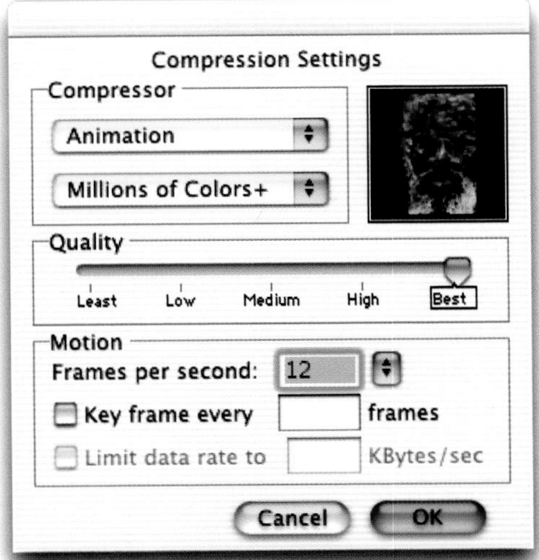

Figure 6.18 The QuickTime Compression Settings window.

Congratulations! You've now succeeded in converting your script into a QuickTime movie. You can now play this movie on any QuickTime player, or integrate it into a movie or film or video, using other software such as Apple Final Cut Pro, Adobe Premiere, or Adobe After Effects. If you ever wish to re-create the frame stack without going to the time-consuming effort of replaying the script again, you can just open the QuickTime movie from within Painter and it will open as a frame stack.

The flipbook animation that you see in the top corner of the pages of this book is an example of a script converted into individual frames using the same technique as described previously.

6.6 Revealing a Photo

One of the great things you can do with scripting is to record the creation of a painting where you use Painter's Tracing Paper to trace and/or clone from a source photo (or several source photos) and then replay the painting without the Tracing Paper visible. This allows you to create animation that magically reveals a photo, or that shows a series of transitions between a sequence of photos (like a video photo-montage).

In this exercise you will create a painting animation in which a single photographic image is magically revealed.

Preparation for Recording a Photo-Reveal Script

1. Open your original source photo in Painter. I shall refer to this as "orig.tif."

   The example I show here is based on a project I did for Apple Computer in 1998. Apple wanted me to create a script replay that could demonstrate the fast speed of the top-of-the-line Apple computer. The original source photo used in this project was the *Think Different* campaign image of Albert Einstein (Figure 6.19).

2. Set up a palette arrangement (Window > Arrange Palettes > Save Layout) that includes the Tools, Property Bar, Brush Selector, and Colors and Scripts palettes.

3. Choose Cmd/Ctrl-E (Effect > Tonal Control > Equalize). See if the automatic equalize effect improves your image. If so click OK, otherwise click Cancel. Make any other final enhancements you wish to your original source image.

4. Drag the Crop tool (keyboard shortcut "c") in the image, adjust the control handles in the sides of the crop marquee to select the ideal crop for that

Continued

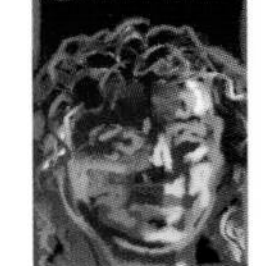

particular image, and then click inside the crop area to complete the crop operation. Ignore this step if you're already perfectly happy with the way the image is cropped.

5 Choose File > Clone. This makes a duplicate image ("Clone of orig.tif") of exactly the same size and resolution as the original image ("orig.tif"), and also automatically assigns orig.tif to be the current clone source (you will see a checkmark by orig.tif in the File > Clone Source menu).

6 Choose File > Save As.

7 Rename "Clone of orig.tif" with a name that includes the subject title and the version number (e.g., photoreveal-01.rif). Save this file in RIFF format into an appropriate project folder. This will be your working image.

8 Choose Cmd/Ctrl-A (Select > All). This selects the whole of photoreveal-01.rif.

9 Choose your Delete/Backspace key. This clears the canvas of the duplicate image.

10 Choose Cmd/Ctrl-S. This updates the file.

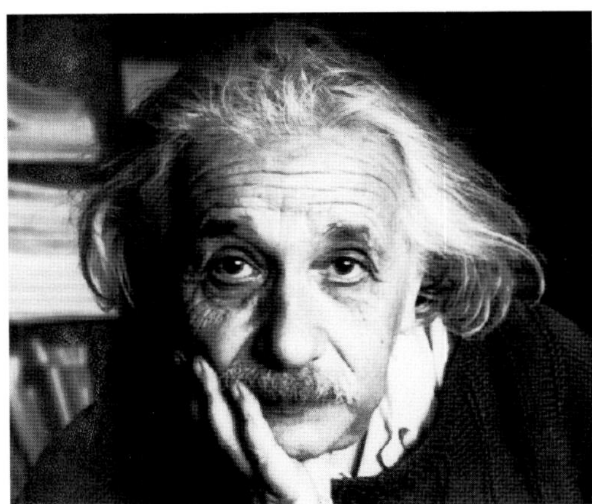

Figure 6.19 The original source image.

Recording a Photo-Reveal Script

1. Choose Cmd/Ctrl-A (Select > All). This selects the whole of photoreveal-01.rif.
2. Click on the central dark red, solid circular record button in the center of the five Scripts control buttons (Scripts palette). The button goes bright red, indicating that recording has begun.
3. Minimize the Scripts palette by clicking once on the little triangle on the top left of the palette. This is for safety to prevent you accidentally turning off the recorder before your image is complete.
4. Choose Cmd/Ctrl-D (Select > None). This gets rid of the selection and the dancing ants.
5. Choose Cmd/Ctrl-T (Canvas > Tracing Paper). You now see a 50 percent opacity view of the source image, the current clone source, orig.tif, superimposed over a 50 percent opacity view of the plain white working image, photoreveal-01.rif (Figure 6.20).
6. Use any brushes you choose to paint on your image, using the Tracing Paper view of your source photo as a visual reference. Start off with artistic brush strokes and only clone in more precise detail from the source photo toward the end.
7. Regularly turn off Tracing Paper by choosing Cmd/Ctrl-T (Canvas > Tracing Paper). This command toggles the Tracing Paper function on and off. Be aware that when Tracing Paper is on, you are *not* seeing an accurate representation of your actual image.

   To base your brush stroke colors on the clone source image colors, either choose a brush Variant from the Cloners brush category in the Brush Selector, or click on the Clone Color icon in the bottom of the Colors Art Materials palette. Mix in your own color choices as well as using clone color. In the case of the Einstein image, I was using a black-and-white original and I chose to use my own selection of bright colors, rather than basing color on the grays of the original image (Figures 6.21 and 6.22).

   If you wish, toward the end start selectively revealing accurate photographic detail from the source image by selecting the Soft Cloner variant from the Cloners brush category (Figure 6.23).
8. Regularly choose File > Save As and save sequentially numbered versions of your working image (e.g., photomontage-02.rif, etc.).

Continued

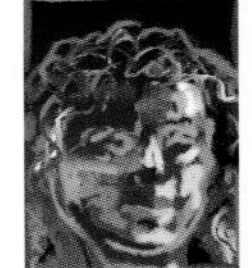

9. When you have completed your photo-reveal painting and are ready to stop the recorder, reopen the Scripts palette.
10. Click on the black square button on the left of the five Scripts buttons.
11. In the Script Name window you will see "Save As: Untitled." Untitled is highlighted.
12. Type in the name of your script, which will replace the default script name "Untitled." I suggest a name that includes the reverse date and .subject.
13. Select OK.

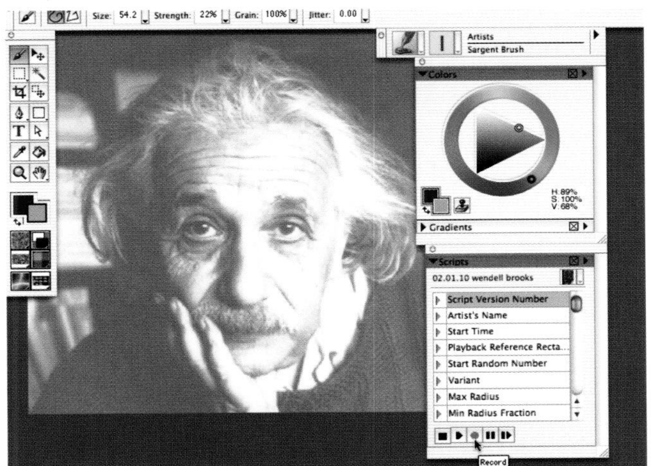

Figure 6.20 The clone image with tracing paper turned on.

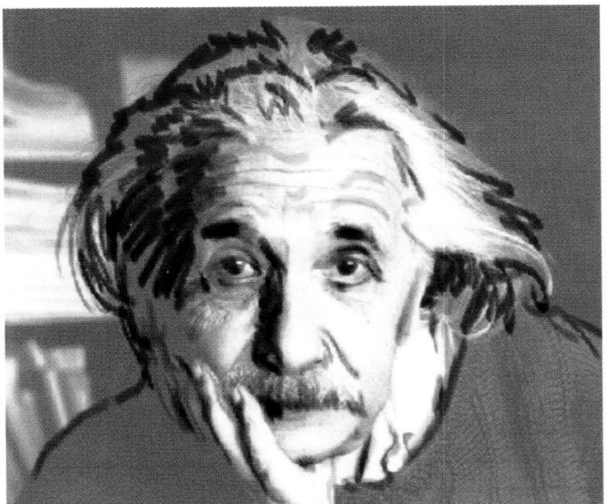

Figure 6.21 With tracing paper turned on.

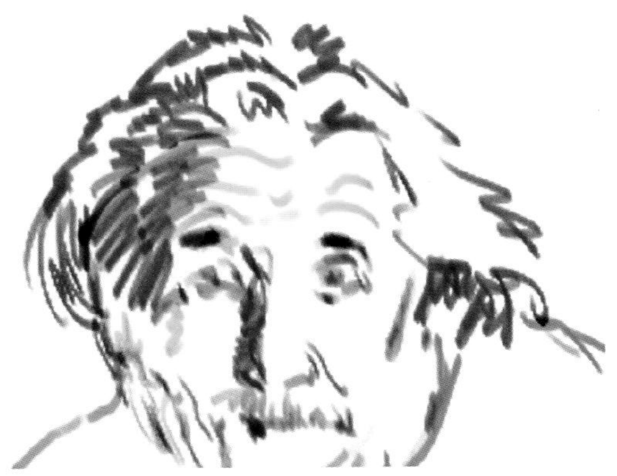

Figure 6.22 With tracing paper turned off.

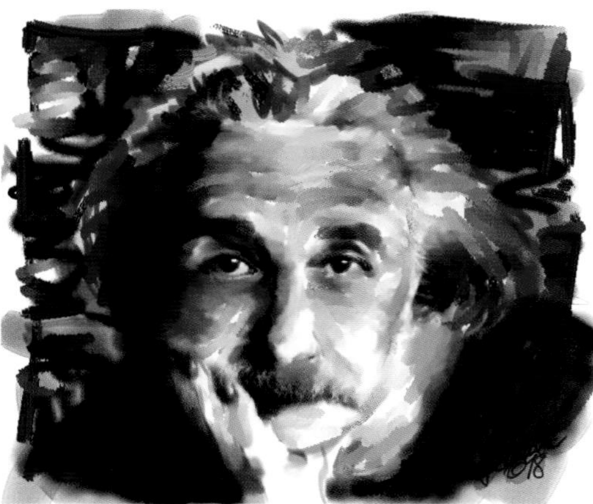

Figure 6.23 The final image with the eyes cloned in from the original source photo using the Soft Cloner variant.

Converting a Photo-Reveal Script into a Movie

Before replaying a photo-reveal script, and converting it into a movie, you first need to set everything up as it was when you started the script originally. That means you should have your working file background (photoreveal-01B.rif) as the active file in Painter, open in screen mode and filled with black. Also open in Painter, but not active, you should have your source image, orig.tif. When you go to File > Clone Source you should see the source image name (e.g., orig.tif) with a checkmark by it, indicating that it is assigned to be the clone source. If not, drag down to the source image name in the Clone Source pop-up menu and make sure there is a checkmark by the file name. Make sure Painter's Tracing Paper function is turned off.

Once all this is ready, follow the instructions earlier in this session (Converting a Script to a Movie) for converting a script to a frame stack and then saving the frame stack as a QuickTime movie. The Tracing Paper does not appear during the script replay. Thus your photo appears to be revealed by your paint strokes (Figure 6.24).

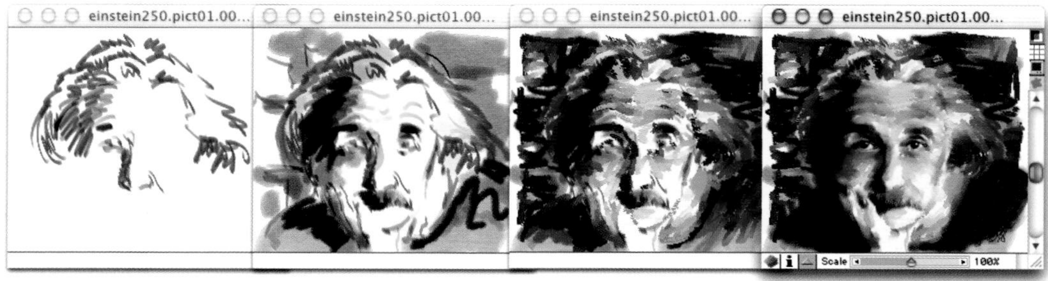

Figure 6.24 A sequence of frames from the final QuickTime movie showing the photo being gradually revealed.

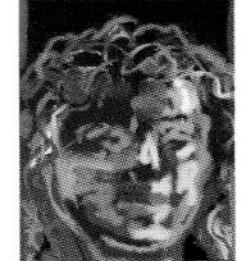

Stitching Frame Stacks Together

If you are wanting to generate many hundreds of frames, I recommend making your recording in stages, saving the script at each stage with a clear name that defines what order it is in the sequence of scripts. Make sure you can recall what files need to be opened when replaying each script. After you have generated several frame stacks (one for each script), you can "stitch" them together by opening the first frame stack, and choose Movie > Insert Movie. In the Insert Movie window select the last option "Insert movie: At end of Movie." Click OK and locate the next frame stack in the sequence (on your hard drive, not already open in Painter). The frames of the second frame stack will be added onto those of the first. Continue this process until you have stitched all of your frame stacks into a master frame stack, from which you can save a master QuickTime movie. An alternative to this approach is to save each frame stack as different QuickTime movies and then stitch the movies together in a video editing program outside Painter. Either way you will need a lot of RAM and storage space.

Resizing a Frame Stack

Sometimes you will create an original script at high resolution and want to end up with a much smaller final movie or set of frames. Within the frame stack mode you do not have access to the Canvas > Resize command. You can resize the frame stack by first playing back into a smaller file choosing Cmd/Ctrl-A (Select > All) before you start the playback (provided you remembered to originally select all before starting your script recording). Alternately, you can save the frame stack as a QuickTime movie and then use a program like Adobe Premiere to resize the QuickTime movie (as I did in the case of the flip-book animation in the top corner of this book). If you wish, you can then open the resized QuickTime movie from within Painter. This will generate a resized frame stack.

6.7 Transitioning between Photos

In this exercise you will create a painting animation that shows painterly transitions between a series of photographs. Choose your own series of images to reveal and transition between. You could use source images depicting a common subject taken at different times. For instance, you could use photographs of a person showing different facial expressions or taken at different stages in life. You could use photographs of a landscape scene taken at different times of the year, or you could choose a series of contrasting images representing, for instance, different places, elements, seasons, moods, people, and so on. Imagine the effect that transforming one image into the next will have on a viewer. Do you want to convey a story or an emotion? Do you want to surprise or amuse your audience?

Preparation for Recording a Photo-Transition Script

To make an effective animation, you have to put some work in upfront. You need to be careful about preparing all your files before starting to record a painting session. Don't be intimidated by the large number of steps in this section!

1. Choose three original source photos and decide on the order in which they will be used in the animation. The three original source photos can be different sizes and resolutions. I shall refer to these three original source images as orig1.tif, orig2.tif, and orig3.tif. Open your three chosen original source photos in Painter. Note that three is an arbitrary number, and this technique can be applied to any number of photographs.
2. Set up a palette arrangement (Window > Arrange Palettes > Save Layout) that includes Tools, Property Bar, Brush Selector, and Colors an Scripts palettes.
3. Select black as the current color (in the Regular color rectangle of the Colors section of the Art Materials palette).
4. With each original source image in turn, choose Cmd/Ctrl-E (Effect > Tonal Control > Equalize). See if the automatic equalize effect improves your image. If so click OK, otherwise click Cancel. Make any other final enhancements to your original source images.
5. With each original source image in turn, drag the Crop tool (keyboard shortcut "c") in the image, adjust the control handles in the sides of the crop marquee to select the ideal crop for that particular image, and then click inside the crop area to complete the crop operation. Ignore this step if you're already perfectly happy with the way the image is copped.
6. Choose one of your original source images, say orig1.tif, to be the size of final file you wish to work on. Make this your active image in Painter.
7. Choose File > Clone. This makes a duplicate image ("Clone of orig1.tif") of exactly the same size and resolution as the original image ("orig1.tif").

   If you wish to make your final working image a different size from any of your source images, then just open a new canvas (Cmd/Ctrl-N or File > New) of the appropriate size.
8. Choose Cmd/Ctrl-M (Window > Screen Mode Toggle).
9. Select black in the Colors palette.
10. Choose Cmd/Ctrl-F (Effects > Fill). Make sure Fill With: Current Color is checked.

Continued

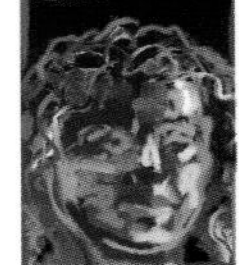

11 Click OK. The background canvas will now be filled with black. Black is an arbitrary choice; you could use any color as your background color.

12 Choose File > Save As.

13 Save the file with a name that includes the subject title and the version number (e.g., photomontage-01B.rif, where "B" is for base, background, or beginning). Save this file in RIFF format into an appropriate project folder.

The next stage is to ensure that all of the source images you will clone from are the exact same size (pixels wide by pixels high) as your final working image. If all of your original source images are already exactly the same size as your final working image, then ignore steps 14 to 25 and skip forward to step 26.

14 Choose File > Clone. This makes a duplicate image ("Clone of photomontage-01B.rif") of exactly the same size and resolution as your working image ("photomontage-01B.rif").

15 Choose File > Save As.

16 Rename the file source2.rif.

17 Select image orig2.tif.

18 Choose Cmd/Ctrl-A (Select > All).

19 Choose Cmd/Ctrl-C (Edit > Copy).

20 Select image source2.rif.

21 Choose Cmd/Ctrl-V (Edit > Paste).

The orig2.tif image will appear in source2.rif as an active layer (highlighted in the Layers section of the Objects palette).

22 Select Effects > Orientation > Free Transform. The orig2 layer is now converted to a Free Transform or reference layer with a yellow and black police tape marquee.

23 Hold down the Shift key and drag on the corner control handles. This rescales your layer without distorting the aspect ratio. Adjust the scale of the layer to suit how you wish it to appear in the final composition.

24 Use the Object Adjuster tool (keyboard shortcut "f") to reposition the layer if needed.

25 Choose Cmd/Ctrl-S (File > Save) to update the source2.rif image.

Repeat steps 14 through 25 for the orig3.tif image if it is a different size from the final working image. You will end up with three source images (orig1.tif, source2.rif, and source3.rif) all exactly the same size and resolution as

Continued

the final image you will paint. Keep all three identically sized source files (orig1.tif, source2.rif, and source3.rif) and the working image file (photomontage-01B.rif) open in Painter. Close all other files.

26 Select the first source image you wish to work from (e.g., orig1.tif).

27 Select your working file (photomontage-01B.rif), open in screen mode and filled with black, as the active file in Painter. Also open in Painter, but not active, you should have your three source images, all exactly the same size as the working file.

28 Choose File > Clone Source and make sure the first source image name (e.g., orig1.tif) has a checkmark by it, indicating that it is assigned to be the clone source. If not, drag down to that name in the Clone Source pop-up menu.

You are now ready to start recording your script.

Recording a Photo-Transition Script

1 Choose Cmd/Ctrl-A (Select > All). This selects the whole of photomontage-01B.rif.

2 Click on the central dark red, solid circular record button in the center of the five Scripts control buttons (Scripts palette). The button goes bright red, indicating that the recording has begun.

3 Close, or minimize, the Scripts section by clicking once on the little triangle on the top left of the section. This is for safety to prevent you accidentally turning off the recorder before your image is complete.

4 Choose Cmd/Ctrl-D (Select > None). This gets rid of the selection and the dancing ants.

5 Choose Cmd/Ctrl-T (Canvas > Tracing Paper). You now see a 50 percent opacity view of the first source image (the current clone source) superimposed over a 50 percent opacity view of the working image.

6 Use any brushes you choose to paint on your image, using the Tracing Paper view of your source photo as a visual reference. Start off with artistic brush strokes and only clone in more precise detail from the source photo toward the end.

Continued

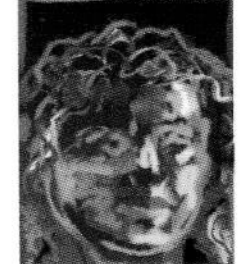

7 Regularly turn off Tracing Paper by choosing Cmd/Ctrl-T (Canvas > Tracing Paper). This command toggles the Tracing Paper function on and off. Be aware that when Tracing Paper is on, you are *not* seeing an accurate representation of your actual image.

To base your brush stroke colors on the clone source image colors, either choose a brush Variant from the Cloners brush category in the Brushes palette or check the Clone Color checkbox in the bottom of the Colors section of the Art Materials palette. Mix in your own color choices as well as using clone color.

If you wish, toward the end start selectively revealing accurate photographic detail from the source image by selecting the Soft Cloner variant from the Cloners brush category.

8 Regularly choose Save As and save sequentially numbered versions of your working image (e.g., photomontage-02.rif).

9 Continue painting until you have completed the version of the image based on your first source image, orig1.tif.

10 Choose File > Clone Source and drag (Macintosh), or click (Windows), on the name of the second source image you wish to use (e.g., source2.rif). This second image will now have the checkmark by its name and is now assigned to be the new clone source.

Repeat the painting process you followed for the first source image, only this time you are working directly on top of the first set of brush strokes. Continue this process until you have reached the stage where you wish to transition to an image based on your third and final source image. Then repeat the same steps as before, reassigning the clone source to be your third source image.

11 When you have completed your third and final transition and are ready to stop the recorder, reopen the Scripts palette.

12 Click on the black square button on the left of the five Scripts buttons.

13 In the Script Name window you will see "Save As: Untitled." Untitled is highlighted.

14 Type in the name of your script, which will replace the default script name "Untitled." I suggest a name that includes the reverse date and subject.

15 Select OK.

Converting a Photo-Transition Script into a Movie

Before replaying a photo-transition script and converting it into a movie, you first need to set everything up as it was when you started the script originally. That means you should have your working file background (photomontage-01B.rif) as the active file in Painter, open in screen mode and filled with black. Also open in Painter, but not active, you should have your three source images, all exactly the same size as the working file. When you go to File > Clone Source, you should see the first source image name (e.g., source1.tif) with a checkmark by it, indicating that it is assigned to be the clone source. Make sure Painter's Tracing Paper function is turned off.

Once all this is ready, follow the instructions earlier in this session (Converting a Script to a Movie) for converting a script to a frame stack and then saving the frame stack as a movie. The Tracing Paper does not appear during the script replay.

Here are frames (Figures 6.25) from a movie I created, using the technique described previously. They show the jazz musician, Ornette Coleman, at various stages in his life. You can see this movie as part of the slide show included on the Painter Creativity Companion CD.

Stitching Frame Stacks Together

Multiple photo transitions will usually involve generating many hundreds of frames. As mentioned earlier for the photo-reveal, in such circumstances I recommend making your recording in stages,

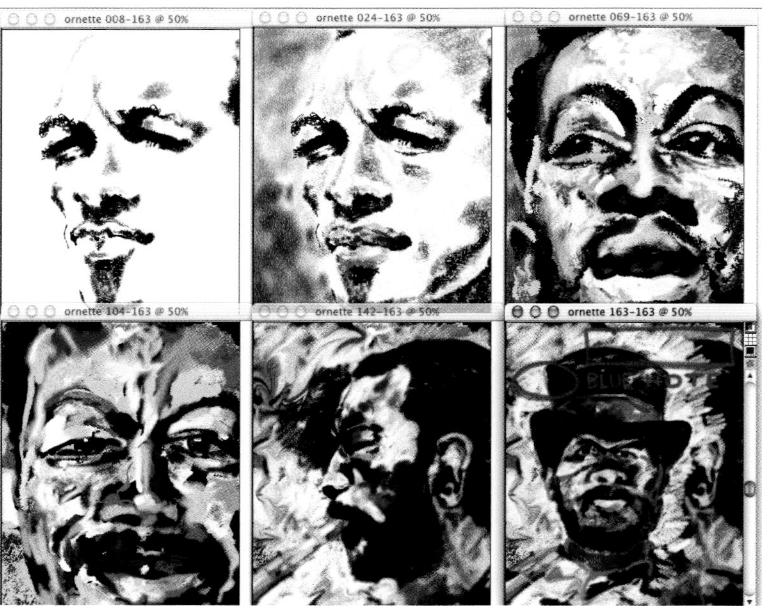

Figure 6.25 Sequence of frames from a movie showing different stages in Ornette Coleman's life.

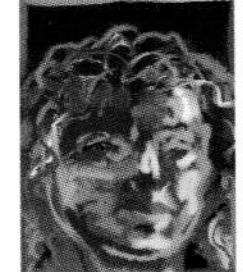

saving the script at each stage with a clear name that defines what order it is in the sequence of scripts. In the case of multiple photo transitions I recommend making each transition a self-contained script. Make sure you can recall what files need to be opened when replaying each script.

After you have generated several frame stacks (one for each script), you can stitch them together by opening the first frame stack, and choose Movie > Insert Movie. In the Insert Movie window, select the last option "Insert movie: At end of Movie." Click OK and locate the next frame stack in the sequence (on your hard drive, not already open in Painter). The frames of the second frame stack will be added onto those of the first. Continue this process until you have stitched all of your frame stacks into a master frame stack, from which you can save a master QuickTime movie. An alternative to this approach is to save each frame stack as different QuickTime movies and then stitch the movies together in a video editing program outside Painter. Either way you will need a lot of RAM and storage space.

Layers in Frame Stacks

Always flatten layers immediately when working in frame stacks. If you get into adding layers into your frame stacks, even if you are just pasting additional images at the end of the frame stack, you must be very careful *not* to run the frame stack, or forward the frames, before you drop the layer. Otherwise you will inadvertently, and irreversibly, drop the layer onto every frame and ruin your frame stack! Therefore, I always recommend backing up and archiving your animations as QuickTime movies rather than frame stacks.

6.8 Painting on Video

You can open QuickTime movies within Painter. When you choose Cmd/Ctrl-O (File > Open) and locate and select a QuickTime movie, Painter will ask you to name and save a frame stack, with the same options for the New Frame Stack window as you encountered earlier. The QuickTime movie will then be converted into a frame stack. Within the frame stack mode of Painter you can apply all of Painter's brushes and effects on each frame or apply them as scripts or brush strokes automatically across all the frames (see options under the Movie menu).

Conversely you can generate a movie from within Painter, as explained earlier in this session, and apply it to a movie in a special effects or video editing program such as Adobe After Effects or Apple Final Cut Pro. It can be useful in this case to generate a mask on each frame, which is the equivalent of an alpha channel. This allows you to selectively superimpose your Painter animation over video.

It can be fun working with layers in creating special video effects. If you want to create an animated heading or title, use a text layer, convert it to a bitmap image layer, and combine paint and special effects. Remember to drop the layer on the last frame before you replay the animation. The results can be dramatic! There is much more that you can explore in this area of Painter.

6.9 Background Scripts

Last Resort Lifeboat

Think of Painter's background scripts (or "Auto-Save scripts," as they are referred to in Painter) as your lifeboat of last resort in the event of a disaster, such as a computer crash. Every time you start Painter, a background script is automatically recorded without you needing to turn on any recorder. The recording session continues in the background (hence "background scripts") until Painter closes (either because you quit out of Painter or because the program or the computer crashes). This recording is saved as a background script that can be replayed. The background script contains everything you did from the moment you opened Painter to the moment it closed (with some exceptions: Painter's scripts do not work with all the plug-in dynamic layers). The background script can allow you to rescue a piece of artwork you had failed to save. It can also allow you to replay a sequence of steps and pause the sequence so you can identify a particular brush you used at one point. But be cautioned: the background scripts do not always work. They are sometimes corrupted by a bad crash. Never rely on them for your back-up. Always save methodically as you work.

Open the Painter General Preferences window (Edit > Preferences > General) and you will see "Auto-Save scripts for 1 days(s)." This means that each background, or Auto-Save, script will be automatically destroyed 24 hours from the time Painter closes, unless you rename the script before that time. The purpose of destroying the scripts is to prevent your computer from getting clogged up with thousands of scripts. Close the Painter General Preferences window.

Playing Back a Background Script

1. Open the Scripts palette.
2. Select the appropriate script name in the scripts drop-down menu (the menu under the scripts library drawer, to the immediate right of the script control buttons). Background scripts are automatically named with the date and time that you initially opened Painter for that session (e.g., 6/9/03 7:11 PM).
3. Click the play button (the black triangle second from the left in the row of script control buttons). The play button turns bright green as the script replays.
4. Pause the script by clicking on the pause button (the two vertical black lines, second from the right in the row of script control buttons). The pause button turns bright orange while the script pauses. This allows you to save the current image or look at the brush settings.
5. Click on the pause button a second time to continue the script replay.

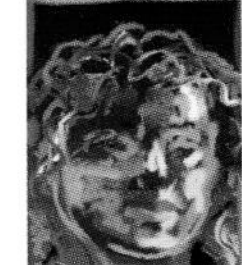

Saving a Background Script

When your replay has finished, if you wish to save the background script from being destroyed automatically, you need to either save a copy of the script in a separate scripts library or change the script name. Both of those actions are achieved in the Script Mover.

1. Select Script Mover from the bottom of the scripts pop-up menu, which is accessible by clicking on the small triangle in the top right corner of the Scripts palette.
2. In the Script Mover, select the appropriate background script in the current script library. The default library name is Painter Script Data. On the left side of the Script Mover window you will see the little icons that correspond to all the scripts in the current script library. The background scripts have blank icons; they just look like white squares. Unfortunately there is no drop-down menu with all the script names listed in the Script Mover (note to Painter developers: please add a drop-down menu!). Thus you just need to identify the correct background script by trial and error. The name of each script you click on will appear in the center of the Script Mover window.
3. When you have selected the appropriate background script, click on the Change Name button (Figure 6.26).
4. In the Change Script Name window, alter the background script name. This will prevent it from being automatically deleted.

   You can also create a new script library, by clicking on the New button on the right side of the Script Mover window, and drag the script from the left to the right of the window. This makes a copy of the script in the new library.

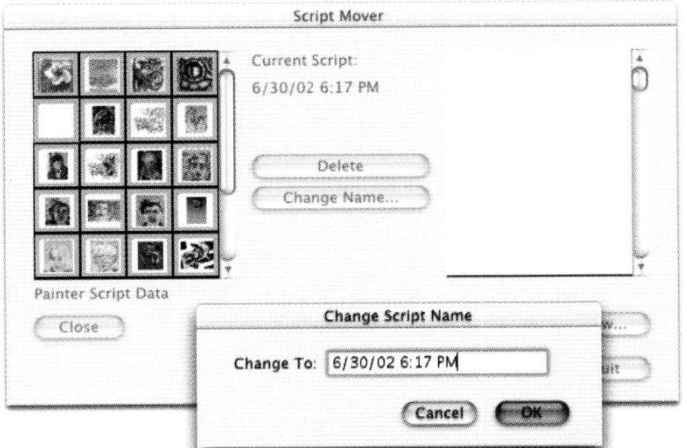

Figure 6.26 The Change Script Name window.

6.10 Wrap

This session has just touched on the powerful creative potential offered by using scripts. I encourage you to experiment with them and make them an integral part of the way you work with Painter.

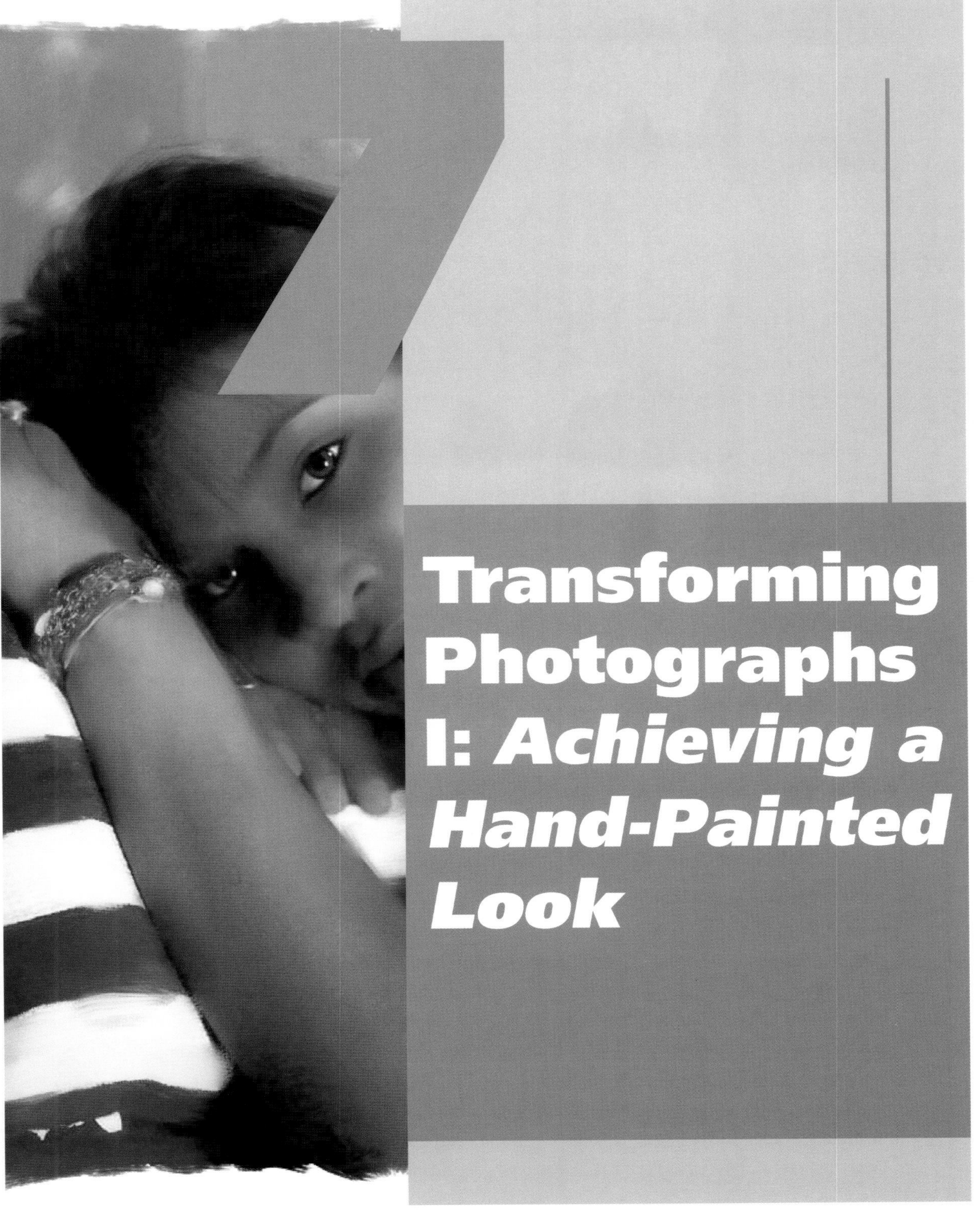

7

Transforming Photographs I: *Achieving a Hand-Painted Look*

7.1 Introduction

Painter offers an unparalleled level of freedom and power to transform your photographs into unique hand-painted images. In this session we will explore ways to generate attractive artistic paintings based on your photographs. The beauty of Painter is the way you can apply transforming brush strokes by hand using almost any of the unlimited range of brushes, rather than just applying global special effects. The use of your hand adds personality and flair to your artwork. With the powerful Painter cloning tools you can alter, add, edit, and bring back your original image at any point. Thus you have full flexibility to make as large or as small changes to your photograph as you wish.

Before I outline what this session shall cover, I wish to acknowledge and thank my friend, Jane Conner-ziser, for introducing me to the professional photography industry and for kindly giving me permission to reproduce in this session techniques, particularly regarding facial retouching, eye enhancements, and creating traditional photo watercolor and oils, that are based on her wonderful lessons. The Rough Out, Pump Up, Smooth Over section of this session is based on Jane's methodology. Jane, who I highly recommend as a teacher and who is coming out with a set of Painter/Photoshop CDs (check out her web site www.janesdigitalart.com for information on her classes and CDs), has kindly contributed an excellent essay that you'll find at the end of this session. The essay discusses the idea and tradition behind photo oils and pastels in the professional photography industry and her thoughts and action process for doing her own paintings. It provides fascinating insight that you may find useful to read before diving into the step-by-step exercises.

This session is focused primarily on the needs of the professional portrait and wedding photographer who wishes to quickly, efficiently, and consistently transform a photograph into a hand-painted image that can be printed out on canvas or watercolor paper and offered to clients as a high-value gift print or wall portrait. By following the principles and techniques shared here, you can do all the handpainting, rather than have to send your photos out to third-party artists or photo labs.

I have structured this session into four parts:

Part 1, "Simple Oil and Watercolor Techniques," shares quick, simple ways to turn your photos into paintings.

Part 2, "Basics and Loosening Up," is a review of the basic principles of working with photos followed by a loosening up self-portrait exercise that I have found useful for all my students. In this exercise you will experience the freedom of departing from the photographic image while having the safety net of always being able to return to it.

Part 3, "Rough Out, Pump Up, Smooth Over," goes into detailed techniques for turning your photographs into paintings, and includes a gallery of real-life examples. You will find some repetition of material between Parts 1 and 3, although Part 3 goes into a more involved process that includes layers, whereas all work in Part 1 is on the background canvas.

Part 4 "Classical Photo Portrait Painting," is the essay by Jane.

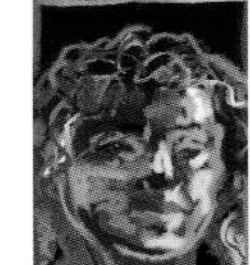

This session makes use of Cloning, a powerful technique for transforming imagery in Painter that was introduced in session 1. Cloning is the process of taking imagery, or more specifically color information, from one area of an image (the clone source) and re-creating the imagery, or applying that color information, in another area of an image (the destination). In cloning you first set the clone source image and then you work in the destination image (which can be the same as the clone source image or, as in the examples in this session, can be a different image). The cloning brush variants let you filter the source imagery, basing their color on the source rather than the regular color picker. One of the beauties of Painter is that you can easily turn any brush that paints color into a cloner just by clicking the Clone Color box in the Colors palette. This means there are almost unlimited ways you can transform photographic imagery into a natural media painting.

7.2 Instructor Notes

If you are making a short presentation that covers the basics to students who are new to Painter, then Part 1 of this session is the simplest and quickest way to show how easily and effectively Painter can be applied to a photograph.

I have found that many people are initially timid about applying brushes and altering their photographs, especially when they are concerned about (1) not being an "artist" and (2) ruining their photographs or producing something that is too wild for their client's taste. I start off my courses for professional wedding and portrait photographers by reassuring them that everyone is an artist and that it's safe and okay for them to be bold and daring, because they always have the safety net of cloning back to their original images ("erase to save").

If there is any component of your course devoted to detail-oriented photoretouching, I recommend completing that first and then doing the free-form self-portrait exercise (Part 2 of this session) to loosen your students up and wean them away from being timid and attached to pure photographic representation. On the first day of class, students will take digital photographs of each other. These are downloaded to a computer and distributed among the class on a CD. Occasionally students have found it difficult working on an image of themselves, because they've felt reticent to "ruin" their own images. In such cases I always encourage them to persevere. The freedom that students experience in this self-portrait exercise reflects in their bolder and more confident use of paint in more conservative and conventional photo-transformations. My experience with the self-portrait exercise has been that almost every student lets go of the photograph and ends up creating the most wonderful painting!

Part 3 offers more involved techniques directly relevant to photographers and follows on naturally after the loosening up exercise.

Part 1: Simple Oil and Watercolor Techniques

The simple approaches described here use only standard default palettes and brushes (from the default Painter Brushes library). You will find all the same brushes in my custom library if you have already installed that. There is minimal explanation of the steps. My intention is to provide you with a basic step-by-step formula you can follow quickly and easily.

7.3 Oil Interpretation

Works well with mid- to low-key images where there are rich, dense, saturated colors and deep tones.

Starting Off: Making a Clone Copy

1. Open the project file kelley.jpg in Painter. You will find this file in the Painter Creativity Companion CD > Creativity Projects > Photography I > 7.3 Oil project folder. This is a senior portrait by Gisele Bonds.
2. Arrange the palettes as you see here (Figure 7.1).
3. Choose File > Clone. This makes a clone copy, or duplicate, of the original photo.
4. Choose Cmd/Ctrl-M (Window > Screen Mode Toggle). This mounts the clone copy and simplifies your desktop.

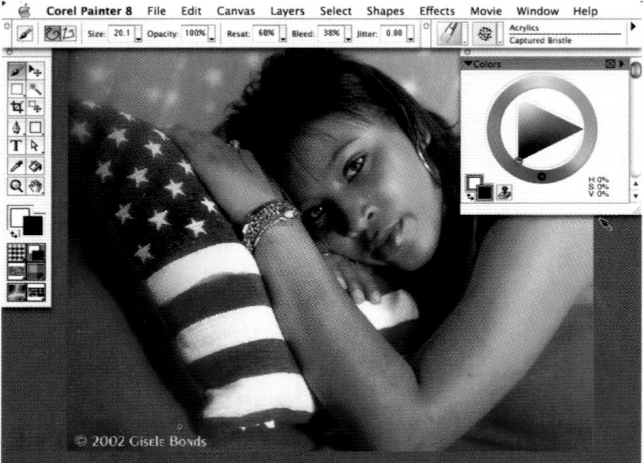

Figure 7.1 Simple palette layout.

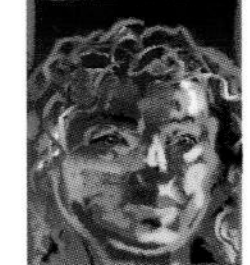

Oily Brush Strokes: Captured Bristle (Acrylics)

1. Choose the Captured Bristle variant in the Acrylics category of the Brush Selector.
2. Check the Clone Color box in the Colors palette. Checking this box turns almost any brush in Painter into a cloner brush.
3. Hold down the space bar and click and drag your image so it is repositioned with the American flag centrally on your screen.
4. Lower the opacity slider in the brushes Property Bar from 100 percent to about 50 percent.
5. Make short brush strokes along the direction of the thread and pattern in the flag (Figure 7.2). Adjust the brush size in the brushes Property Bar to suit the scale of the feature in which you are painting. For instance, on the stars I used a brush size as small as about 5, while on the stripes I increased the brush size to about 23.
6. Continue this process in the rest of the background.
7. Lower the brush opacity to about 20 percent.

Continued

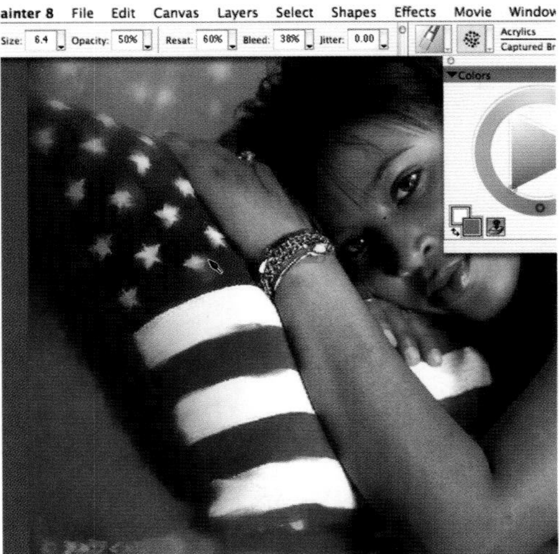

Figure 7.2 Adding brush strokes to the background.

8. Work into the hair (Figure 7.3), following the direction of the hairs with your brush strokes. Use the brush strokes to gently tease the hair out and add a painterly feel to it. As before, adjust the brush size to suit the scale of the features you are painting over.
9. Lower the brush opacity to about 10 percent.
10. Brush very lightly over the skin (Figure 7.4), following the contours of the hands, arms, shoulders, and face. Imagine you are sculpting the form with your brush strokes. The skin takes on a smooth, silky appearance. You can think of this stage as equivalent in the world of cosmetics to putting on a subtle foundation. Use a small brush size and short brush strokes on the lips and in the eyes.

Bringing Back Original: Soft Cloner (Cloners)

1. Any time you wish to bring back some of the original photo, just choose the Soft Cloner variant from the Cloners category. You may find this useful for the eyes and lips to bring back some of the original shine.
2. Adjust the brush size to suit the area you wish to apply the brush to.
3. Apply the Soft Cloner very lightly, gently bringing back the original photo. This tool gives you complete flexibility and freedom since you can always return any region of the image back to its original state.

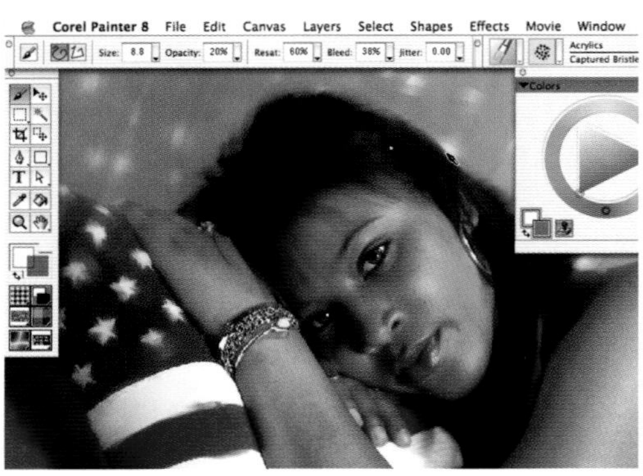

Figure 7.3 Adding brush strokes to the hair.

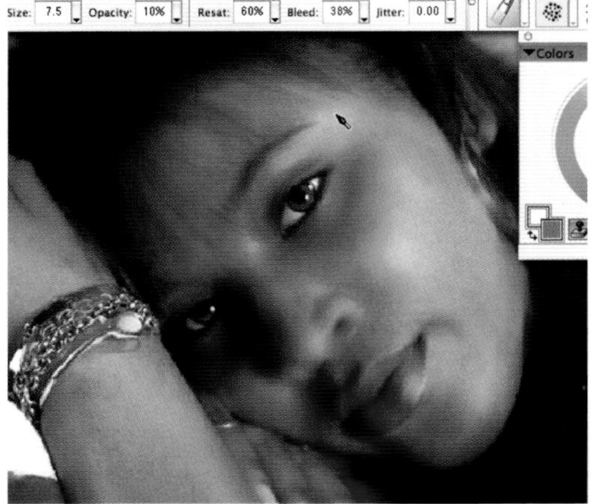

Figure 7.4 Light brush strokes over the skin.

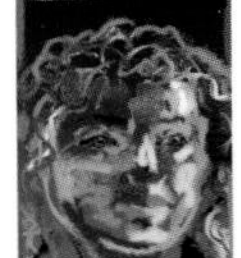

Adding Color, Contrast, and Detail

The goal here is to bring out the key features, particularly the eyes, and enhance the beauty of your subject. Although the details here apply to a female subject, similar basic principles can be applied to a male subject.

1. Choose the Captured Bristle variant in the Acrylics category.
2. Uncheck Clone Color in the Colors palette.
3. Reduce the brush opacity to about 2 percent.
4. Hold the Option/Alt key down, which changes the brush tool into a Dropper tool, and click in the image just below the outer part (i.e., the part closer to the ear) of Kelley's left eyebrow to sample the color there.
5. Reposition the Saturation-Value triangle cursor toward the upper right to lighten the tone.
6. Gently brush on the lighter color immediately below the outer part of the brow with strokes that follow the direction of the brow. This creates a subtle brow bone highlight (Figure 7.5). You may wish to zoom in on the eye at this stage (Cmd/Ctrl-+ or Window > Zoom In).
7. Hold the Option/Alt key down and click in the iris to sample the iris color.

Continued

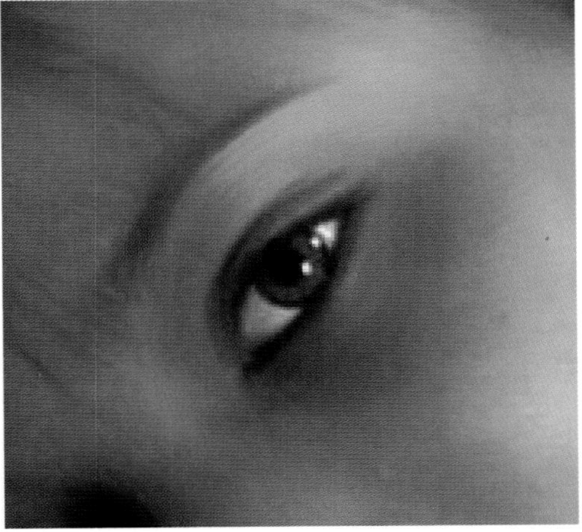

Figure 7.5 Subtle brow bone highlight.

8. Drag the Hue Ring cursor in the Color Picker to the opposite side of the Hue Ring. This automatically gives you the complementary color. Green eyes look good with purples and reds; blue eyes with pinks, browns, and blues; and brown eyes with greens, purples, and light colors. Jewel tones (blues, purples, greens, and burgundy) go well with darker skins.
9. Slightly lighten the color (move the Saturation-Value triangle cursor to the upper right).
10. Apply this color very lightly to the outer part of the eyelid just above the eyelashes (Figure 7.6).
11. Hold the Option/Alt key down and click in a mid-tone region of the lips to sample the lip color.
12. Slightly lighten the color (move the Saturation-Value triangle cursor to the upper right).
13. Apply this color very lightly to the inner part of the eyelid, over the crease (Figure 7.7).

Continued

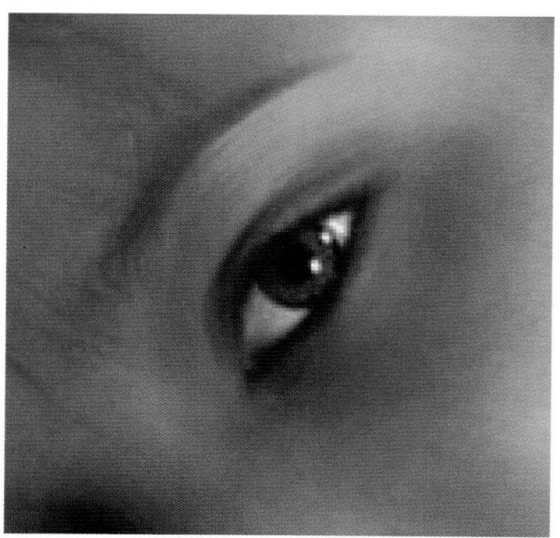

Figure 7.6 Contrasting outer eyelid color.

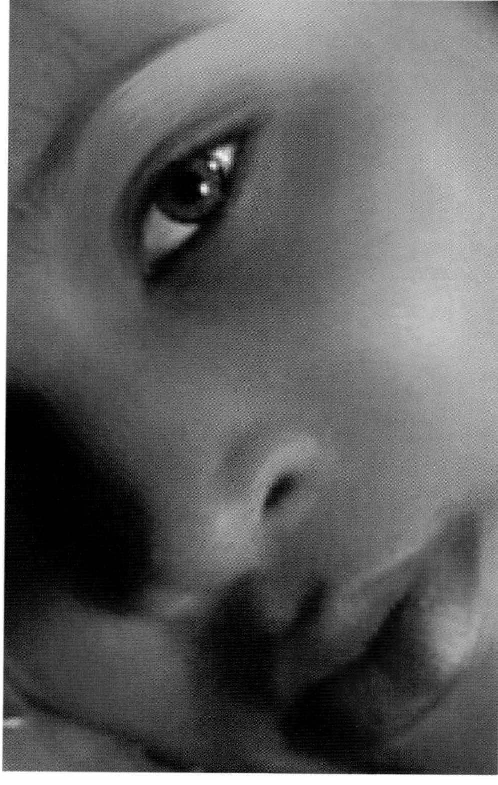

Figure 7.7 Inner eyelid color mirroring lip color.

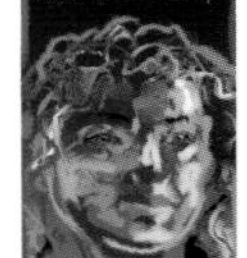

14 Choose the Digital Airbrush variant in the Airbrushes category.

15 Reduce the brush size to minimum.

16 Hold the Option/Alt key down and click in the eyelash region to sample the eyelash color.

17 With gentle "c" strokes add to and emphasize the outer eyelashes (Figure 7.8).

You can continue this process of selectively adding color (such as blush to the cheeks), enhancing contrasts, emphasizing highlights, and adding to detail.

Softening Skin: Just Add Water (Blenders)

1 Choose the Just Add Water variant from the Blenders category.

2 Reduce the brush opacity to about 10 percent.

3 Lightly apply the Just Add Water brush to the skin areas, gently blending in colors and smoothing the skin surface into a porcelain-like finish (Figure 7.9). Make brush strokes that follow the contours of the form, as before, and adjust the brush size to suit the features you are painting over.

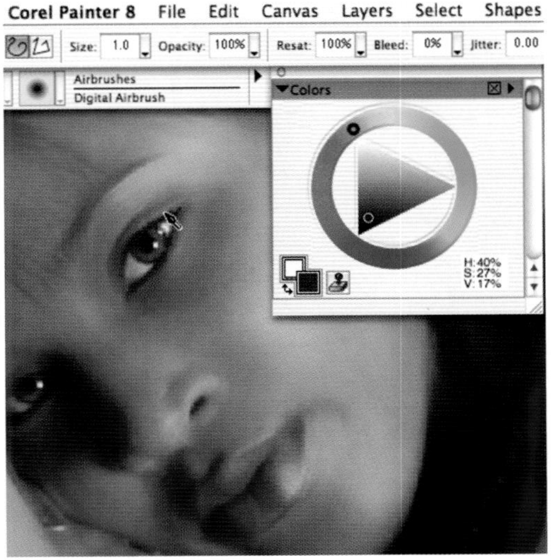

Figure 7.8 Emphasizing eyelashes.

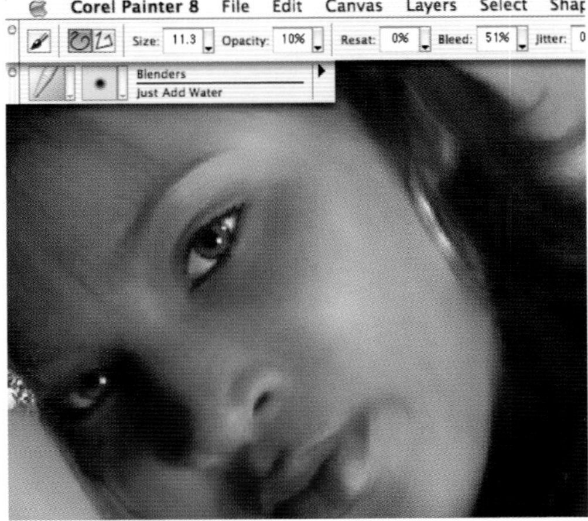

Figure 7.9 Smooth porcelain skin.

Adding Artistic Edge: Blunt Soft Pastel 40 (Pastels) and Captured Bristle (Arylics)

1. Choose the Blunt Soft Pastel 40 variant in the Pastels category.
2. Choose white in the Color Picker.
3. Choose the Basic Paper texture in the Papers selector in Tools palette.
4. Choose Cmd/Ctrl-A (Select > All).
5. Choose Select > Stroke Selection. The brush is automatically applied in a single stroke around the perimeter of the image, thereby creating an instant border (Figure 7.10).
6. Choose the Captured Bristle variant (Acrylics category).
7. Ensure that Clone Color is checked in the Colors palette.
8. Make short brush strokes along the edge of the picture to create a rough painterly edge effect (Figure 7.11). Vary the size and direction of the brush strokes according to the feature that is bleeding into the edge.
9. Choose File > Save As. Rename the file kelley-oil.rif and save this file as a RIFF file in your project folder.

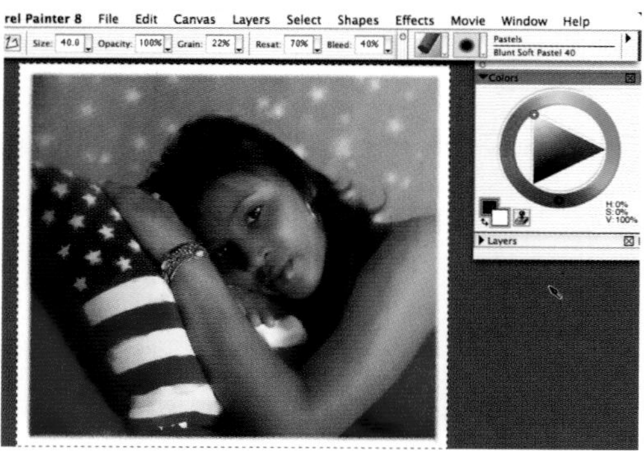

Figure 7.10 Rough edge added using stroke selection.

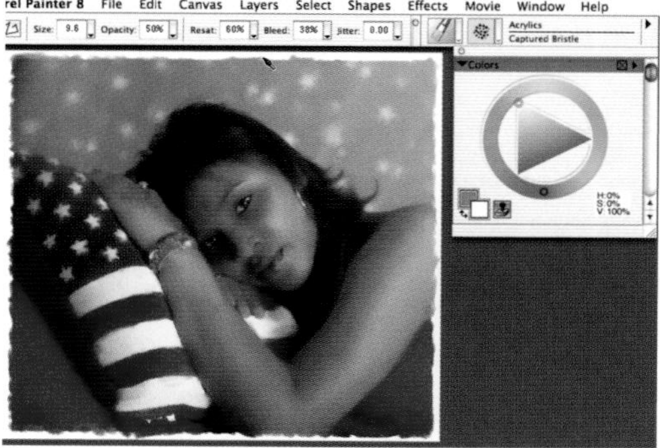

Figure 7.11 Roughening the edge with Captured Bristle cloner.

7.4 Watercolor Interpretation

Works well with mid- to high-key images where there are soft contrasts and light tones.

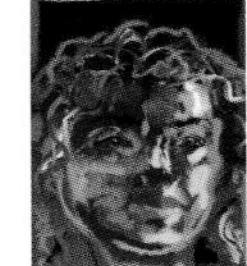

Starting Off: Making a Clone Copy

1. Open the project file bailey.jpg in Painter. You will find this file in the Photography I > 7.4 Watercolor project folder. This is a child fantasy portrait by Laura Ruppersberger.
2. Choose File > Clone.
3. Choose Cmd/Ctrl-M (Window > Screen Mode Toggle).
4. Arrange your palettes as shown here (Figure 7.12).

Clearing the Clone Copy: Using Tracing Paper

1. Choose Cmd/Ctrl-A (Select > All).
2. Choose Delete/Backspace. This clears the canvas.
3. Choose Cmd/Ctrl-T (Canvas > Tracing Paper). This toggles the Tracing Paper on and off. When Tracing Paper is on, you see a 50 percent opacity representation of the original clone source image superimposed over a 50 percent opacity representation of the clone copy image. Note where the child's face is.
4. Choose Cmd/Ctrl-T (Canvas > Tracing Paper) again. This turned the Tracing Paper off, so you just see a blank white canvas.

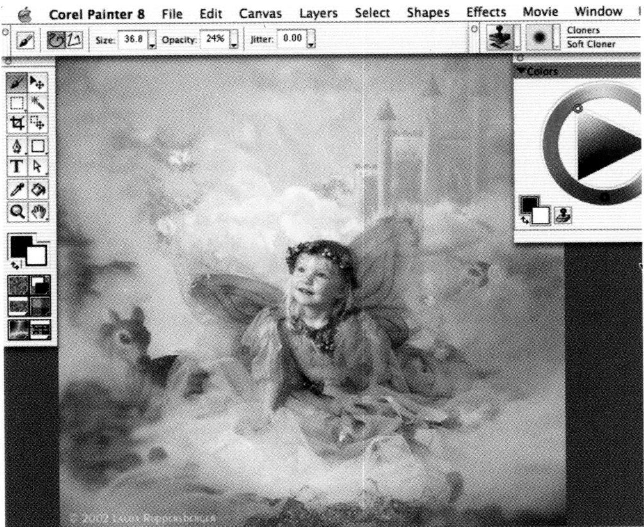

Figure 7.12 Palette arrangement.

Easy Vignette: Soft Cloner (Cloners)

1. Choose the Soft Cloner variant in the Cloners category.
2. Lightly brush in the little girl, working out from her face (Figure 7.13).
3. If you overextend with the Soft Cloner, choose the Digital Airbrush variant in the Airbrushes category.
4. Select white in the Color Picker.
5. Make the opacity about 17 percent.
6. Adjust the brush size to suit. Lightly brush back in white over the image (Figure 7.14).

Blending Colors and Adding Watery Edges: Just Add Water (Blenders)

1. Choose the Just Add Water variant in the Blenders category.
2. Reduce the opacity slider to about 23 percent.
3. Lightly apply the Just Add Water variant throughout the background and the clothing (Figure 7.15). Use the brush to blend the edges into the white canvas to give a watercolor effect.

Continued

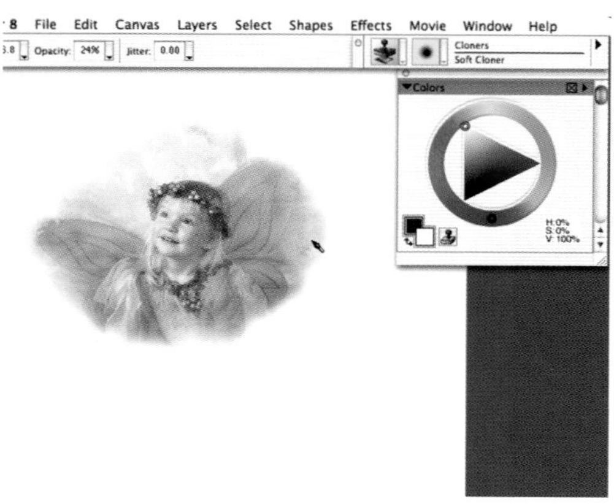

Figure 7.13 Soft cloner vignette.

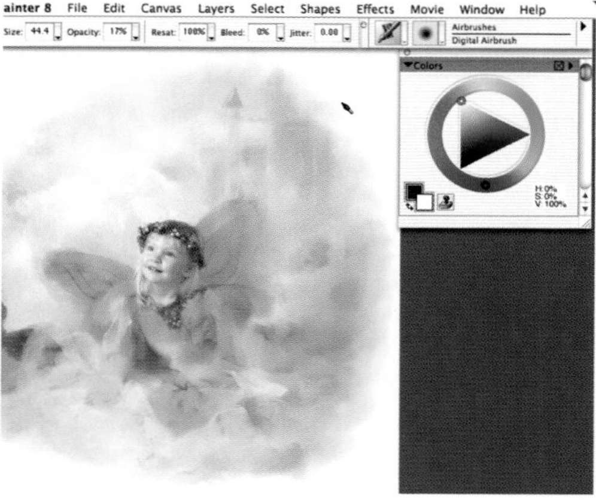

Figure 7.14 Airbrushing white back in to fine-tune edge.

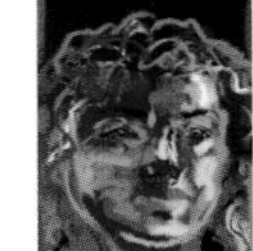

4. Choose Cmd/Ctrl-+ (Window > Zoom In) to zoom in on the face.
5. Use light, small, low-opacity Just Add Water brush strokes over the face, following the contours of the face, until the skin has a luminescent porcelain quality.

Adding Color, Contrast, and Detail

1. Choose the Digital Airbrush variant (Airbrushes category).
2. Choose Option/Alt and click in the iris.
3. Lighten the color in the Saturation-Value triangle.
4. Adjust the brush diameter to approximately the radius of the iris.
5. Lower the brush opacity down to about 8 percent.
6. Gently brush in the lightened color over the right side of the iris.
7. Repeat this step for the left side with slightly darker tonal value and different hue.
8. Continue working into the pupils and catchlights. In the example shown here (Figure 7.16), the pupils were slightly enlarged and the catchlights shifted to the upper right.

Continued

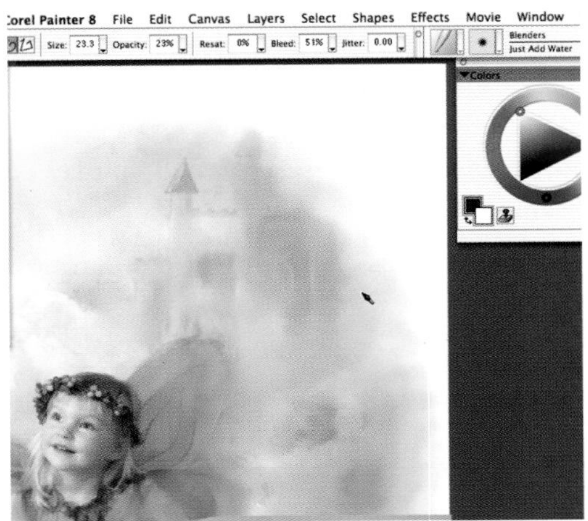

Figure 7.15 Blending colors with the Just Add Water.

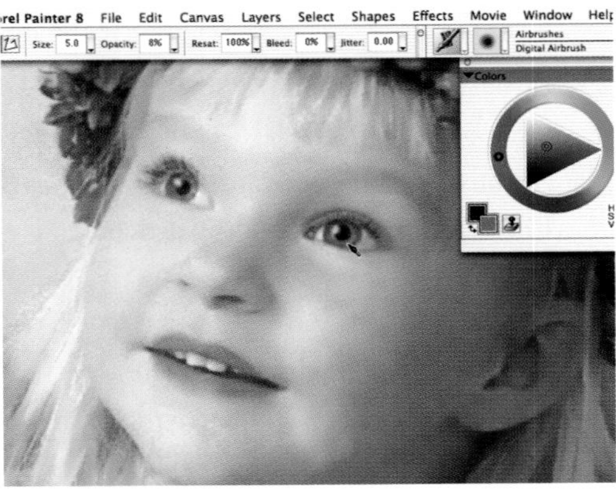

Figure 7.16 Enhancing the face and eyes.

9 This process of adding color, contrast, and detail can be continued in bringing out emphasis to the eyelashes, warmth to the cheeks, and color to the lips. You can see the overall result here (Figure 7.17).

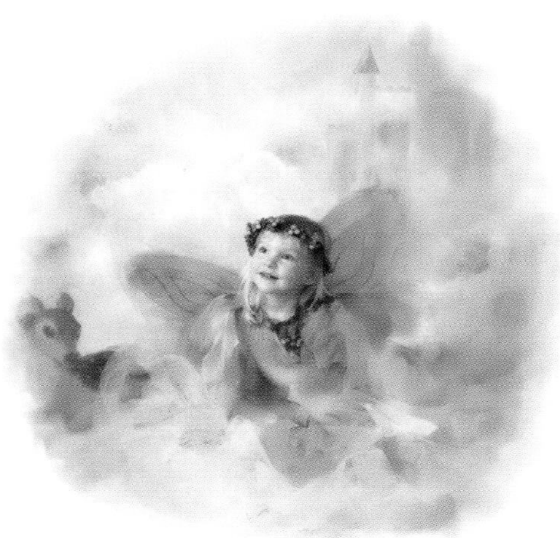

Figure 7.17 The final watercolor painting.

Part 2: Basics and Loosening Up

7.5 Golden Rules

Here are three golden rules for working with photographs in Painter:

1. *Always work on a copy.* Whenever you are working from photographs in Painter, *always* work on a clone copy; *never* work on an original image.
2. *Always rename the file right away.* Always *immediately* rename your clone copies and your layers. Give them meaningful, organized, and consistent names.
3. *Always save sequentially numbered versions.* Always save versions of your work in progress as RIFF files, especially prior to dropping layers.

7.6 Setting Up a Clone Copy

The following steps outline the standard procedure for working from a photograph and embody the golden rule of always working from a clone copy. These steps also prepare you for the first project of this session, the free-form self-portrait.

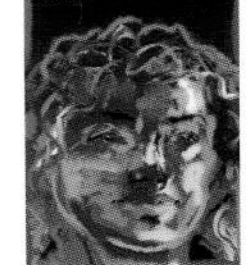

1. Open a photograph of yourself. This image will be your original image for this exercise. You can also follow these project instructions using any choice of photograph as an original image.
2. Choose Cmd/Ctrl-M. This places the image in screen mode.
3. Set up a palette arrangement as shown here (Figure 7.18).
4. Choose Window > Arrange Palettes > Save Layout.
5. Name the palette arrangement Photo.
6. Choose OK in the Palette Layout window. Your Photo palette layout is now saved for convenient future use (accessed at any time through the Window > Arrange Palettes menu).
7. Choose File > Clone. This generates a duplicate of the original image.
8. Choose File > Save As.
9. Rename your file *yourname-self-portrait-01.rif*. You could use the reverse date notation (YY-MM-DD) at the beginning of the file name if you wish. so all your files line up chronologically by name. It is important to get rid of the "Clone of . . . " default file name (or you end up with numerous confusing "clone of clone of . . . " file names!)
10. Save the renamed clone copy image (which will be your working file) as a RIFF format image.
11. Choose Cmd/Ctrl-M. This places the image in screen mode.

Continued

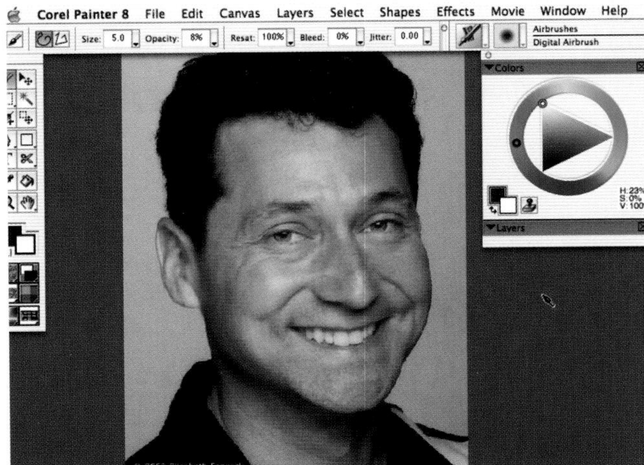

Figure 7.18 Basic palette layout for transforming a photograph.

12 Repeatedly click Cmd/Ctrl-"–" to zoom out until you can see your entire image unobscured by palettes. If your image is much larger than your screen, you can also choose "m" on the keyboard, which is the shortcut for the Magnifier tool, and use the Zoom Level pop-up menu in the Controls:Magnifier palette to drastically zoom out in one step. If needed, hold down the space bar and drag on your image with your cursor to reposition your image for convenience.

The simple procedure, described previously, of generating and renaming a clone copy, will be repeated again and again whenever you are working from photographs.

7.7 Free-form Self-portrait

This free-form self-portrait exercise is designed to give you the freedom to be wild and explore. Don't be timid! Whatever you do here can always be cloned back toward the original photo, so don't hold back. Make sure you fill the entire canvas with paint, and remember to have fun!

1 Make sure you have an original photographic image and a clone copy duplicate of that image open in Painter (see previous section). Your clone source should automatically be set to your original image. You can double-check this by viewing the File > Clone Source pop-up menu and ensuring there is a check mark by the original file name.

2 With the clone copy image active and in screen mode, choose a color in the Color Picker to use as a canvas background color for your self-portrait.

3 Choose Cmd/Ctrl-F (Edit > Fill). You should see Fill With: Current Color checked.

4 Choose OK.

5 Choose Cmd/Ctrl-T (Canvas > Tracing Paper). This turns on the Tracing Paper function in Painter, which shows a 50 percent opacity representation of the clone source image superimposed over a 50 percent opacity representation of the current active image, provided both images are exactly the same pixel size (which they are automatically when you create a clone copy). Holding the Cmd/Ctrl key down, click a few times on the "T" key so you can see the Tracing Paper toggled on and off.

Continued

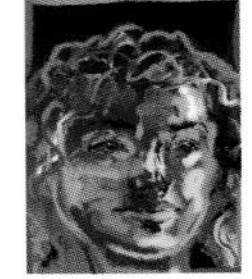

If you are going to record a script of your painting process, this is the time to set the recorder going. Please refer to the previous session for details on recording and playing back scripts in Painter. One advantage of recording what you paint, besides the fun of watching your painting play back, is that the script will record all the brushes you use and allow you to conveniently find out exactly what you used at every stage.

6 Starting off with Tracing Paper turned on, use any brushes, with or without clone color, to build up a painting based on your photo portrait. Fill the whole canvas with paint. Intermittently turn off Tracing Paper so you can see what is really on your canvas. You can see in this example (Figure 7.19) how Tracing Paper hides what's really happening in your image.

As the painting progresses, turn off Tracing Paper and allow yourself to break free from relying on the original photo. Remember to use your Save As button regularly and save sequential versions of your image. If you are recording a script, remember to back up all your saved versions prior to replaying the script. Also make sure you save a final version outside the script (i.e., after stopping the recorder and after naming the script).

7 Spend at least an hour on this project. Make use of different brushes. If you find yourself staying safe and not wanting to depart from the original photo, just try to be wild! Remember you can always bring the painting back to the original photo at any time just by using the Soft Cloner variant in the Cloners brush category.

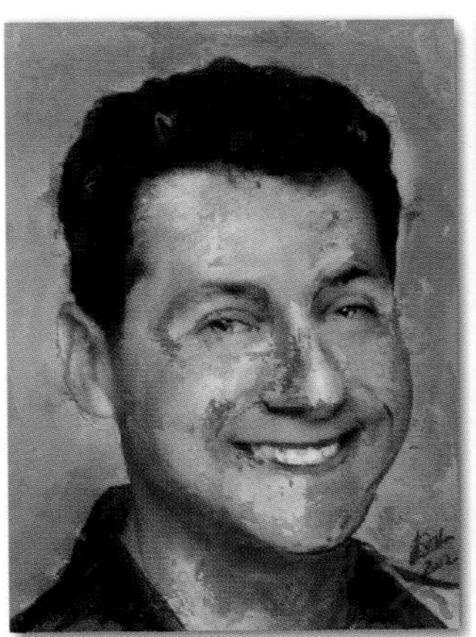

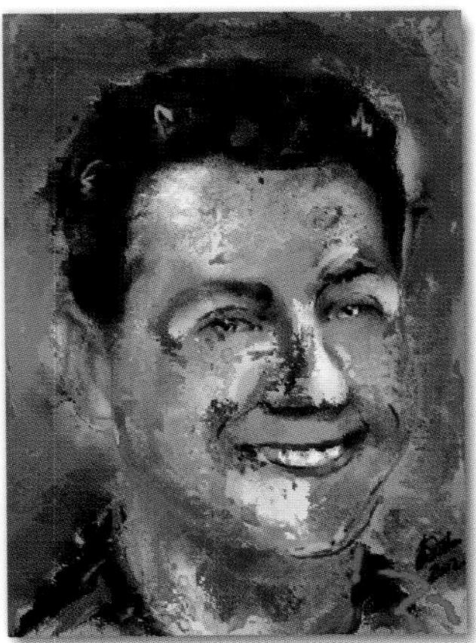

Figure 7.19 What you see with Tracing Paper turned on (*left*) and turned off (*right*).

Questions

1. What did you feel about your resulting self-portrait?
2. How did you feel about letting go of relying on the original photo?

Here are some examples of source photos and final self-portraits from a few of my students (Figures 7.20 to 7.23).

You can see here how Marge made a painting that, while being very colorful, was initially kept fairly close to the original photo in terms of composition (second stage shown in the upper right corner). By the third stage shown here (lower left corner), she was completely transforming the portrait into something looser and more playful and imaginary. It is inspiring to see the creative transformations in this image. I encourage you to push beyond the literal with this exercise. Allow yourself the freedom to go wild, to explore beyond the confines of the photograph.

It was wonderful watching Giselle's portrait develop and seeing the way she really got into this project. Notice the way your attention is drawn to the eye by use of sharper contrast and greater detail.

Lorne succeeded in being very loose and expressive in his brush strokes. The empty space at the top and the bottom of his canvas indicates that he may have inadvertently had the top and the

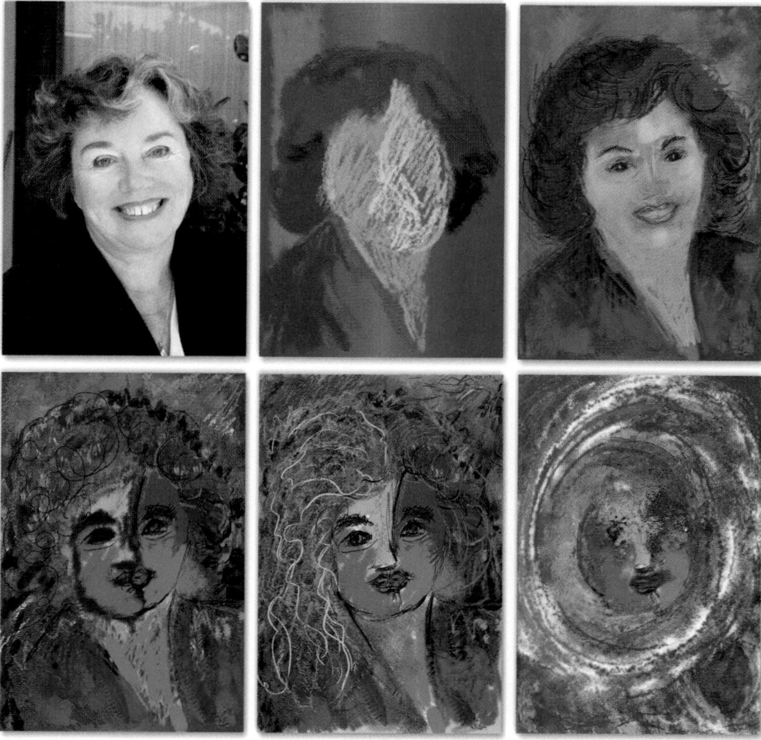

Figure 7.20 Marge's original photo and five stages of her self-portrait.

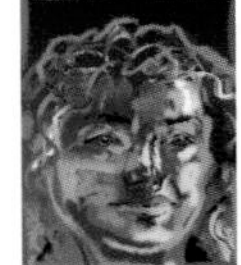

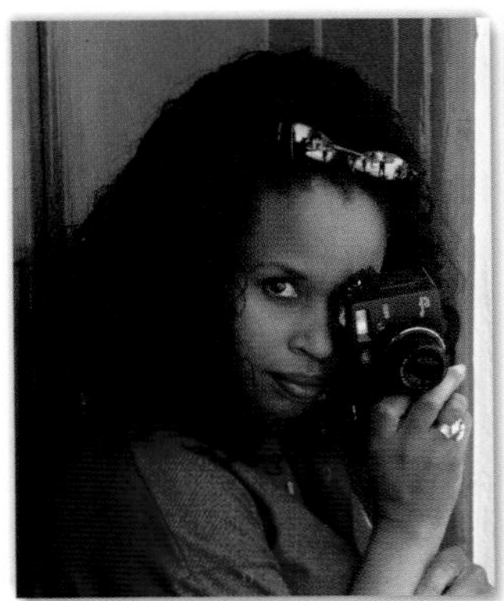
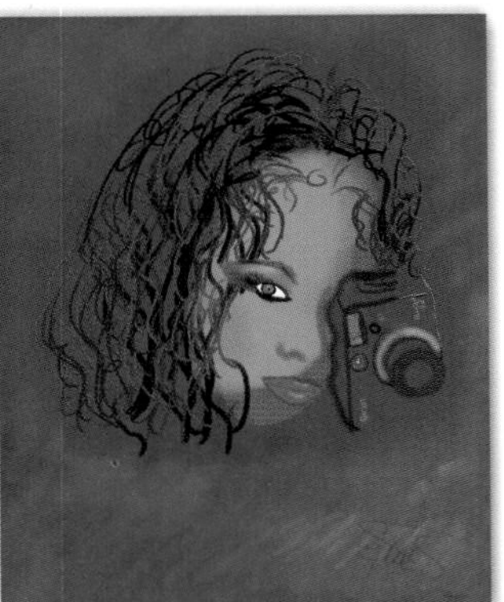

Figure 7.21 Giselle's original photo and self-portrait.

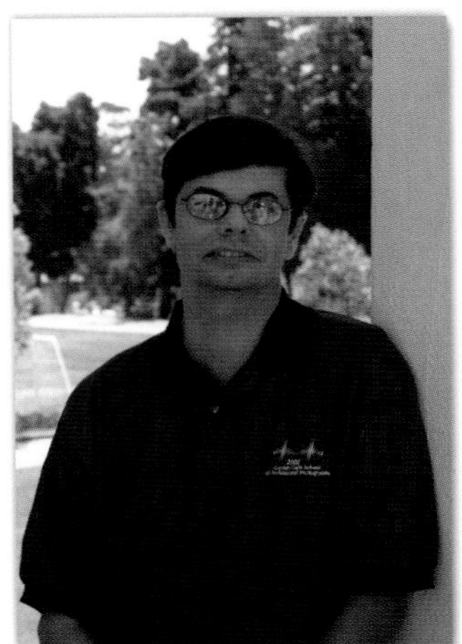
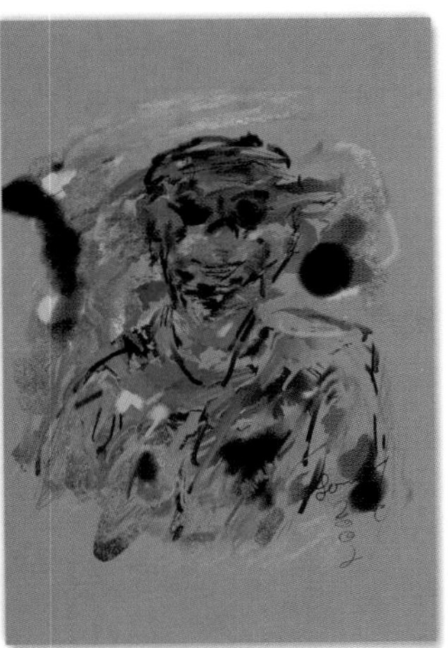

Figure 7.22 Lorne's original photo and self-portrait.

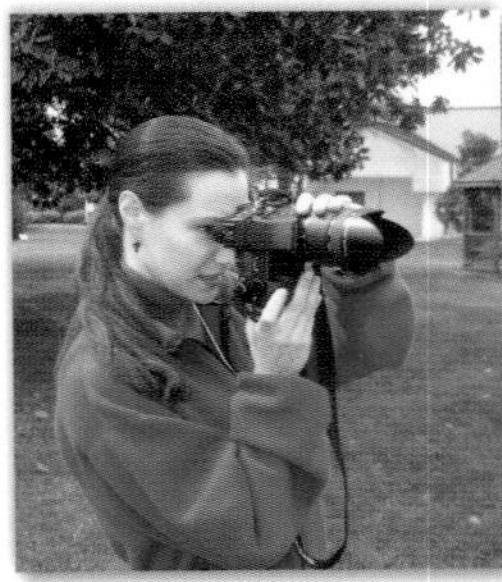
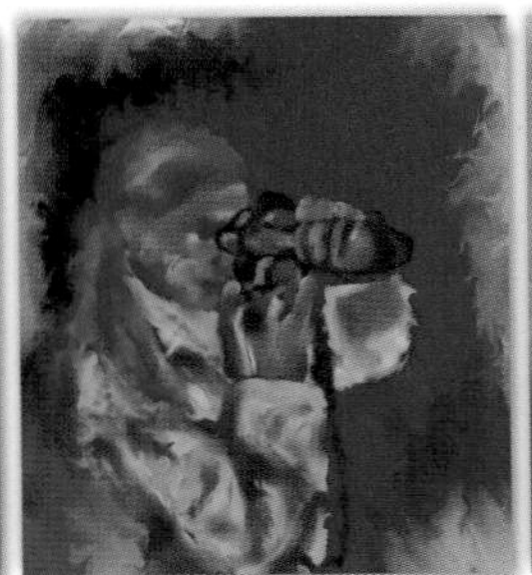
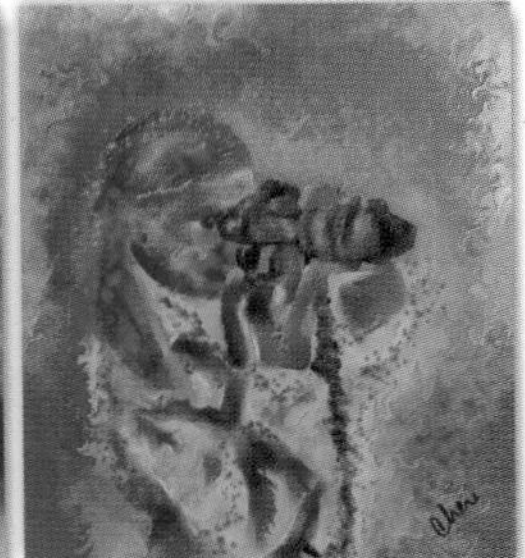

Figure 7.23 Cheri's original photo and self-portrait.

bottom of the canvas off the screen. It is always useful to zoom out (or use the Window > Zoom to Fit menu command) intermittently to see what your overall composition looks like. I encourage you to fill the whole canvas with paint in this exercise.

Cheri did a great job experimenting with color and texture in this project. Push yourself to create a work you would not normally create. This exercise is an excuse to explore new creative territory.

Part 3: Rough Out, Pump Up, Smooth Over

The basic process described in this part of the session for turning a portrait photograph into a classic photo painting is based on Jane Conner-ziser's methodology (see her essay at the end of this session). The process, in a nutshell, is:

1. *Rough out* the background and work on the border look. Several options are considered, including a soft vignette and a more painterly edge.
2. *Pump up* the contrast and saturation of the highlights and shadows and selectively enhance details, working from the background into clothing, followed by the hair, followed by the skin, followed by the eyes. Most detailing is left to the regions you wish to draw most attention to, such as the eyes.
3. *Smooth over* the skin and add final touches.

The techniques described here, some of which overlap with retouching techniques, can be applied very subtly, leaving the photographic integrity and realism of the picture intact, or could be applied more boldly, transforming the photograph into a more natural media hand-painted look.

As a last step, you can add final touches such as texture, more brushwork, and edge enhancement. Of course, you can do these actions in any order you choose. I suggest you first follow the step-by-step instructions and then, as you work on your own projects, develop your own personal preferred methodology. You may find that you like to work into the shadows before the highlights, or do the eyes first, or the background last. You may also find that, if you're used to working with Photoshop, you may find the highlight and shadow adjustments most easily done in that program. There are no right and wrong ways, only what works best for you.

7.8 Backgrounds and Borders

Vignette: Soft Background Fade

In this project you will create a simple photographic vignette that fades off gradually into the background canvas.

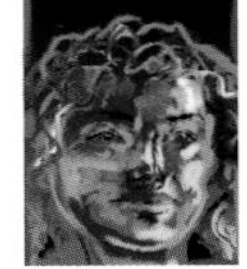

1. Open Painter afresh. If Painter is already open, quit out of Painter and reopen it. It is important to always start Painter afresh whenever you are starting on a new project.
2. Open the project file Elizabeth.jpg which you will find in the Creativity Projects > 7-Photography I > 7-6 to 7-11 Watercolor & Chalk folder on the Painter Creativity Companion CD. This is a photograph of Jane Conner-ziser's daughter, Elizabeth, taken by Eddie Tapp. This image will be your original image for this exercise. You can also follow the project instructions using your own choice of photograph as an original image.
3. Choose Window > Arrange Palettes > Photo (Figure 7.24). This resets the palette arrangement to be the same as shown earlier in this session.
4. Choose File > Clone. This generates a duplicate of the original image.
5. Choose Cmd/Ctrl-A (Select > All).
6. Choose Delete/Backspace. This clears the canvas to the default paper color, which should be white. (If it clears your canvas to a color other than white, then select white in the Colors palette and choose Canvas > Set Paper Color).
7. Choose Cmd/Ctrl-D (Select > None).
8. Choose File > Save As.

Continued

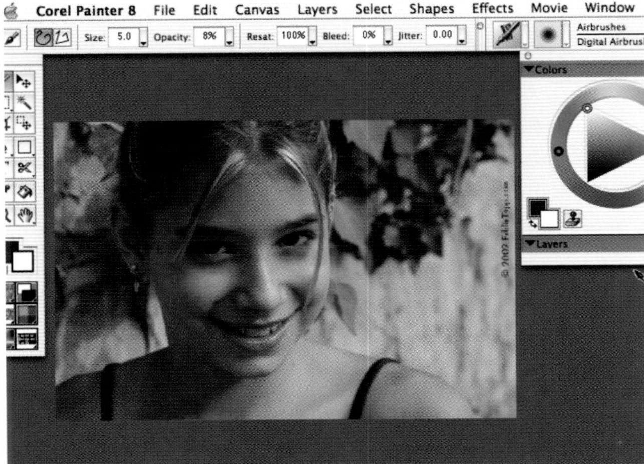

Figure 7.24 Basic palette layout for transforming a photograph.

9. Rename your file with reverse date, main subject, version number, keyword, and format tag (e.g., 03-07-25elzbth-01-vignette.rif). The keyword follows the version number as a convenient reminder to you of what was in that version. These keywords are useful when you're looking back through a large number of versions to find one particular stage.
10. Save the newly renamed clone copy image into the appropriate project folder.
11. Choose Cmd/Ctrl-M. This places the image in screen mode.
12. Hold the space bar down on your keyboard while you click and drag your canvas into a convenient position on the screen.
13. Choose Cmd/Ctrl-T (Canvas > Tracing Paper). This turns on the Tracing Paper (see above). You will see a 50 percent opacity representation of the clone source image (Elizabeth.jpg). Holding the Cmd/Ctrl key down and clicking on the "T" key toggles Tracing Paper on and off. Leave the Tracing Paper turned on.
14. Choose the Soft Cloner variant in the Cloners category of the Brush Selector.
15. Adjust the brush size in the brush Property Bar to about 30 (or a size suitable for the scale and resolution of your image).
16. Reduce the Opacity slider in the Brush Property Bar to about 40 percent.
17. Working your way out from the center of the face, slowly and softly brush into the image. You'll see the image deepen in intensity where you paint (Figure 7.25, upper image).
18. Choose Cmd/Ctrl-T (Canvas > Tracing Paper). This turns the Tracing Paper mode off (Figure 7.25, lower image).
19. Choose Cmd/Ctrl-S (File > Save). This updates your version -01 to be the vignette stage.

This process is a simple, fast way to create a photographic vignette. You can always select white in the Colors section and apply the Digital Airbush (Airbrushes category) to paint back white. For added flexibility you could first create a new layer (New Layer option in pop-up menu accessed by clicking third button from left at bottom of Layers section). You can apply the Soft Cloner on the new layer. The advantage of this approach is that you can adjust the opacity of the whole layer, and paint into its mask to selectively control the opacity of any regions.

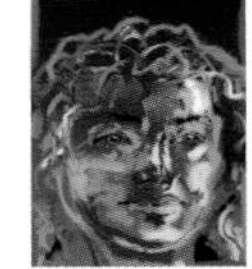

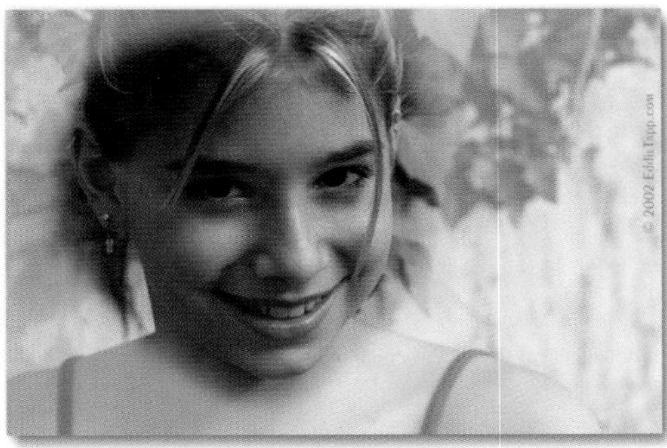

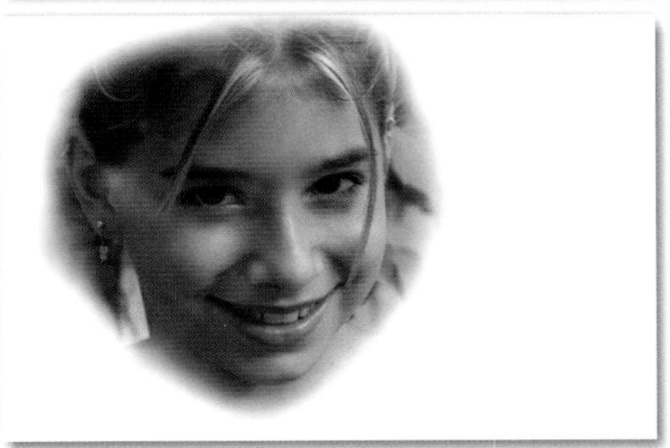

Figure 7.25 Tracing Paper turned on (*upper image*) and off (*lower image*).

Soft, Watery Look

1. Continue working on the same photo vignette you created in the previous project, keeping the original photograph (elizabeth.jpg) open in Painter and defined as clone source (File > Clone Source).
2. Choose the Just Add Water variant (Blenders category) and start blending the edges of your vignette image into the background.
3. Choose the Smear variant (Blenders category) with about 50 percent opacity (adjust Opacity slider in the Controls:Brush palette) and continue working into the background.
4. Choose the Grainy Water variant (Blenders category).
5. Make soft dabs and light brush strokes in the background with Grainy Water to soften and texturize the edges (Figure 7.26).
6. If you go too far with the blending, softening, and texturizing and you wish to bring back to the original photographic image, just choose the Soft Cloner (Cloners category) and gently paint back the photograph.

Continued

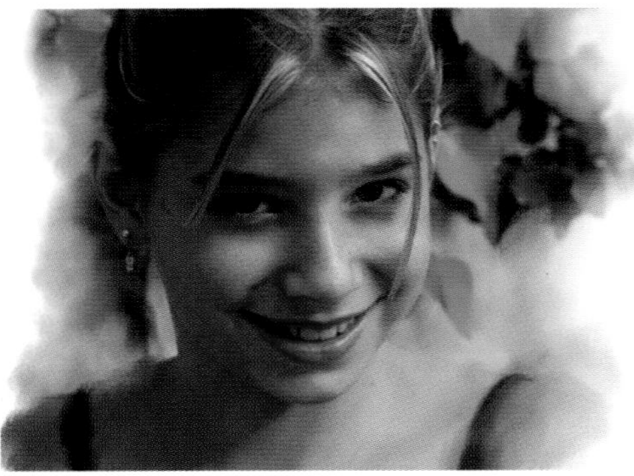

Figure 7.26 Softly blended background and border.

7 If you extend too far out into the white canvas and wish to bring the edge in, or just lighten the edge, then choose the Digital Airbrush variant (Airbrushes category), make it large with low opacity, and gently paint white over the edges.

8 Choose File > Save As.

9 Save your file with the next version number and the keyword wtrbkgnd (e.g., elzbth-02-wtrbkgnd.rif).

Thus using the combination of the Soft Cloner, the Blenders brushes (Just Add Water, Smear, and Grainy Water) and the Digital Airbrush, you can exert complete control over the quality and feel of your background and edges.

Wilder, Rougher Look

1 Open your vignette image (elzbth-01-vignette.rif). This is the file you will be painting on. It should be the active image in Painter.

2 Make sure the original photograph (elizabeth.jpg) is also open in Painter (check by looking at the bottom of the Windows menu) and defined as clone source (check by looking at File > Clone Source).

3 Choose the Sargent variant (Artists category) or the Oil Pencil variant (Graphic Design category in the Creativity Brushes custom brush library contained on the Painter Creativity Companion CD).

Continued

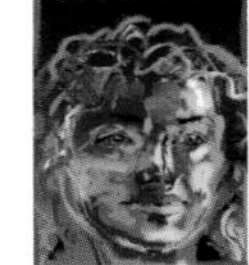

4 Check the Clone Color checkbox in the Colors palette.

5 Apply brisk, loose, gestural brush strokes in your image. Don't worry about obscuring the face. Where possible, apply your brush strokes in a direction that matches the underlying form (turn Tracing Paper on using Cmd/Ctrl-T if you need to reference the original image).

6 Select the Soft Cloner variant (Cloners category) and brush back in the face and hair (Figure 7.27).

7 Choose File > Save As.

8 Save your file with the next version number and the keyword wildbkgnd (e.g., elzbth-03-wildbkgnd.rif).

The Instant Artistic Border

1 Open the project file Elizabeth.jpg.

2 Choose Cmd/Ctrl-M.

3 Choose File > Clone. This generates a duplicate of the original image.

4 Choose File > Save As.

5 Rename your file with reverse date, main subject, version number, keyword and format tag (e.g., 03-07-25elzbth-04-instntborder.rif).

6 Save the renamed clone copy image into the appropriate project folder.

7 Choose Cmd/Ctrl-M (mount image in screen mode).

Continued

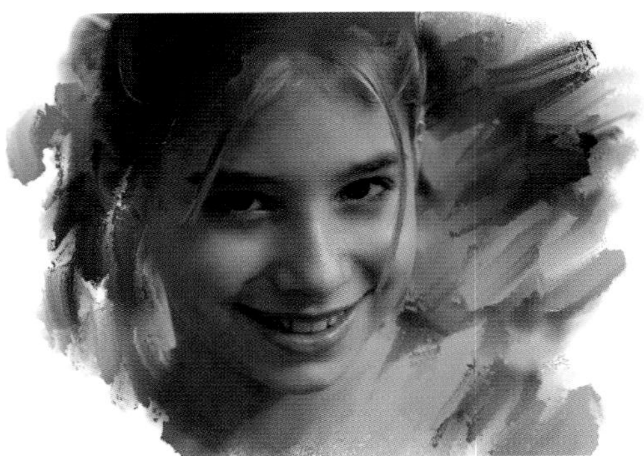

Figure 7.27 Looser, wilder background and border.

8. Choose Window > Zoom to Fit so you can see the complete edge of the image. (I recommend adding a Zoom to Fit button to your custom Shortcuts palette.)
9. Choose the Artist Pastel Chalk (Pastels category). There are some good alternatives to this in my Creativity Brushes library contained on the companion CD such as Oil Pencil variant (Graphic Design category) or Oil Funky Chunky (Den's Oil Brushes).
10. Select white in the Color picker. Make sure the opacity is set at 100 percent (see the Opacity slider in the Controls:Brush palette).
11. Make test marks in your image, adjusting the brush size, until you make a mark that is the right thickness to act as a good border. Undo (Cmd/Ctrl-Z) after making each test mark.
12. Choose Cmd/Ctrl-A (Select All).
13. Choose Select > Stroke Selection. You will now see your instant artistic border magically appear (Figure 7.28). Voila!
14. Choose Cmd/Ctrl-S (File > Save).

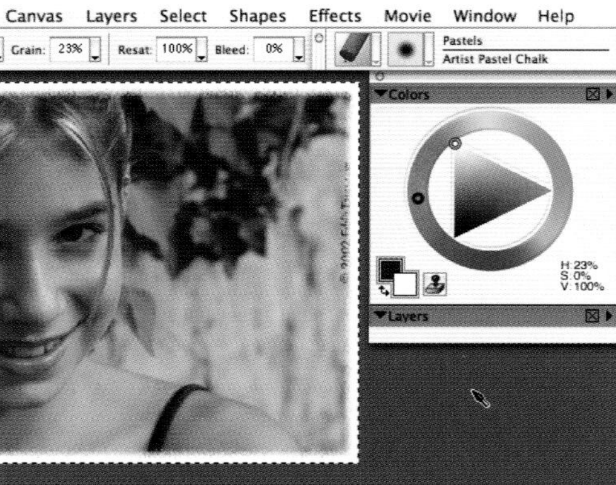

Figure 7.28 Instant Oil Pencil border.

All the border techniques discussed here can also be applied as a last step in your image creation process.

7.9 Pumping up Highlights

The following techniques described can be applied either directly onto the clone copy photographic image on the background canvas or onto a separate layer. Painting onto a layer gives you the advantage of being able to conveniently observe the effect of your brush strokes on the underlying

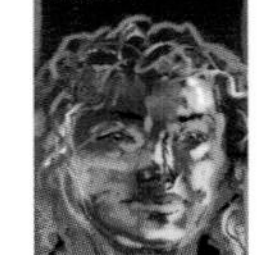

image (by comparing with the layer visibility turned on and off). Layers also give the benefit of being able to scale back the effect of your brush strokes simply by lowering the layer opacity.

The disadvantage of layers is that there's no blending and mixing of your new paint with the color already on the canvas. In this example I create separate layers for each of the highlight and shadow adjustments and for the various eye enhancements (e.g., catchlights, iris, pupil). I recommend having separate layers for the highlight and shadow adjustments to each section of the picture, and for each section of the eye, each with an appropriate descriptive name such as Clothing Highlights, Clothing Shadows, Hair Highlights, Hair Shadows, Skin Highlights, Skin Shadows, Eye: Catchlights, Eye: Iris, and Eye: Pupils. Naming layers in this situation is vitally important. The benefit of breaking down your adjustments into so many layers is the amount of control and editability you have. The difficulty is the room for confusion if you get the layers mixed up (due to not having clear names).

1. Make sure the original photograph (Elizabeth.jpg) is open in Painter (check by looking at the bottom of the Windows menu) and defined as clone source (check by looking at File > Clone Source).
2. Open your file elzbth-02-wtrbkgnd.rif. This is the file you will be painting on. It should be the active image in Painter.
3. Choose File > Save As.
4. Rename this file as elzbth-06-highlts.rif.
5. Choose Cmd/Ctrl-M (Window > Screen Mode Toggle).
6. Select New Layer (Figure 7.29) from the third button from the left in the bottom of the Layers palette. You will see a new layer, called Layer 1, appear in the Layers list.
7. Double-click on Layer 1 in the Layers list. This brings up the Layers Attributes window.
8. Rename Layer 1 as highlights (Figure 7.30).
9. Choose OK.
10. Make sure that the Preserve Transparency checkbox is unchecked. If it is checked, you won't be able to see any paint on that layer.
11. Choose Cmd/Ctrl-"+" and click a few times on the face (while holding down the Cmd/Ctrl-"+" keys). Zoom in until the face and hair fills your screen.
12. Choose the Digital Airbrush variant (Airbrushes category) and make sure the Clone Color is inactive in the Colors palette.

Continued

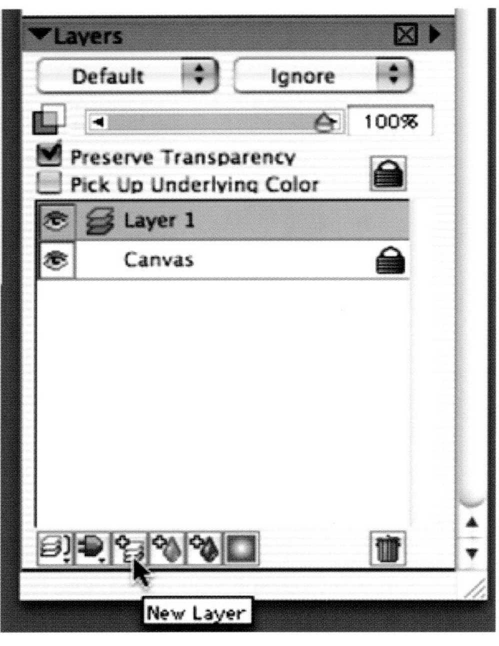

Figure 7.29 New Layer command.

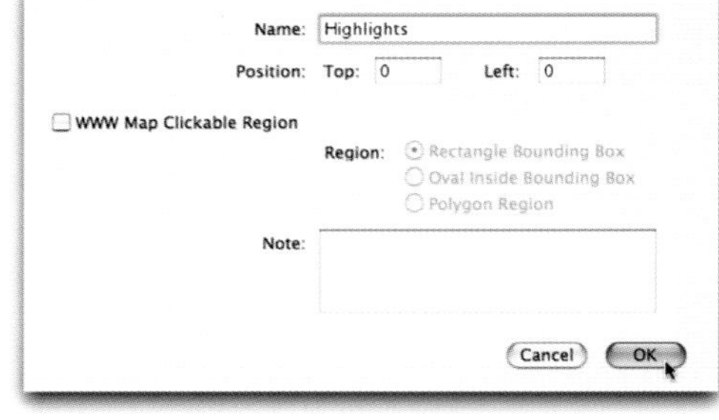

Figure 7.30 Layers Attributes window.

13 Reduce the brush size (Size slider in the Size section of the Brush Controls palette) so that it is comparable with, or slightly smaller than, the level of detail in the highlight regions you are working on. For instance, if we start off working into the highlights in the hair, then a brush size of about 2 seems to work well.

14 Reduce the brush opacity (Opacity slider in the Controls: Brush palette) to about 40 percent.

15 Hold down the Option/Alt key. This turns your Brush tool into a Dropper tool that samples color from wherever you click in the image.

16 Keeping the Option/Alt key held down, click in the highlight on the hair.

17 Release the Option/Alt key.

18 In the Colors palette, move the Saturation Value triangle cursor slightly upward (this lightens) and slightly to the right (this increases the saturation or intensity of the color). The overall effect is to slightly brighten the selected highlight color.

Continued

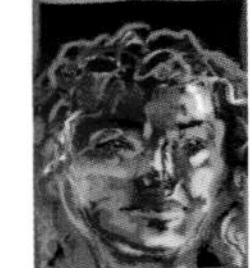

19 Lightly stroke the airbrush along the hair highlight region centered at the place where you sampled the color, with your strokes following the direction of the hair.

20 Make several samplings (followed by brightening adjustments) down the length of the hair as you paint so your color varies along the length of the hair.

21 Choose Cmd/Ctrl-S (File > Save). This updates your file. Regularly select Cmd/Ctrl-S as you work so you are continuously updating your file until you are satisfied with it.

22 Continue the sampling and painting process described previously until you have pumped up all the main highlights in the face (except the eyes, see following section) and hair.

23 Turn off, and then back on, the small eye icon to the left of the Highlights name in the Layers list. This allows you to judge the effect of your highlights layer brush marks. You see them disappear and then reappear.

24 Slowly drag the Layer Opacity slider, located in the Layers section, all the way to the left (0%) and then back all the way to the right (100%). Decide visually what level of opacity looks best (Figure 7.31). Sometimes subtle is better.

While recommending layers for working on certain clear features such as the highlights (discussed previously) and the eyes (discussed later), there are some effects and some brushes that you may find work better directly on the background canvas than on a layer (or that need the Pick Up Underlying Color box checked in the Layers palette). Whether you're working on a layer or on the background canvas, you can always choose Cmd/Ctrl-Z to undo your most recent brush strokes. If you're working directly on the background layer, you also have the possibility of using the Soft Cloner variant (Cloners category) to gently clone back your original image (in this case Elizabeth. jpg).

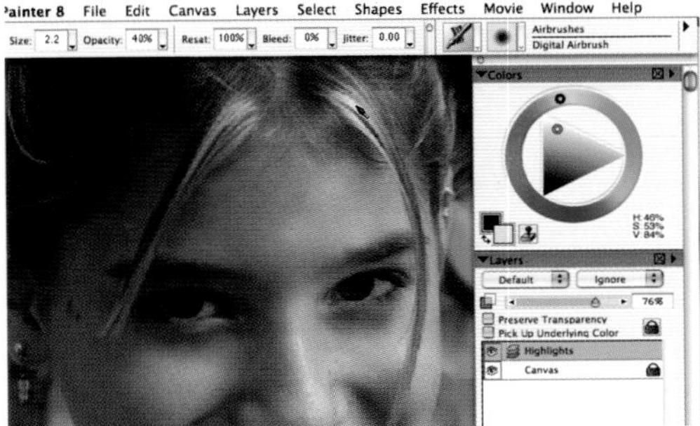

Figure 7.31 Brightening the hair highlights.

7.10 Deepening Shadows

For this example you will work on the shadows directly on the background canvas so you get an idea of the comparison with working on layers. Work on the darker areas of the face and hair, excluding the pupils, which you will work on separately.

1. Make sure the original photograph (Elizabeth.jpg) is still open in Painter (check by looking at the bottom of the Windows menu) and defined as clone source (check by looking at File > Clone Source).
2. Continue working on your file elzbth-06-highlts.rif. This is the file you will be painting on. It should be the active image in Painter and the Canvas should be highlighted in the Layers list.
3. Choose File > Save As.
4. Rename this file as elzbth-07-shdws.rif.
5. Continue using the Digital Airbrush variant (Airbrushes category).
6. As before with the highlights, adjust the brush size so that it is comparable with, or slightly smaller than, the level of detail in the shadow regions you are working on. For instance, if we start off working into the shadows in the hair, then a brush size of about 2 seems to work well.
7. Adjust the brush opacity (Opacity slider in the Controls: Brush palette) to about 40 percent.
8. Hold down the Option/Alt key. This turns your Brush tool into a Dropper tool that samples color from wherever you click in the image.
9. Keeping the Option/Alt key held down, click in the shadows in the hair.
10. Release the Option/Alt key.
11. In the Colors palette, move the Saturation Value triangle cursor slightly downward (this darkens) and slightly to the right (this increases the saturation or intensity of the color). The overall effect is to slightly darken and deepen the selected shadow color.
12. Lightly stroke the airbrush in the shadow region centered at the place where you sampled the color.
13. Continue until you have pumped up the shadows sufficiently. If you overdo it, you can always either choose Cmd/Ctrl-Z to undo your most recent brush strokes or use the Soft Cloner variant (Cloners category) to gently clone back the original image (Elizabeth.jpg).
14. Choose Cmd/Ctrl-S (File > Save). This updates your file.

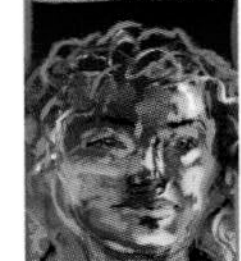

7.11 Enhancing Eyes

As you work into the eyes to bring out color, contrast, and detail, treat each eye individually. The asymmetry between eyes is important in conveying character and bringing your portraits to life. Avoid the temptation to artificially create symmetry. The asymmetry and imperfections in a face give character.

The eye techniques described as follows are all done using the Digital Airbrush variant (Airbrushes category). This variant has the benefit of offering fine control and also working well on layers, which gives an additional level of editability and fine tuning. The methodology followed here is to work on a separate layer for each element of eye enhancement (e.g., catchlights, iris coloration, and pupil darkening), as you did for the highlights. It is common to overdo an effect initially, and the layer allows you to easily scale back the effect in a controlled way and compare with what it looked like previously.

An alternative that I like for detailed eyework is a small modification of the Distorto variant in the Distortion brush category. Adjust the Distorto variant to size about 1 and opacity about 30 percent for catchlights and pupil enhancement, and size 3 and opacity 2 percent for iris coloration. This modified variant, which can help define the delicate striations that you see in the iris, works best on the background canvas since it interacts with paint already on the canvas. It is not suitable for working on a layer. I recommend you follow the steps below with the Digital Airbrush on layers as instructed and try out the modified Distorto on another project. I also recommend you save the customized Distorto by choosing Save Variant from the Brush Selector pop-up menu.

Catchlights

Catchlights are the bright sparkles in the eyes that bring a picture to life. The brightest catchlight is the specular highlight, which reflects light directly from the main light source (see the Five Lights of Nature explanation in session 3). There are secondary catchlights that reflect other light sources and bright surfaces in the environment (these are the refracted light in the Five Lights of Nature). Brightening and emphasizing these multiple catchlights, with their irregular shapes and varying degrees of brightness, will bring added life and sparkle to your image.

Avoid creating two identical, perfectly round, pure white idealized catchlights, one in each eye. The result looks unreal and does not evoke character or personality.

1. Select New Layer from the Layers pop-up menu or by clicking the third button from the left in the Layers palette. You will see a new layer appear in the Layers list.

Continued

2 Double-click on the new layer in the Layers list. This brings up the Layers Attributes window.

3 Rename the new layer as Catchlight.

4 Choose OK.

5 Choose Cmd/Ctrl-"+" and click between the eyes. Zoom in until the eyes almost fill your screen.

6 Adjust the Digital Airbrush size to about 1.3 (Size slider in the Size section of the Brush Controls palette).

7 Adjust the brush opacity to about 20 percent (Opacity slider in the Controls: Brush palette).

8 Hold down the Option/Alt key and click on the brightest point in the catchlight in one eye. This samples that color.

9 Move the SV triangle cursor up and slightly to the right.

10 Gently brush in over the catchlight region. The catchlight layer should be highlighted in the Layers list as you paint (to ensure you are painting on the layer, not on the background canvas).

11 Sample a region in the iris where some light is reflected but it is not the brightest catchlight.

12 Lighten the sampled color (move the SV triangle cursor up slightly).

13 Gently paint over the secondary catchlights.

14 Turn off, and then back on, the small eye icon to the left of the Catchlight name in the Layers list. This allows you to judge the effect of your catchlight layer brush marks. You see them disappear and then reappear.

15 Slowly drag the layer opacity slider, located in the Layers palette, all the way to the left (0%) and then back all the way to the right (100%). Decide visually what level of opacity looks best. In the example shown here I found that about 70 percent opacity worked best (Figure 7.32).

16 Choose Cmd/Ctrl-S (File > Save) to update your file.

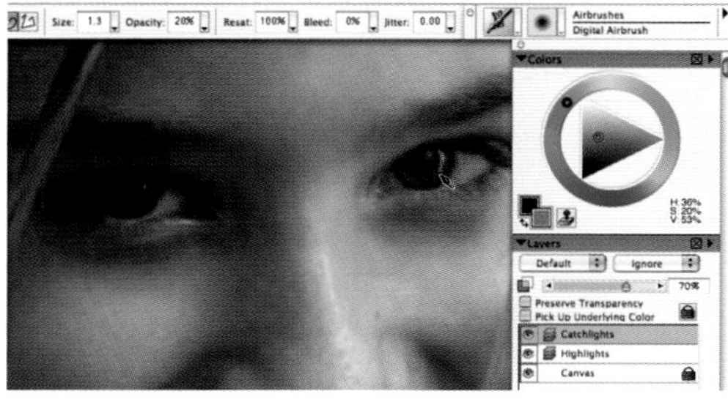

Figure 7.32 Brightening and emphasizing catchlights.

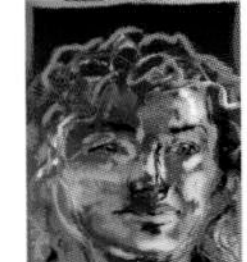

Iris Coloration

While the bright, sparkling catchlights in the eyes are important, the luminous glow of the multiple colors and subtle striations and variations in the iris are equally valuable in conveying character and making a picture jump out at the viewer.

1. Select New Layer from the Layers pop-up menu (as before). A new layer, also called Layer 1, will appear above the catchlight layer.
2. Double-click on the new layer in the Layers list. This brings up the Layers Attributes window.
3. Rename the new layer as Iris.
4. Choose OK.
5. Hold down the Option/Alt key while you click in the iris (avoiding the catchlights).
6. Move the Saturation Value (SV) triangle cursor in the Colors palette up very slightly to lighten, and to the right to saturate or intensify the color.
7. Adjust the Digital Airbrush size to about 3.5.
8. Brush very lightly over the non-catchlight parts of the iris, resampling and adjusting color as you go (Figure 7.33).
9. Adjust the layer opacity slider to the level of opacity that looks best.
10. Choose Cmd/Ctrl-S (File > Save) to update the file.

Note that by changing your iris layer Composite Method (pop-up menu near top of Layers palette) from Default to Colorize you can preserve the underlying tonal detail while just altering the hue. You may find it interesting to experiment with this aspect.

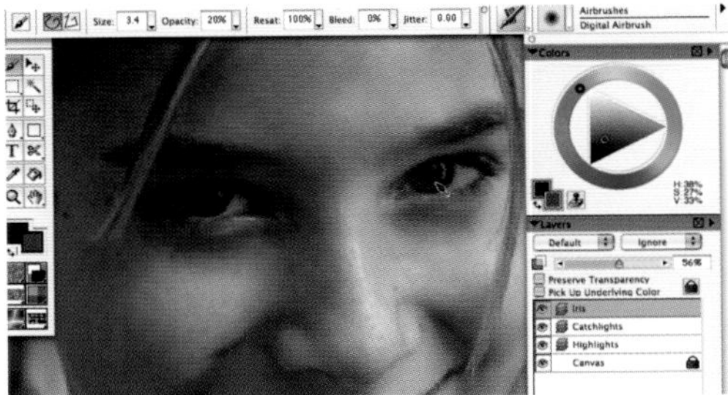

Figure 7.33 Pumping up the iris coloration.

When I colorize irises I like to add subtle specks and hints of colors from the environment. I will often sample colors from other parts of the picture. Take the time to look deeply into people's eyes (not just looking at photographs) and carefully observe the complex patterns and myriad of colors.

Pupil Darkening and Enlarging

Darker pupils set up a greater contrast with the catchlights, which often overlap the pupils, and bring added emphasis to the eyes. Slightly larger pupils also have the effect of giving the portrait a friendlier feeling (our pupils usually dilate slightly when we like the person we are looking at).

1. Select New Layer from the Layers pop-up menu (as before). A new layer, again called Layer 1, will appear above the iris and catchlights layers.
2. Double-click on the new layer in the Layers list. This brings up the Layers Attributes window.
3. Rename the new layer as Pupils.
4. Choose OK.
5. Hold down the Option/Alt key while you click in one pupil (avoiding the catchlights).
6. Move the Saturation Value (SV) triangle cursor in the Colors palette down slightly to darken the color.
7. Adjust the Digital Airbrush size to about 1.3.
8. Brush gently over the non-catchlight parts of the pupil, expanding the outer limits of the pupil slightly.
9. Repeat this process for the second pupil. Pupils are rarely exactly the same color or darkness because a light source is usually closer to one eye than the other and the nose may be casting a shadow over one pupil.
10. Choose Cmd/Ctrl-S (File > Save) to update the file.

7.12 Smooth Watercolor Look

This final stage of the hand-painting process requires a flattened image. As a golden rule, always save a RIFF version of your files before flattening them. This is important so you have the flexibility to go back and edit layers at a later date.

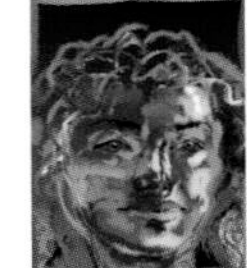

1. Choose Drop All from the Layers pop-up menu (accessed by clicking on the small triangle in the upper right corner of the Layers palette).
2. Click on your Save As button (File > Save As) and rename your file elzbth-07-smooth.rif. It is important that you save the flattened file with a different file name so the last version has the layers preserved.
3. Choose the Just Add Water variant from the Blenders category.
4. Adjust the Brush Size slider, located in the Size section of the Brush Controls palette, to about 17 or 18.
5. Adjust the Opacity slider to about 14 percent.
6. Very lightly apply gentle strokes to the skin areas (Figure 7.34). Make your stroke directions follow the contours of the form of the face, neck, and shoulders as you do so.
7. Choose Cmd/Ctrl-S (File > Save) to update your file.

Note that in softly applying the Just Add Water in this manner you lose much of the skin surface detail. This results in a smooth, watercolor paint look. Here is an example (Figure 7.35) of this technique from Cheri, who created this painting during a lesson taught by Jane Conner-ziser at the Georgia Photographic School.

To bring back more realism, you could use the Soft Cloner (Cloners category) to subtly reintroduce either the original photograph or any saved versions (just make sure the version is open in Painter, go to File > Clone Source, and select the version name to be the clone source).

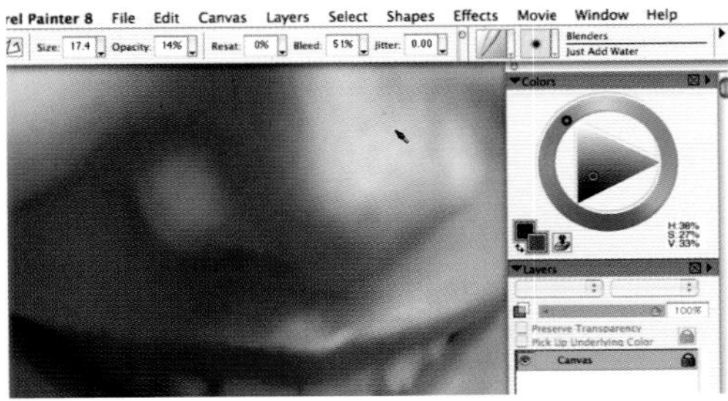

Figure 7.34 Applying Just Add Water to soften the skin.

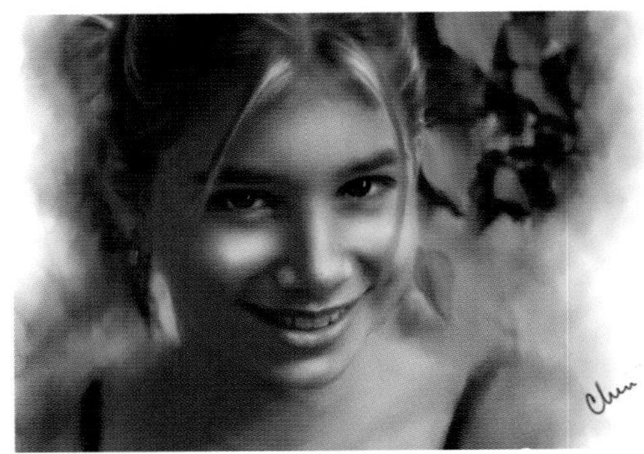

Figure 7.35 Cheri's version of Elizabeth.

7.13 Grainy Pastel Chalk Look

Here you will explore a pastel chalky look, taking one more step from photographic realism toward the look of an original fine art drawing.

1. Open the file elzbth-07-smooth.rif in Painter.
2. Choose File > Clone.
3. Choose File > Save As.
4. Save the clone copy file as elzbth-08-chalk.rif.
5. Choose Save in the Save As window.
6. Choose Cmd/Ctrl-M (Window > Screen Mode Toggle).
7. Choose the Variable Oil Pastel variant in the Oil Pastel brush category (other variants in this category will also work fine). This is a grainy brush that reflects the current paper texture (Papers selector in the Tools palette). The Basic Paper in the default Paper Textures papers library works well (though you may wish to experiment with other textures).
8. Click the Clone Color box in the Colors palette.
9. Adjust the Brush Size slider in the Size section of the brush Property Bar to about 20.
10. Adjust the Opacity slider in the brush Property Bar to about 50 percent.
11. Go over the whole image with gentle brush strokes, following the form of the face and background (Figure 7.36).
12. Click again on the Clone Color box in the Colors palette to disable Clone Color and activate the regular Color Picker.
13. Select bright, warm pastel colors in the color picker, and apply dabs of these colors in the skin regions and the hair (Figure 7.37). I find that warm, light yellows, oranges, and reds work well in the highlight regions and warm, medium tone reds, purples, and blues work well in the shadow areas. Don't worry about the dabs appearing to stand out. You will blend them in shortly.
14. Click on the Clone Color box in the Colors palette to enable clone color.
15. Use the Oil Pastel variant in the Oil Pastels brush category to blend the pastel color dabs (Figure 7.38).
16. Choose Cmd/Ctrl-S (File > Save). This updates your file.
17. Choose File > Save As.

Continued

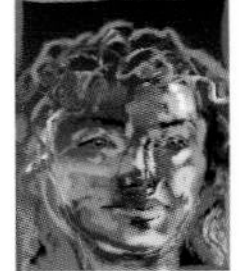

18. Rename your file elzbth-09-chalktxtr.rif. It is important to save a new version of your file at this stage since you are about to apply a surface texture effect. Whenever you are about to apply a major global effect to the whole image, you should always save a safe version of the image prior to applying the effect. This gives you the flexibility later on to retrieve the image without the effect.
19. Choose Save.
20. Choose Load Library from the bottom of the Papers selector pop-up menu.
21. Select the French Watercolor Paper from the Papers selector in the Tools palette.
22. Choose Effects > Surface Control > Apply Surface Texture.
23. In the Apply Surface Texture window (Figure 7.39) leave the default settings Using: Paper and Softness 0.0. Adjust the Amount slider to 10 percent and the Shine slider to 0 percent.
24. Choose OK. You will see the texture now applied subtly to the whole of your canvas surface. If you find the effect a little overwhelming, just choose Edit > Fade and adjust the fade slider until you are satisfied. The Fade allows you to fade back the last brush stroke or effect by any amount between 0 percent and 100 percent. I find that a subtle paper texture works much better than a stronger one that distracts from the image. Always leave this operation to last.
25. Choose Cmd/Ctrl-S.

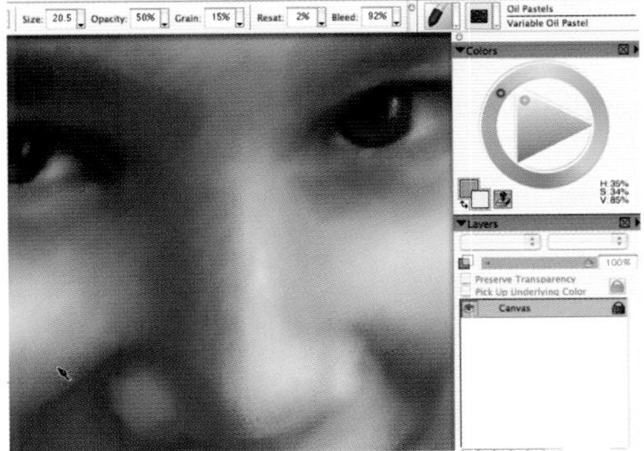

Figure 7.36 Applying Oil Pastel as Cloner.

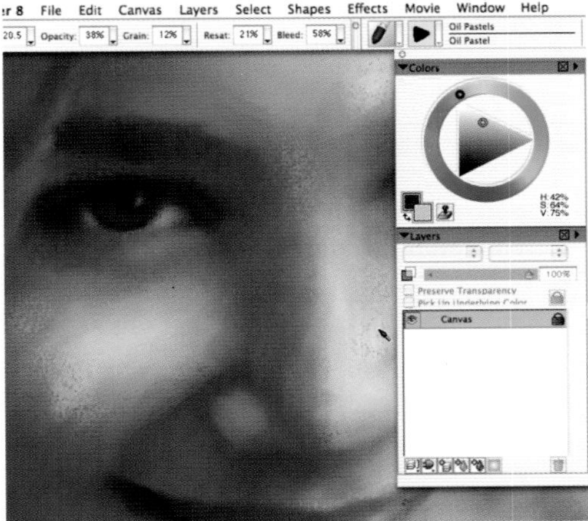

Figure 7.37 Adding pastel color patches.

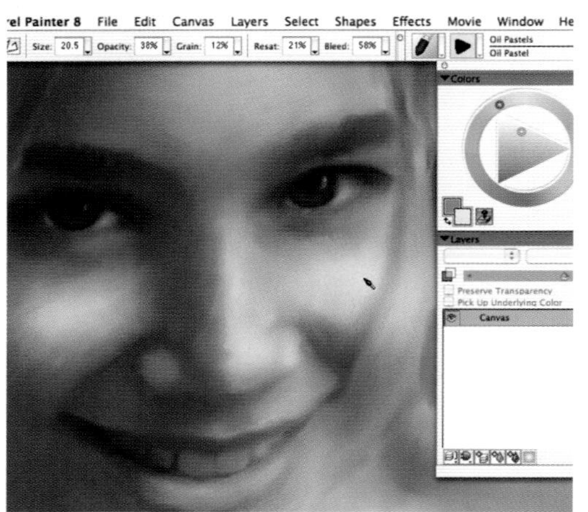

Figure 7.38 Blending the pastel color into the image.

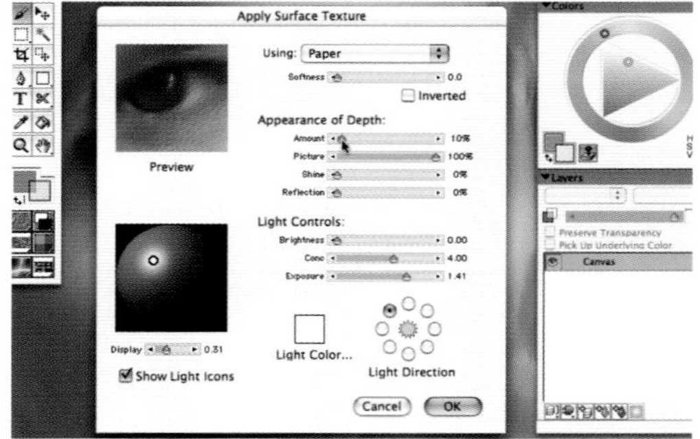

Figure 7.39 Applying Surface Texture.

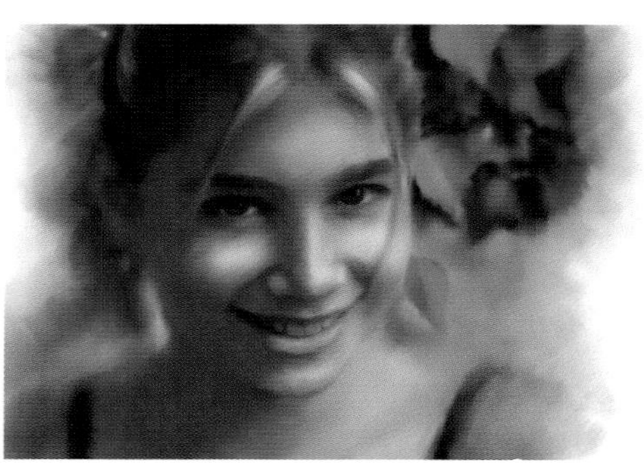

Figure 7.40 Pastel Chalk version of Elizabeth.

Here is the final version of the image with the texture applied (Figure 7.40).

Note that you may find it more satisfying to simply print the image on watercolor paper and use the real paper texture rather than impose an artificial one digitally.

7.14 Thick Oil Paint Look

Thus far the look and feel of the photo transformations you've been doing resemble more the traditional watercolor and chalk rather than traditional oil paint. In this project you will transform a photograph into an image with a thick hand-painted oil look.

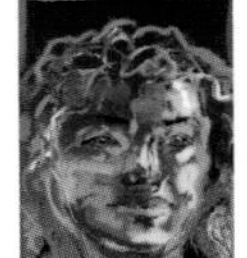

Preparation

1. Open Painter afresh. If Painter is already open, Quit out of Painter and reopen it. It is important to always start Painter afresh whenever you are starting on a new project.
2. Open the tutorial file specialmoment.jpg, a photograph by Jim Paliungas, that you will find in the Creativity Projects > 7-Photography I > 7.12 Oil Paint folder (on the Painter Creativity Companion CD).
3. Choose Cmd/Ctrl-M (Window > Screen Mode Toggle).
4. Choose Window > Arrange Palettes > Photo (the same palette arrangement shown earlier in this session on page 179).
5. Hold the space bar down on your keyboard while you click and drag your canvas into a convenient position on the screen.
6. Choose Canvas > Canvas Size.
7. In the Canvas Size window add 50 pixels to all four sides (Figure 7.41). Use the tab key to go from one side to the next when entering the "50" on your keyboard.
8. Choose OK. You have now added a white border all the way around the edge of the image.
9. Choose File > Save As.
10. Rename the file photo-oil-original.rif.
11. Choose Save in the Save As window.
12. Choose File > Clone.
13. Choose File > Save As.
14. Rename the file photo-oil-01.rif.
15. Save the newly renamed clone copy image into the appropriate project folder.
16. Choose Cmd/Ctrl-M (Window > Screen Mode Toggle).
17. Hold the space bar down on your keyboard while you click and drag your photo-oil-01.rif file into a convenient position on the screen.

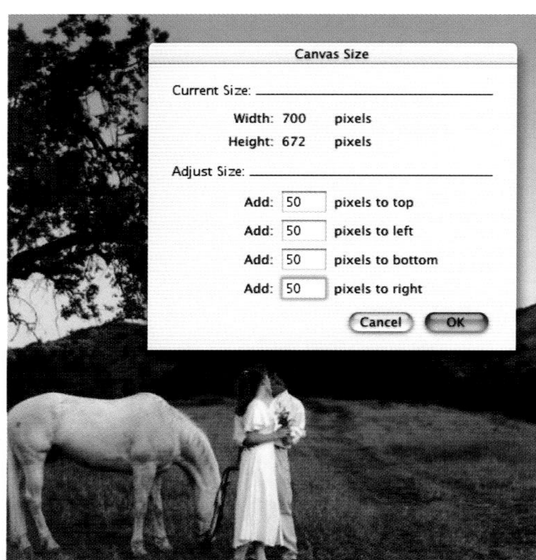

Figure 7.41 Canvas Size window.

An aside on canvas size and paper color

The Canvas Size command automatically fills the extra space you define in the border with the current paper color (which is white by default). If you ever wish to add plain borders of other colors, you can do this with the Canvas Size command. You first need to select the color in the color picker (or color set) that you wish to use for the border, and then choose Canvas > Set Paper Color. You then apply the Canvas Size command and you will have a plain border filled with that color. You can always reset the paper color to white, or any other color you wish, afterward. Paper color in Painter is related to the specific canvas that happens to be active. You can have two or more images open in Painter at the same time, each with different colors set for paper color. When you clear a canvas using Cmd/Ctrl-A followed by Delete/Backspace, the canvas is also automatically filled with the current Paper color setting for that particular canvas.

This addition of extra canvas size is also a useful technique for blending and softening the sharp, harsh edge of an image. If you add a white border and then use some of the Blenders brush variants (for instance Smear, Just Add Water, and so on) you can merge the edge into the white with a rough organic edge. Adding the white border may be something to consider doing at the very beginning of the painting process, rather than at the end, so you can use Tracing Paper (which only works when the source and destination images are exactly the same size).

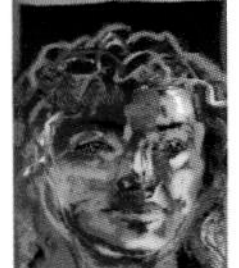

Oil Brush Cloning

1. Choose the Captured Bristle variant in the Acrylics category and click on the Clone Color box in the Colors palette. An alternative would be to choose the Oil Brush Cloner variant in the Cloners brush category and modify the impasto settings in the Brush Creator > Stroke Designer (Cmd/Ctrl-B), changing the Draw To setting from Color and Depth to just Color. The Bristle Brush Cloner and the Camel Oil Cloner variants will also work fine for this project.
2. Adjust the Opacity slider in the Controls: Brush palette to 100 percent.
3. Start painting over the image (Figure 7.42). Adjust the brush size to suit the features you are painting (I found I used sizes as large as 30 for the sky and as small as 6 for the woman's dress). Apply your brush strokes in directions that flow around the natural contours and emphasize the forms in the image. Use bigger brush strokes in the background to create a more diffuse look that focuses the viewer's eyes toward the central figures. At the outer edges of the image, bring some brush strokes in from the white toward the center of the image. This will create a nice oily border.
4. Choose Cmd/Ctrl-S (File > Save).

At this stage you could leave the picture as it is, or you could use the Soft Cloner variant (Cloners category) to bring back some of the original photograph, or use Blenders brushes to smear and blend the paint.

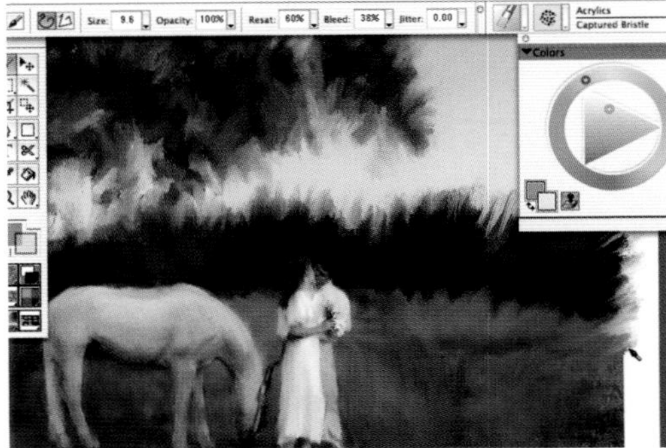

Figure 7.42 After Judi Paliungas started applying oily cloner brushes.

Blending and Smearing

1. Choose File > Save As.
2. Rename the file photo-oil-02-smear.rif.
3. Choose the Sable Chisel Tip Water variant in the Blenders category.
4. Apply blending brush strokes in the image, varying the brush size to suit the features.
5. Choose Cmd/Ctrl-S (File > Save).

Three versions based on the same original image are shown in Figure 7.43. The two versions on the left are by me and the right-hand version is by Judi Paliungas.

7.15 Gallery

In the example shown in Figure 7.44 I used a slightly more conservative (i.e., less expressionistic) photo oil approach on another photograph by Jim Paliungas.

After applying a modified Oil Brush Cloner (with no impasto depth) over the whole image for about 30 minutes, I added the final touch of Effects > Surface Control > Apply Surface Texture using Image Luminance (Figure 7.45) followed by a 50 percent Edit > Fade.

When the Apply Surface Texture effect is set to Using: Image Luminance, as in this example, it creates an embossment of the brush strokes, which can give the sense of thick oil paint. This contrasts with a watercolor effect, where you would want the grain of the paper showing through (Apply Surface Texture effect set to Using: Paper). You'll find the original photo as a tutorial image (winningsmile.jpg) in the PainterCreativityProjects > 7-Photography I > 7.13 Gallery folder.

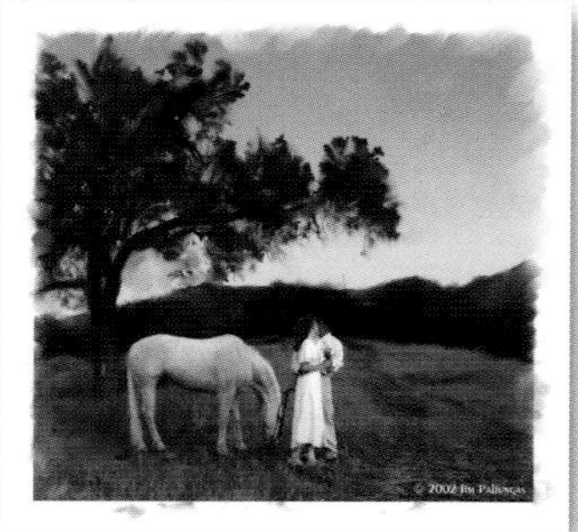

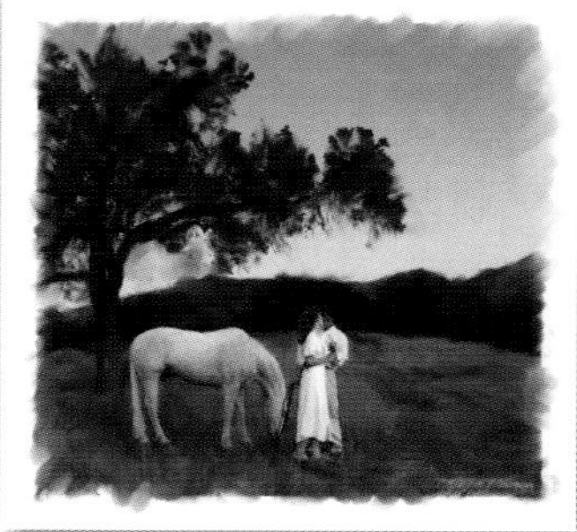

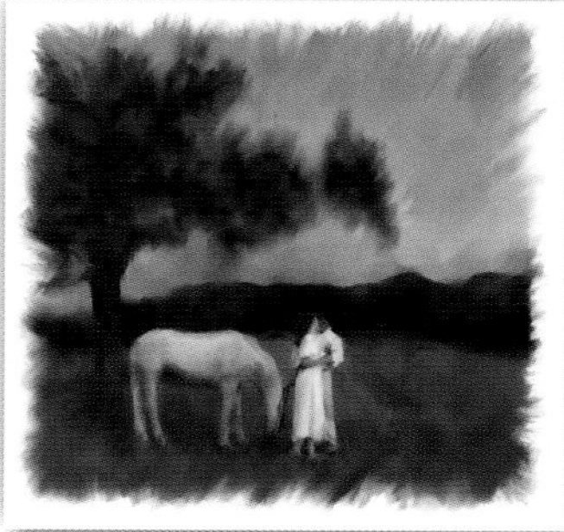

Figure 7.43 Photo Oil renditions.

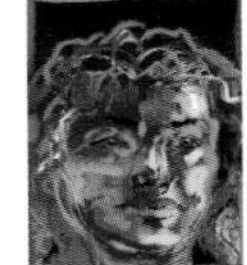

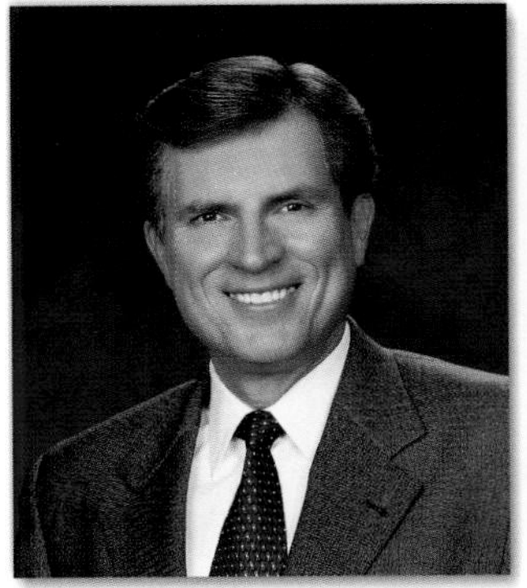

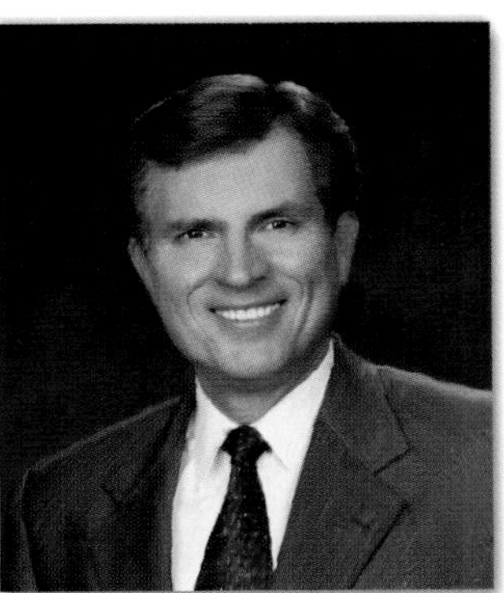

Figure 7.44 The original photo and the photo oil rendition.

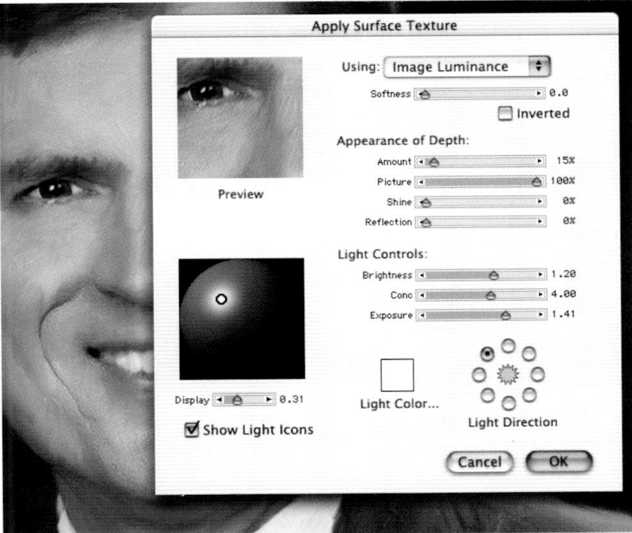

Figure 7.45 Apply Surface Texture using Image Luminance.

Figure 7.46 is an example of a photo oil transformation created by Sherron Sheppard based on one of her infrared photographs of a boat on Morro Bay, California.

You will find the original Morro Bay image as a tutorial file (morrobay.jpg) in the tutorial folder (PainterCreativityProjects > 7-Photography I > 7.15 Gallery). You can follow Sherron's example (Figure 7.47) or create your own rendition. Notice how Sherron first painted bold brush strokes and added dabs of color, and then blended the paint and brought back some of the original photograph.

If you wish to create a looser, more expressionistic effect, you can start with a low-resolution candid shot and use wilder colors and brush strokes. Figure 7.48 is an example of a photo oil I painted based on a photograph by Victor de Leon of saxophonist Jules Broussard.

Figure 7.49 shows the original photo and an intermediate stage.

If you'd like to experiment with expressionistic photo oils, take some pictures of musicians playing live and then have fun with the images! I've also included the original photo used here as a

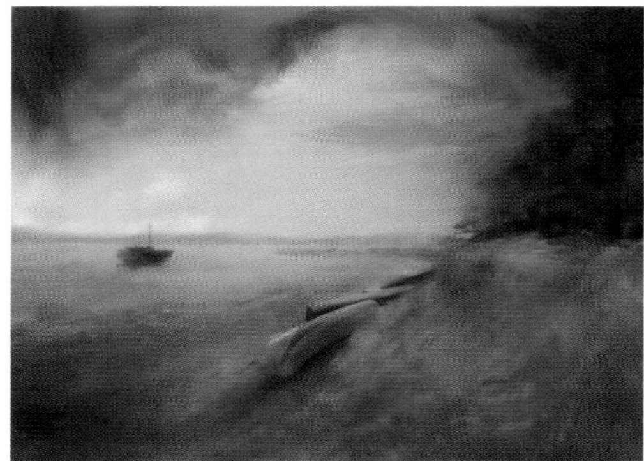

Figure 7.46 Morro Bay: The photo oil rendition.

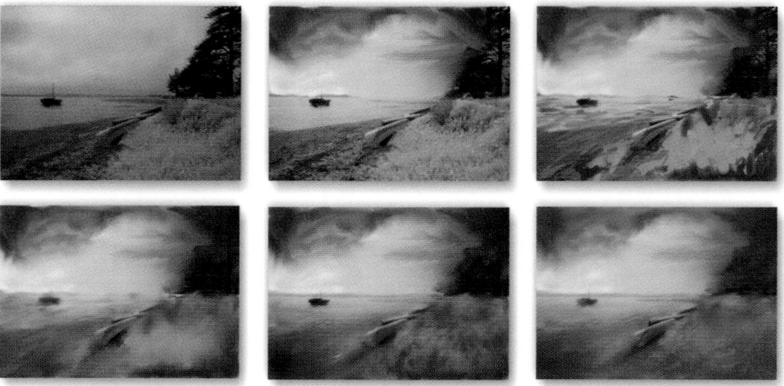

Figure 7.47 Morro Bay: The creative process.

tutorial image (sax.jpg) in the tutorial folder (PainterCreativityProjects > 7-Photography I > 7.15 Gallery) for you to experiment with.

Departing from the human subject, Figure 7.50 shows a lovely hand-painted rendition of white orchids based on a photograph by Jane Conner-ziser. The rendition shown here is by Leslie Jacob, one of Jane's students at the Georgia Photographic School.

This painting of white orchids was created during one of Jane's exercises for practicing the Five Lights of Nature. A version of the original file (orchids.jpg) is included in the tutorial folder for you to use as a basis for your own painting.

Figure 7.51 is an example I like in which Judi Paliungas applied a combination of watercolor and oil effects, plus added a little coloring and tinting.

The original photograph is by Jim Paliungas, and a tutorial version (embrace.jpg) has been included in your tutorial folder for you to experiment with.

Figure 7.52 is Cheri MacCallum's watercolor rendition of a photograph by Valerie Markle.

Cheri used the multi-layered technique described earlier to create this rendition.

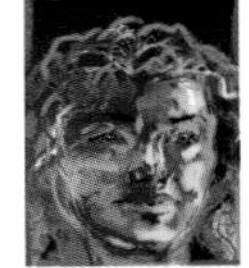

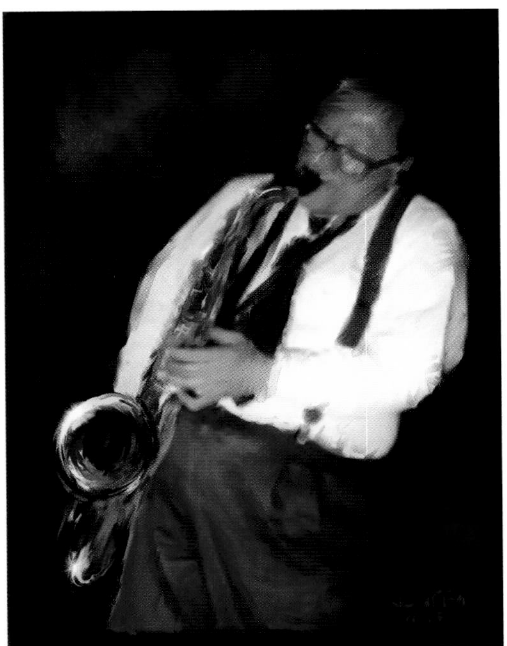

Figure 7.48 Sax!

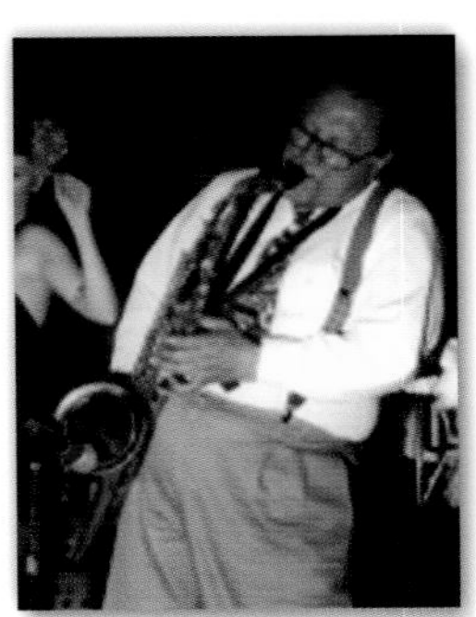
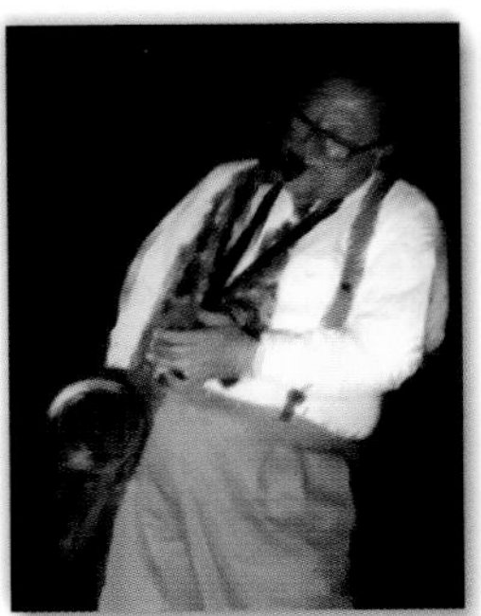
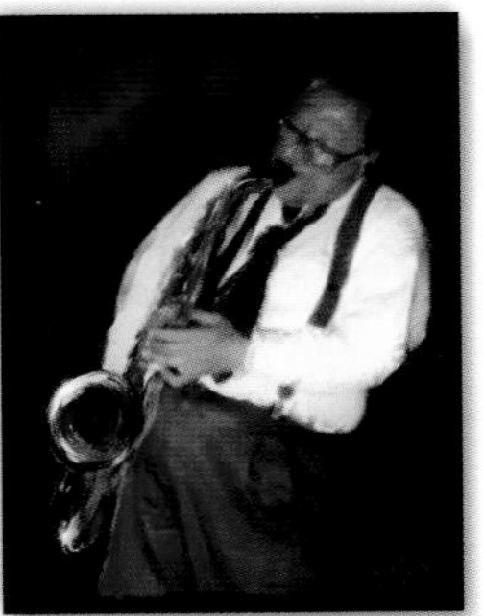

Figure 7.49 Sax!: The creative process.

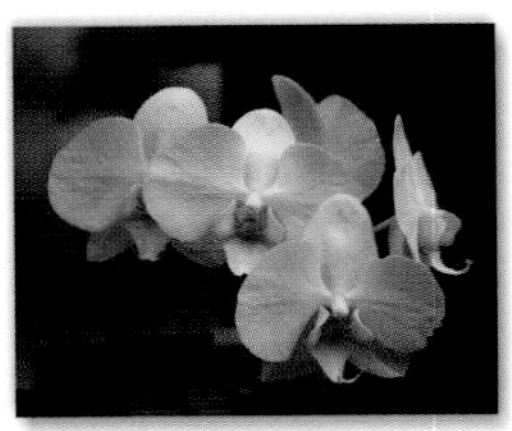
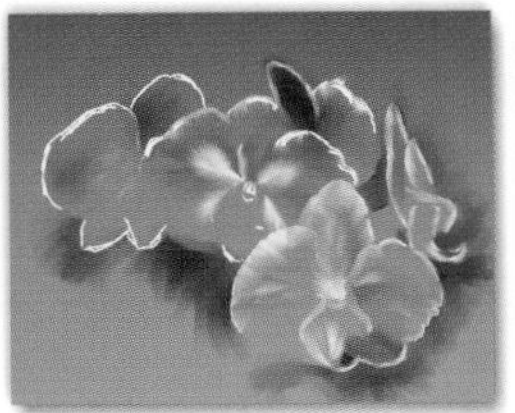
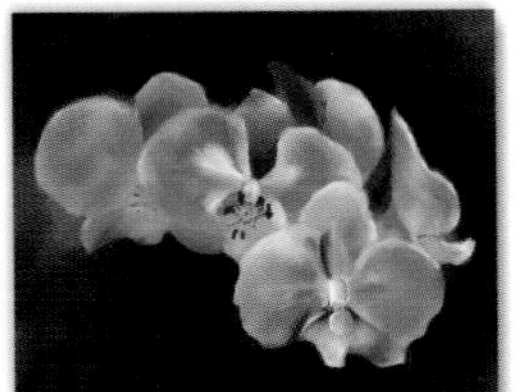

Figure 7.50 Painterly rendition of white orchids.

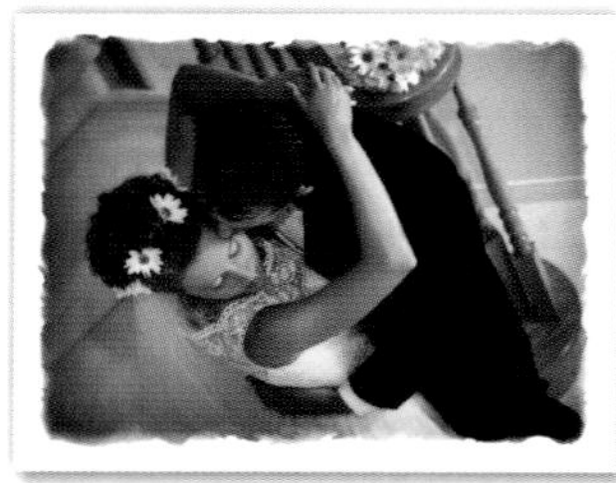

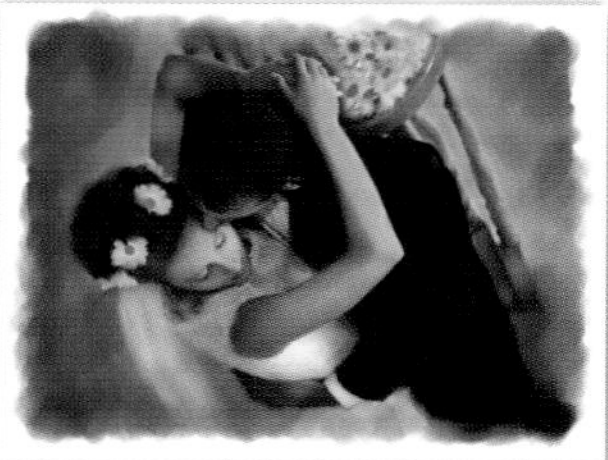

Figure 7.51 Embrace: Original photo and painterly rendition.

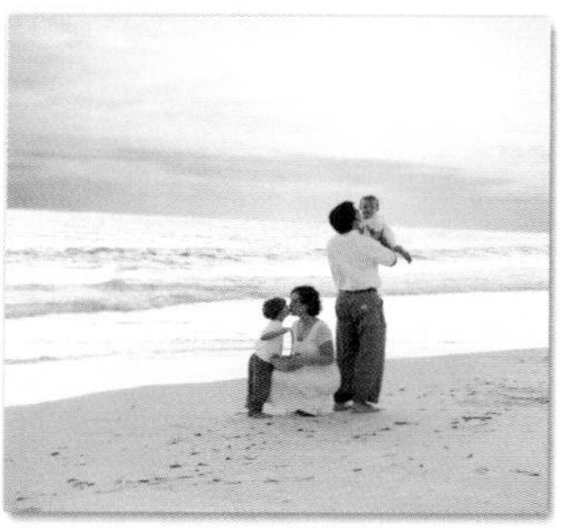

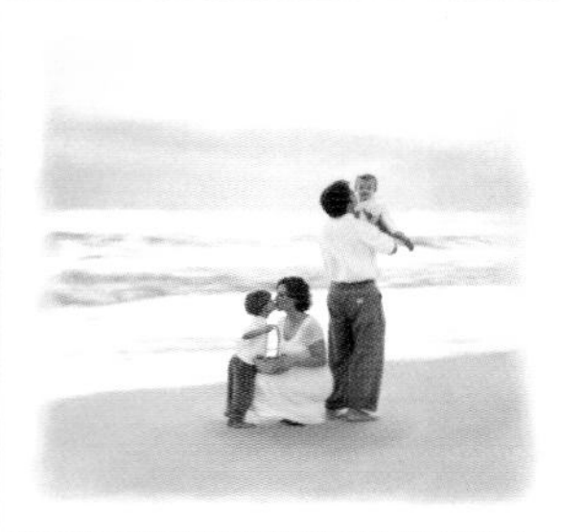

Figure 7.52 Beach: Original photo and watercolor rendition.

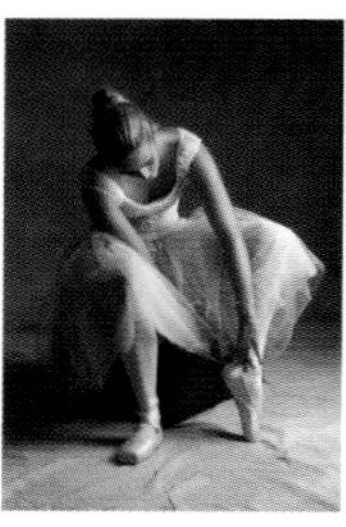

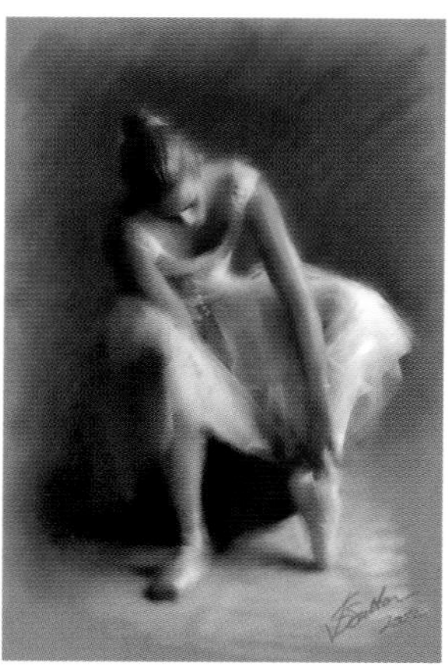

Figure 7.53 Ballerina Sitting. Original photo and pastel rendition.

This rendition of a ballerina sitting (Figure 7.53). is based on a photograph by Hawaii photographer David Taylor. When David took the original photograph he was looking for an image with a Degas feel to use to promote the Mavis Tracy Ballet School. The model is Lindsay McGlinn, a Ballet Instructor at the school. I reinterpreted David's original photograph as a pastel drawing in the Degas style.

The image in Figure 7.54. is based on a photograph that I took of Lisa and her daughter Quinn. Initially I cloned the color from the original photo, and then I started adding color. The original

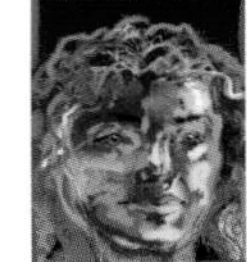

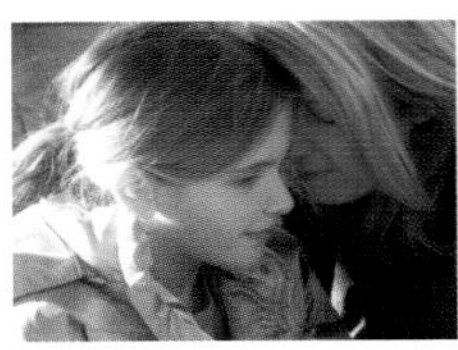

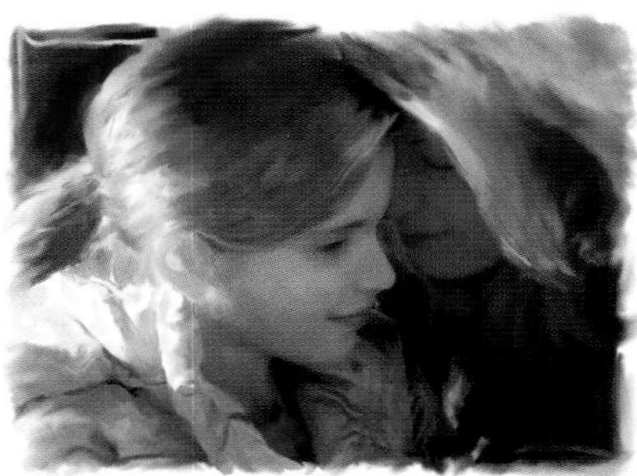

Figure 7.54 Precious: Original photo and watercolor rendition.

photo was rather cool with a blue-gray cast and a limited tonal range. With my brush strokes I added a greater variety of warmer, more saturated colors and increased the tonal contrasts in selected places. I also smeared and blended the image, especially at the edge.

Part 4: Classical Photo Portrait Painting—an essay by Jane Conner-ziser

Introduction

I met Jeremy Sutton about four years ago, when I was actively looking for the best instructor of Painter, a program that I was very interested in learning more about. I have been a fine artist most of my life, and a professional photographer and retouching/photo painting artist for over 25 years, using both optical and digital media. I had been using and teaching digital technology for almost twelve years for portrait retouching, enhancements, and other photo related arts, but had not found a program that could satisfy my desire to paint with the quality I could achieve with "real" paints and brushes.

I had heard about Painter—even purchased it and played around with it for several months, but wanted some expert instruction. I set out to find the best teacher on the program. I went to the creator's web site, called the company personally, and asked for the best Painter instructor in the world. They gave me the name of Jeremy Sutton and I searched him out on-line.

Arriving at Portrayals.com, I was excited to see his remarkable work—Jeremy's mastery of brushes and his abundance of color remain thrilling to me today, but the reason I actually telephoned him and arranged private instruction was that his paintings sing with the life of his subjects—the essence of professional portraiture. We've been friends now for three years and I've added to my previous impressions that he's also a very nice person and a great teacher—I couldn't wait to introduce him to the professional portrait photography industry!

I feel that Jeremy and I are enriched by our friendship and the openness of our mutual sharing. I think both of our worlds have gotten a little bit bigger thanks to technology, the Internet and art.

I've written this essay as a classical portrait photo painter—a traditionalist in the essence of photo "oils" and "watercolors." There are many new styles of painting now, but the classic pieces still remain close to my heart. They are also top of the line products for most portrait photography studios.

The Art of Photo Portrait Painting

The art of photo portrait painting is based upon the professional photographer's desire to create a photograph that looks like a painting, the mirror reflection of the photo realist painter who wants to create a painting that looks like a photograph.

In either case, the photographic likeness and photographic qualities are equally important to creating a successful image. Traditionally, a photo painter starts with a photograph and literally paints on top of it, gradually building up layers of paint while being careful to use the lighting, composition and details of the original image. Ideally, the end result should be such a delicate mixing of both paint and image that they are indistinguishable from each other.

Technology makes it possible for photo painters to go even farther with their art, incorporating digital effects, composite tools and distortions to create base images that never existed until the artist brings the dream to life. In addition, though the traditional medium for photo painting was oils, Painter opens magical doors to chalks, inks and watercolors, with brushes that apply "paint" like a fine artist expects them to; paint that blends with natural hand movements.

Image Selection

For me, a photo painting always starts with the proper image selection. I find that an image is more successful through the years when it is composed according to classical fine art principles of lighting, posing, props, and attire. If you need reference, art galleries offer tremendous education in classical portraiture and many of the best portrait photographers emulate the timeless elements of classical portrait painters. The example I show in Figure 7.55 was selected for its character and personality.

Deciding on Output

Once I've selected a suitable image, my next decision is choosing how I wish to paint the portrait and what output will be consistent with the medium I select.

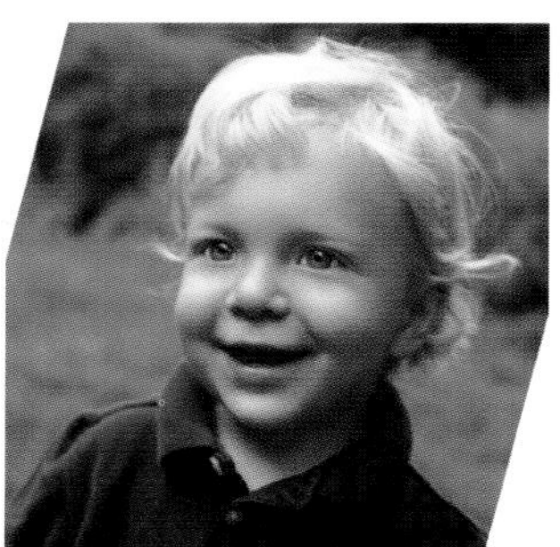

Figure 7.55 Image selected for character.

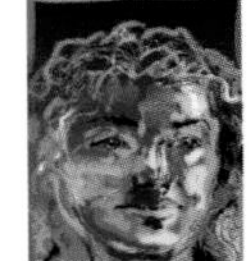

It's my opinion that medium- to high-key images make the best watercolors and light pastels. Part of my feeling is just that a light image naturally flows into water or dusts into the airy feeling of chalk, but the other reason is that I will likely want to output on watercolor or art papers which tend to drink up a lot of ink, thus "killing" the blacks and color saturations. In my opinion, most low-key and highly saturated images look dull and uninteresting when output onto art papers.

However, low key and saturated images make beautiful oil paintings! And I've seen some oil pastel presentations that are also very exciting. These are traditionally printed on photographic or ink jet paper that will be mounted on canvas and stretched onto stretcher bars to finish the illusion of an oil painting.

Composition and Balance

The next decision is how the image should be cropped for best composition and balance. I want to make sure that I include everything I want and need in the image and that I've made the most out of my focal points and compositional elements.

The Painting Process

Then I retouch the overall image to achieve complete balance of contrast, color, and detail so my painting can incorporate as much of the original photograph as possible. It's not my goal to really alter the photograph unless there are problems in the composition, but I do want to make it look like a painting.

My final preparation for photo painting is facial retouching, hair, clothing and eye enhancement, and careful blending of the subject's skin tones. It's important to me to structure the facial features and accomplish some cosmetic retouching without losing the character of the subject. Many times I add contrast to the highlights and shaded sides according to the natural lighting (Five Lights of Nature) and bone structure of the subject. This begins to eliminate pore structure lending the skin a more painted look while still maintaining photographic quality. Finally, I begin adding a few accent colors and brush details to lead me gracefully into the paint.

Part of the goal of digital photo painting is to combine photograph and paint. I like to intensify highlights and shadows, plus add accents colors with paint, using the selection of brushes I've determined are the best for the image. Next I use distortion, effect cloners, and Blenders brushes to melt, blend, and push the photograph and paint together—the base image becomes the diffused highlight (or mid tone) areas. For a realistic effect it is important to work with the contours of the original image and feel like you are painting it freehand. Comb the hair with small brushes, blending out irregular-looking areas and enhancing the flow of the hair. Move gracefully with folds of fabric and more staccato on objects with texture.

While you are doing this, remember that you have another goal that is crucial to the success of the painting. It is to work on edges and fabrics to remove or modify textures and details that are telltale photographic signs. The usual array of small stray hairs blending into the background is a good example of this as is the vast repetitive detail in the weave of a sweater. It would be very rare for a painter to describe an object or edge with that many pieces in that degree of detail and regularity unless the goal goes beyond photo realism to photo surrealism—in which case it wouldn't contain the "imperfections" of real life photography.

I also like to vary the brushes and the sizes of my brushes while I'm painting. I find that I like the look of choosing a few styles of brushes for a particular painting and using them in a variety of sizes and opacities, much like I would if I were using brushes from my art table. Remember that the difference between a good painting and a great one is in the planning and also the attention to technique and detail throughout the creative process. When I'm painting, I organize the project, set up the workspace—and then I try to leave the software program behind and get into the experience of the paint and technique.

There comes a point in every painting where you begin to lose the photograph (sometimes many times during the painting session!). Depending on what your goal is—a traditional photo portrait painting or a freehand painting based upon a photograph—you can choose to either clone back from the original (I use the retouched and enhanced version as my original) or keep going and not look back. If you keep going, you leave the realm of photo painting and enter the realm of interpretive painting based upon a photograph. Both can be beautiful, but they yield different products.

In either case, the most successful images have a definite focal point and a pleasing feeling to the paint. Considering that you have contrast, color, and detail as your tools, working these elements to perfection in the focal point area and gradually loosening up as you move away from the focal point will help you achieve the effect you want. This can mean that smaller brushes, more pieces, and more colors, or more saturated colors, are used in the focal point area, graduating to larger brushes, less definition, and fewer, or less saturated, colors as you work away from it.

Style and Presentation

I like to paint in a variety of styles but I gravitate to a classic look in my photo portrait paintings because I enjoy creating the illusion of the photograph—no, is it paint?—and I love the warm timelessness of the style. Depending on the image and the people I am painting for, I'll push the technique toward impressionism or abstract, but I'll preserve the community between photograph and paint.

To complement this type of portrait, choose traditional presentations. Soft vignettes and fade outs are pleasing on medium to high key paintings (Figure 7.56), but I like to paint to the edge with my oils. Decorative edges and other digital techniques lend themselves seamlessly to contemporary pieces . . . choose a presentation that works well with your style and compliments your work.

It would be my encouragement to you to find your path to paint and develop your style, whether it is watercolors, oils, pastels, or mixed mediums. Leave your comfort zone often to experiment, learn, and grow as an artist, yet do the things that feel natural to you. Remember, there's nobody just like you!

Finally . . .

And finally, when you are given the trust of painting a person's face, honor them with your work. Preserve the character and expression of your subjects and be aware that your brushes caress the faces of beautiful people who deserve your best work and your respect for who they are.

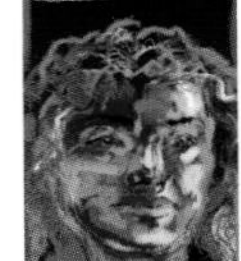

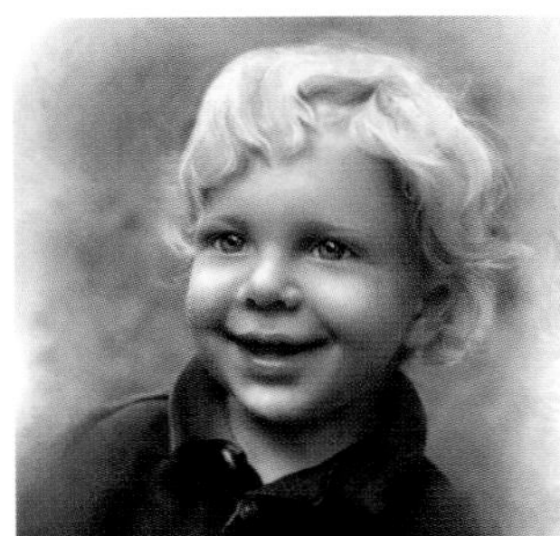

Figure 7.56 Soft vignette and fade out works well for this medium key painting.

Jane Conner-ziser (www.janesdigitalart.com) is an independent consultant and teacher for the professional photography industry. With 25 years of experience, 16 of them in digital imaging and evolving technologies, Jane's projects have spanned across a large segment of the studio photography market, freelance art, photography, lab systems, digital imaging, Internet, teaching PhotoShop and Painter, fine arts, writing for industry publications and developing/educating on marketing/selling images with new technologies. Jane is on the Digital and Advanced Imaging Committee for the Professional Photographers of America. Considered to be one of the most versatile experts in the industry, her clients include Canon, Art Leather Manufacturing Co., Marathon Press, Kodak, many of the nation's largest professional color labs, and many studios of fine portrait and commercial photography.

7.16 Wrap

This session has just touched the surface of what is possible. I encourage you to experiment with different brushes and techniques. Depending on what you wish to achieve, just as Jane says in her essay, you will eventually find certain approaches work for you better than others. You don't have to be a trained "fine artist" to be able to create wonderful painterly renditions of your photographs with Painter. If you are a professional photographer, you will find that Painter allows you to add that special "hand-painted" look in an efficient, consistent way that you can offer to your clients as a higher-value product.

The next session, Transforming Photography II: *Walking on the Wilder Side*, takes the departure from your original photograph a step further and includes applying some of the wonderful special effects that Painter has up its sleeves!

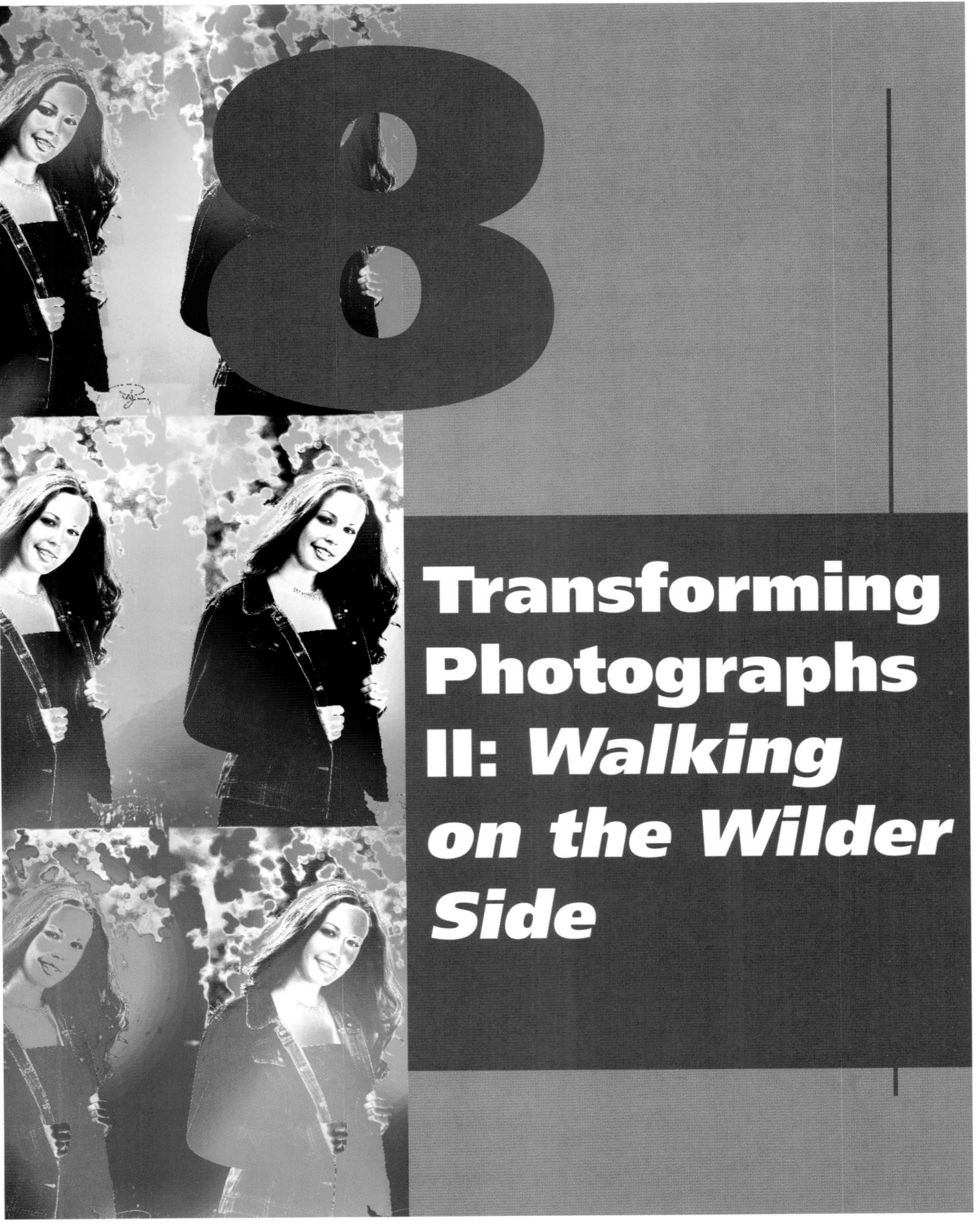

8 Transforming Photographs II: *Walking on the Wilder Side*

8.1 Introduction

Are you ready for even more fun with photographs? Now is your opportunity to really play with your images and explore the full range of possibilities. I have structured this session around specific case studies, grouped in general topics. In each case the original photograph has been included in your tutorial folder (look under Creativity Projects > 8-Photography II) so you can follow along with the techniques used. One of the reasons I am using the case study approach here is that my artwork does not follow generic formulae. I cannot say, "This is the general way to apply the serigraphy effect in an image to create an interesting result." Every image suggests its own path of transformation that may include experimenting with several different effects and brushes. My creative process is intuitive and spontaneous, rather than preplanned and calculated. I embrace serendipity and treat every unexpected result as an opportunity to explore a direction I may not have previously considered.

By sharing specific examples in this session, I don't expect you to simply copy the exact same procedures on your own images. I hope that you will experiment and discover your own unique methods and techniques (and then please drop me a line, send me a small JPEG, and share them with me!). With Painter almost anything is possible. You are only limited by your imagination.

Please note that some of the case studies in this session utilize my custom library of brushes, Creativity Brushes, which is found on the Painter Creativity Companion CD that comes with this book. My custom brush library includes many wonderful Painter brushes that are not automatically installed in the default brush library, plus a number of fabulous unique brushes made by artists around the world who have kindly given their permission for me to share them with you. For detailed instructions as to how to load the extra brushes and art materials from the Painter Creativity Companion CD, see Appendix IV, Loading Extra Brushes and Art Materials.

8.2 Instructor Notes

This session is a series of real-life case studies, each of which utilizes different Painter tools and techniques. All of the tutorial files are included in the Painter Creativity Companion CD so that your students can follow along with the case studies. I suggest you look through all the case studies prior to deciding which ones to use in your class. They could be tackled in any order. You could also easily adapt them to be topical to your students. For instance, instead of using my Holiday Gala Postcard original photograph, you could assign your students the task of designing their own postcards for an imaginary (or real) event of their own and get them to use their own source material. I find that students love to work on their own imagery, and I encourage them to do so. In a class setting I typically have all the students follow along on a common image to initially learn the technique, and then do a project on their own image that applies that technique.

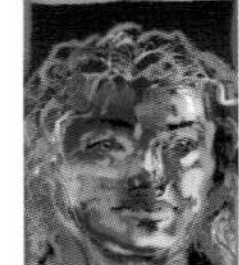

8.3 Luscious Oil: *Laying It on Thick 'n' Wild*

Dwight's Balinese Dancer

In this example the source photograph, which shows a Balinese dancer, suggested a treatment where the background acquires an abstract oily look while the central figure remains undistorted. It also suggested brush strokes and colors that radiate from the dancer.

1. In Painter, open the project file balidancer.jpg from the Painter Projects > 8-Photography II > 8.3.1 Balinese Dancer project folder. This is a photo of a Balinese dancer taken by Dwight Goode in Thailand. Set up a palette arrangement similar to the one you see in Figure 8.1.
2. Choose File > Clone. This generates a duplicate of the original image.
3. Choose File > Save As.
4. Rename your file with the subsequent version number and RIFF file format tag (e.g., balidancer-01.rif).
5. Save the renamed clone copy image as a RIFF file into the project folder 8.3.1 Balinese Dancer.
6. Choose Cmd/Ctrl-M (Window > Screen Mode Toggle).

Continued

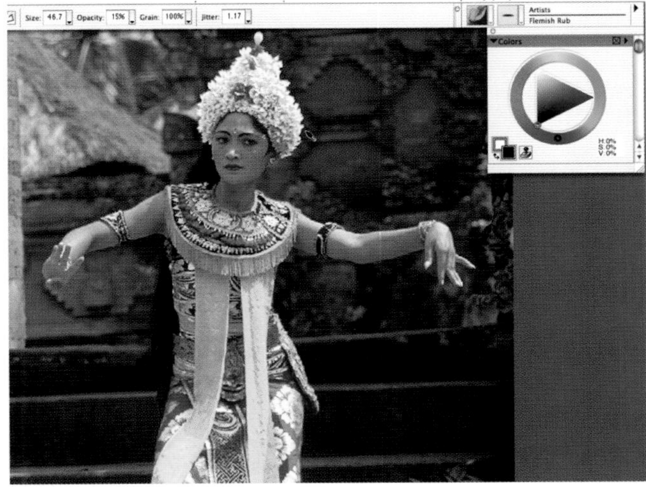

Figure 8.1 Simple palette arrangement.

7. Choose Window > Zoom to Fit so you can see the complete edge of the image. (I recommend adding a Zoom to Fit button to your custom Shortcuts palette.)
8. Choose the Flemish Rub variant (Artists category of the custom Creativity Brushes library that you will find on the companion CD). Note that for the remainder of this case study it is assumed you are using my custom Creativity Brushes brush library and all variant/category references apply to that custom library.
9. Click on the Clone Color icon in the Colors palette.
10. Brush into the background of the image with the Flemish Rub cloner, varying the brush size to suit the scale of the features. I used size about 46 for most of the background in the example shown here (Figure 8.2). You can also get interesting results using the Big Wet Luscious variant (Artists category) with Clone Color active. Make your brush strokes begin close to the dancer and end off the canvas so they create the effect of energy radiating out of the dancer. Be loose and fluid with your brush strokes. Don't worry about distorting the central figure; you can always clone back the figure with the Soft Cloner (Cloners category) at any time.
11. Choose Cmd/Ctrl-S (File > Save). This updates your file.
12. Choose Window > balidancer-00.jpg. This makes the original photograph the active image.

Continued

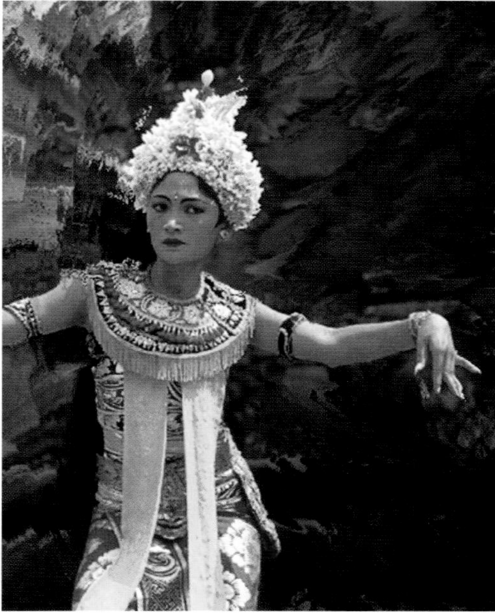

Figure 8.2 Flemish Rub radiance.

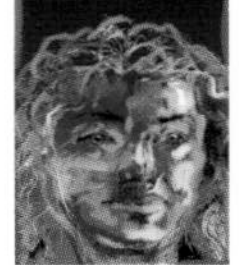

13 Choose File > Clone.

14 Choose File > Save As.

15 Rename your file with the subsequent version number, zoom blur (the effect you are about to apply), and RIFF file format tag (e.g., balidancer-02-zoom blur.rif).

16 Choose Cmd/Ctrl-M (Window > Screen Mode Toggle).

17 Choose Effects > Focus > Zoom Blur.

18 Click in the neck of the dancer on the main image.

19 Adjust the Amount slider in the Zoom Blur window to about 15 percent (Figure 8.3).

20 Choose OK. This effect is quite slow, so on a very large image you may wish to take a short tea or coffee break!

21 Choose Cmd/Ctrl-S (File > Save).

22 Hold the Option/Alt key down (turns the cursor into a Dropper tool when Clone Color is *not* active) and click on a bright yellow part of the image. Increase the brightness and saturation of the color on the Saturation-Value triangle of the Color Picker.

23 Click on the color changer arrows in the Color Picker, so that yellow color goes to the additional color (back) rectangle.

24 Hold the Option/Alt key down and click on a bright red part of the image. This color now appears in the Regular color (front) rectangle.

25 Choose the Two-Point gradation in the Gradients selector (located in the bottom of the Tools palette).

26 Choose Express in Image from the Gradients pop-up menu (Figure 8.4).

27 Click OK.

28 Choose File > Save As. Rename the file balidancer-03-xprsgrad.rif.

29 Choose Window > balidancer-01.rif. This makes the cloned image with the Flemish Rub brush strokes the active image.

30 Choose File > Clone Source and set the clone source to be balidancer-02-zoom blur.rif.

31 Choose the Soft Cloner (Cloners category). Gently brush in radiant brush strokes (Figure 8.5).

32 Choose the Sunburst variant in the F-X category.

Continued

33 Choose a bright yellow color in the Color Picker and adjust the brush size to about 100 (in practice you'll need to experiment with brush size for each image).

34 Lightly dab the stylus on a few select places where you want the sunburst glistening effect (Figure 8.6).

35 Choose File > Clone Source and set the clone source to be the original photograph, balidancer-00.jpg.

36 Choose the Captured Bristle variant of the Brushes category of the Creativity Brushes library (the same variant is in the Acrylics category of the default Painter 8 brush library).

37 Click on the Clone Color icon in the Colors palette.

38 Lightly brush over the skin to make it look like it is painted.

39 Choose the Soft Cloner in the Cloners category.

40 Use the Soft Cloner to restore the edges of the figure.

41 Choose File > Save As. Rename the file balidancer-04-details.rif.

42 Choose white in the Color Picker.

43 Choose the Flemish Rub variant in the Artists category and set the Opacity slider to 100 percent.

44 Experiment with different brush sizes as you make strokes on the very edge of the image. Here's the final result (Figure 8.7).

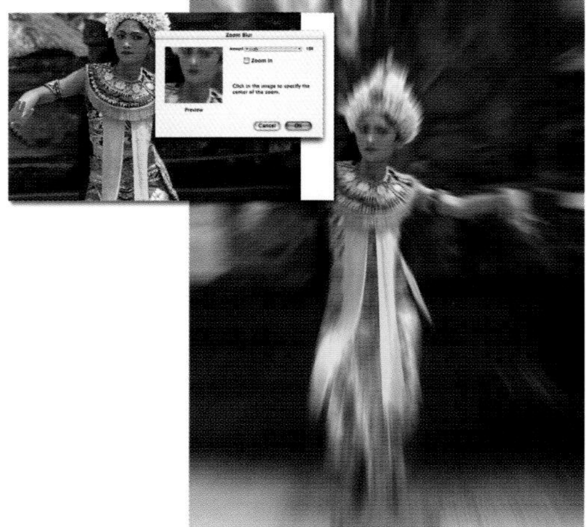

Figure 8.3 Zoom Blur effect.

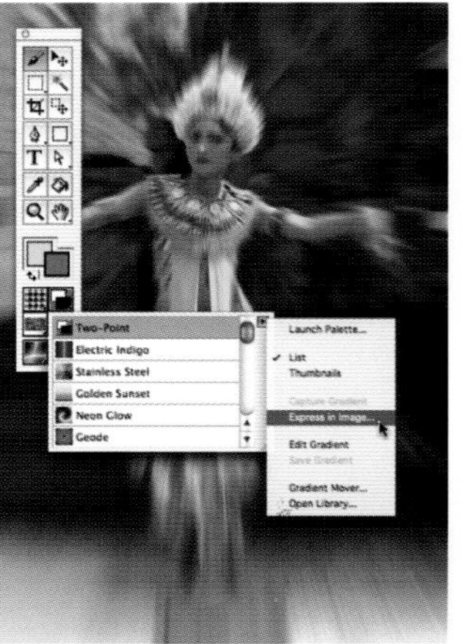

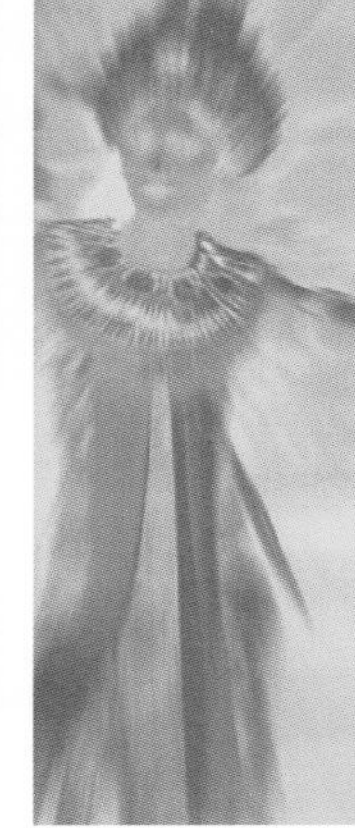

Figure 8.4 Express Gradient in image.

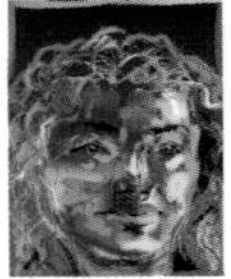

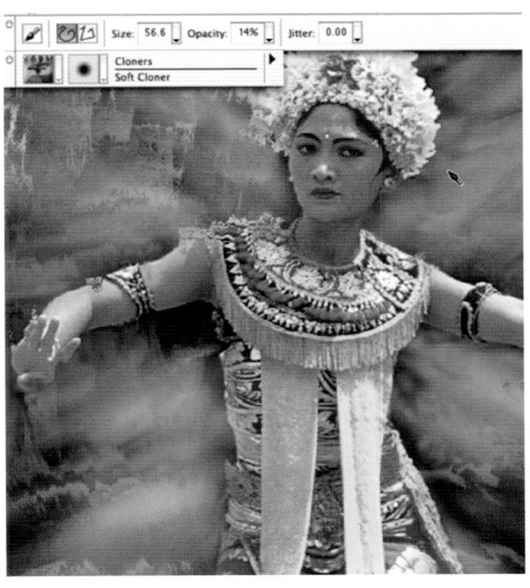

Figure 8.5 Brush in radiant brush strokes.

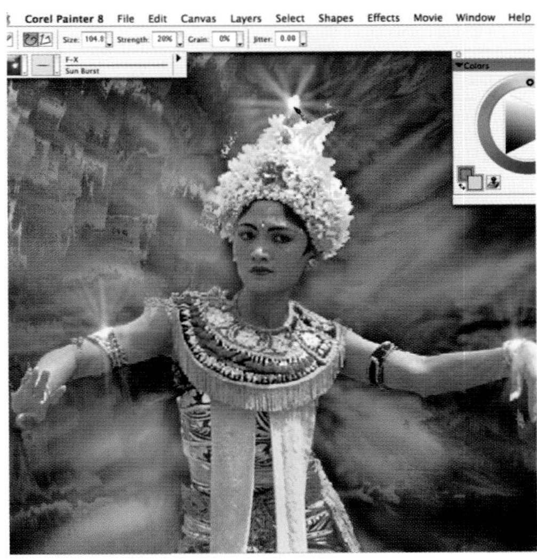

Figure 8.6 Lightly apply Sunburst.

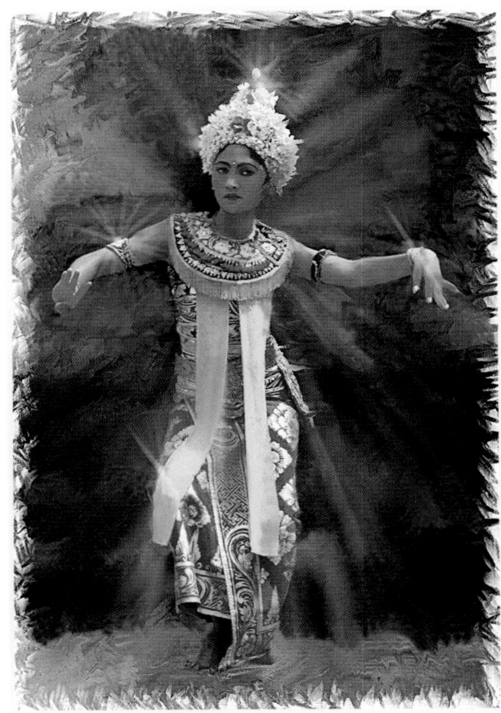

Figure 8.7 The completed painting.

Cheri's Canoe

The source image for this project is a Polaroid SX-70 manipulation by Cheri MacCallum. The photograph was taken with a Polaroid SX-70 camera with Time-Zero film, and the print was manipulated with a small sculpting tool that has a small ball on the end of it, making it great for moving the emulsion around.

1. Open the project file canoe.jpg from the Painter Projects > 8-Photography II > 8.3.2 Canoe project folder. Set up a palette arrangement similar to the one you see in Figure 8.8.
2. Choose File > Clone.
3. Choose File > Save As.
4. Rename your file with the subsequent version number and RIFF file format tag (e.g., canoe-01.rif). Subsequently throughout this project choose Cmd/Ctrl-S (File > Save) regularly to update your work. If you wish to save separate versions for different stages, you could do so.
5. Choose Cmd/Ctrl-M (Window > Screen Mode Toggle).
6. Choose Window > Zoom to Fit so you can see the complete edge of the image.
7. Choose the Artists > Flemish Rub variant from the Creativity Brushes custom brush library. For the remainder of this case study it is assumed you are using the Creativity Brushes library.
8. Click on the Clone Color icon in the Colors palette.
9. Brush into the background foliage of the image with the Flemish Rub cloner, varying the brush size to suit the scale of the features. Use your brush direction to create a sense of movement in the image (Figure 8.9).
10. Choose the Blenders > Smeary Bristle variant.
11. Apply the Smeary Bristle in the canoe with brush strokes that flow along the hull (Figure 8.10). Experiment with the brush size and opacity.
12. Choose the Blenders > Thick Oil variant.
13. Apply the Thick Oil in the water (Figure 8.11). Experiment with the brush size and opacity.
14. Choose the Blenders > Runny variant. Make sure the brush opacity is set to zero and brush size to about 14.
15. Apply the Runny variant along the rough edge (Figure 8.12).
16. Choose Cmd/Ctrl-S (File > Save) for your final update.

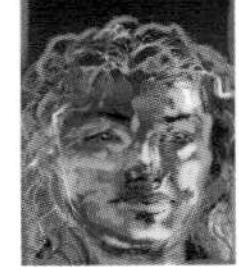

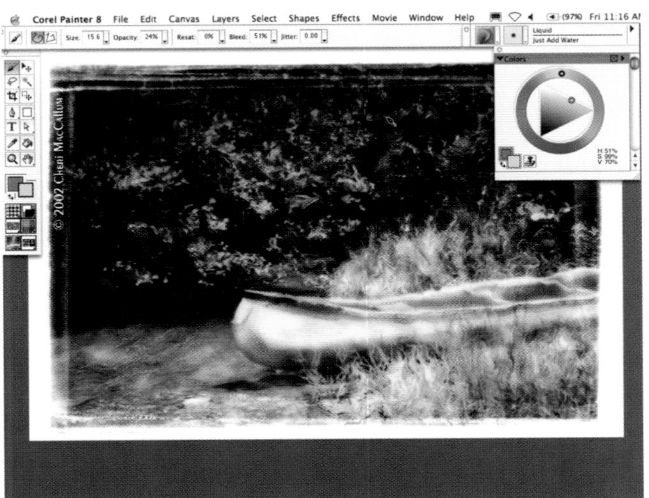

Figure 8.8 Simple palette arrangement.

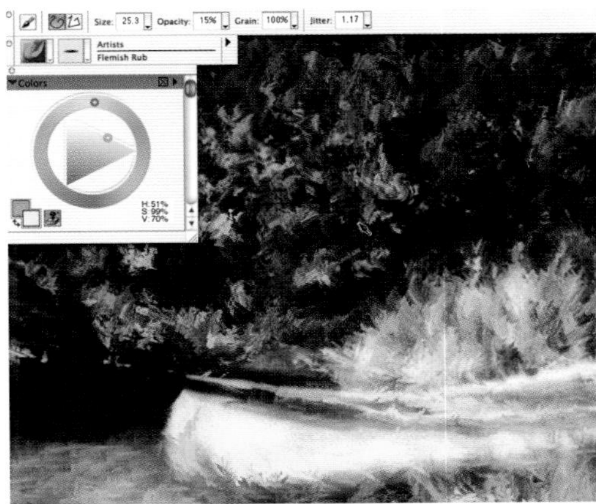

Figure 8.9 Applying the Flemish Rub cloner in the foliage.

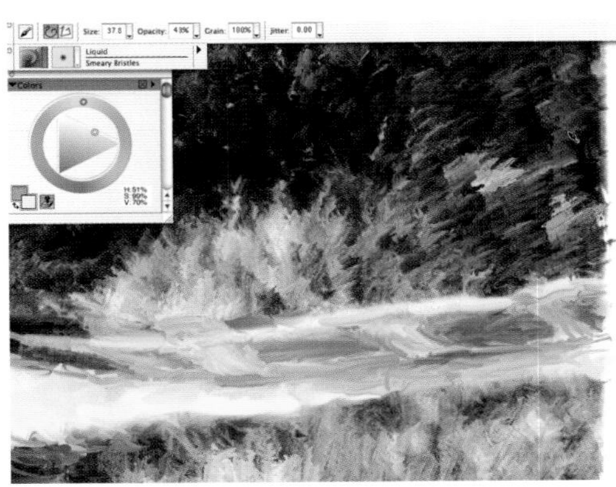

Figure 8.10 Applying the Smeary Bristle brush in the canoe.

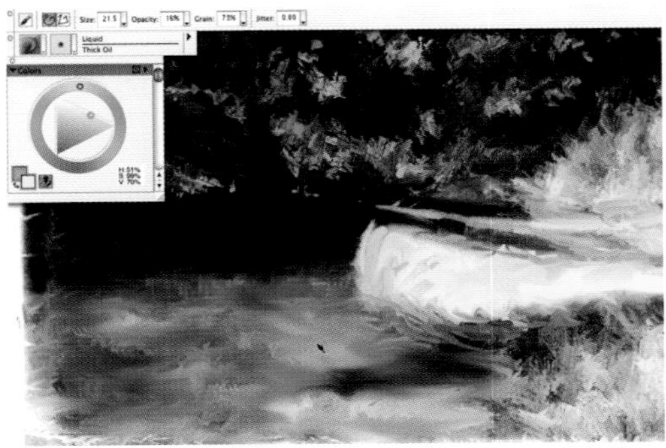

Figure 8.11 Applying the Thick Oil brush in the water.

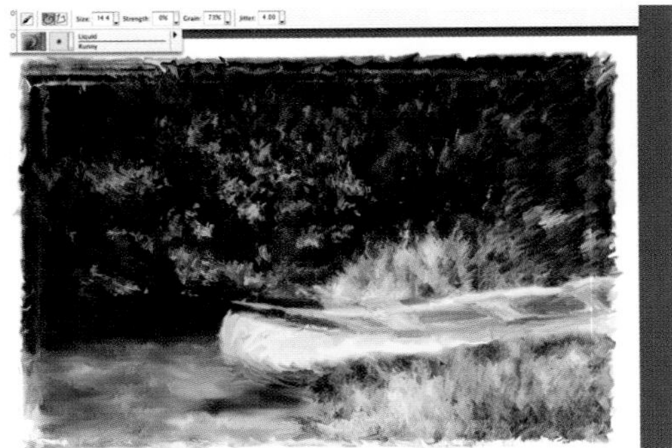

Figure 8.12 Applying the Runny brush along the edge.

The approach used in this oily example can also be used to create impressionistic versions of photos. Here is an example (Figure 8.13) where a combination of Artists > Flemish Rub, Blenders > Distorto, Brushes > Captured Bristle, and Cloners > Oil Brush Cloner were used. The original photograph is by Lisa Evans.

If you just want a straight mimic of a classical painting technique like the pointillist style of George Seurat, then you can apply the Artists > Seurat brush using clone color. Here is an example (Figure 8.14) applied to a photograph of magician Robert Strong. The background has been changed to resemble a painting in the style of Seurat.

Here is another image (Figure 8.15) based on the same photo, this time transformed, using the Captured Bristle and Sargent brushes, to resemble the style of Henri Renoir.

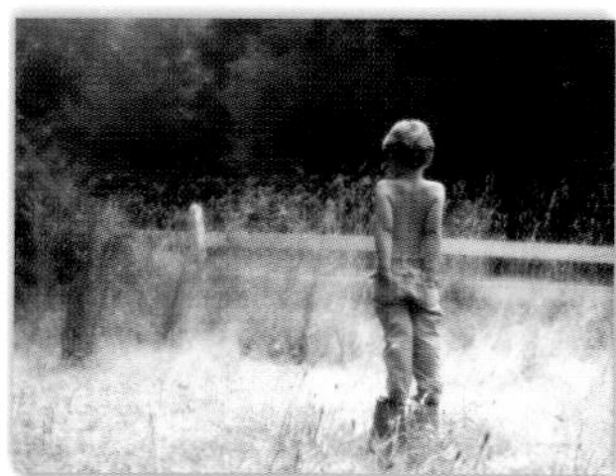

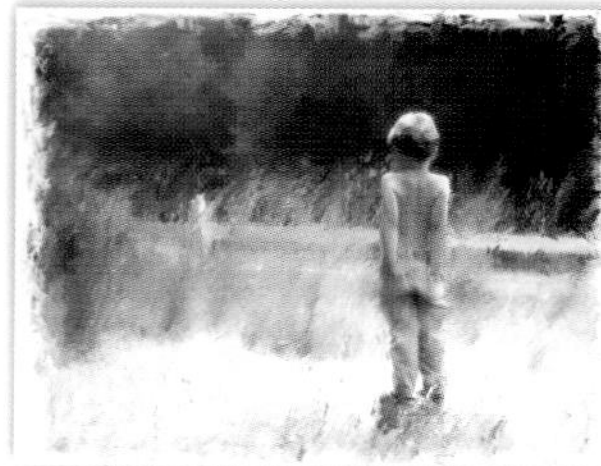

Figure 8.13 Impressionistic oily effect: Before and after.

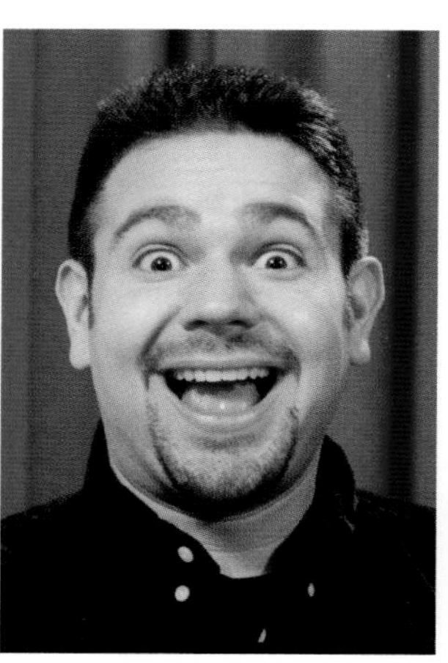

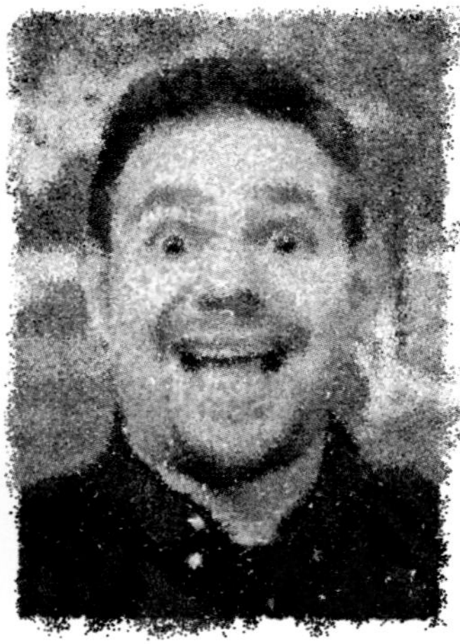

Figure 8.14 Seurat pointillist style.

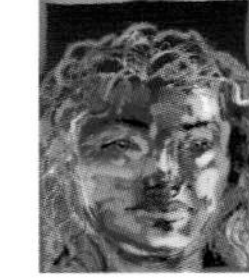

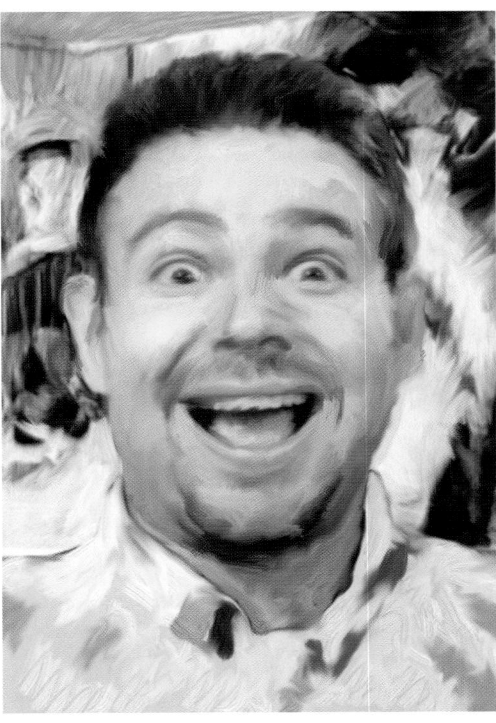

Figure 8.15 Renoir style.

8.4 Blur Dynamism: *Adding Motion with Blur Effects*

Celeste's Love Riders

This project uses a beautiful photograph of a wedding couple riding away from the church on a Harley motorcycle. The photo was taken by Celeste Dobbins. This example shows how the Zoom Blur effect can add dynamism and motion to a picture. You experienced an earlier example of this effect as part of the balidancer project.

1. Open the project file loveriders.jpg from the Painter Projects > 8-Photography II > 8.5.1 Loveriders project folder.
2. Choose File > Clone.
3. Choose File > Save As.
4. Rename your file with the subsequent version number and RIFF file format tag (e.g., loveriders-01-zoomblur.rif). Subsequently throughout this project, choose Cmd/Ctrl-S (File > Save) regularly to update your work.

Continued

5 Choose Cmd/Ctrl-M (Window > Screen Mode Toggle).

6 Choose Window > Zoom to Fit so you can see the complete edge of the image.

7 Choose Effects > Focus > Zoom Blur.

8 Click in the image at a point between the groom and bride's heads.

9 Adjust the amount slider in the Zoom Blur window to about 22 percent (Figure 8.16).

10 Click OK (Figure 8.17).

11 Choose Cmd/Ctrl-S.

12 Choose Window > loveriders.jpg.

13 Choose File > Clone.

14 Choose File > Save As.

15 Rename your file with the subsequent version number and RIFF file format tag (e.g., loveriders-02-zoomblurmix.rif).

16 Choose File > Clone Source > loveriders-01-zoomblur.rif. This sets your zoom blur image as clone source.

17 Choose the Cloners > Soft Cloner variant.

18 Clone in the zoom blurred image into the background (Figure 8.18). Make brush strokes that radiate outward from the center. Don't worry about losing detail in the groom and bride. You can always change the clone source back to the original photo, loveriders.jpg, and use the Soft Cloner at any time to clone back the original detail.

19 Open the Color Sets palette.

20 Choose Open Color Set from the Colors Sets palette pop-up menu.

21 Locate the ArtDeco Grande color set that you copied over from the Painter Creativity companion CD within the Extra Color Sets folder in the Painter 8 application folder.

22 Click OK. You see the ArtDeco Grande color set appear on your desktop.

23 Open the Layers palette.

24 Click on the third button to the right at the bottom of the Layers palette. This generates a new layer called Layer 1.

25 Double-click on the Layer 1 name and rename the layer Colorize.

26 In the Layers palette change the Composite Method (left hand pop-up menu near top of Layers palette) from Default to Colorize, make sure the Preserve Transparency box is unchecked, and lower the Layer Opacity slider to about 55 percent.

Continued

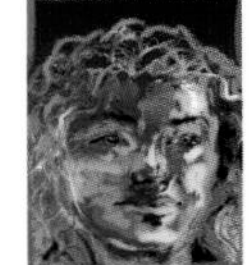

27 Choose the Airbrushes > Digital Airbrush variant.

28 Click in the ArtDeco Grande color set to choose colors and then paint those colors into the background with radial brush strokes (Figure 8.19).

29 At this point you could use the Photo > Burn and Dodge variants to emphasize the tonal contrast in the bride and groom's faces and clothing. Don't overdo it. Use low opacity and light pressure.

30 Choose File > Save As.

31 Rename the file loveriders-03-colorize.rif.

32 Choose Canvas > Canvas Size.

33 Add 100 pixels to all four directions (click in the first Adjust Size box and type in 100, then use the tab key to go down the other three boxes).

34 Click OK. Note that once you have changed the canvas size, the cloning from the original will not work (it'll be off-center).

35 Select the Colorize layer in the Layers palette.

36 Click on the first button on the left at the bottom of the Layers palette and choose Drop. This flattens your image.

37 Choose the Blenders > Runny variant.

38 Go around and roughen up the edge of the image with short radial brush strokes (Figure 8.20).

39 Choose Liquid > Bulge from the Creativity Brushes custom brush library. Experiment with lightly brushing the Bulge brush along the edges. You'll see the edge forms become elongated and distorted. This is an optional effect that you may choose to apply if you like the result. I sometimes apply it just on the sides.

40 As a final touch, choose the Blenders > Smear variant. Work over the edge with Smear using both radial strokes to blur the edge outward and contour strokes (along the edge) to soften the raggedness of the edge (Figure 8.21).

41 Choose File > Save As.

42 Rename the file loveriders-04-edgeFINAL.rif.

Figure 8.22 is another variation of the same image.

In the example of the loveriders image, the Zoom Blur succeeded in adding dynamism and a sense of motion to the picture. Another blur effect that can be good to use is the Effects > Focus > Camera Motion Blur. In the case of the Camera Motion Blur, you drag your cursor in the image to

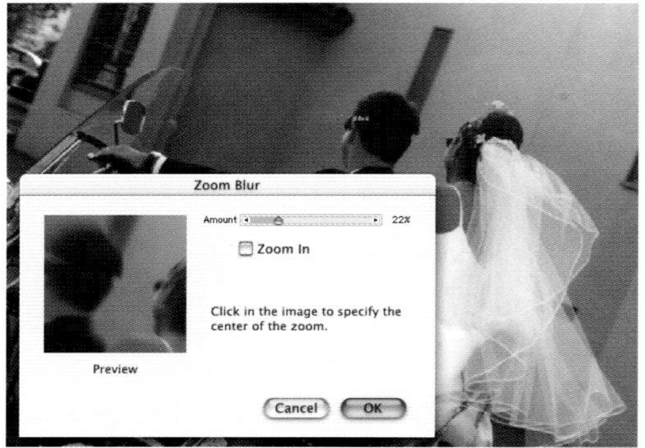

Figure 8.16 Zoom Blur window.

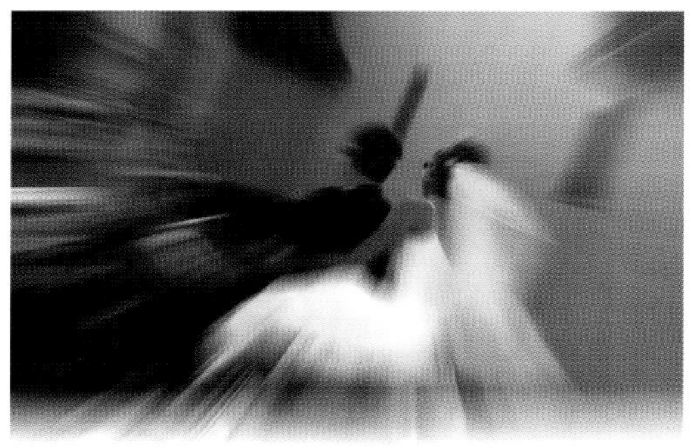

Figure 8.17 Zoom Blur applied.

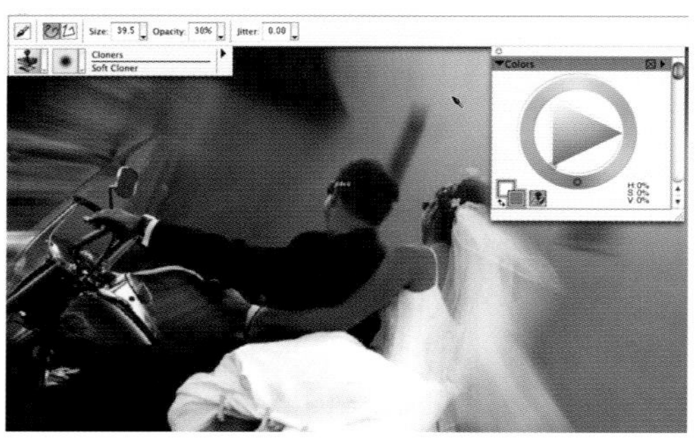

Figure 8.18 Zoom Blur cloned into the background with the Soft Cloner.

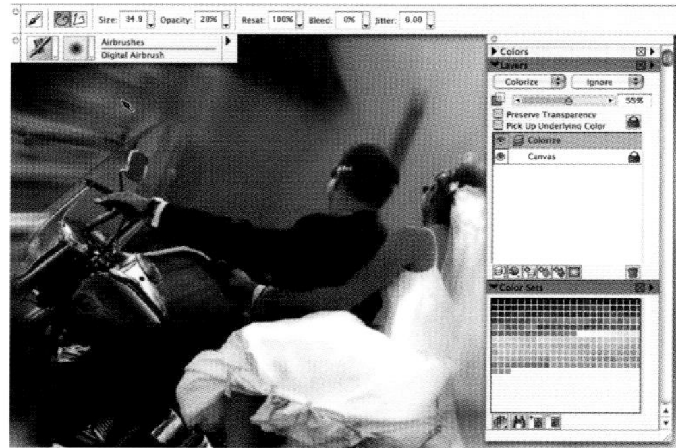

Figure 8.19 Colorizing the background.

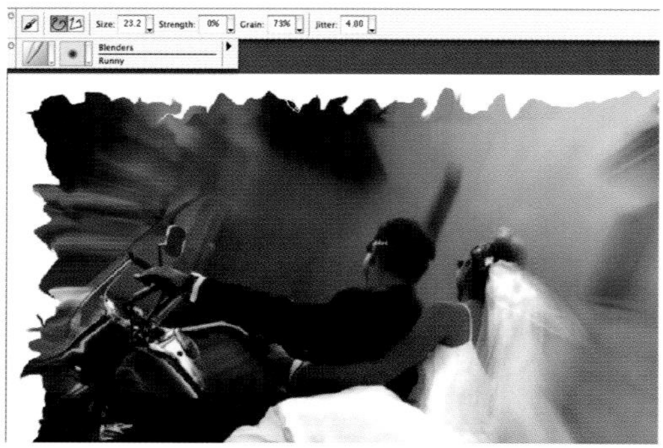

Figure 8.20 Working the edge with Runny.

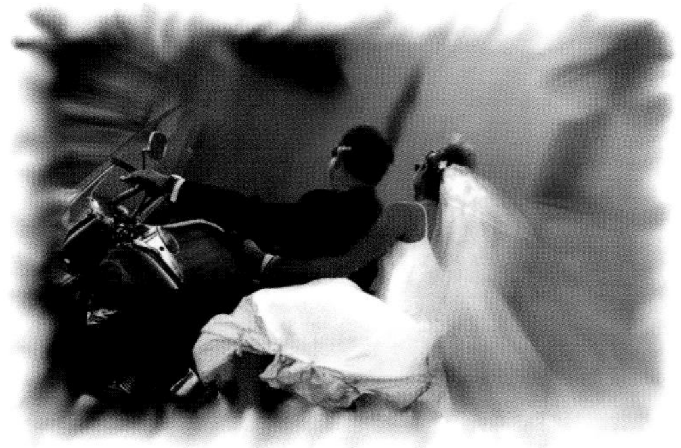

Figure 8.21 Completed image.

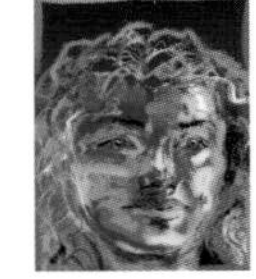

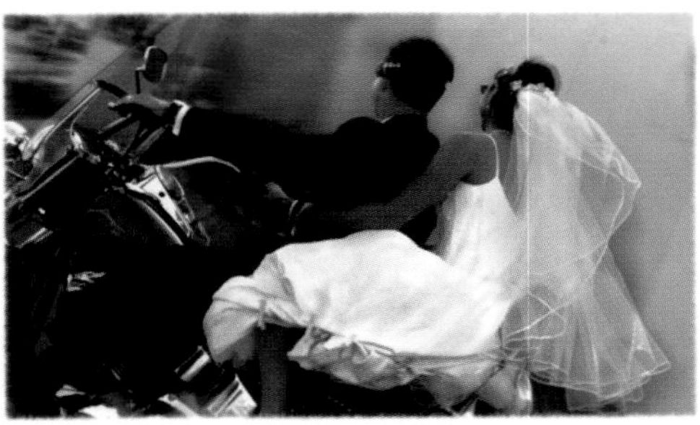

Figure 8.22 Another variation.

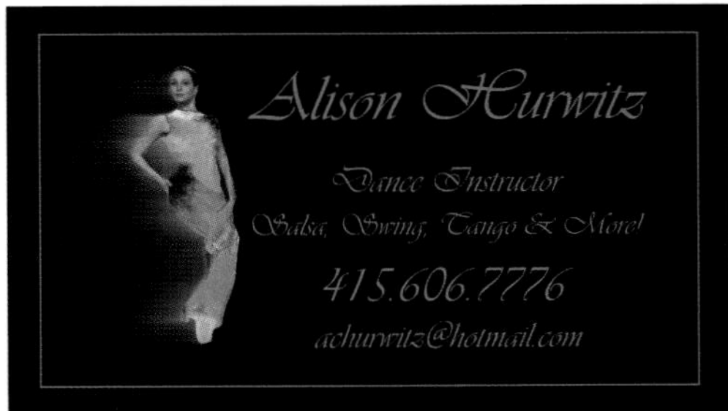

Figure 8.23 An example of Camera Motion Blur effect: Alison's card.

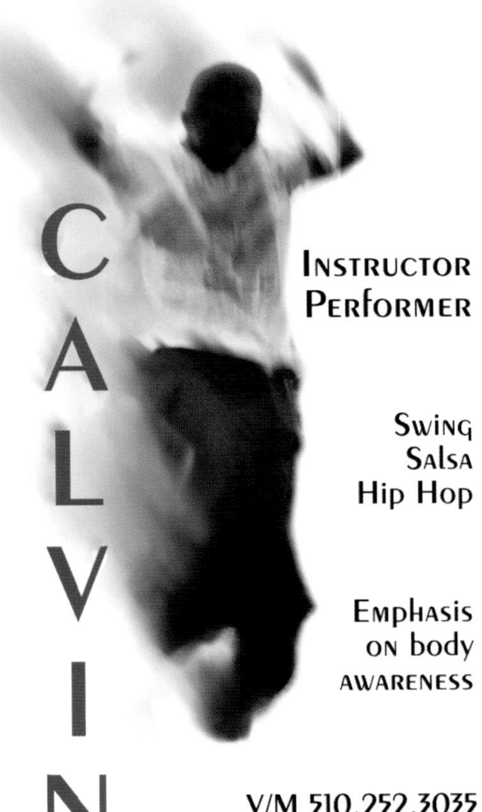

Figure 8.24 Another example of Camera Motion Blur effect: Calvin's card.

determine the extent and direction of the blur. This is best used to create a blurred clone copy, which you then clone to another (unblurred) copy of the photo, just like the methodology used in the loveriders project. Examples where the Camera Motion Blur effect have been used include the two business cards (Figures 8.23 and 8.24) that I designed for dancers Alison (www.secondglancedance.com) and Calvin.

8.5 Mosaic Magic: *Modern Edge to Ancient Craft*

This project takes you through the steps to transform your photo into a mosaic. In creating a mosaic interpretation in Painter, you enter a special mode of Painter where only mosaics work and most of the normal tools and functions, such as zoom in and zoom out, do not work.

1. Open the project file clown.jpg from the Painter Projects > 8-Photography II > 8.5 Clown project folder. This is a photo by Dwight Goode.
2. Choose File > Clone.
3. Choose File > Save As.
4. Rename your file clown-01.rif.
5. Choose Cmd/Ctrl-M (Window > Screen Mode Toggle).
6. Choose Window > Zoom to Fit so you can see the complete edge of the image. This is particularly important in mosaics, because you can't zoom in and out while in Make Mosaic mode. To do so you have to click Done, come out of Make Mosaic mode, zoom in or out, and then return to Canvas > Make Mosaic mode.
7. Choose Canvas > Make Mosaic. Your clone copy canvas will become white and a Make Mosaic window will appear.
8. Check the Tracing Paper checkbox in the Make Mosaic window. You will see the underlying original photo show through at 50 percent opacity.
9. Click on the Clone Color icon in the Colors palette. This enables Clone Color and disables the Color Picker.
10. Start painting in mosaic tiles into your image.
11. Adjust the Settings: Dimensions (sliders that determine the size of each tile) to suit the features you are painting (Figure 8.25).
12. Continue until the canvas is filled with mosaic tiles.
13. Choose the third button to the right in the Make Mosaic window, and select Tint from the pop-up menu.
14. Click on the Clone Color icon in the Color palette, which enables the Color Picker, and select colors you wish to add tints with.
15. Apply selective color tinting of the tiles to enhance the composition. In this case I tinted the apple.

Continued

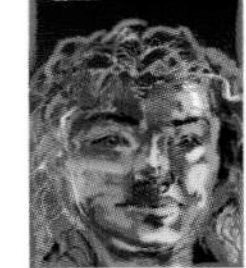

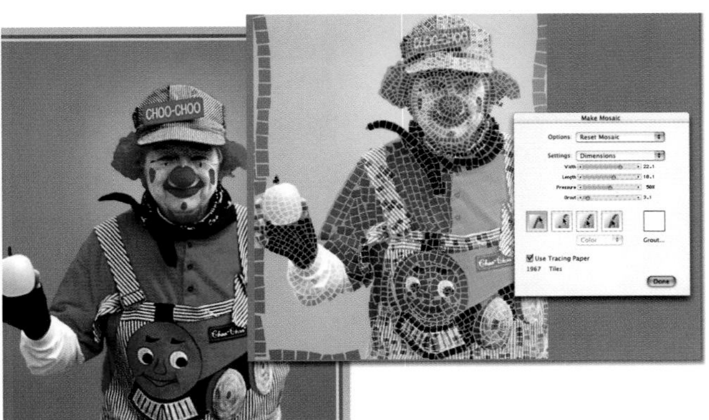

Figure 8.25 Painting mosaic tiles with Tracing Paper on.

16 Double-click on the grout color swatch in the make Mosaic window. (Grout is the material between the tiles.)

17 Select black in the grout Color Picker (slider all the way to the left, Figure 8.26).

18 When you've completed the mosaic, select Render Tiles into Mask from the Options pop-up menu (Figure 8.27). Although nothing visible happens, this is an important step.

19 Choose Done. You now return to the non-mosaic mode and have access to all the normal tools and functions.

20 Open the Channels palette (Window > Show Channels). Click on the first button on the left in the bottom of the Channels palette. This is the Load Selection button and allows you to load any mask (also known as channel) that you choose from the Load From pop-up menu as an active selection in the image.

21 Choose Mosaic Mask from the Load From pop-up menu (Figure 8.28).

22 Click OK. You'll see a complex array of dancing ants appear around the contours of every tile.

23 Choose Selection > Hide Marquee. The dancing ants disappear even though the selection of all the mosaic tiles is still active. You can now work into the tiles with any effects or brushes, leaving the grout untouched. Sometimes selectively using the Cloners > Soft Cloner can give interesting results.

24 Choose Effects > Surface Control > Apply Surface Texture.

25 Make sure the Using menu is set to Paper, and that the Softness slider is all the way to the left (0.0). These are the default settings. Reduce the Amount slider to about 25 percent.

26 Choose OK. You have now added a little roughness to the tile surface.

Continued

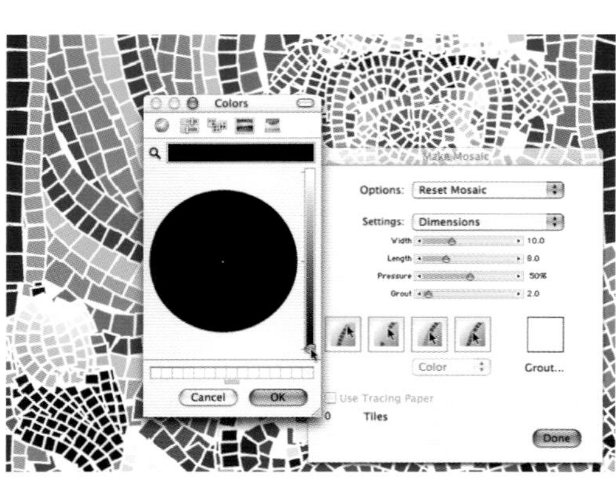

Figure 8.26 Setting grout color to black.

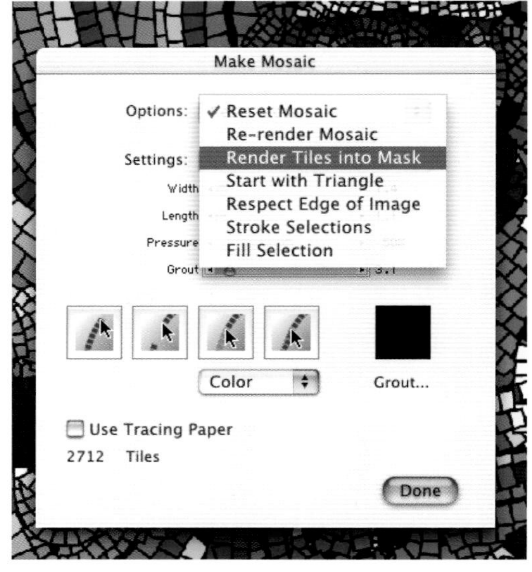

Figure 8.27 Rendering Tiles into Mask.

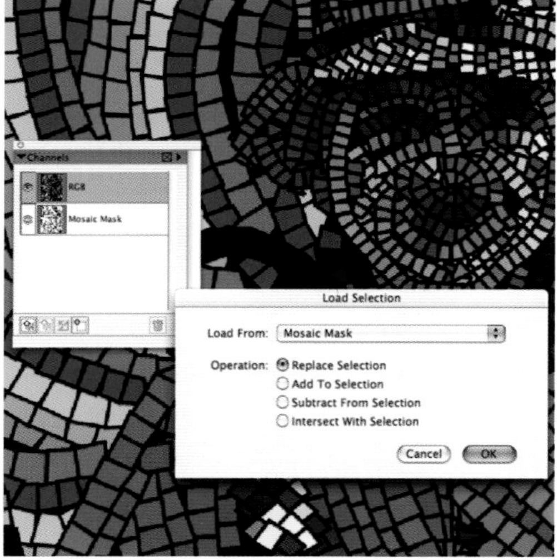

Figure 8.28 Loading the mosaic mask as a selection.

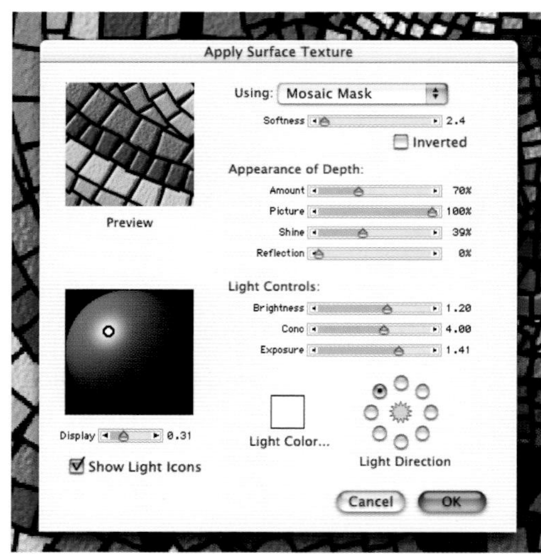

Figure 8.29 Applying Surface Texture using the mosaic mask.

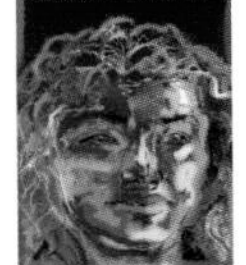

27 Choose Effects > Apply Surface Texture (the most recent effect always becomes the first menu item).

28 Select Using: Mosaic Mask.

29 Adjust the Softness slider to about 2.4 (Figure 8.29).

30 Click OK.

31 Choose File > Save As and rename the file clown-01-mosaic.rif. Note that only the RIFF file format preserves the editability of the mosaic mode. Figure 8.30 shows the final result.

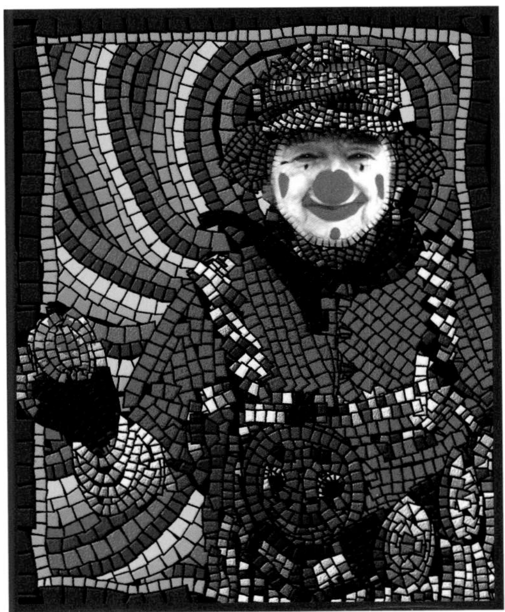

Figure 8.30 Finished mosaic.

8.6 Gradient Expressionism: *Instant Psychedelia*

In this project you apply the Zoom Blur effect, which was used in the earlier balidancer and loveriders projects, followed by the Gradients > Express in Image effect, which is a great way to colorize an image.

1. Open the project file fatherandbride.jpg from the Painter Projects > 8-Photography II > 8.6 Father and Bride project folder. This is a photo showing a bride, Gracie, and her father, Anesto, taken by Ernest Love.
2. Choose File > Clone.
3. Choose File > Save As.
4. Rename your file fatherandbride-01-zoomblur.rif.
5. Choose Cmd/Ctrl-M (Window > Screen Mode Toggle).
6. Choose Window > Zoom to Fit so you can see the complete edge of the image.
7. Choose Effects > Focus > Zoom Blur.
8. Click between the father and the bride.
9. Adjust the Amount slider in the Zoom Blur window to about 15 percent.
10. Choose OK.
11. Open the Gradients selector (located in the bottom of the Tools palette).
12. Choose an appropriately colored gradient from the Gradients library drawer that contains colors you would like to express in the image. In the example shown in Figure 8.31, I created a custom gradient by adding colors from a Color Set using the Edit Gradient command from the Gradient pop-up menu.
13. Choose Express in Image from the Gradients pop-up menu (click on the small triangle in the top right corner of the Gradients selector to access this menu).

Continued

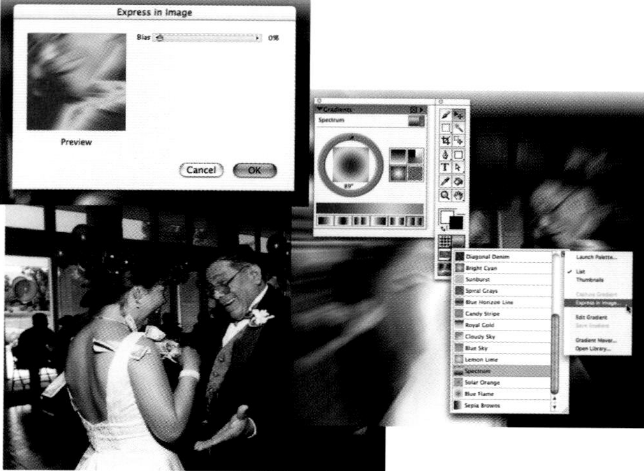

Figure 8.31 Original photo and expressing gradient in zoom blurred version.

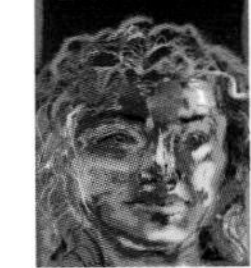

14 If, as in my case, the resulting colors are a bit dull, choose Effects > Tonal Control > Adjust Color. Then adjust the Saturation slider all the way to the right (Figure 8.32).

15 Choose Cmd/Ctrl-S (File > Save).

16 Choose Window > fatherandbride.jpg. This returns you to the original photo as the active image.

17 Choose File > Clone.

18 Choose File > Save As.

19 Rename your file fatherandbride-02-mix.rif.

20 Choose the Cloners > Soft Cloner variant.

21 Choose File > Clone Source > fatherandbride-01-zoomblur.rif.

22 Use the Soft Cloner to clone in the colorful zoom blurred version around the main figures. If you need to restore the original photo, just change the clone source back to the original photo (File > Clone Source > fatherandbride.jpg) and clone back in the original. In this way you can go back and forth cloning in from one source image or another until you are satisfied.

23 Choose Cmd/Ctrl-S (File > Save).

24 Choose Canvas > Canvas Size.

25 Add 100 pixels to all four directions (click in the first Adjust Size box and type in 100, then use the tab key to go down the other three boxes).

Continued

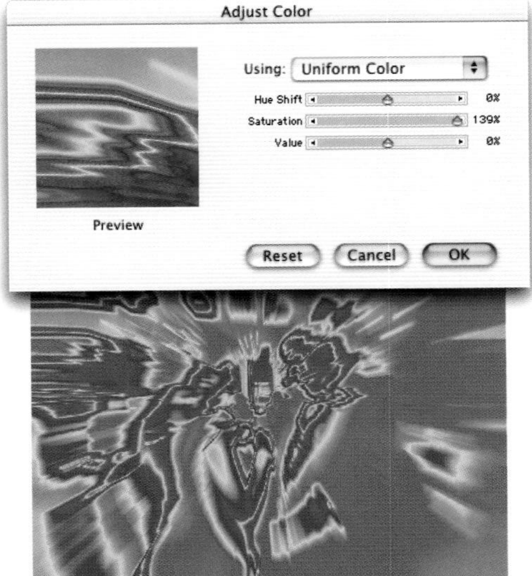

Figure 8.32 Saturating color in the image.

26. Click OK. Note that once you have changed the canvas size, the cloning from the original will not work (it'll be off center).
27. Choose File > Save As.
28. Rename your file fatherandbride-03-mixwithborder.rif.
29. Choose File > Clone.
30. Choose Effects > Focus > Zoom Blur.
31. Click between the father and the bride.
32. Adjust the Amount slider in the Zoom Blur window to about 45 percent.
33. Choose OK.
34. Choose File > Save As.
35. Rename your file fatherandbride-04-mixwithborderzoom.rif.
36. Choose Window > fatherandbride-03-mixwithborder.rif.
37. Choose File > Clone Source > fatherandbride-04-mixwithborderzoom.rif.
38. Use the Soft Cloner to clone in the blurred border.
39. Choose the Blenders > Smear variant to complete the smearing of the border (Figure 8.33).

Figure 8.34 is another example of a photo transformation where the Gradient > Express in Image effect was used. This image is based on the same photograph by CelestePhotoArt.com that was used earlier.

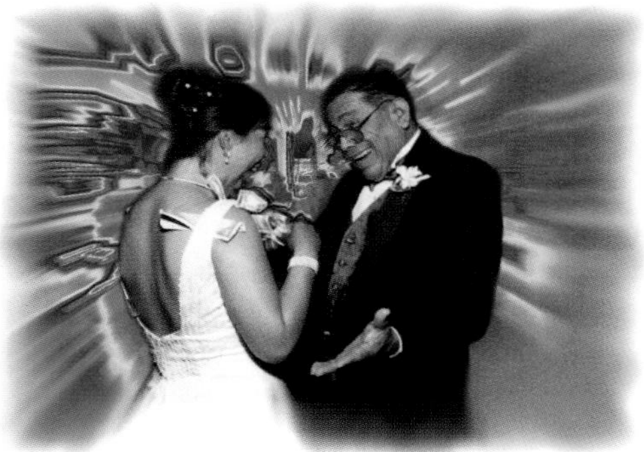

Figure 8.33 Completed artwork.

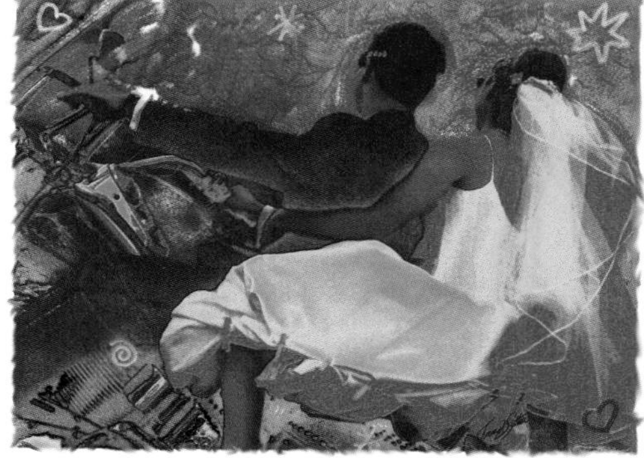

Figure 8.34 Version of Celeste's LoveRiders created using Gradients > Express in Image.

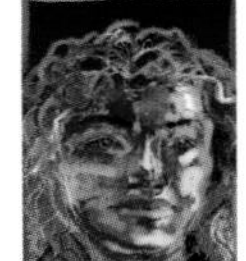

8.7 Sensational Serigraphy Meets Woodcut Wizardry

This project uses as its basis a photograph by Elsa Vera taken at an open-air swing event in Santa Rosa. I used this image to create a postcard for a dance party. This project shows you how to use two wonderful effects in Painter 8: the Serigraphy and Woodcut effects.

1. Open the project file santarosadance.jpg from the Painter Projects > 8-Photography II > 8.7 Santa Rosa Dance project folder. This is a photo by Elsa Vera.
2. Choose File > Clone.
3. Choose File > Save As.
4. Rename your file santarosadance-01-serigraphy.rif.
5. Choose Cmd/Ctrl-M (Window > Screen Mode Toggle).
6. Choose Window > Zoom to Fit.
7. Choose Effects > Surface Control > Serigraphy. A Spot Color window appears.
8. Select a color in the Color Picker or from a Color Set (in this example I used colors from the ArtDeco Grande color set that comes with the Painter Creativity Companion CD).
9. Adjust the Threshold slider until you are satisfied with the resulting preview (Figure 8.35).
10. Choose Create Spot Layer. When you click this button, a new layer appears in your layers list (Objects > Layers palette) with a name like "Red Spot Layer 1." Do *not* click Done at this stage (if you do accidentally click Done, just reselect the Serigraphy effect).
11. Continue this process with other colors until you have built up a series of spot color layers. In this example I ended up with 11 spot color layers (Figure 8.36).
12. Click Done.
13. Choose Window > santarosadance.jpg. This makes the original photo the active picture in Painter.
14. Choose File > Clone.
15. Choose File > Save As.
16. Rename your file santarosadance-02-woodcut.rif.
17. Choose Cmd/Ctrl-M (Window > Screen Mode Toggle).

Continued

18 Choose Effects > Surface Control > Woodcut.

19 In the Woodcut window uncheck Output Color (so only Output Black is checked) and experiment with the sliders until you see a result in the preview window you like. In this case (Figure 8.37), the slider settings I used were Black Edge 18.53, Erosion Time 0, Erosion Edge 2.0, and Heaviness 32 percent.

20 Choose OK.

21 Choose Cmd/Ctrl-S (File > Save).

22 Choose the Airbrushes > Digital Airbrush variant.

Continued

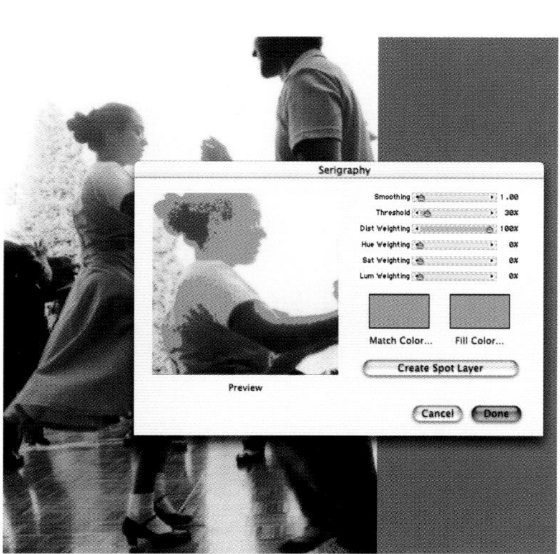

Figure 8.35 Serigraphy Spot Color window.

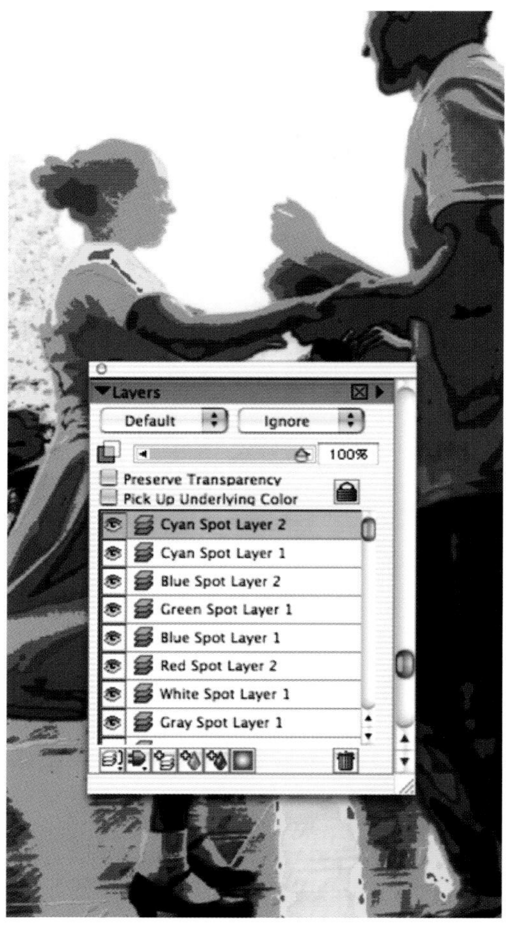

Figure 8.36 Multiple spot color layers.

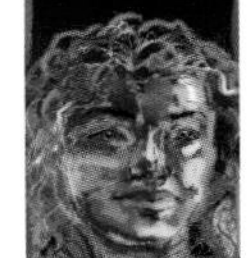

23 Choose white in the Color Picker.

24 Paint out all the black lines besides the dancing figures. The remaining black lines will be used to bring visual emphasis to the dancing figures.

25 Choose Select > Auto Select.

26 Select Using: Image Luminance in the Auto Select window.

27 Choose OK. Dancing ants appear around the black lines.

28 Choose Cmd/Ctrl-C (Edit > Copy).

29 Choose Window > santarosadance-01-serigraphy.rif. This makes the multilayered multicolored serigraphy image the active image. To make sure this image is centered, click once with the Grabber Hand tool (hold down the space bar to turn the brush cursor temporarily into the grabber hand cursor). Centering the image is important to ensure that the black lines generated in the Woodcut effect are pasted in with perfect registration.

30 Choose Cmd/Ctrl-V (Edit > Paste). This pastes the black lines onto the multicolored image (Figure 8.38). If any repositioning of the pasted layer is needed, use the arrow keys.

31 Select a spot color layer in the Objects > Layers palette that you wish to accentuate.

32 Choose a bright color in the Color Picker.

33 Choose Cmd/Ctrl-F (Effects > Fill). Make sure the Fill window has Fill With: Current Color selected.

Continued

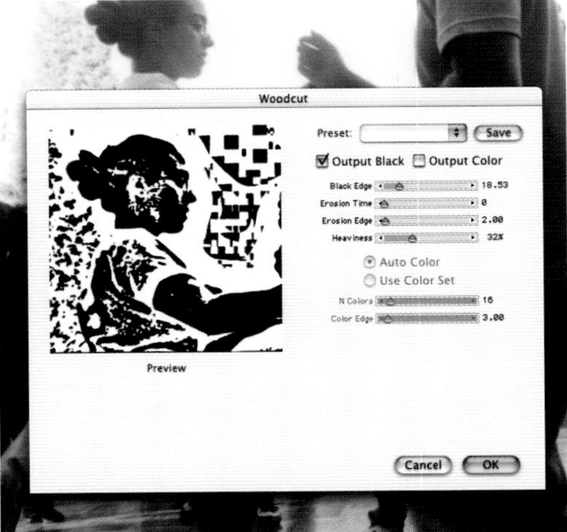

Figure 8.37 Woodcut window.

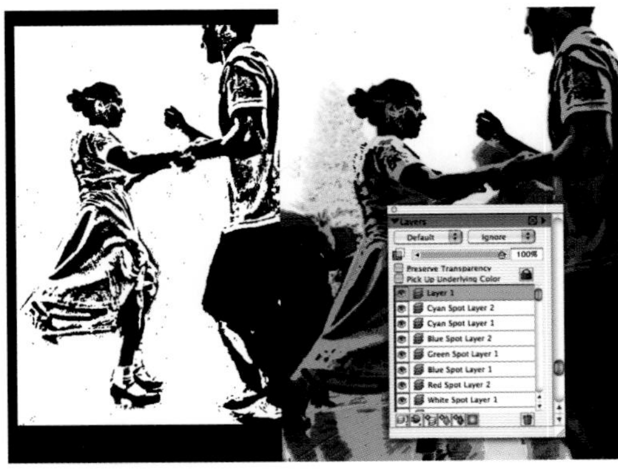

Figure 8.38 Woodcut black lines (*left*) pasted into multicolored serigraphy image (*right*) as a new layer.

34 Choose OK.

35 Repeat with different colors for a few other spot color layers (Figure 8.39).

36 Choose File > Save As.

37 Rename your file santarosadance-03-colorlayers.rif.

38 Choose Drop All from the Objects > Layers pop-up menu.

39 Choose the Blenders > Runny variant.

40 Use the Runny variant to smear some of the background coloring.

41 Choose other brushes to blur and smear and slightly distort the background imagery. Leave the figures untouched. This helps bring emphasis and attention to them.

42 Choose File > Save As.

43 Rename your file santarosadance-04-distortbkgnd.rif.

44 Add any text or logos to the final design (Figure 8.40).

45 Choose File > Save As.

46 Rename your file santarosadance-04-textFINAL.rif.

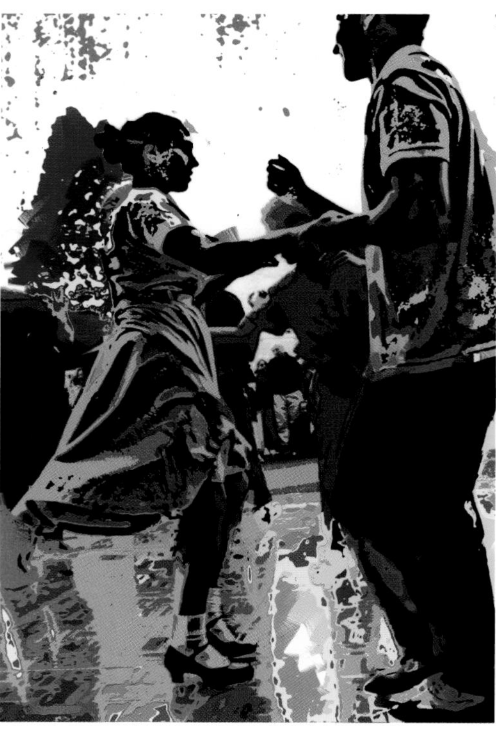

Figure 8.39 After coloring selected layers.

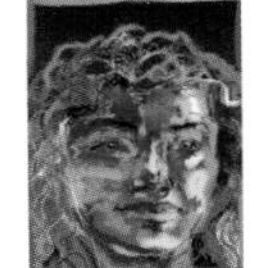

This project shows the way you can selectively weave together multiple effects, in this case the Serigraphy and the Woodcut effects, plus the organic hand-painted feel of original brush work, to create a powerful, beautiful image. Another example of this approach is the "Andy Warhol pop-art" version of the Robert Strong portrait (Figure 8.41). In this case I used the Woodcut effect with Output Color unchecked to produce the black line work, and then mixed Liquid Ink brushwork with regular paint. See Figures 8.14 and 8.15 for other versions of the Strong portrait.

This image leads us into the next project where you'll learn a very easy, fast, and fun way to transform any photo into an "Andy Warhol pop-art" style of image.

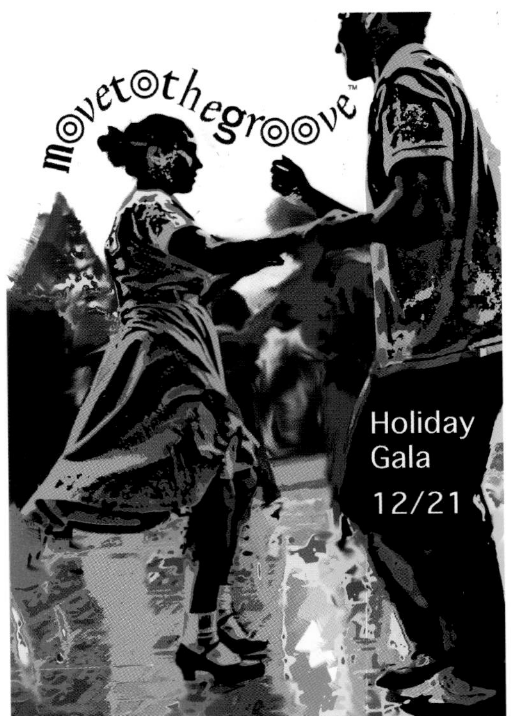

Figure 8.40 The final design.

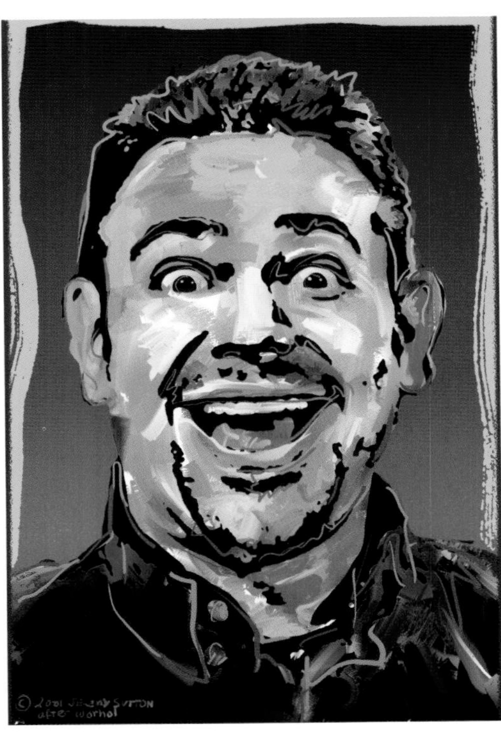

Figure 8.41 "Andy Warhol pop-art" style of Robert Strong portrait.

8.8 Pop Art à la Warhol: *Inverse Texture Technique*

This project uses a high school senior photograph of Melyssa taken by Peg Buckner. I felt that the mood and feel of the portrait lent itself to a less traditional, more "pop-art" type of transformation. The inverse texture technique described here is easy and fast to apply to any photo. It also is versatile and allows you to quickly generate variations and produce repeating designs.

In essence you will be generating a paper texture from a photo and then using a chalk brush to paint into the positive and negative spaces of the paper grain with different colors.

Paper Texture in Painter (also referred to as Paper Grain) is actually a repeating gray-scale tile that modulates the way certain grainy brushes (those that have Grainy in their Method Subcategory, a characteristic found in the Brush Creator > Stroke Designer > General section) apply paint onto the canvas.

Single Melyssa

1. Open the project file melyssa.jpg from the Painter Projects > 8-Photography II > 8.7 Melyssa project folder. This is a photo by Peg Buckner.
2. Choose File > Clone.
3. Choose File > Save As.
4. Rename your file melyssa-01-texture.rif.
5. Choose Cmd/Ctrl-M (Window > Screen Mode Toggle).
6. Choose Window > Zoom to Fit.
7. Choose Effects > Tonal Control > Express Texture.
8. Click and drag in the Express Texture preview window until you see a key feature, such as an eye, visible.
9. Select Using: Image Luminance.
10. Adjust the slider settings slowly from one extreme to another until you get a clear gray-scale image that keeps detail in the mid-tones but has good contrast (deep blacks and pure whites). This is the quality we want for an effective paper texture (in Painter the paper texture and paper grain are often used interchangeably). In this case I chose the slider settings Gray Threshold 104 percent, Grain 155 percent and Contrast 75 percent (Figure 8.42).
11. Click OK. Note that although the clone image looks like it's been converted into a gray-scale image, it is in fact still an RGB image. All images in Painter are RGB. If you wish to convert an image to any other color mode, it is best to do so in Photoshop.
12. Choose Cmd/Ctrl-A (Select > All).
13. Choose Capture Paper from the Papers pop-up menu in the upper right corner of the Papers selector (located in the Tools palette) (Figure 8.43).

Continued

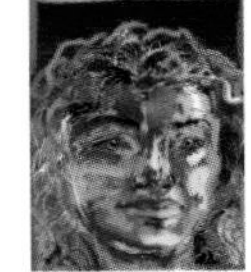

14 Name the paper "melyssa." Adjust the Crossfade slider all the way to the left (0.00). The Crossfade setting, the default value of which is 16.00, determines how much overlap there is between adjacent repeating tiles of paper texture. In this case we will initially only have one tile filling the entire image. If you choose to reduce the scale of the paper texture later and create multiple portraits, then making the Crossfade 0.00 is needed to ensure that you can accurately clone in the original photo, also at the same scale. This is explained in greater detail below.

15 Choose OK. The paper now appears in the Papers selector preview. To see a larger preview and access more controls choose Window > Open Papers. This opens the Papers palette. Drag in the Papers palette preview window to see the eyes in the captured texture.

16 Choose Cmd/Ctrl-S (File > Save).

17 Choose Delete/Backspace. This clears the canvas to white. If you wish to paint your pop-art image onto any background other than white, this is the time to fill the canvas with your desired background color or gradient (gradients can look very effective).

18 Choose File > Save As.

19 Rename your file melyssa-02-background.rif.

20 Choose the Chalk > Large Chalk variant.

21 Adjust the brush size to about 85, the Grain slider to about 9 percent, and the opacity to about 24 percent.

Continued

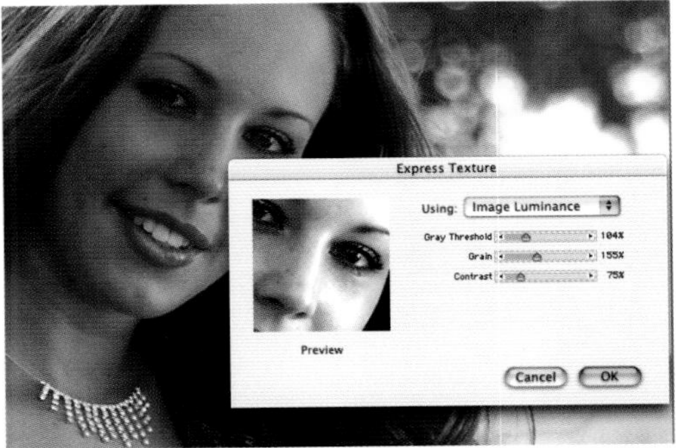

Figure 8.42 Convert image into "gray-scale" using Express Texture.

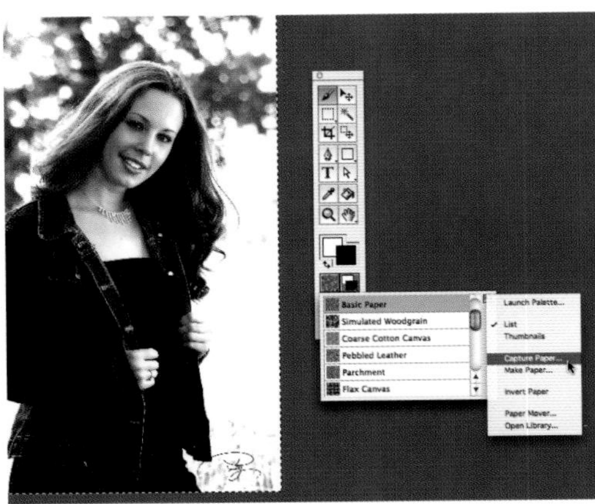

Figure 8.43 Capture Paper.

22 Start painting into the canvas. In effect you are painting into the positive space (i.e., the "mountain tops" of the texture), where the original image was dark. Vary the colors as you paint (Figure 8.44).

23 Choose File > Save As.

24 Rename your file melyssa-03-paint.rif.

25 Click on the Papers Palette > Invert Paper icon (right hand of the two icons that are located to the right of the preview window in the Papers palette).

26 Choose appropriate colors and paint into the negative spaces of the texture (i.e., where the "valleys" were), which correspond to where the original image was light (Figure 8.45).

27 Choose Cmd/Ctrl-S (File > Save).

28 Choose File > Clone.

29 Choose File > Save As.

30 Rename your file melyssa-04-softcloner.rif.

Continued

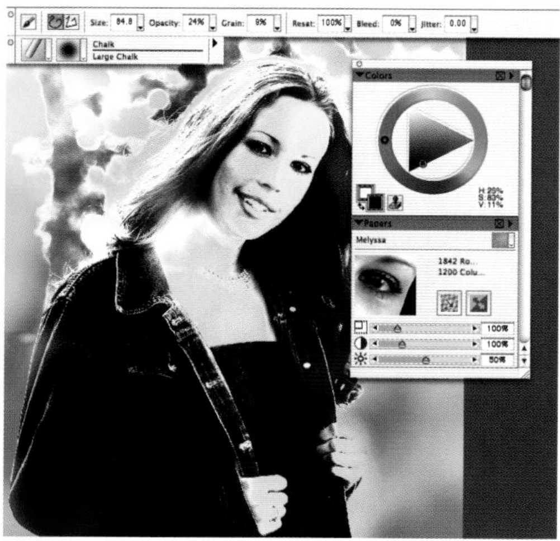

Figure 8.44 Painting into the positive space.

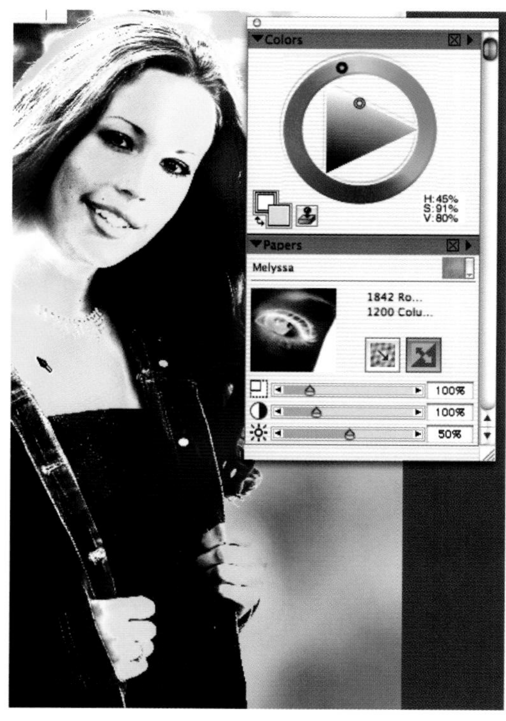

Figure 8.45 Painting into the negative space.

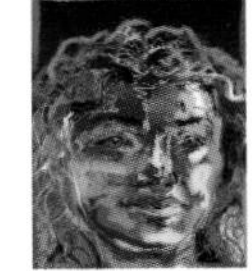

31 Choose File > Clone Source > melyssa.jpg. This resets the original photo to be the clone source.

32 Choose the Cloners > Soft Cloner variant.

33 Lightly clone back in some of the original image (Figure 8.46).

If you overdo it, just choose File > Clone Source > melyssa-03-paint.rif and paint back in the painted version. You can go back and forth between clone sources until you are satisfied. This way you have complete control.

34 Choose Cmd/Ctrl-S (File > Save).

35 Choose Canvas > Canvas Size.

36 Add 100 pixels to all four directions (click in the first Adjust Size box and type in 100, then use the tab key to go down the other three boxes).

37 Click OK. Note that once you have changed the canvas size, cloning from the original will not work (it'll be off center).

38 Choose File > Save As.

39 Rename your file melyssa-05-edges.rif.

40 Choose Liquid > Bulge (from Creativity Brushes library). Lightly brush the Bulge brush along the edges. The final result may look something like Figure 8.47.

Note that the word *finished* should be taken as a relative term. In reality there are always more permutations that can be done, more fine-tuning, and so on. In this case you can experiment in

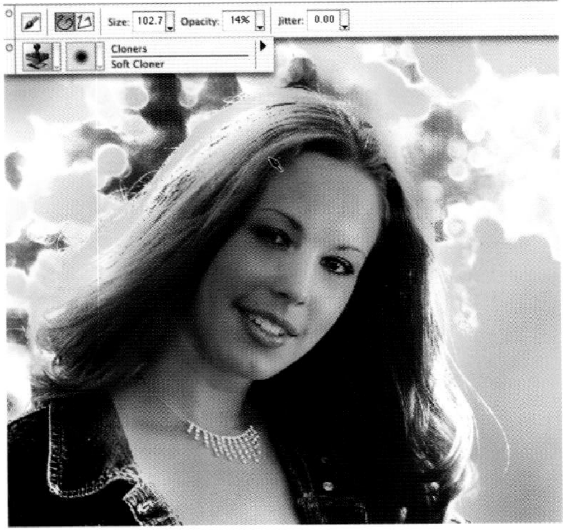

Figure 8.46 Cloning back the original photo.

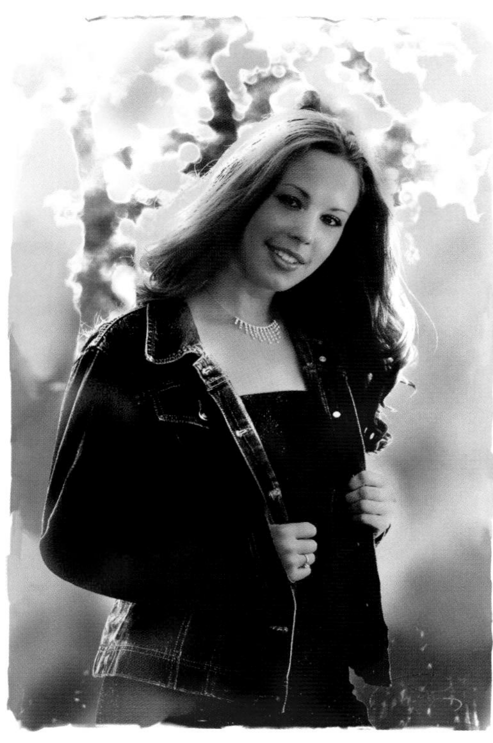

Figure 8.47 The finished version of Melyssa.

many ways with the newly created paper texture, for instance, by using different color combinations or by creating multiples on a single image.

Multiple Melyssas

1. With melyssa-05-edges.rif as your active image, choose File > Clone.
2. Choose File > Save As.
3. Rename your file melyssa-06-multiple.rif.
4. Choose Cmd/Ctrl-A (Select > All).
5. Choose Delete/Backspace.
6. Lower the Scale slider in the Papers palette from 100 percent down to 34 percent. You can also just click on the number box and type in the required number, in this case 34. Note that a 33 or 34 percent Paper scale will result in

Continued

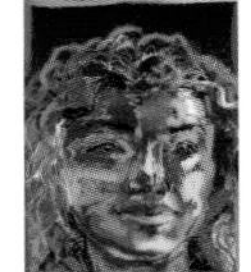

three portraits across by three up, which means a total of nine repeating portraits in the multiple. If you wanted just four portraits (two along by two up) you'd then make the Paper scale 50 percent.

7 Experiment with some chalk brush strokes across the whole canvas and see how many multiples fit into the canvas vertically and horizontally. You may need to adjust the Scale slider by trial and error to get a suitable scale of image. Remember you can always crop down to clean up the edges later. When you do settle on a paper scale, make a note of it, because it is likely to change as you work on other projects. If you ever wish to return to working on this image, you'll need to reset the exact paper scale.

8 When you are satisfied with your paper scale, reclear the canvas (Cmd/Ctrl-A followed by Delete/Backspace). You could also fill (Cmd/Ctrl-F) with any color or gradient.

9 Paint into the positive and negative spaces, as you did before, using the Invert Paper checkbox in the Papers section. In the example shown here (Figure 8.48), I played complementary colors off against each other (e.g., reds against greens, blues against oranges). I also used a very large chalk brush size (almost 250) to work into the background negative space.

10 Choose Cmd/Ctrl-S (File > Save).

An attractive embellishment to this multiples technique is to clone in some of the original photograph at the same reduced scale into the multiples image. To do this, follow these steps.

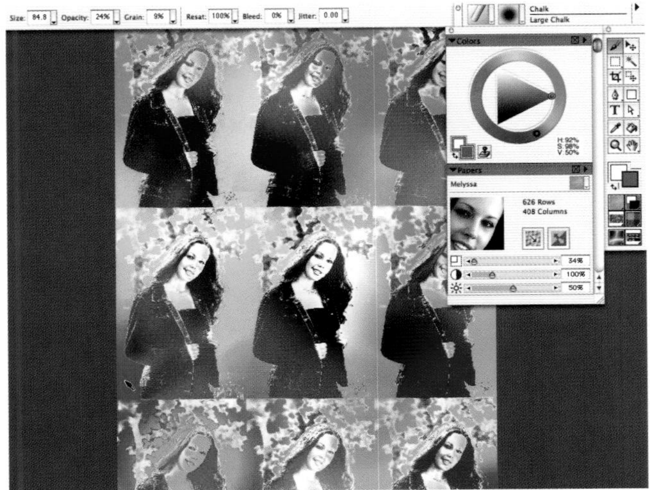

Figure 8.48 Melyssa multiples.

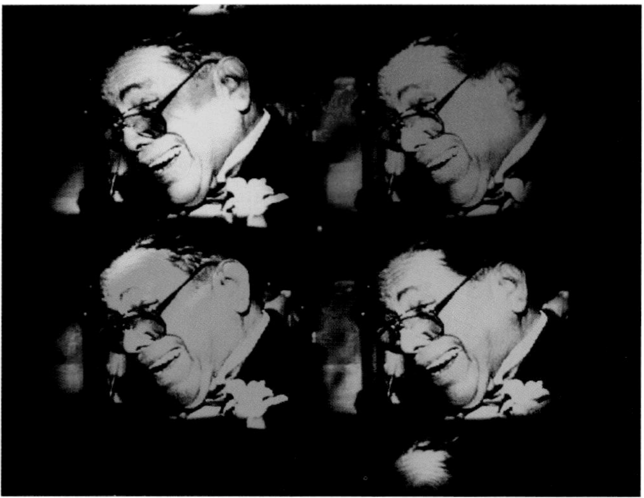

Figure 8.49 Anesto multiples.

1. Capture your original photograph as a pattern (Select > All, followed by Patterns palette pop-up menu > Capture Pattern, very similar to the way you captured the paper texture, except that patterns include color information). The Clone Source will automatically be reset to be the current pattern, which happens to be your captured pattern of Melyssa.
2. Adjust the pattern scale to be exactly the same as the paper scale.
3. Use the soft cloner to selectively clone in the rescaled captured pattern into the multiples image created earlier.

I find that subtly cloning back into the faces can work very effectively. This technique only works if the Crossfade slider was set to 0.00 when you first captured the paper texture. Otherwise the pattern and the texture don't match up precisely.

Figure 8.49 is another example of the same multiple technique, this time starting with a black background and using a section of the fatherandbride.jpg image, which showed the father, Anesto.

8.9 Wrap

I hope you have thoroughly enjoyed this session's exploration through various combinations of Painter's wonderful brushes and effects. The case studies used here only touch the surface of what is possible. There is still much left for you to discover!

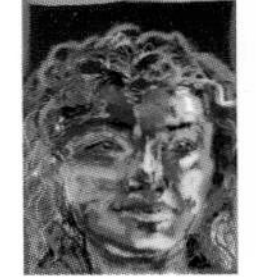

Beyond learning specific techniques, the most important lesson of this session is adopting an open-minded creative approach to transforming your imagery. Think beyond just applying a single effect or technique. Think, instead, of entering a journey of transformation in which you may use several effects in addition to hand painting. Along the journey you may create many variations which you can clone into one another. You may generate multiple layers, and then flatten your image to blend and smear, and so on. Be open-minded and allow your creativity to flow.

Now that you have tasted the joy of transforming single images, the next step is to work with multiple images and explore ways to bring them together into powerful, dramatic, evocative collages.

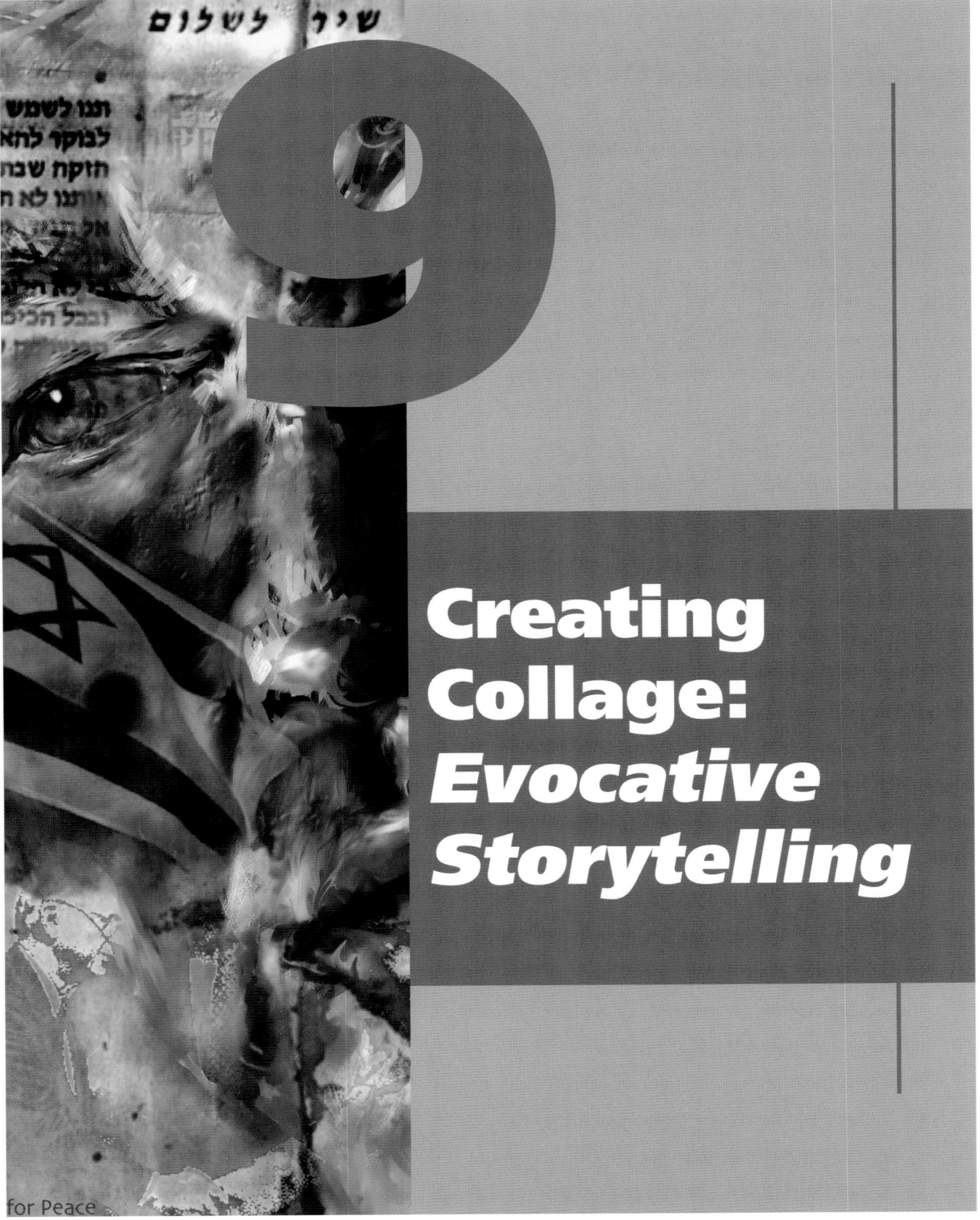

9

Creating Collage: *Evocative Storytelling*

9.1 Introduction

A collage is an assembly, or composition, of diverse elements. Traditionally, gluing various materials, such as paper, cloth, and wood, onto a surface has created collages. With the advent of programs like Photoshop and Painter, we can now easily combine diverse elements on the digital canvas with great flexibility and ease.

No matter whether we create a collage traditionally or on the computer, our starting point remains the same: What is it we wish to say? Collages tell stories, whether intentionally or not. Our minds naturally seek meaning and patterns. When we see a variety of diverse elements brought together, we infer meaning into those spatial and visual relationships. The juxtaposition of different elements causes a subliminal linkage in our mind. It is important to start with a goal and a vision.

Regarding the composition itself, all the principles of traditional art and composition apply: the use of line, shape, and direction to guide the eye; the use of color, contrast, and detail to bring focus to certain elements; the use of balance and harmony in combining elements and forms and textures; and so on.

Within the technical details of the "how to," there are many choices to be made along the way. The first choice is medium: whether to work traditionally, digitally, or with a combination of both (e.g., by scanning traditional work and adding it to the digital canvas, or painting on and adding elements to a digital print). Once you have decided to use the digital medium, your next choice is: Which tool to use? With Photoshop you can easily combine image elements together as layers, an approach that offers great versatility for controlling the layer opacity and experimenting with layer blending modes. With Painter you can follow a multilayer collage approach similar to what you may do in Photoshop. With Painter you have the additional versatility of mixing and blending imagery with hand-painted brush strokes by using Painter's phenomenal range of organic, natural media brushes. These hand-painted strokes can be applied on layers or on the flat canvas; used to add new color or introduce clone color from a source image; or used simply to move, smear, and distort imagery. The artistic texturing and brush effects possible with Painter are unparalleled. Thus Painter can add a whole level of richness to collage that is unattainable with any other graphics software.

In the first part of this session you will go through a step by step case study of one collage I made, called "Song for Peace." In the Song for Peace project you will learn powerful and expressive ways that you can mix, overlay, and compose multiple images together in a single image. The specific skills, strategies, and techniques you will learn in this project include the following:

Working with multiple source images

Making selections with the Pen tool

Working with layer masks and channels

Cloning from multiple sources

Creating a soft, grainy border

Although the Song for Peace project is just one sample, the principles and techniques used can be applied to any collage project. In dissecting and analyzing the steps that went into making this

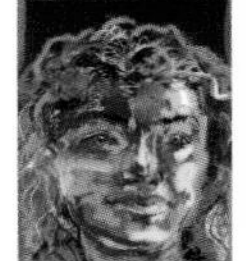

collage, I want to share an intuitive creative approach to combining imagery. I also want to empower you to make decisions in the future as to which technique is best for what you wish to achieve (e.g., when to clone versus when to paste as a layer). There are no hard and fast rules. Every process of creation is full of unexpected twists and turns. You will find each project has its own unique path.

After the Song for Peace project, you will work on a collage of your own theme. For this project I want you to choose any theme you feel highly motivated and passionate about. This is your opportunity to express your voice.

If you are a professional photographer, potential products you could create using these collage techniques are "personality pages" for high school seniors; "memory lane montages" for birthdays, special events, and weddings; greeting cards and invitations; and so on.

Painter offers ease and versatility in creating beautiful digital collages. Enjoy exploring this wonderful form of visual storytelling.

9.2 Instructor Notes

I recommend a two-part session on collage for a group class. In the first part follow a step-by-step case study in which the students all work with the same images and follow the same steps together. You can use my Song for Peace example given here, which I have found to be instructive for students, or you can create your own case study example. Allow about two to three hours to go through these steps thoroughly with a group class. At the conclusion of this first exercise, brainstorm with the students regarding themes for the independent collage exercise, which will follow as the second part of the class.

In the independent collage exercise, students choose their own themes, gather their own source material, and use the techniques appropriate to meet their goals and help them express their voice. This gives students freedom to follow their passions and thus work on a project they are highly motivated about. For those students who have a hard time coming up with their own theme, you could suggest themes such as "Family," "Joy," "Metamorphosis," "Fantasy," "Freedom," and so on.

Using Painter's Text tool is not addressed directly in the Song for Peace case study, although it is mentioned briefly in the next section, General Principles and Techniques. Typography can be a powerful element to incorporate into collage. You may wish to suggest a collage project to your students based on working with type as a visual element in the composition.

9.3 General Principles and Techniques

Principles

Here are six basic principles that will help you with any collage project. When working on complex, multilayered, multiple clone source projects, these basic organizational and strategic principles make an enormous difference to the ease and efficiency of your creative process.

1 *Set a goal, have a vision.* Start off your collage project with a goal in mind. What would you like to express? What is your goal? What is important to you? Research your imagery. Visualize what imagery you wish to create, what your base image will be that you can build upon, and what you want to communicate. Even though your goals may change as the project progresses and the end result may differ considerably from what you initially visualized, having that initial goal and vision is still important.

2 *Work at maximum quality.* Scan source material at resolutions at least as high as you will need. Save scans as TIFF files rather than JPEGs. Work at the size and resolution you want to end up at. See Appendix II for comments on deciding what resolution to work at.

3 *Organize palettes.* Make sure you have all the palettes showing that you will need. This will include the Property Bar, Tools, Brushes, Colors, Layers, and Channels. Save the palette arrangement for easy recall (Window > Arrange Palettes > Save Layout).

4 *Work on clone copies.* Always work on clone copies, rather than originals, for added flexibility. Besides protecting your originals, it allows the convenient "erase to save" function with Cloners > Soft Cloner.

5 *Document meticulously.* Periodically save sequentially numbered versions as you work. Always Save As or Save immediately before applying any effect or dropping layers, and then Save As with a new version number after applying the effect or dropping the layers. Keep all of the saved versions in a project folder that you archive for future reference.

6 *Rename consistently and meaningfully.* Always rename clone copies and new layers immediately, consistently, and meaningfully.

Blending Techniques

There are two basic techniques for introducing and blending image elements into a collage composition: (1) subtracting from a layer and (2) revealing from a clone source.

Subtracting from a Layer

The simplest, quickest way to introduce an image element is to copy and paste from one image into another (or select a region in one image and hold the Option/Alt key down while you drag and drop the selection from one image into another). A pasted image automatically appears as a layer. Layers have the advantage of flexibility. You can continually reposition, reorient, and resize layers (although repeated resizing and rotating will reduce image quality, unless you keep the layer as a Free Transform). You can adjust layer opacity and composite method, and rearrange the ordering of layers. You can also control which parts of a layer are visible by painting black (to take away or conceal) or white (to add or reveal) in the layer mask using a soft, low-opacity Airbrushes > Digital Airbrush variant. You generate a layer mask by clicking on the mask icon (right-hand square button at the bottom of the Layers palette) while the layer is selected. You activate the mask mode (i.e., the mode where black takes away layer visibility and white adds layer visibility) by clicking on the mask

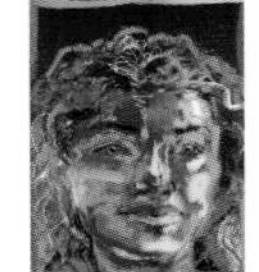

icon that appears immediately to the left of the layer name in the Layers palette layers list. You return to regular mode (i.e., the mode where you can paint and apply effects directly on the layer) by clicking on the regular mode icon to the left of the mask mode icon in the layers list.

Revealing from a Clone Source

With this technique you place each image element you wish to add to the collage as a layer in a clone source file that is the exact size as the working image. You generate the identically sized clone source by cloning from the working image. You resize, reorient, and reposition the element as needed and then clone from that source image into the background canvas of the main working image, which can remain a flat image (no need for layers in the working image in this technique). The clone source approach allows an intuitive way of gradually revealing imagery rather than making it disappear. It also allows a more painterly feel to the introduction of imagery than layers, because you can use almost any brush as a clone brush (click the clone color icon in the Colors palette). It also has the advantage that you can integrate blending and smearing brushes into the way you manipulate the paint on the background canvas.

Both of these techniques are employed in the Song for Peace project.

Text

The Text tool in Painter is fairly self-explanatory and there is a thorough description in the User Manual. The Text tool generates a special text layer.

Choosing Your Font

There is a Text palette (Window > Show Text) where you control the point size, font, and so on. I recommend starting in the Text palette by setting up your choice of font. You can type lettering and then adjust the font choice and see it dynamically reflected in the type on your canvas. Select a color in the Color Picker to ensure you can clearly see the text when you first type it (you can always add other coloring later). Always save a version of your file at each stage of the process and before converting the text layer to shapes or bitmap.

Rotating and Skewing Lettering

The next step is rescaling, rotating, skewing, and distorting individual letters or groups of letters. To do this, choose the Convert Text to Shapes option from the bottom of the Layers palette pop-up menu. This converts the text layer into a group of vector-based shapes that can be individually selected and manipulated (independent of resolution).

Painting and Applying Effects

Once you have completed any rescaling and rotating of letters, the final step with text is to close the group of shapes and then choose Collapse from the left-hand side of the six square buttons at the bottom of the Layers palette. This turns the group of shapes into a regular bitmap image layer, also known as default layer, which you can paint on and apply effects to (e.g., embossment, drop shadows, texture). You can also convert a text layer directly into a default layer (if you don't need to do any shape manipulations) by selecting Convert to Default Layer in the Layers pop-up menu.

Finishing Touches

I recommend concluding your collage process by flattening your image (ensuring you save the multilayered stage before flattening) and working on the flat background with tools for blending (Blenders category) and enhancement (such as Dodge and Burn from the Photo category). You can also add an artistic border as a last step (an easy way is to Select All, choose a brush such as Chalks > Large Chalk, select white in the Color Picker, and then choose Select > Stroke Selection).

9.4 Case Study: *Song for Peace*

The Background to Song for Peace

The imagery used in this project is based on a collage portrait I created of Yitzhak Rabin, the Israeli Prime Minister who was shot by an assassin at a peace rally in Tel Aviv, Israel, on November 4, 1995 (Figure 9.1). I wanted to create a portrait that expressed the horror of the murder; the shock that

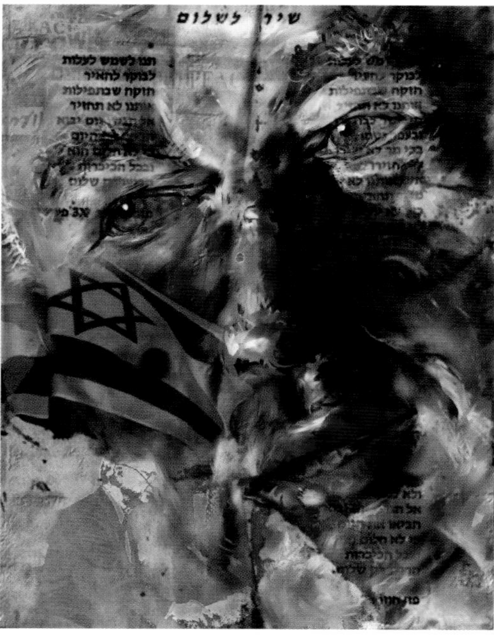

Figure 9.1 Song for Peace.

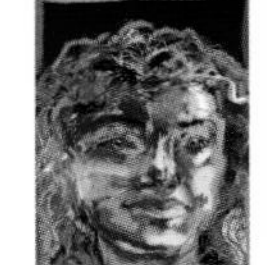

Israeli society had become so polarized; the miracle that a peace process had been initiated; and the hope that it would continue despite Rabin's death.

I was particularly struck by the powerful image of the blood-soaked song sheet that had been in Rabin's pocket when the fatal bullet passed right through it. A photograph of the bloodied song sheet appeared in a British newspaper called *The European* the week after Rabin was assassinated. Here is what the newspaper said about it:

> The Hebrew lyrics of the Song of Peace, partly obscured by blood and a bullet hole, were on a sheet of paper retrieved from the pocket of Yitzhak Rabin after his assassination. Written after the 1967 Arab-Israeli war, the song was banned, only later to become the rallying cry of the peace movement. The words, the last to be uttered by Rabin before his death, proved grimly poignant.

The Song for Peace (sometimes referred to as the Song of Peace) was written by Jacob Rotblit. Here's an English translation (thanks to Miri Skoriak):

Song for Peace

Let the sun rise
Let the morning shine
The purest of prayers
Will not bring us back

He whose candle has been snuffed out
And was buried in the ground
Bitter tears will not wake him up
Will not bring him back

No one will resurrect us
From the depths of darkness
Neither the victory cheer
Nor songs of praise will help

So, sing a song for peace
Don't whisper a prayer
Better to cry aloud
A song for peace

Let the sunshine penetrate
Through the flowers
Don't look back in worry
Let the deceased rest

Raise your eyes and
Look ahead with hope
Sing a song for love
Not for wars

Don't say the day will come
Make it happen now
It's not a dream
When in all quarters
The praise for peace will sound

So, sing a song for peace
Don't whisper a prayer
Better to cry aloud
A song for peace

It really is a song for peace as if sung by the deceased (i.e., a plea from the grave) to the next generation to pursue peace. The dead are asking the living to concentrate on the future (rather than on the past and the victims) and to not be afraid to express their wishes for peace strongly. Sadly, this song is just as relevant at the time of writing this book as when Rabin was assassinated.

When I saw the song sheet (which was inadvertently reproduced in the newspaper upside down), I said to myself, "This is my canvas." I kept the cutting and from that moment started working on the portrait in my mind, collecting material along the way.

Nine months later I was asked to submit an image for an exhibition at the headquarters of Scitex (makers of Iris printers) in Herzlia, Israel. I knew this was the image I needed to submit and started work on the portrait.

Symbols and elements in the collage include the crowds who were at the rally where Rabin was killed, the hand-shake with Yasser Arafat that broke the years of enmity and hate, the Western Wall in Jerusalem pockmarked with bullet holes just after the Six Day War in 1967, and a photo of Rabin at age 18 taken in 1940 when he was involved with the underground fight against the British mandate in Palestine. The Israeli flag flying at half-mast, with the fatal bullet hole passing through it, is a metaphor for the way the bullet ripped a hole through the fabric of the Israeli society.

The portrait itself is a freehand painting based on an image I saw on the cover of *Newsweek* magazine. It was an image that spoke to me, where I saw the eyes express sensitivity, strength, hope, sadness, dreams, and courage. I decided not to simply scan the portrait, but to do a freehand painting, so that the final painting would speak more personally of how I felt.

I presented an Iris print (courtesy of the Image House, Santa Fe) to Rabin's widow, Lea Rabin, in January 1998. She looked at it in silence and then said: "Those eyes . . . ."

Song Sheet

1. Open Painter. Make a point of closing Painter after completing every project and reopening Painter afresh whenever you start a new project.
2. Have the following palettes visible: Tools, Property Bar, Brush Selector, Colors, Layers, and Channels. Save this palette arrangement for easy recall (Window > Arrange Palettes > Save Layout). I suggest calling the layout "collage."
3. Open the project file "1 song sheet.tif" from the Painter Projects > 9-Collage > 9.4 Song for Peace project folder. This is an image of the bloodied song sheet that was in Rabin's pocket when he was killed.
4. Choose Cmd/Ctrl-A (Select > All).
5. Choose Cmd/Ctrl-C (Edit > Copy).
6. Choose Cmd/Ctrl-W (File > Close).
7. Choose Don't Save (so the file closes without saving changes).
8. Choose Cmd/Ctrl-N (File > New).

Continued

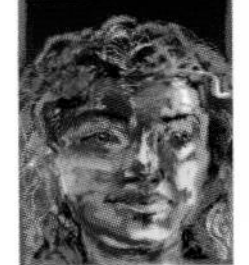

9 In the New Picture window, set the Width to 700 pixels, Height to 1000 pixels, and Resolution to 100 pixels per inch. Leave the paper color as white. Click OK.

10 Choose File > Save As.

11 Name the new image songforpeace-base-01.rif. The naming convention used here is subject ("songforpeace")-indication that this is the main working image ("base")-version number (01). All working files are saved in RIFF file format to ensure the editability of all data is preserved. Think carefully about how you name your collage files. Organized file naming makes it much easier to work with complex projects.

12 Choose Cmd/Ctrl-M (Window > Screen Mode Toggle).

13 Choose Cmd/Ctrl-V (Edit > Paste). The song sheet image is pasted in as a new layer named Layer 1.

14 Double-click on Layer 1 in the Layers palette.

15 In the Layer Attributes window, rename Layer 1 as "song sheet."

16 Click OK.

17 Choose Effects > Orientation > Free Transform. Note that a different icon appears next to the "song sheet" layer name in the Layers palette. The Free Transform mode allows you to experiment with rotating, skewing, distorting, and resizing a layer without actually making any changes to the original layer information. What you see when you are working with a Free Transform layer is a reference layer, a representation of the layer (this is why the quality of the Free Transform layer seems low). It is only when you commit the transform that the changes are applied and the reference layer becomes a regular image layer. Because the quality of an image is reduced every time you resize, rotate, and so on, Free Transform allows you to minimize the reduction in quality.

18 Hold the Cmd/Ctrl key down while tapping on the minus ("–") key to zoom out (Window > Zoom Out). Zoom out until you can see small, faint, square control handles in the corners and midpoints at the boundary of the pasted layer. These control handles will be outside the visible image because the pasted layer is larger than your canvas. Note that these control handles are only visible when the Free Transform layer is selected (highlighted in the Layers palette) and the Layer Adjuster tool is selected.

19 Continue to hold the Cmd/Ctrl key down and click and drag on a corner control point with the tip of the Layer Adjuster tool (pointing finger tool). This tool, located in the top right of the Tools palette, is automatically selected when you paste in a new layer or generate a Free Transform. As you click and drag, the

Continued

pointed finger cursor changes into a faint circular cursor, barely visible against the gray background. Drag and rotate the layer 180 degrees (to correct for the song sheet being reproduced in the newspaper upside down), making sure the columns of writing are aligned vertically. Let go of the Cmd/Ctrl key when done.

20 Click and drag in the song sheet layer to center the writing in the image (Figure 9.2). Use the arrow keys for fine adjustments.

21 Choose Cmd/Ctrl-S (File > Save).

22 When the position and angle of the song sheet is correct, select Effects > Orientation > Commit Transform. Note that the symbol next to the Layer name returns to the image layer symbol.

23 Select the variant Cloners > Soft Cloner. This automatically selects the Brush tool. Set the brush size in the Brush Property Bar to be about 30 pixels and the opacity to be about 50 percent.

24 Hold down the Option/Alt key while clicking on the song sheet background paper in a light colored region near the lower left corner. This sets the clone source location.

25 Clean up the black corners by cloning the light paper over the dark regions in the lower left and lower right corners, resetting the clone source location (Option/Alt-click) as necessary. Make sure the song sheet layer, not the background canvas, is selected (highlighted in the Layers palette).

26 Click once on the padlock icon located in the upper right of the Layers palette, just above the layers list. You will see a padlock icon appear to the right of the song sheet name in the layers list. This locks the layer in place and prevents any accidental moving or altering of the layer. To unlock at any time, just click again on the padlock icon while the song sheet layer is selected. You can toggle

Continued

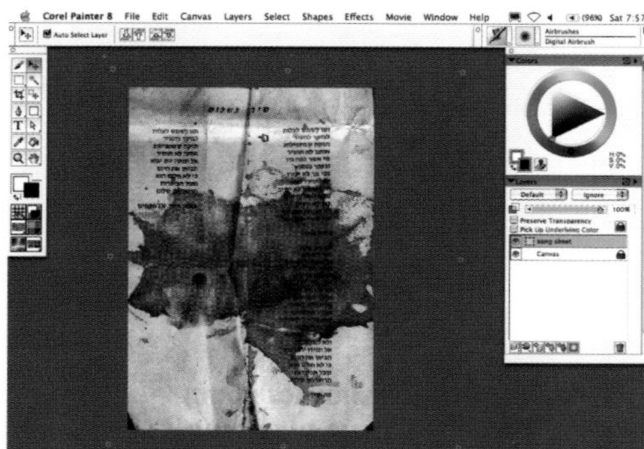

Figure 9.2 Rotated song sheet.

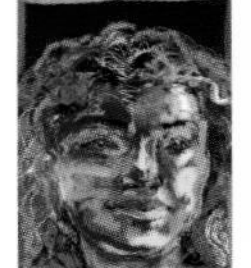

any layer between locked and unlocked modes by clicking on the far right hand end of the layer name bar in the layers list. This will cause the padlock icon to appear and disappear.

27 Choose Cmd/Ctrl-S (File > Save).

Flag

1 Open "2 flag.tif" from the "9.4 Song for Peace" folder. This shows the Israeli flag.

2 Select the Pen tool in the Tools palette (keyboard shortcut "p").

3 Use the Pen tool to click on points around the contour of the flag, excluding the flagpole. The pen tool generates a vector-based shape, and you will see a new layer, Shape 1, appear in the Layers palette with a shape icon next to it. Where you want curvature, just drag the cursor after placing a point on the canvas. Don't worry about precision in this case because you will be feathering the edges later.

4 Close the contour path around the flag (Figure 9.3) by clicking with the Pen tool on the initial control point where you started the path. If the closed path suddenly fills with the current color then choose Edit > Preferences > Shapes and uncheck the Fill in and Stroke to checkboxes.

Continued

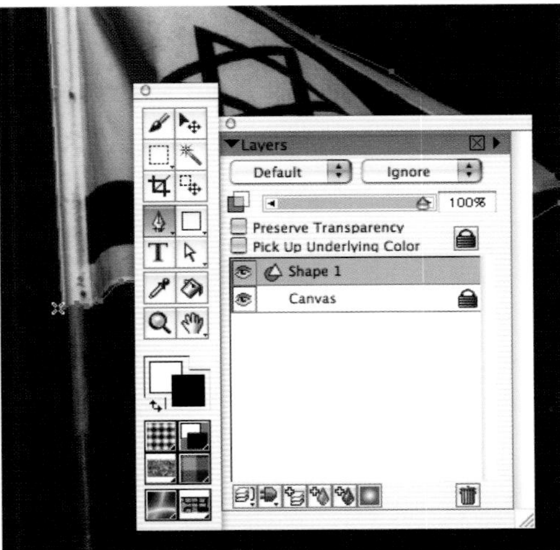

Figure 9.3 Creating a closed path around the flag with the Pen tool.

5 Choose Shapes > Convert to Selection. When you generate a selection you automatically generate an Alpha channel, visible in the Channels palette, that allows you to go back and reactivate that same selection (by clicking on the left hand load selection button at the bottom of the Channels palette). This is useful if you inadvertently deselect your flag selection.

6 Choose Cmd/Ctrl-C (Edit > Copy).

7 Choose Cmd/Ctrl-W (File > Close).

8 Choose Don't Save (so the 2 flag.tif image closes without saving changes).

9 With the songforpeace-base-01.rif image now being the only active image open in Painter, choose Cmd/Ctrl-V (Edit > Paste). The flag becomes a new layer. An alternative to copying and pasting, is to use the Layer Adjuster tool to drag the flag selection from the 2 flag.tif image onto the songforpeace-base-01.rif image.

10 Double-click on the new layer name in the Layers palette.

11 Rename Layer 1 as "flag."

12 In the Layers palette, with the "flag" layer active, reduce the Opacity slider from 100 percent to about 60 percent.

13 Use the Layer Adjuster tool to position the flag so it is located on top of the bullet hole in the underlying song sheet layer. With this and other image elements, you can refer to the finished collage for reference regarding placement of the elements. You don't have to place things exactly as I originally did. The important thing is that you practice using the techniques, not that your picture ends up looking exactly like mine.

14 Choose Cmd/Ctrl-S (File > Save).

15 Make sure that Preserve Transparency is unchecked in the Layers palette.

If black and white are not your current regular and additional colors, then follow the next three steps. If black and white are your current regular and additional colors, then make sure black is the regular color and skip ahead to step 19.

16 Select white in the Colors palette.

17 Click on the exchange arrows that swap the regular and additional color squares in the Colors palette. This places white in the additional color square.

18 Select black in the Color picker. You should now see a white square behind a black square. Always make sure the front square is the active square (by clicking on it).

Continued

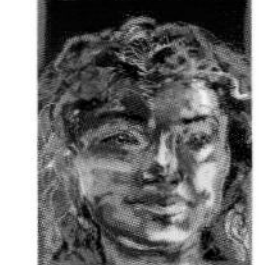

19 Airbrushes > Digital Airbrush in the Brushes palette. In the Brush Property Bar set the brush size to about 30 pixels and the opacity to about 30 percent.

20 Ensuring the flag layer is selected (highlighted in the Layers palette), click once on the right hand of the six small buttons at the bottom of the Layers palette. This is the mask button, and it generates a layer mask which appears as an icon to the immediate left of the word flag in the Layers list. There are now three small icons to the left of the word flag, an eye symbol that makes the whole layer visible or invisible; a default layer symbol (looks like a three layered sandwich); and the mask symbol (looks like a soft circular sun in a gray background). Click on the mask symbol next to the word flag. This activates the layer mask mode which allows you to selectively add or take away from the layer visibility. If you open the Channels palette you will see the flag layer mask channel beneath the RGB channel. By clicking on the channels you can control whether you see the RGB image or a representation of the layer mask.

21 Softly paint with the Digital Airbrush around edges of the flag to make it fade away. If you overdo it, change color from white to black to bring the image back (white conceals what's behind the layer, black reveals what's behind the layer).

22 Softly paint with white over the bullet hole so that it shows through (Figure 9.4).

23 When completed, click once on the padlock icon above the layer list to lock the changes in the flag layer. You'll see a padlock symbol appear to the right of the word flag.

24 Choose Cmd/Ctrl-S (File > Save).

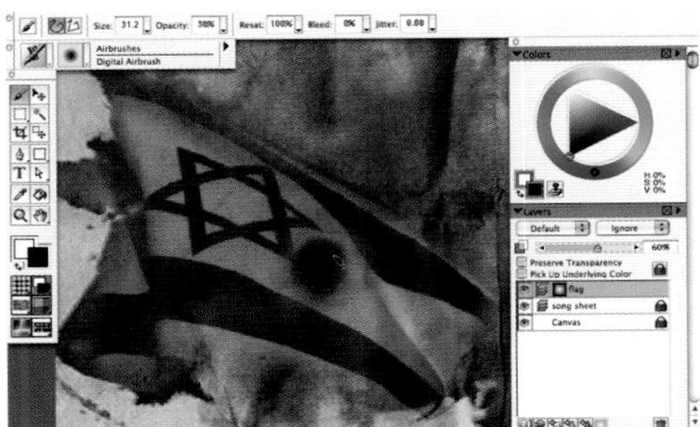

Figure 9.4 Painting into the flag layer mask.

Rally

1. Open "3 rally.tif" from the "9.4 Song for Peace" folder. This shows the peace rally in Tel Aviv, Israel, at which Rabin was assassinated.
2. Choose Cmd/Ctrl-A (Select > All).
3. Choose Cmd/Ctrl-C (Edit > Copy).
4. Choose Cmd/Ctrl-W (File > Close).
5. Choose Don't Save (so the 3 rally.tif image closes without saving changes).
6. Choose Cmd/Ctrl-V (Edit > Paste) and paste the rally as a new layer in the songforpeace-base-01.rif image.
7. Double-click on the new layer name in the Layers palette.
8. Rename Layer 1 as "rally."
9. In the Layers palette, with the "rally" layer active, reduce the Opacity slider from 100 percent to about 40 percent.
10. Drag the rally layer to the top of the image.
11. Choose Cmd/Ctrl-S (File > Save).
12. Choose Effects > Orientation > Free Transform.
13. Hold the Shift key down while clicking and dragging the Layer Adjuster tool on a corner control handle. Drag the control handle inward toward the center of the rally layer to reduce its size (holding the Shift key down ensures you maintain the proportions).
14. Choose Effects > Orientation > Commit Transform when satisfied with the scale of the rally layer. It is important to commit the transform, which converts the Free Transform reference layer into a regular image layer, because you cannot paint in the layer mask while the layer is a reference layer. If you try you will get the error message: "Commit reference layer to an image layer?".
15. Using the same technique as with the flag, generate a layer mask, activate the layer mask, select the brush tool (keyboard shortcut "b") and then paint in the rally layer mask with a black airbrush to make it fade at the edges and disappear into the fabric of the song sheet background layer (Figure 9.5). Try to avoid obscuring the song title. With this layer, and others where you select all and then copy and paste, pay special attention to ensuring that the straight edges of the rectangular pasted layer completely disappear.

Continued

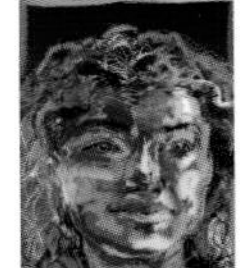

16 When completed, click once on the padlock icon above the layer list to lock the changes in the rally layer. You'll see a padlock symbol appear to the right of the word rally.

17 Choose Cmd/Ctrl-S (File > Save).

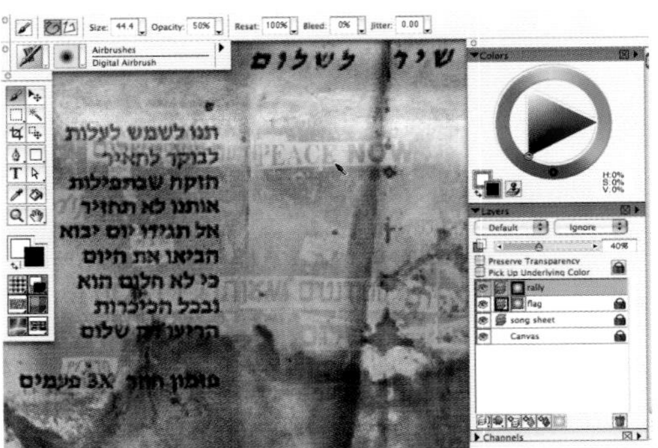

Figure 9.5 Painting into the rally layer mask.

Young Rabin

1 Open "4 young rabin.tif" from the "9.4 Song for Peace" folder. This shows Rabin as a young man a few years before the founding of the state of Israel.

2 Choose Cmd/Ctrl-A (Select > All).

3 Choose Cmd/Ctrl-C (Edit > Copy).

4 Choose Cmd/Ctrl-W (File > Close).

5 Choose Don't Save (so the 4 young rabin.tif image closes without saving changes).

6 Choose Cmd/Ctrl-V (Edit > Paste). This pastes the young rabin image as a new layer in the songforpeace-base-01.rif image.

7 Double-click on the new layer name in the Layers palette.

8 Rename Layer 1 as "young rabin."

9 In the Layers palette, with the "young rabin" layer active, reduce the Opacity slider from 100 percent to about 40 percent.

10 Drag the young rabin layer to the right of the image.

11 Choose Cmd/Ctrl-S (File > Save).

Continued

12. Choose Effects > Orientation > Free Transform.
13. Hold the Shift key down while clicking and dragging the Layer Adjuster tool in a corner control handle. Drag the control handle inward toward the center of the young rabin layer to reduce its size.
14. Choose Effects > Orientation > Commit Transform when satisfied with scale.
15. Using the same technique as with the flag and rally, generate a layer mask, activate the layer mask, select the brush tool, and then paint in the young rabin layer mask with a black airbrush to make it fade at the edges and disappear into the fabric of the song sheet background layer.
16. When completed, click once on the padlock icon above the layer list to lock the changes in the young rabin layer. You'll see a padlock symbol appear to the right of the words young rabin.
17. Choose Cmd/Ctrl-S (File > Save).

Handshake

1. Open "5 handshake.tif" from the "9.4 Song for Peace" folder. This shows the historic handshake between Yitzhak Rabin and Yasser Arafat outside the White House with President Bill Clinton in the background.
2. Choose Cmd/Ctrl-A (Select > All).
3. Choose Cmd/Ctrl-C (Edit > Copy).
4. Choose Cmd/Ctrl-W (File > Close).
5. Choose Don't Save (so the 5 handshake.tif image closes without saving changes).
6. Choose Cmd/Ctrl-V (Edit > Paste). This pastes the handshake image as a new layer in the songforpeace-base-01.rif image.
7. Double-click on the new layer name in the Layers palette.
8. Rename Layer 1 as "handshake."
9. In the Layers palette, with the "handshake" layer active, reduce the Opacity slider from 100 percent to about 50 percent.
10. Drag the handshake layer to the lower left of the image.
11. Choose Effects > Orientation > Free Transform.

Continued

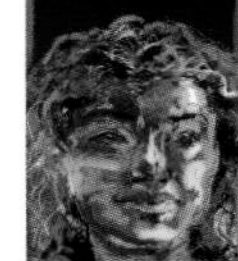

12 Hold the Shift key down while clicking and dragging the Layer Adjuster tool in a corner control handle. Drag the control handle inward toward the center of the handshake layer to reduce its size while maintaining its proportions.

13 Choose Effects > Orientation > Commit Transform when satisfied with scale.

14 Make sure black and white are the two colors in the regular and additional color rectangles in the Colors palette.

15 Make sure the Two-Point gradient is selected in the Gradient Selector in the Tools palette (the Two-Point gradient is the default so it is probably already selected).

16 Select Express in Image from the Gradient pop-up menu which you can access through the Gradient Selector.

17 Drag in Express in Image window preview so you can see Rabin's profile.

18 Adjust Bias slider in Express in Image window until you see an effect you like (Figure 9.6).

19 Click OK.

20 You may need to experiment with this effect to get the best result. Undo (Cmd/Ctrl-Z) and repeat if necessary. You can also experiment at this stage with changing the Composite Method for the handshake layer.

21 Using the same technique as used previously, generate a layer mask, activate the layer mask, select the brush tool, and then paint in the handshake layer mask with a black airbrush to fade away the edges and the images of President Bill Clinton and Yasser Arafat. I find making soft (low pressure) circular brush strokes with a relatively large (50 pixels or so) airbrush with low opacity (about 30 percent) works well for achieving a subtle fading effect.

22 When completed, click once on the padlock icon above the layer list to lock the changes in the handshake layer.

23 Choose Cmd/Ctrl-S (File > Save).

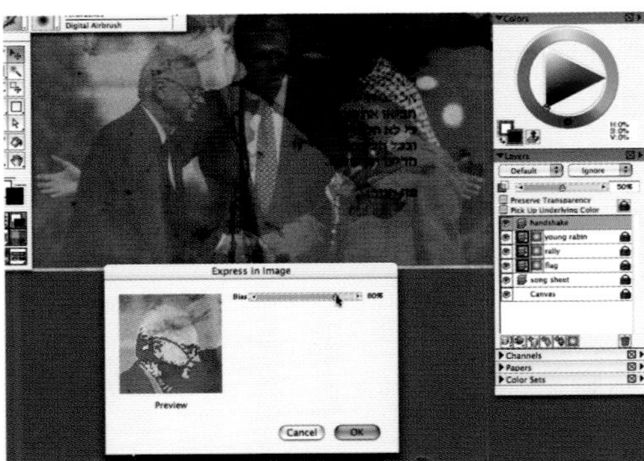

Figure 9.6 Expressing Two-Point gradient in Handshake image.

Wall Texture

1. Click once on the padlock icons on the right of each layer listed in the Layers palette. This unlocks each layer (which we need to do to be able to drop the layers and flatten the image). Each padlock icon will disappear when the layer is unlocked.
2. In the Layers palette pop-up menu, select Drop All. This flattens your image.
3. Choose File > Save As.
4. Rename the image as songforpeace-base-02-flat.rif.
5. Choose File > Clone.
6. Choose File > Save As.
7. Rename the clone copy image as songforpeace-walltexture.rif.
8. Choose Cmd/Ctrl-M (Window > Screen Mode Toggle).
9. Open "6 wailing wall.tif" from the "9.4 Song for Peace" folder. This is a photograph showing an Israeli soldier carrying a baby past the historic Western Wall, also known as the Wailing Wall, of the former temple in Jerusalem, just after the 1967 Six Day War.
10. Select Cloners > Soft Cloner in brushes palette.
11. Hold down the Option/Alt key while clicking in the 6 wailing wall.tif image in a region of wall texture to set the clone source point.
12. Clone away the soldier with child and replace with surrounding wall texture. Don't worry about making it perfect.
13. Choose Cmd/Ctrl-E (Effects > Tonal Control > Equalize).
14. Click OK (leave the Equalize default settings as is).
15. Cmd/Ctrl-A (select all).
16. Choose Capture Paper from the Paper pop-up menu, located in the upper right corner of the Paper Selector, which is the top left of the six selectors in the bottom of the Tools palette (Figure 9.7).
17. Name paper as "wall."
18. Click OK. You will now see the texture of the wall appearing as the currently selected paper texture in the Paper Selector.
19. Cmd-W/Ctrl-W.

Continued

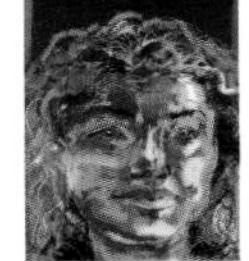

20 Choose Don't Save. This closes the 6 wailing wall.tif image without saving changes. The songforpeace-walltexture.rif will now be the active image.

21 Choose Effects > Surface Control > Apply Surface Texture. Ensure the Using: Paper option is selected in the Apply Surface Texture window. This is the default setting, so you probably won't need to adjust the Using menu.

22 In the Apply Surface Texture window, reduce Amount to about 30 percent and Shine to 0 percent (Figure 9.8).

23 Click OK.

24 Choose Edit > Fade if you wish to fade the effect back. This is a useful feature any time you apply an effect because it is easy to underestimate the visual impact of an effect from the small Apply Surface Texture preview window.

25 Choose Cmd/Ctrl-S (File > Save). This updates the songforpeace-walltexture.rif image.

26 Choose File > Clone.

27 Choose File > Save As.

28 Save the clone copy as songforpeace-base-03-textured.rif. This will become the next stage of our working file.

29 Choose Cmd/Ctrl-M (Window > Screen Mode Toggle).

30 Choose File > Clone Source > songforpeace-base-02-flat.rif.

Continued

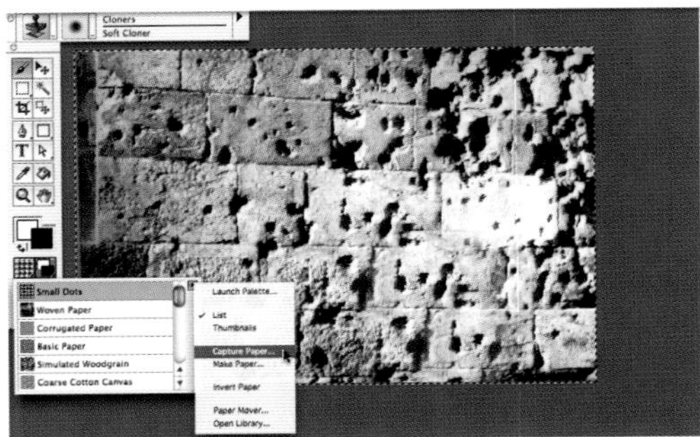

Figure 9.7 Capturing the Wailing Wall image as a paper texture.

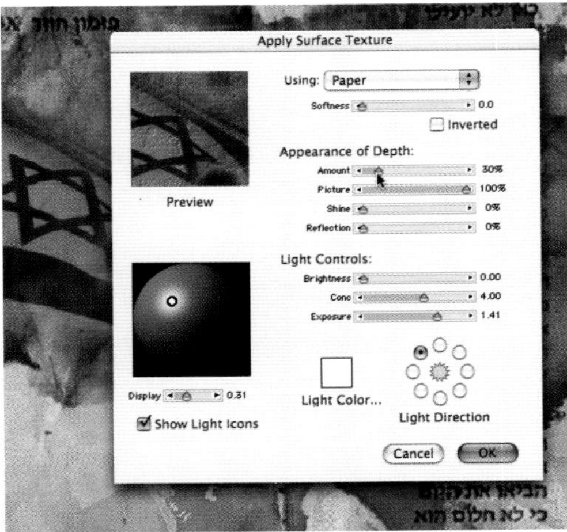

Figure 9.8 Applying the wall texture to the flat working image.

31 Select Cloners > Soft Cloner in the Brushes palette.

32 Choose Restore Default Variant from the Brush Selector pop-up menu. This resets the clone source starting point so when you clone from the clone source, songforpeace-base-flat.rif., the clone image will be perfectly aligned with the current file, songforpeace-base-03-textured.rif.

33 Clone selected areas of the smooth songforpeace-base-02-flat.rif image into the textured songforpeace-base-03-textured.rif image. Create a more organic variation of texture across the image (less uniform). A large low-opacity Soft Cloner will help achieve this effect.

34 To undo (i.e., bring back texture) just change the clone source (using File > Clone Source) from songforpeace-base02-flat.rif to songforpeace-walltexture.rif and clone the texture back in. This dual clone source technique, where I generate two alternative clone source images (in this instance one with texture applied, one without) and then clone selectively from either source into my working image, gives me a lot of flexibility to fine tune how much of an effect I want to appear in my image. I use this same technique later to selectively clone in the painted portrait of Rabin using two alternative clone sources, one with the portrait and one without.

35 Choose Cmd/Ctrl-S (File > Save). This updates the songforpeace-base-03-textured.rif image.

Painted Portrait

As I mentioned in the introduction to this case study, I painted the portrait of Rabin from visual reference, without the use of any cloning. You are welcome to print out the "7 contemplative rabin.tif" image and do the same. However in the following section is an alternative approach that uses cloning as a basis. While the free-hand painting approach is more challenging, it also offers the greatest opportunity to put your soul into your work.

1 With songforpeace-base-03-textured.rif as the active image in Painter, choose File > Clone.

2 Choose Cmd/Ctrl-M.

3 Save As songforpeace-portraitsource.rif.

4 Open "7 contemplative rabin.tif" from the "9.4 Song for Peace" folder.

Continued

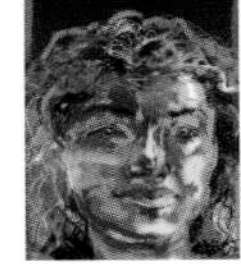

5 Choose Cmd/Ctrl-A (Select > All).

6 Choose Cmd/Ctrl-C (Edit > Copy).

7 Choose Cmd/Ctrl-W (File > Close).

8 Choose Don't Save (so the "7 contemplative rabin.tif" image closes without saving changes).

9 Choose Cmd/Ctrl-V (Edit > Paste) and paste the contemplative rabin image into the songforpeace-portraitsource.rif as a new layer.

10 Double-click on the new layer name in the Layers palette.

11 Rename the layer as "rabin."

12 With the songforpeace-portraitsource.rif image now being the active image in Painter, and the new layer rabin being selected in the Layers palette, reduce the Opacity slider from 100 percent to about 50 percent.

13 Drag the layer in the image to position Rabin's right eye (i.e., on the left of the photo layer) just above and slightly to the right of the Star of David in the flag (Figure 9.9).

14 When the portrait layer is correctly positioned, adjust the layer opacity back to 100 percent.

15 Click once on the padlock icon above the layer list to lock the rabin layer in place. You'll see a padlock symbol appear to the right of the word rabin.

16 Choose Cmd/Ctrl-S (File > Save).

17 Choose File > Clone.

18 Choose Cmd/Ctrl-M.

19 Save As songforpeace-portraitpaint.rif.

20 Select the Cloners > Flat Oil Cloner in the Brush Selector.

21 Paint everywhere in the image with this brush to convert the photo to oil. Adjust the brush size and stroke directions to suit the features and form. Don't worry about the writing and other features that will need painting over.

22 When the whole image has been treated with the Flat Oil Cloner, click on the clone color icon in the Color Picker. This deactivates the clone color and activates the Color Picker. Now you can bring the portrait to life by applying your own color choices using this and other brushes. In the process cover up the magazine lettering and other features that distract from the portrait (Figure 9.10).

23 Choose Cmd/Ctrl-S (File > Save).

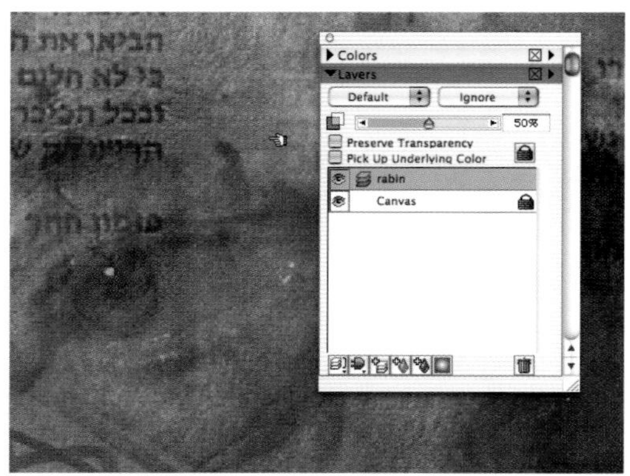

Figure 9.9 Reduced opacity for repositioning layer.

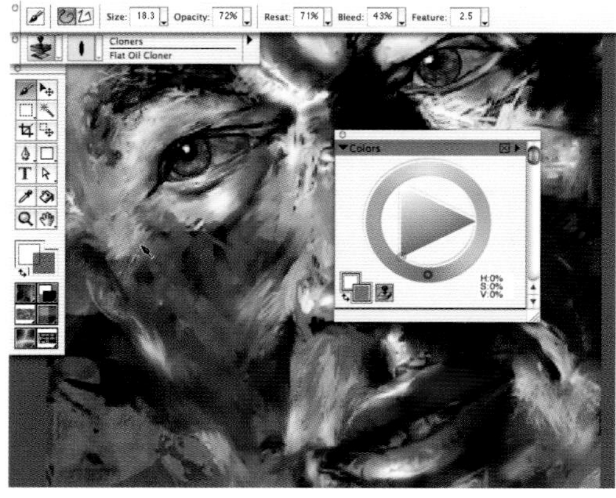

Figure 9.10 Painting the portrait.

Final Mix

1. Select the image songforpeace-base-03-textured.rif.
2. Choose File > Clone.
3. Choose Cmd/Ctrl-M.
4. Choose File > Save As. Save the image as songforpeace-base-04-final.rif.
5. Choose File > Clone Source > songforpeace-portraitpaint.rif.
6. Use the Cloners > Soft Cloner variant to bring the painted portrait into the textured photo collage.
7. To take away the portrait and bring back the textured collage background, just change the clone source from songforpeace-portraitpaint.rif to songforpeace-base-03-textured.rif. This is the same dual clone source technique used previously for the wall texture.
8. Choose Cmd/Ctrl-S (File > Save).

Adding a Border

If I am intending to print out on water color paper I like to soften the border of my image. Here is a fast simple technique I applied in the final version of this collage.

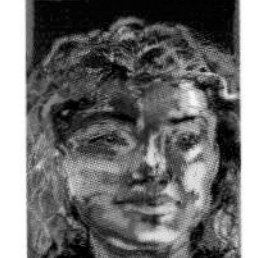

1. Choose the Chalk > Large Chalk variant. There are other brushes that can work well for borders, depending on the type of effect you're looking for. I recommend experimenting to find a brush stroke that suits the feel of your image. In this case the simple grainy chalk seemed to work well.
2. Choose Basic Paper in the Paper Selector (in the Tools palette).
3. Select white in the Color Picker.
4. In the Brush Property Bar, experiment with brush size, opacity, and grain.
5. Make a test brush stroke with this chalk to check its suitability with respect to scale and graininess for use as a border (Figure 9.11).
6. Choose Cmd/Ctrl-Z. Undo the brushstroke.
7. Choose Cmd/Ctrl-A (File > Select All).
8. Choose Select > Stroke Selection (Figure 9.12).

   If the brush opacity is low, you may wish to repeat the Select > Stroke Selection a few times to get the best results.
9. Choose File > Save As. Save the image as songforpeace-base-04-final-brdr.rif.
10. Choose File > Quit/Exit.

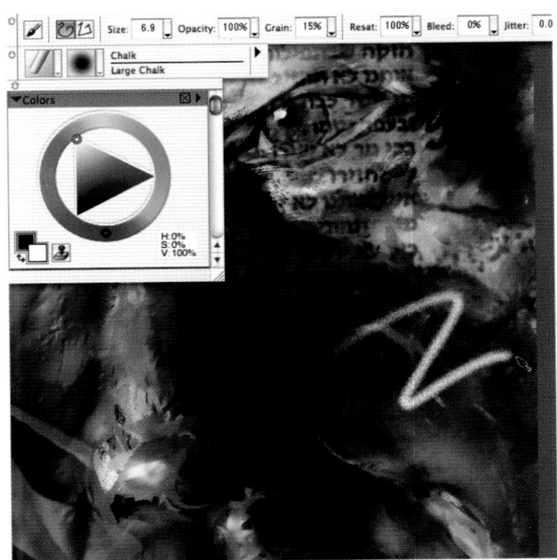

Figure 9.11 Making a test brush stroke.

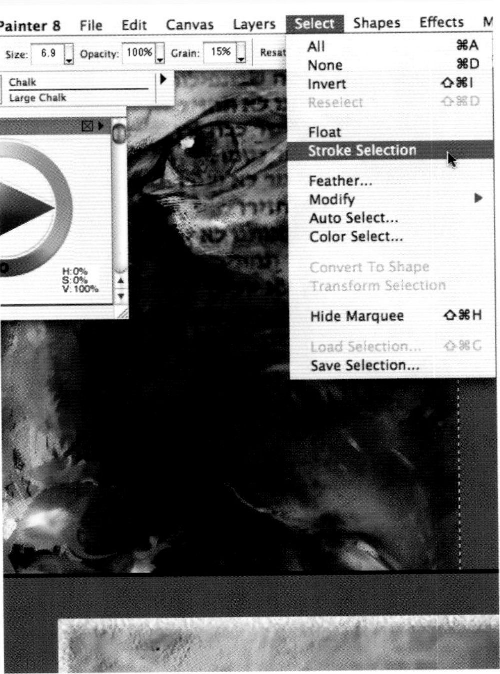

Figure 9.12 Stroking the selection to soften the border.

9.5 Your Voice: *Independent Collage Project*

This is your opportunity to express your own voice. Choose a collage theme and title that inspires you and that you are passionate about. It doesn't matter what the theme is; it is more important that you are passionate about it. Your theme could be about a particular person, about your life, about events, social issues, or about concepts or feelings. Examples are "Family," "Joy," "Metamorphosis," "Fantasy," "Freedom," and so on.

Research imagery for the collage. Go to the library, go on the Web, look through books, and so on. Use all the resources at your disposal. Sketch out ideas. Brainstorm. Ask yourself what it is you wish to say. Think about a base image, something that can tie other images together, a central image that unifies the composition, that conveys the essence of your message.

Plan your collage carefully. Think about how large a print you may want and create an initial file that will be large enough. If you are unsure, check with a printer first.

Feel free to use any techniques in Painter as part of this project. Remember to document meticulously and archive all versions and source imagery. Save your versions in the Painter Projects > 9-Collage > 9.5 Your Voice project folder.

9.6 Wrap

Congratulations on concluding the final session of this course. This is not an ending, merely a beginning. I wish you much joy, success, and satisfaction in applying all the skills you have learned along the way and in continuing to expand your creativity.

Appendix I
Painter, Photoshop, and Illustrator: Which Software to Use When

Photographic Capture, Cropping, and Orientation

For scanning, cropping, and rotating photographs, Photoshop is often the best tool for the job, especially if you are already familiar with Photoshop. Although Painter can adequately accomplish some of these tasks, such as cropping, retouching, and adjusting levels, Photoshop may be faster if you are used to it. Other tasks, such as changing from RGB to CMYK, cannot be done within Painter.

Basic Image Manipulation and Enhancement

Photoshop is great for almost any kind of image-editing need, such as enhancing your source image, adjusting levels, hue, saturation, contrast, and brightness (use Adjustment Layers for maximum versatility), except when you need organic and painterly effects, where Painter is necessary. If you are already working on an image in Painter and want to make tonal or color adjustments, then you may find it most convenient to use Painter's built-in tools under Effects > Tonal Control.

Hand-painted Artistic Effects

Any time you want an organic, artistic, hand-painted look and feel to your work, then Painter is the tool to use. This applies equally whether you are creating a painting from scratch or transforming a photographic image. While Photoshop 7 has an expanded brush set and numerous wonderful built-in and third-party filters and effects, there is no substitute for the versatility, variety, and richness of Painter's brushes and textures.

Selections and Layers

Both Painter and Photoshop have comparable and compatible facilities for making and saving selections and for controlling, adjusting, and organizing layers. My approach is always to aim at simplicity and to making any task as easy as possible. Therefore I would suggest that if you are already in one program, then use that same program for your selections and layering (although I have found Photoshop users often prefer the Photoshop selection tools to those in Painter). You can always save the files as a Photoshop format file and go from one program to the other while maintaining the saved selections (alpha channels in Photoshop, channels in Painter) and the editability of bitmap layers. Note that the editability of some special layers and modes in Painter (Watercolor, Liquid Ink, Impasto, and Mosaic) are lost when you convert to a Photoshop format file (the full editability of these special layers and modes is only preserved in the RIFF format).

Type

Generally, vector programs, such as Illustrator, are great for sharp, editable, scalable type and small file sizes. Only use type in Photoshop or Painter when you wish to apply a special effect to it.

Both Photoshop 7 and Painter 8 have versatile text tools that allow you to experiment with different fonts, orientation, positioning, alignment, and spacing. In Painter, by converting to Shapes you can also skew and distort lettering individually or as a group. By converting to a default image layer in Painter (either from Text or Shapes), you can apply all of Painter's brushes and effects, including great three-dimensional embossment (Effects > Surface Control > Apply Surface Texture using Mask and a little Softness) and instant drop shadows (Effects > Objects > Create Drop Shadow).

If you want to wrap text accurately around a circle or a path, then you should create the text in a vector-based program like Adobe Illustrator or Macromedia Freehand. If you wish to add effects to the text or integrate the text into a bitmap (pixel) image in Painter, then you can always import the Illustrator- or Freehand-generated text as a layer, or series of layers, into either Photoshop or Painter. In Painter, Illustrator text is imported as a group of Shapes (File > Acquire > Adobe Illustrator File).

If you are preparing a piece for print and want the most precise, accurate, sharp-looking text possible and the text will be a plain color without gradients, transparency, or drop shadows, then you are better off creating the text in Illustrator (or other vector program) and converting it to outlines. Keep a copy of the original (nonoutline) document for your records for future editing and resolution-independent resizing.

Printing and Color Modes

I recommend printing from Photoshop. While working in Painter, save your files as RIFF files. Resave the final version as an RGB TIFF file. Reopen that final TIFF in Photoshop. Many printers give superb results printing directly from RGB files (Painter is an RGB program). If you are working with traditional offset lithography printers, you may be required to convert your files into CMYK color mode. In that case, convert from RGB to CMYK in Photoshop; however, be aware that many options

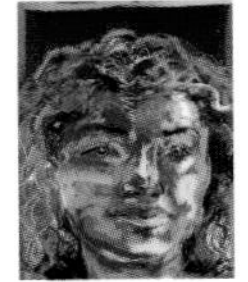

and filters are not available in Photoshop when working in CMYK, so, unless you are starting from a high-resolution scan that is already CMYK, keep your image in RGB mode and only save a flattened, CMYK copy of the file if needed. When saving for Web in Photoshop or Illustrator, use the "Save for Web" options, as this leaves the original file untouched.

Appendix II What Size to Make Your Files

When deciding what size to make your files, always start with the end in mind. Think through what your final usage will be and ensure that you start with sufficient resolution for that final usage.

In this appendix I simply share my own approach to file size. In my case I have four distinct situations: (1) painting portraits from life as performance art, (2) creating an image for print, (3) creating an image for the Web, or (4) creating images for video.

Painting Portraits from Life as Performance Art

In the first case, live performance portraits, I typically use a relatively small canvas of about 7 inches by 10 inches at 100 pixels per inch (700 by 1000 pixels). Such a small file size means that all of the brushes and effects respond immediately. It also provides enough resolution for a good-quality print on letter-size paper with an inexpensive inkjet printer. My imagery is quite expressionistic and painterly, and this allows it to print well even with relatively low resolution.

Creating an Image for Print

In the second case, where I specifically have a printed end product in mind, I generally work at the final size and 300 pixels per inch (ppi). With large-format prints (20 inches by 24 inches and larger), 150 ppi may be sufficient. You should check with your printer or service bureau first.

Creating an Image for the Web

Both Illustrator and Photoshop have an option called "Save for Web," which allows you to see how your image will look depending on what quality or format you choose. I recommend that you use this option when saving from either program. There are ways to minimize the file sizes further and optimize the colors for the Web (e.g., using Adobe Image Ready), which you may wish to look into.

My Web gallery images typically end up being about 400 to 600 pixels in the maximum dimension at 72 ppi. I normally create my original images at higher resolution (see above) as RIFF files in Painter and then resized and resaved (also in Painter) as High-Quality JPEGs. As a word of warning, every time you save anything as a JPEG, the quality of the file is reduced, and if you resave as a JPEG, then the quality is reduced even more. Only save as a JPEG once, if you can help it. Creating images at higher resolution gives me the flexibility to reuse the images for printing at a later time.

Creating Images for Video

When working on a QuickTime movie for video, I generally start my projects in Painter at the required final video resolution, typically 720 pixels by 480 pixels at 72 ppi. This keeps everything simple and straightforward and allows me to directly use the resulting QuickTime movie without any need for resizing.

Appendix III
Getting Colors to Look Right When You Print

Matching the colors on your screen with the color output from your printer is an issue close to the heart of any digital artist. I will always recall my disappointment the first time I saw an inkjet print of one of my portraits where all the colors looked so much duller than on the screen and the blues had become purple and the yellows green! To get the closest and most consistent correspondence between the colors you see on your screen and how they appear on your print, you will need to understand and address the issues of color management. Two books that you may find helpful are:

Real World Color Management by Bruce Fraser, Chris Murphy, and Fred Bunting (Peachpit Press 2003) ISBN 0-201-77340-6.

Mastering Digital Printing: The Photographer's and Artist's Guide to High-Quality Digital Output by Harald Johnson (Musk & Lipman 2002) ISBN 1-929685-65-3.

You will also find useful links on this subject on the *www.paintercreativity.com* web site resources page. I recommend investing some time in understanding how you can manage the color of your images in Photoshop to prepare them for printing after you've created them in Painter. Calibrating your screen can also make a significant difference. There are many factors and details to consider which are better dealt with by experts in the field (please refer to the books mentioned above and the web links).

Appendix IV Loading Extra Brushes and Art Materials

Your Painter 8 CD2 (that comes with Painter) contains a wealth of fabulous extra brushes, papers, patterns, gradients, and more, that do not get installed automatically when you install Painter on your computer hard drive. On the Painter Creativity Companion CD that comes with this book, I have put together a collection of my favorite brushes and art materials, including unique custom-made brushes and color sets that you will not find anywhere else (thanks to the artists around the world, such as Chris, Den, Don, Marge, Paulo, Ron, and Sherron, who have kindly given permission for me to share their custom brushes and art materials with you). I explain in this appendix exactly where to copy the files from the Painter Creativity Companion CD and how you can load the extra brushes and art materials and set them to be your defaults every time you open Painter.

Where to Copy Files from the Painter Creativity Companion CD

1. Locate the Painter Creativity Companion CD > Goodies folder appropriate to your operating system (there are two choices of Goodies folders, one for Mac OS 9 and 10 and Win XP; and one for Win 98, ME, and 2000).
2. Copy the *contents* of the Goodies > Art Materials folder (Extra Color Sets, Papers Artsy, Papers Decorative, Papers Metal Liquid, Papers Wood Stone, and Patterns Taster) into the Corel Painter 8 application folder on your hard drive. Do not copy the Art Materials folder itself—just its contents.
3. Copy the *contents* of the Goodies > Brush Category folder (Jeremy Faves folder and Jeremy Faves.jpg file) into the Corel Painter 8 > Brushes > Painter Brushes library folder. Do not copy the Brush Category folder itself—just its contents.
4. Copy the *contents* of the Goodies > Brush Libraries folder (Basic Brushes and Creativity Brushes) into the Corel Painter 8 > Brushes folder. Do not copy the Brush Libraries folder itself—just its contents.

Note that the precise location of these files and folders is crucial for the extra brushes and art materials to be accessible from within Painter. Whenever you are loading extra brushes into Painter, whether from my Creativity Brushes library or Jeremy Faves category, or brushes you have downloaded from the Internet, always be sure to identify whether you are loading a brush Library (as in the case of Creativity Brushes), a brush Category (as in the case of my Jeremy Faves folder accompanied by the Jeremy Faves.jpg icon), or a brush Variant (usually a file ending with .xml and sometimes accompanied by a .jpg file). Each of these—the Library, Category, or Variant—needs to be copied to the correct level in the folder hierarchy in the Corel Painter 8 application folder on your hard drive (see Looking Under the Hood on pages 17–18).

Windows users may need to go through each folder and file that they copy to uncheck the Read Only property. To do this, select all the contents of each folder, right-click to get the Properties window, uncheck the Read Only check box, and then click Apply, selecting the option to apply to the contents of all folders.

Using the Jeremy Faves Brush Category

If you follow the previous instructions you should find the Jeremy Faves brush category automatically appearing in your list of Categories in the default Painter Brushes library. The Jeremy Faves category contains a small sampling of my favorite brushes picked from my Creativity Brushes library.

Loading the Creativity Brushes Library

1. Select Load Library from the bottom of the pop-up menu on the right of the Brush Selector.
2. Locate and select the "Creativity Brushes" Brush Library in the Brush Libraries window.
3. Click Load. You'll now see that the Brush Library has become the "Creativity Brushes."

Setting Creativity Brushes as the Default Library

If you wish to use this library as your default brush library (i.e., the library that appears in the Brushes palette every time you open Painter), then:

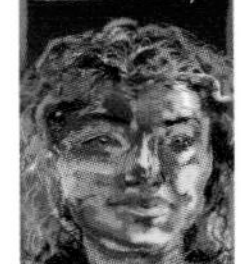

1. Select Edit (Corel Painter 8 on Mac OS X) > Preferences > General.
2. You will see the default brush library name, "Painter Brushes," next to Brushes and under Libraries on the top right of the General Preferences window. Replace the library name "Painter Brushes" with "Creativity Brushes."

If you wish to return to having the regular Painter Brushes library be the default Brush Library, just type "Painter Brushes" next to Brushes.

Using Extra Color Sets

To use one of the custom Color Sets in the Extra Color Sets folder, choose Open Color Set from the Color Sets palette pop-up menu and select the color set you wish to use from the Extra Color Sets folder in the Corel Painter 8 application folder.

Setting a Color Set as Default

To make one of the custom color sets your default color set every time you open Painter, choose Edit > Preferences > General and type in the exact color set name in the Libraries: Color Set section in the top right of the General Preferences window.

Using Extra Papers and Patterns

To access one of the custom libraries of papers or patterns, choose Open Library from the bottom of the Paper or Pattern Selector pop-up menus and then select the library from within the Corel Painter 8 application folder. You will find the Paper and Pattern Selectors in the lower part of the Tools palette, as well as in the Papers and Patterns palettes.

Setting a Custom Papers Library to be the Default

To make one of the custom papers libraries your default papers library every time you open Painter, then choose Edit > Preferences > General and type in the exact papers library name in the Libraries:Papers section in the top right of the General Preferences window.

Appendix V
Painting Portraits: Principles and Actions

Preparation *Principles*

Principle	How To	Things to Consider
Think ahead	Plan for future versatility.	The only guaranteed thing in life and creativity is change. You can't always predict the ways you may want to recycle or reuse your artwork in the future. Build in future versatility into everything you do.
Be comfortable	Be physically comfortable. Minimize distractions, both visually on the screen and externally in your space.	The tools should assist your creativity, not get in your way. Ideally they should become invisible. Being physically comfortable is a very important aspect of allowing you to focus 100 percent on your painting.
Simplify	Simplify your palettes and interface. Avoid overlapping palettes.	Only have visible what you need to access or observe at any time.
Document obsessively!	Save versions as you go. Record scripts.	"Save as, save as, save as" is the mantra!

Preparation *Actions*

Action	How To	Things to Consider
Make time	Put aside a block of undisturbed time.	Turn your phone off. Be focused. Allow time for preparation and transformation.
Select subject	Look for a subject that speaks to you.	Do you have a detail that you are drawn to? Be in tune with your choices.
Prepare subject	Ask for model's release (details on digital ownership). Tell subject he or she will receive (for personal use) a copy of the portrait. Look at artist, not screen. Be relaxed and comfortable. Position subject close to screen so you don't have to crook your neck looking back and forth between subject and screen.	It's important for the subject to understand his or her participatory role in the creative process, and for you to develop a rapport with the model. Be sure to explain the rights and responsibilities as a model upfront. The model's release should be short, simple, and clear. Sample wording may be: "I, (name of model), give (name of artist) permission to paint my portrait and use, display, transfer, or reproduce the completed image, or any stage or derivative version of it, in any way they wish. The artist retains full copyright over their artwork. No payment is owed for use of my likeness. I will receive a signed free color print for personal use." The model should sign and date the release, which you keep in your records.
Set up technology	If Painter is open, quit and reopen. Customize screen to show only palettes and tools you will use.	Technology shouldn't inhibit the decision-making process. It should make decisions faster and simpler. Arranging palettes so the screen is uncluttered and inviting to the eye helps creative decision making.
Prepare the canvas	Fill with color. Apply texture.	The background color gives the artist something to work against. Overcomes the fear factor of facing a blank white canvas.

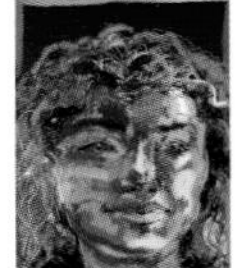

Save the canvas	Use Save As. Name methodically.	Select consistent file and folder naming protocols that make it easy to identify, access, and retrieve files. Sample file name 03.11.05-xena smith-01.rif (reverse date—subject—version number—format).
Relate to tablet	Stroke the tablet with both hands, as if it were paper. Move the stylus, without touching the tablet, so the cursor follows the edge of the canvas.	Leave the tip of your left thumb gently resting on the tablet at the location corresponding to the top left corner of the canvas. This serves as a useful reference as you paint with your right hand. Reverse these instructions if you're left handed.
Begin documentation process	Set recorder going. Technique: select all, start recorder, and deselect. This increases versatility.	Documenting the process (using scripts), as well as saving the intermediate stages, maximizes versatility at the end of the day.

Looking *Principles*

Principle	How To	Things to Consider
Observe accurately	Look carefully at what you see. Focus on relationships and contrasts.	Observe the relationships of contrasting areas of light and dark. What shapes are they? What relative size are they? How do they intersect and fit together? What areas and contrasts stand out?
Observe frequently	Continually look back and forth at your subject as you paint.	Try to spend at least as much time looking at your subject as at your screen. Continue to make marks as you look at your subject.
Observe fully	Observe with all senses. Take sufficient time to look at your subject.	Don't let technology distract you from the tactile and sensual nature of observation and painting. Use all of your senses to take in the subject.

Looking *Actions*

Action	How To	Things to Consider
Tune into subject	Take a deep breath. Rest your hands palm down on the tablet. Close your eyes. Let go of all the trivia and noise in your mind. Be still. Open your eyes. Look at subject as if for the first time, with freshness and openness. Visualize the feeling of the final picture.	What does the subject express to you? In your mind, sculpt the final result. Visualize the final canvas (picture the feeling of the picture, not necessarily what it looks like). What does the portrait say, convey, evoke? Decide where to focus the viewer's attention and how to lead the eye around. Be selective in use of color, contrast, and detail to draw attention to selected regions of the portrait (such as the eyes).
Look for darks and lights	Observe shapes of dark and light areas. Identify specular highlights, diffuse highlights (base tones), shaded sides, refractive highlights, and cast shadows.	Compare the relative lightness and darkness of different areas. Note the contrasts along borders of these areas. Where are the lightest and darkest areas?
Compare relative proportions	Compare the sizes and shapes of the areas you see and observe the way they fit together.	Look for shapes, whether defined by darkness and lightness or by distinct contrasting colors. The relative dimensions and positioning of neighboring shapes gives you a way to start depicting your subject on the canvas.

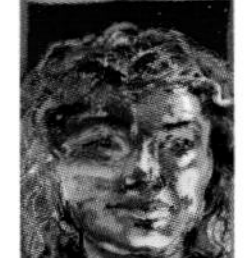

Making Marks *Principles*

Principle	How To	Things to Consider
Be committed	Don't use undo. If a brush stroke seems messy or wrong, paint over it (it will add to the richness of the canvas). Don't get attached to what you've done or haven't done. Trust in your intuitive self. Accept what unfolds and look forward, knowing that everything can be transformed.	Never panic about a mistake. Everything is liquid (it can and will change). Trust in continual transformation.
Maximize versatility	Make the most of the dynamic range of marks you can get from every brush you choose. Select fewer brushes and achieve more versatility with each brush.	Get the maximum out of the chosen brushes, rather than use a lot of different brushes. Technology can overwhelm you with too many choices that are too easy to access. Capture complexity through simplicity.
Make marks with your hand	Avoid applying special effects to the whole image or to selections. Stick to handmade brush strokes.	By using your hand you transfer your feelings and your soul into the picture. As soon as an automated or mechanical means of mark making is used, the artist detaches himself or herself emotionally from what is conveyed in the picture.
Stay playful	Have fun! Don't get attached to detail or the end result. Always experiment.	Don't get too serious. Playfulness is a key to accessing your intuitive creativity.

Making Marks *Actions*

Action	How To	Things to Consider
Begin with gestural movement	Choose a large, flowing expressive brush such as the Artists > Sargent. Engage in gestural movements to capture the energy and feel of the subject. Start these gestures with the stylus just above the tablet so you see the cursor move but no paint. Then continue the gestures in paint.	The gestures create the energy spine of the drawing.
Rough out blocks of tone	Select larger, cruder brushes that force you to work abstractly. Half-close eyes to see tonal values. Rough out blocks of tone.	Work over the entire canvas, roughly and abstractly. Don't dive into details yet. This forces you to face your fears head on. Once you have entered the space, you have the freedom/license to get started, and to make it more or less chaotic.
Work on color, detail and contrast	Draw attention by highlighting contrasts, using warm and complementary colors, and being selective in details.	Choose to make things stand out specifically. Don't have everything stand out. Identify what's really important. Add warm hues in specular highlights and complementary cool hues in shaded sides.
Strive for essence	Create order and harmony out of chaos and disorder. Focus on bringing the power of the picture out—the essence of the subject.	

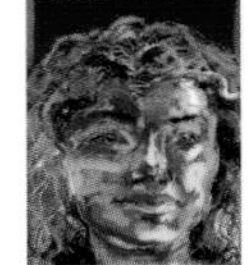

The end game	Sign the portrait to signal the end. Stop the script recorder and name the script. Save the current version of the picture. Quit Painter.	When should you stop? There is no right answer. You have to feel it intuitively. Deadlines often drive the ending. Quitting Painter resets the memory put aside for Painter and also ensures that you have the back-up of the background script in case of emergency. Painter always records a background script every time it is opened. The script stops when Painter is closed. Background scripts last 24 hours only unless they are renamed using the Script Mover.

Transforming Marks *Principles*

Principle	How To	Things to Consider
Treat your canvas as a malleable clay or liquid	See your marks as ever-changing, nonpermanent. Use your creative process as an ongoing means of expression, rather than just as a means of producing a single final result.	Use the brushes that alter and interact with existing marks on your canvas. Also use the script replay to change, or add to, your paintings.

Transforming Marks *Actions*

Action	How To	Things to Consider
Replay the script	Reopen Painter. Open a new sheet of paper, the same size as your original painting. Replay the script using a different background, perhaps the favorite color of the subject. Pause the script, change brushes, and continue the script.	Because you took the time to build in flexibility from the beginning (by setting the recorder), you have the power to extend your creative process and create variations. Shows the power of documentation; it allows you replay and stop at any time.

Appendix VI Troubleshooting

The World's Greatest Troubleshooters

I would like to begin this appendix on Troubleshooting by sharing a story from my friend Olaf about the world's greatest troubleshooters, the Eskimos, also known as the Inuits. The Inuits have survived in some of the most stressful conditions. Every day presents them with troubleshooting challenges, whether it is a boat's outboard motor stopping without a garage in sight or a sudden snowstorm and subfreezing temperatures. They adapted to surviving and thriving in harsh conditions over thousands of years by following three rules. These rules are surprisingly relevant to surviving and thriving in Painter.

Eskimo Survival Rule #1: Be Alert

The Inuits are at all times fully aware of their complete environment. They are at one with nature and respectful of nature. They are constantly observing the land and the sky, seeing potential dangers near and far, sensing what weather is coming. They are also constantly in touch with their bodies, heading off any chance of frostbite or injury. They are alert inside and outside.

This links up to the Painter Feng Shui discussed earlier in this book (session 2). Be aware of the clutter and distractions in your environment and your Painter workspace and, where possible, take actions to eliminate them. This will prevent many problems that arise out of confusion, such as hiding one palette behind another. Pay attention to giving meaningful names to files and layers; this saves a lot of time and effort spent trying to work out what's what. It's easy to get so absorbed on the computer that you lose track of time. Hours can pass with little body awareness or movement. Make sure you stretch and get fresh air regularly.

Eskimo Survival Rule #2: Be Practical

Inuits live in desolate, isolated conditions. They cannot rely on handy technicians, mechanics, garages, or repair shops to solve their problems. When anything goes wrong, no matter what it is or how simple or complicated, they repair it. They recycle almost everything and improvise constantly with whatever is at hand.

In our busy lives we can become reliant on quick fixes and always having someone else around to take care of practical matters. In Painter, think like the Eskimo. When you run into a problem, improvise and experiment. You'll find that whatever the outcome of the improvisation and experimentation, you will always learn something along the way. You will deepen your understanding of Painter.

Eskimo Survival Rule #3: Have a Sense of Humor

When all else fails, if the Inuits are in a situation they can't fix, they *laugh*! They grab every opportunity offered by adversity to laugh. They are very jolly people despite great hardships. Humor is their emotional valve—their way of externalizing rather than bottling up.

When you run into a problem, just as *The Hitchhiker's Guide to the Galaxy* says, don't panic! Instead pause, relax, reflect, and, if you feel totally lost, laugh! Don't give up in despair or frustration. If necessary, take a break and come back to Painter later. It's amazing what a bit of subconscious processing can do to help your brain come up with solutions.

Ounce of Prevention Is Worth a Pound of Cure

As the saying goes, "an ounce of prevention is worth a pound of cure." By thorough preparation and organization, and by following the troubleshooting precautions covered here, you'll be able to minimize the amount of trouble you need to shoot. Just like a trained streetwise martial artist is much less likely to be picked on than a naive head-in-map tourist, a well-prepared, organized Painter artist is much less likely to run into problems than an unprepared, disorganized one.

Structure

However prepared you are, it is almost inevitable that, at some time, you'll get stuck or confused by something that happens (or doesn't happen) on your screen. I encourage you to take risks and experiment. That means inevitably that at some time you will try something and what you expect to happen won't happen. That may mean that you try to paint a brush stroke and nothing appears on your canvas, or you try to clear your canvas and something's left behind that you don't want. Whatever form trouble takes, there are some simple steps to sorting it out. That's where this section comes into play. I've divided this section into five topics:

Precautions

Brush or effect not working?

Painter display not looking right?

Tablet not working?

Crashes and launch errors

In Precautions I suggest some simple things to do before you run into problems. The other topics each have a list of suggested actions. Follow these actions in sequence. After the first action, each

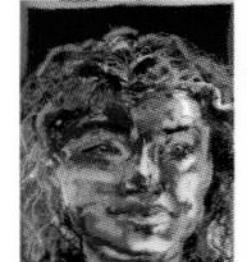

subsequent step can be thought of as being prefaced by "if you still have a problem . . ." Some actions are repeated in different sections. Fortunately you'll find that 99 percent of problems are solved before you go through all the actions.

Precautions

1. *Close any nonessential applications.* As a general rule I suggest that you close any other nonessential applications when working in Painter.
2. *Disable any nonessential extensions and control panels.* Keep your system as clean and lean as possible. Free up as much memory and hard drive space. Disable any nonessential Extensions and Control Panels. This will help avoid conflicts with Painter.
3. *Reopen Painter with every new project.* Always start and quit Painter at the beginning and end of any project. This helps memory management and also allows you to conveniently use the background script to rescue unsaved artwork in the event of a computer crash. See lesson 6.9: Background Script. As an additional safety feature, set the number of levels of undo (Edit > Preferences > Undo) to the maximum your memory will allow.

Troubleshooting Tips

Brush or Effect Not Working?

1. *Quit any other applications that are open.* If Painter is struggling for memory, it is worthwhile making sure that you do not have other applications running at the same time. For Mac OS 9 make sure there is sufficient memory allocated to Painter and that Virtual Memory is turned off.
2. *Select a simple palette arrangement.* Make sure you can see the Tools, Property Bar, Brush Selector, Colors, and Layers palettes.
3. *Check which file you're working on.* Go to the Window drop-down menu and check which file (at the bottom of the menu) has a check by it. This is the file that is currently active. If it is not the file you thought you were working on, drag down to the file name of the file you want to work on. If there are any files open in Painter that you are not using, and that are not needed as clone sources, close them. Make sure that Painter is active and that you haven't accidentally selected the Finder or another application.
4. *Check your tool.* Are you using the tool you thought you were? If painting, make sure the Brush tool is selected.
5. *Check for selections.* Is there a current selection on the canvas? It's possible that you may have accidentally created a tiny selection by brushing the Lasso tool on the canvas inadvertently. If you don't want a selection, then deselect with Cmd/Ctrl-D to be sure.

6 *Check Brush Category, Variant, and settings.* Confirm the Brush Category and Variant. It may be that your variant settings have been changed. If in doubt, go to the Brushes palette and select Variant > Restore Default Variant.

7 *Check the Colors palette.* Look at the Regular/Additional Color squares. What is the Regular (primary) Color? Make sure the Regular Color square (the foremost one) is selected (Figure AP6.1). If in doubt, click on the Regular Color square.

Are you painting white on white? Is the Clone Color icon in the Colors palette active? If so, do you want to be using Clone Color? If you are using Clone Color, reset the clone source in File > Clone Source (unless you want the current pattern to be a clone source, in which case just reselect the pattern in the Patterns palette).

8 *Check the brush Size in the Brush Property Bar.* How large is your current brush? Adjust size if necessary.

9 *Check the Layers palette.* Carefully check what, if any, layers there are and which, if any, are selected in the Layers palette. One by one, go through all the layers and turn the eye of each one off so it disappears. Then reopen the eyes one at a time to make sure you know what each layer is. Now select what you want selected. If you do not want any layer or mask selected, click on the Canvas in the Layers section. Make sure any layer you want to effect has the padlock icon open. It's easy to accidentally lock a layer. Also check that the Preserve Transparency checkbox is unchecked. It is easy to accidentally check it or for it to be checked when you open Painter.

10 *Check for active Layer Masks in the Layers palette.* Check if any Layer Mask layer is selected. If you have an image layer selected, make sure the eye next to the image layer mask in the Channels palette is closed.

The next four suggestions (11–14) are common for almost any problem once you've tried everything else.

11 *Quit out of Painter.* Quit out of Painter File > Quit. If you are frozen in Painter, you can try a forced quit out of the program. To force quit out of Painter for Mac, users choose Option-Cmd-Esc. To force quit out of Painter for Windows, users choose Ctrl-Alt-Delete and select the

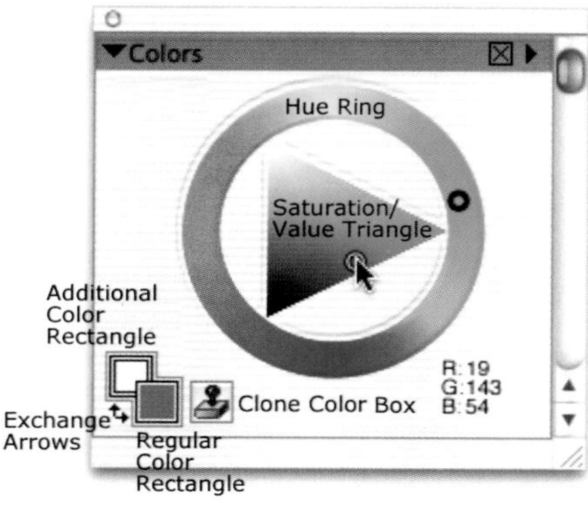

Figure AP6.1 The Standard Colors Color Picker.

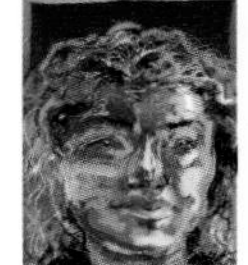

Task Manager. The Task Manager will let you quit a program that's not responding. Choose the Applications tab and select Painter in the Task list and click the End Task button. It might take a few moments to quit Painter. If that doesn't work, then Ctrl-Alt-Delete a second time will reboot your system.

12 *Restart computer.* Restart your computer (Mac users choose Ctrl-Cmd-Start to force a restart on the Mac, Windows users hit the power button or the reboot button, depending on what computer you have).

13 *Consult Help Topics.* Within Painter select Help > Help Topics. This gives you an on-screen version of the User Guide. Look up the topic of concern. The Help Topics are very thorough.

14 *Contact Painter technical support.* Within Painter select Help > Tech Support for a summary of support options. The direct phone number for Painter technical support is +1-613-274-0500. You are entitled to 30 days of free telephone technical support (the Classic level of service). The 30 days commences from your first call. Follow the prompts. Have the following information at hand: Painter serial number, operating system version number, exact description of the problem, list of actions that led up to the crash, any error messages that appeared, and what you've tried as solutions. You will be given a PIN number, which you will need to give if you make any future calls.

15 *Post a message on the Painter List, Painter Forum, or other online Painter community.* See the resources link from www.paintercreativity.com. Describe your system, the exact symptoms, and what you've tried as solutions.

Painter Display Not Looking Right?

1 *Quit out of Painter.* Quit out of Painter File > Quit. Reopen Painter.

2 *Check all connections.* Check all connections between your monitor and your computer.

3 *Restart computer.*

4 In Windows go to Settings > Control Panel > Display and make sure the setting is 32 bit video, not 16 bit.

Tablet Not Working?

1 *Make sure that the tablet in pen mode, not mouse mode.*

2 *Quit out of Painter.* Quit out of Painter File > Quit. Reopen Painter.

3 *Check tablet Control Panel.* If the scaling is off, reset the scaling in the Control Panel.

4 *Restart computer.*

5 *Install the latest driver.* Download the latest driver from the Web (Wacom users go to www.wacom.com). Install the latest driver and restart your computer.

6 *Contact tablet technical support.* Look in your tablet user guide or refer to the tablet manufacturer web site for your local Technical Support contact information. Through the Wacom web site (www.wacom.com), Wacom users can contact technical support, download the latest drivers, and access a Frequently Asked Questions web page. In the United States, Wacom users requiring phone support can call +1-360-896-9833 and dial 4 for Technical Support (7:30 a.m. to 5 p.m. Pacific Time, Monday through Thursday, and 8:30 a.m. to 5 p.m. on Friday). Wacom technical support is excellent and has helped me out during workshops on a number of occasions.

Crashes and Launch Errors

1 *Force quit out of Painter.* If everything has frozen in Painter, then force quit out of Painter (Cmd-Option-Esc on the Mac or Ctrl-Alt-Delete > Task Manager in Windows).

2 *Restart computer.* If your whole computer is locked, then force a restart (Ctrl-Cmd-Esc on the Mac, or power or reboot button with Windows).

3 *Eliminate possible conflicts.* If you continue to have persistent crashes, or if you see an error message come up every time you launch Painter (e.g., "Profile Processor Error: File not found"), try to eliminate possible software conflicts. For Mac OS 9 reduce the Control Panels and Extensions to a minimum and then enable the Control Panels and Extensions one by one until you have full functionality. In general I recommend upgrading to the latest operating system. Mac users will find everything performs better in the latest version of OS X.

4 *Regularly clean up and defragment for hard drive.* Mac users should regularly run a program such as Symantec's Norton Utilities, or something similar, to defragment your hard drive.

5 *Windows disk maintenance.* Are you doing a regular disk cleanup and defragmenting your hard disks to keep your system healthy? Disk Defragmenter rearranges files, programs, and unused space on your computer's hard disk, so that programs run faster and files open more quickly. Disk Cleanup helps free up space on your hard drive. Disk Cleanup searches your drive and then shows you temporary files, Internet cache files, and unnecessary program files that you can safely delete. You can direct Disk Cleanup to delete some or all of those files. You should do this regularly for optimum performance, but beware, Disk Defragmenter can take quite a long time if you have a large hard disk, so plan this kind of housekeeping for a time when you don't have a lot to do on the computer. Find these tools under Start Menu > Programs > Accessories > System Tools.

6 *Windows Troubleshooter.* If you are a Windows user and you continue to have persistent problems, use the Windows Troubleshooter in the Windows Help System to see if you can solve the problem. Go to the Start Menu and choose Help and look for the Troubleshooting section. This will guide you through the process diagnosing and repairing a variety of problems.

Appendix VII Keyboard Shortcuts

Here are a few keyboard shortcuts that you may find handy.

Cmd/Ctrl-M	mount (or unmount) your canvas on the screen
b	Brush tool
Shift-x	exchanges the Regular (Primary) and Additional (Secondary) colors

Space bar held down when the Brush tool is selected turns the cursor into a Grabber Hand that you can use to reposition your canvas (by clicking and dragging on the canvas).

Shift-Option-Cmd/Shift-Alt-Ctrl	allows you to click and drag within image to resize brush when brush tool selected
]	increase brush size
[	decrease brush size
d	Dropper tool
Option/Alt	resets clone source start position if Clone Color active
Option/Alt	turns Brush tool into the Dropper tool if Clone Color not active
r	Rectangular Selection tool
c	Crop tool
f	Layer Adjuster tool (useful when you are working with layers in a photo collage)

The number keys for adjusting brush opacity (1 is the lowest, 0 is the highest)

Cmd/Ctrl-1	show (or hide) the Colors palette
Cmd/Ctrl-2	show (or hide) the Mixer palette
Cmd/Ctrl-3	show (or hide) the Color Sets palette
Cmd/Ctrl-4	show (or hide) the Layers palette
Cmd/Ctrl-5	show (or hide) the Channels palette
Cmd/Ctrl-6	show (or hide) the Text palette
Cmd/Ctrl-7	show (or hide) the Info palette
Cmd/Ctrl-8	show (or hide) the Gradients palette
Cmd/Ctrl-9	show (or hide) the Patterns palette
Cmd/Ctrl-B	show (or hide) the Brush Creator

These, and many other useful keyboard shortcuts, are summarized on the Painter 8 Quick Reference Card, which comes with the Painter 8 User Guide.

Index

This index is designed to provide you with a convenient way to access and cross-reference specific subjects and concepts discussed in this book. It is not intended to be a comprehensive Corel Painter 8 index. If you are looking for specific Painter-related topics and cannot find them in this index, then I recommend you look them up in the excellent Corel Painter 8 User Manual (also available from the www.corel.com web site in PDF format).

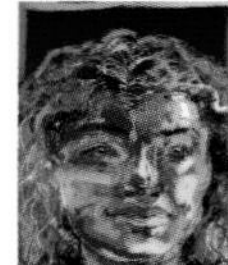

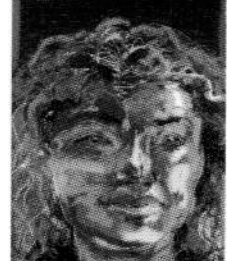

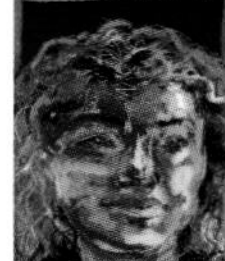

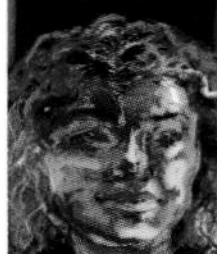

Q

R

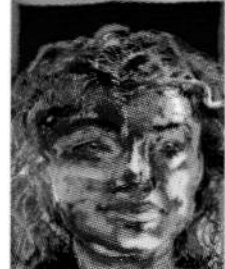

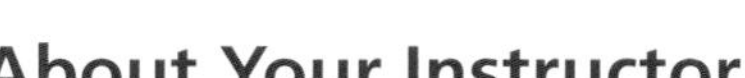

About Your Instructor

Jeremy, former faculty member of the Academy of Art College, San Francisco, is a renowned artist, author, and educator. His publications include the following:

PainterCreativity for Professional Portrait and Wedding Photographers DVD (PhotoVision, 2003)

Secrets of Award-Winning Digital Artists (Wiley, 2002)

Total Painter Video Series (Total Training, 1998)

Painter 4 Video Series (MacAcademy, 1996)

Fractal Design Painter Creative Techniques (Hayden Books, 1996)

Jeremy is currently host of the DMN Forums Worldwide Users Group Painter Forum (www.dmnforums.com) and is an associate editor and regular contributor (PainterView column) for the *EFX Art & Design* magazine (www.macartdesign.matchbox.se).

Currently a resident of San Francisco, Jeremy grew up in London and has drawn since he was three years old. He has a degree in Physics from Oxford University, and he studied art at the Ruskin School for Drawing and Fine Art, Oxford University, and at the Vrije Akademie, the Hague, in the Netherlands. Jeremy is a lively, knowledgeable, and entertaining instructor who teaches Painter Creativity workshops and seminars all over the world. He has performed his unique style of colorful digital portraiture internationally for clients ranging from Industrial Light and Magic and the United Nations to Virgin Atlantic Airlines. You can see samples of Jeremy's paintings and learn about his commissioned portraiture, seminars and publications through the PainterCreativity.com companion web site.

You are welcome to let Jeremy know any thoughts and comments you have regarding this book. Contact Jeremy via e-mail at jeremy@paintercreativity.com.

Contributors

Barbara Buchner
Ormond Beach, Florida
BABINTL@worldnet.att.net
www.crearrtive.com
Figures 5–1 and 5–2 (page 114)

Carol Mooney
Oakville, Ontario
CANADA
Camamoon@aol.com
Figure 5–14 (page 123)

Cathleen C. Savage
Alexandria, Virginia
savage@erols.com
Figure 5–13 (page 123)

Celeste Dobbins
Celeste PhotoArt
Santa Rosa, California
celestephotoart@juno.com
www.CelestePhotoArt.com
Figures 8–16 to 8–22 (pages 227–30) and 8–34 (pages 238)

Cheri MacCallum
Fairburn, Georgia
Cheri@fairburn.com
www.artbycheri.net
Figures 7–23 (page 183), 7–52 (page 210) and 8–8 to 8–12 (page 225)

Chris Cimonetti
PhoenixvillePennsylvania
frodo9f@hotmail.com
http://members.bellatlantic.net/~vze235xx
Custom brushes: Chris' Fine Art

David Taylor
Taylor & Roger's of Kailua
Kailua, Hawaii
info@photokailua.com
www.photokailua.com
Figure 7–53 (page 210)

Denise Laurent
London, UK
den@imagine.co.uk
www.imagine.co.uk
Figure 4–9 (page 101) and custom brushes: Den's Oil Brushes

Dezraye Choi
Piedmont, California
sashachoi@yahoo.com
Figure 3.3 (page 76)

Don Seegmiller
Orem, Utah
don@seegmillerart.com
http://seegmillerart.com
Custom brush: Liquid > Seegmiller Blender

Dwight E. Goode
Northridge, California
goodecpa@pacbell.net
Figures 8–1 to 8–7 (pages 219–23) and 8–25 to 8–30 (pages 232–235)

Eddie Tapp
Atlanta, Georgia
etapp@aol.com
www.eddietapp.com
Figures 7–24 to 7–40 (pages 185–202)

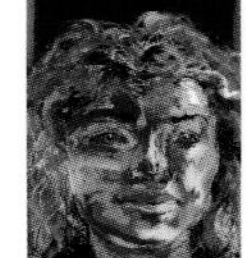

Elizabeth Fenwick
Menlo Park, California
elizabeth@elizabethfenwick.com
www.elizabethfenwick.com
Figures 7–18 and 7–19 (pages 179–80)

Elsa Vera
EVP Events
Santa Rosa, California
EVPevents@aol.com
www.winecountrycelebrations.com
Figures 8–35 to 8–40 (pages 239–43)

Ernest Love
Ernest Love Photography
Pacifica, California
ELuv1Photo@aol.com
www.geocities.com/Eluv1Photo
Figures 8–31 to 8–33 (pages 236–8) and 8–49 (page 250)

Gisele Bonds
Positive Images
Oakland, California
PImages@aol.com
www.positiveimages-portraits.com
Figures 7–1 to 7–11 (pages 169–174) and 7–21 (page 183)

Jane Conner-ziser
Jane's Digital Art School
Ormond Beach, Florida
janecz@shawus.com
www.janesdigitalart.com
Figures 3–19 to 3–24 (pages 84–8), 7–50 (pages 208–9) and essay (page 211–15)

Jeff Peterson
Novato, California
pimage@ix.netcom.com
www.pimaging.com
Figure 5–7 (page 119)

Jenny Lovett
Berkeley, California
jen@jennylovett.com
Figure 3.7 (page 77)

Jim and Judi Paliungas
Palimor Studios
Camarillo, California
judi@palimorstudios.com
www.palimorstudios.com
Figures 1–15 (page 32), 7–41 to 7–45 (pages 203–7) and 7–51 (page 210)

Laura Garner
Berkeley, California
laurlgrnr@aol.com
Figure 3–8 (page 77)

Laura Ruppersberger Photography
New CastlePennsylvania
lrphoto@pathway.net
www.lauraphoto.com
Figures 7–12 to 7–17 (pages 175–8)

Lesley Fountain
Sonoma, California
lesart@weallr1.org
www.weallr1.org
Figure 4–7 (page 101)

Leslie Howard Jacob Portraiture
Palm Beach Gardens, Florida
lesliehjacob@aol.com
www.lesliejacobportraits.com
Figure 7–50 (page 209)

Lisa Evans
Lisa Evans Portrait Design
Lafayette, California
lisaevansart@aol.com
Figure 8–13 (page 226)

Lois Freeman-Fox
Fillmore, California
undergrove@aol.com
Figures 1–19 (page 35), 4–6 (page 100), 5–9, 5–10 (page 120), 5–13 (page 123) and 5–15 (page 128)

Lorne Chisholm
Castro Valley, California
photogoose@earthlink.net
Figure 7–22 (page 183)

Marge Stewart
Mendocino Art Center
Mendocino, California
margecraft@aol.com
Figure 7–20 (page 182), and custom brushes: Marge's Brushes

Paulo Roberto Purim
CuritibaParaná, Brazil
paulo.purim@avalon.sul.com.br
www.jogodeluz.com.br
Custom brushes: Paulo's Brushes

Peg Buckner
Picture This! Studio and Gallery
Fallon, Nevada
PiczurThis@aol.com
www.PictureThisStudio.Com
Figures 8–42 to 8–48 (pages 243–50)

Rheba K. Mitchell
Lampasas, Texas
rkm@starband.net
www.lair-wildscape.com
Assorted color sets

Robert Strong
Powerful Comedy
San Francisco, California
robert@strongentertainment.com
www.strongentertainment.com
Figures 8–14 (page 226), 8–15 (page 227) and 8–41 (page 243)

Ron Kempke
Urbana, Illinois
Custom brushes: Ron's Oil Brushes and assorted color sets

Selina Topham
selina@topham.demon.co.uk
Figure 5–11 (page 122)

Sharon Bing
London, UK
sharonb1@mac.com
Figure 5–12 (page 122)

Sharon Moran
Glenview, Illinois
SMoran2136@aol.com
Figures 1–19 (page 35) and 3–29 (page 91)

Sherron Sheppard
Ventura, California
sheppardphotography@adelphia.net
www.sheppardphotography.com
Figures 5–8 (page 119), 7–46, 7–47 (pages 207–8), custom brushes: Sherron's Brushes and assorted color sets

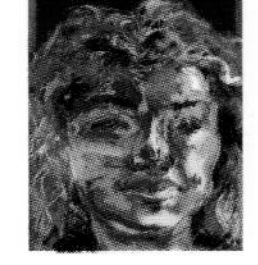

Sidne Teske
Battle Mountain, Nevada
siddo_t@yahoo.com
www.wildwomenartists.com
Figure 4–8 (page 101)

Susan LeVan
LeVan/Barbee Studio
Indianola, Washington
lvbwa@earthlink.net
www.bruckandmoss.com
Custom Color Sets: LeVan's Lively Favorites and LeVan's Lively Mix

Thomas Barron
Novato, California
teb2@usa.com
Figure 3–5 (page 76)

Valerie Markle, M. Photog., Cr.
Acworth, Georgia
valmarkle@aol.com
www.markleportraits.com
Figure 7–52 (page 210)

Victor de Leon
San Francisco, California
vicdeleon@earthlink.net
Figures 7–48, 7–49 (page 209)

LIMITED WARRANTY AND DISCLAIMER OF LIABILITY

FOCAL PRESS AND ANYONE ELSE WHO HAS BEEN INVOLVED IN THE CREATION OR PRODUCTION OF THE ACCOMPANYING CODE ("THE PRODUCT") CANNOT AND DO NOT WARRANT THE PERFORMANCE OR RESULTS THAT MAY BE OBTAINED BY USING THE PRODUCT. THE PRODUCT IS SOLD "AS IS" WITHOUT WARRANTY OF ANY KIND (EXCEPT AS HEREAFTER DESCRIBED), EITHER EXPRESSED OR IMPLIED, INCLUDING, BUT NOT LIMITED TO, ANY WARRANTY OF PERFORMANCE OR ANY IMPLIED WARRANTY OF MERCHANTABILITY OR FITNESS FOR ANY PARTICULAR PURPOSE. FOCAL PRESS WARRANTS ONLY THAT THE MAGNETIC CD-ROM(S) ON WHICH THE CODE IS RECORDED IS FREE FROM DEFECTS IN MATERIAL AND FAULTY WORKMANSHIP UNDER THE NORMAL USE AND SERVICE FOR A PERIOD OF NINETY (90) DAYS FROM THE DATE THE PRODUCT IS DELIVERED. THE PURCHASER'S SOLE AND EXCLUSIVE REMEDY IN THE EVENT OF A DEFECT IS EXPRESSLY LIMITED TO EITHER REPLACEMENT OF THE CD-ROM(S) OR REFUND OF THE PURCHASE PRICE, AT FOCAL PRESS'S SOLE DISCRETION.

IN NO EVENT, WHETHER AS A RESULT OF BREACH OF CONTRACT, WARRANTY OR TORT (INCLUDING NEGLIGENCE), WILL FOCAL PRESS OR ANYONE WHO HAS BEEN INVOLVED IN THE CREATION OR PRODUCTION OF THE PRODUCT BE LIABLE TO PURCHASER FOR ANY DAMAGES, INCLUDING ANY LOST PROFITS, LOST SAVINGS OR OTHER INCIDENTAL OR CONSEQUENTIAL DAMAGES ARISING OUT OF THE USE OR INABILITY TO USE THE PRODUCT OR ANY MODIFICATIONS THEREOF, OR DUE TO THE CONTENTS OF THE CODE, EVEN IF FOCAL PRESS HAS BEEN ADVISED OF THE POSSIBILITY OF SUCH DAMAGES, OR FOR ANY CLAIM BY ANY OTHER PARTY.

ANY REQUEST FOR REPLACEMENT OF A DEFECTIVE CD-ROM MUST BE POSTAGE PREPAID AND MUST BE ACCOMPANIED BY THE ORIGINAL DEFECTIVE CD-ROM, YOUR MAILING ADDRESS AND TELEPHONE NUMBER, AND PROOF OF DATE OF PURCHASE AND PURCHASE PRICE. SEND SUCH REQUESTS, STATING THE NATURE OF THE PROBLEM, TO ELSEVIER SCIENCE CUSTOMER SERVICE, 6277 SEA HARBOR DRIVE, ORLANDO, FL 32887, 1-800-321-5068. FOCAL PRESS SHALL HAVE NO OBLIGATION TO REFUND THE PURCHASE PRICE OR TO REPLACE A CD-ROM BASED ON CLAIMS OF DEFECTS IN THE NATURE OR OPERATION OF THE PRODUCT.

SOME STATES DO NOT ALLOW LIMITATION ON HOW LONG AN IMPLIED WARRANTY LASTS, NOR EXCLUSIONS OR LIMITATIONS OF INCIDENTAL OR CONSEQUENTIAL DAMAGE, SO THE ABOVE LIMITATIONS AND EXCLUSIONS MAY NOT APPLY TO YOU. THIS WARRANTY GIVES YOU SPECIFIC LEGAL RIGHTS, AND YOU MAY ALSO HAVE OTHER RIGHTS THAT VARY FROM JURISDICTION TO JURISDICTION.

THE RE-EXPORT OF UNITED STATES ORIGIN SOFTWARE IS SUBJECT TO THE UNITED STATES LAWS UNDER THE EXPORT ADMINISTRATION ACT OF 1969 AS AMENDED. ANY FURTHER SALE OF THE PRODUCT SHALL BE IN COMPLIANCE WITH THE UNITED STATES DEPARTMENT OF COMMERCE ADMINISTRATION REGULATIONS. COMPLIANCE WITH SUCH REGULATIONS IS YOUR RESPONSIBILITY AND NOT THE RESPONSIBILITY OF FOCAL PRESS.